Wrestling Brothers

Wrestling Brothers

Rethinking Religion-Science Relationships

Bruce Yaeger

ROJNAHY

Wrestling Brothers:
Rethinking Religion-Science Relationships
© 2016 by Bruce Yaeger

Contact:
yaegerbruce@gmail.com

Ordering information:
http://bruceyaeger.blogspot.com

Cover picture: Detail from "Les Jeunes lutteurs"
  ("Young Wrestlers") by Paul Gauguin (1888).
Cover background: Fibonacci spiral.

Unless otherwise indicated, all quotations from the Bible are from the New Revised Standard Version (designated as "NRSV"), copyright 1989 by the Division of Christian Education of the National Council of the Churches of Christ in the U.S.A.

Printed in the United States of America

to
Kathleen

and to
Carol

Contents

Illustrations

Insets

Preface

When did I first became interested in science? Perhaps it was in early elementary school, when I looked at a diagram of our solar system with the Earth and other planets sweeping around the sun in great arcs.

When did I first became interested in religion? Perhaps it was when I was of the same age, or maybe younger, and I looked at a Bible's colored pictures of Jesus with children happily clustered about him.

Whenever it was that I first became interested in science and religion, I know that my interest in both grew as I grew. I was fortunate to have been part of a family and a church where people believed we need not make a choice between science and religion. I was thus able to welcome both the knowledge science provided and the insights faith-traditions offered.

(I do recognize that some people have grown up believing that their faith required them to reject evolution. I empathize with them on the harder life-paths they may have journeyed upon. If you are one of those people, I hope you will still be able to find within the pages of this book insights about the past and guidance for integrating knowledge and faith.)

I have never been able to escape my dual fascination with both science and religion. In college, I first thought I was going to major in biology. But after realizing that I was asking philosophical questions rather than scientific ones, I switched to a combination major of religion and English. Even when I was under the tutelage of the college's religion department, I was not allowed to forget about science. In the theology courses I took, the issue most discussed, second only to questions about God, was the viability of religious language and thought in our scientific age. We grappled with the issue of whether the "God-talk" of religions had become antiquated in a modern world. What role can religious thought play in an age in which we employ mostly scientific language to explain the world around us, and even explain the entire universe?

Is religious language outmoded? Is it just decoration?

I had become so intrigued by such matters that even after college graduation I continued to avidly read anything I could lay my hands on interrelating religion and science. I also discovered that those two fields could not remain apart for many other people. That was because I had become somewhat of an itinerant church-school teacher to adults, creating classes not only for my home-church but also for a number of neighboring churches. Wherever I taught, I encountered adults who could not subscribe to the common depiction of religion and science as combatants engaged in "warfare." That was because those people had also grown up accepting science (including the theory of evolution), even as they had grown within their faith-tradition. Such people wanted to think about interrelations between religion and science. They wanted to talk about the two together.

I was glad to be able create many classes and presentations to address those needs, drawing upon my own continuing study and education. This book is the fruition of my decades of teaching. It covers a variety of topics in which religion and science engage with each other—wrestling with each other so that each enterprise might find its own best identity.

I am grateful to my students for providing me so many opportunities to teach, as well as stimulating me to continue with my own education. As I look back upon over fifty years in which I have thought about religion-science relationships, I am also grateful for professors who encouraged me to reflect upon theology in ways that seek to make religion relevant to our contemporary world. I remember especially Lonnie D. Kliever, John H. Hayes, and John McGee.

I can only hope that readers of this book might find within its pages some insights that will be equally invigorating to their own thinking and spiritual life.

Introduction:

The Need for a New Metaphor

"W ar." "Conflict." "Battle." "Fighting." These words are the mainstays of our contemporary TV, radio, and newspaper diet. The vocabulary of warfare and conflict seems to pop out of reporters' word processors automatically, ready to grab readers' attention. It does not matter whether the news story is about an event overseas or in our own city, whether it involves politics or interpersonal relations. Conflict is the prevalent imagery.

Meanwhile, most of us are able to go about our own lives, even as challenging as they are, without coming to physical blows with anyone. A different vocabulary is needed to describe most of our lives. And that would have been the case with the lives of most people down through the course of human civilization.

The metaphors of "war" and "conflict" are also those most frequently used by today's media in its presentation of issues involving the relationship between religion and science. The media often state or assume that religion and science have been primarily in conflict during their joint histories. The image often put forward by purveyors of this "warfare" model is that of science continuously advancing using reason, while religion, in opposition, insists on unquestioning adherence to beliefs, even if they are naive or ignorant.

This belief that science and religion (particularly Christianity) have usually been in conflict also sometimes intrudes into science books written for general readers. One fairly typical contemporary book on great scientists, for example, inserts into its chapter on Darwin the claim that down through history, "many scientists ... encountered particularly fierce opposition from the Church, whose members preferred the safety of a sacred text to the uncertainties of observation and experiment."[1]

The "Warfare" Model Not Tenable

There is a big problem, however, with that common "warfare" or "conflict" depiction. As one contemporary historian of science, Lawrence Principe, explains:

> Serious modern historians of science have
> unanimously *dismissed* the warfare model as an
> adequate historical description.[2]

Admittedly, some magazine articles do tell us that there might now be a "truce" in the religion-science "wars." Such articles usually contain statements from scientists or religious leaders declaring that the two fields can co-exist after all. But such announcements of a "truce" imply—incorrectly—that warfare is the best description for religion and science's past relationship. That is simply not the case (as will be demonstrated in Chapter 1, which presents a historical overview of Christianity).

The warfare-or-truce imagery is also misleading because it suggests that the primary challenge for religious believers is to "surrender" to science. That is, to accept science's findings (particularly the theory of evolution), the assumption being that religion usually resisted such findings. However, many religious believers found ways to accept the theory of evolution long ago. (This will be explained in Chapter 3, "Tempest in a British Teapot," and Chapter 4, "An Awkward History.") Moreover, there are many easily overlooked matters that followers of a faith-tradition need to address even after accepting the findings of science. And so, even the imagery of "surrender" or signing a "truce" is inadequate.

Historians of science tell us that the word which best describes the interrelationships between religion and science is not "conflict" but "complexity." As the two leading historians of science David Lindberg and Ronald Numbers explain:

> Historical investigation ... has revealed a rich and
> varied interaction between science and Christianity....
> Most important, we will see [in studying history] that
> influence has flowed in both directions, that
> Christianity and science alike have been profoundly
> shaped by their relations with each other.[3]

This complexity, rather than black-and-white warfare, continues even today. Even though debates in the U.S. continue over evolution in public-school textbooks, the relationships between religion and science as a whole are more intricate. Just to begin with, even Christians who are anti-evolutionists accept science in other forms, such as modern medical knowledge and technological knowledge about how automobile engines operate.

Moreover, a recent study of 10,000 Americans made by Rice University's Religion and Public Life Program revealed that "nearly 70 percent of evangelical Christians do not view the two [i.e., science and religion] as being in conflict with each other."[4] As that organization's director Elaine Ecklund pointed out, that sizable number stands "in contrast to the fact that only 38 percent of Americans feel that science and religion can work in collaboration."[5] Similarly, a 2015 Pew Research survey showed that "less than one third of Americans ... (30%) say their personal religious beliefs conflict with science," whereas "a majority of the public says science and religion often conflict."[6] The contrasts in both sets of percentages—a contrast between fact and public perception —demonstrates how wrong an impression is given by the media's overused "warfare" and "conflict" formulations.

There are complexities here that cry out for rethinking religion-science relationships. Complexities that cry out for looking beyond the simplistic "warfare" and "conflict" imagery.

A More Flexible Metaphor

Metaphors matter. Our choice of metaphors to describe any complex phenomenon shapes which aspects we see and which we do not see. We need a new metaphor, therefore, if we are going to be guided by the conclusion of historians of science that complexity, not warfare, has been the primary characteristic of religion-science relationships. We need a new metaphor not only to clarify their historical relationships but also to make our lives of faith relevant to our modern scientific age.

Although other metaphors might be examined, I propose the image of wrestling brothers. To begin to expand that metaphor, I suggest we draw upon one narrative in which we find two siblings, as well as references to wrestling. It is a narrative in the Bible's book of Genesis, but is a story so human that people of any faith-tradition can engage with it. The story is about the twin brothers Jacob and Esau, who wrestle with each other before they are born —a foreshadowing of the struggles between them that continue after their birth. As the narrator looks imaginatively into the womb of their mother Rebekah, it is said that the two brothers "struggled together within her."[7]

Once they are born, there is indeed competition between them for dominance—but neither one kills or even physically strikes the other. Instead, Jacob gains greater power, leaves home, raises a family, becomes successful, and then re-connects with Esau. At that point, readers discover that Esau has also become successful. The two brothers have worked out their different identities.

This engaging ancient story can have many applications, but the imagery it provides is one of the best analogies for comprehending the *true* relationships between science and Western Christianity, both past and present. That is because even though those two enterprises are vastly different (like Jacob and Esau), and even though they have sometimes struggled with how to live peacefully with each other, they have done so in a variety of complex ways. The metaphor of brothers who have sometimes wrestled has the advantage of being flexible in order to depict such variety.

Whereas the "warfare" metaphor suggests only a conflict until the point of death or surrender, the wrestling-brothers metaphor can open us to recognizing different kinds of interactions. In the real world, brothers do not wrestle just as a way of competing (much less wrestle with the aim of destroying). Brothers might wrestle as a way of figuring out their individual abilities and identities. Or they might wrestle just for the fun of it, in the way academic colleagues sometimes debate issues just for intellectual enjoyment.

(I know of two brothers who occasionally wrestled for fun while growing up. One day, the younger sibling paid the older a great compliment by telling him, "You're my favorite person to fight with!")

Dictionaries recognize such flexibility in the way we use the word "wrestle." They offer such synonyms as "to contend with," "to struggle," "grapple," "strive," "joust." Even the playful "tussle." That is the very mixture of words needed to describe the multiplicity of religion-science interactions that historians of science have uncovered. That mixture of words also better describes today's religion-science interplay: Christians and other religious people struggle with how to understand God's presence in a world described so much by science. We contend with ethical questions about genetic cloning and other technologies. We grapple with how to make our religions' best values relevant to a scientific age.

The wrestling-brothers metaphor points us to another significant matter: Like Jacob and Esau, the enterprises of religion and science are intimate at their origins. Modern science, which has its origins in 17th-century Europe, grew out of a predominantly Christian culture. It even has elements of Christian thought as some of its assumptions about the orderliness of the world and the ability of human reason to comprehend it. Religion and science have, so to speak, some "genes" and life-experiences in common. They have more shared life-experiences that did Jacob and Esau.

Another inadequacy of the warfare-conflict imagery is that it does not allow for a depiction of much growth in the two parties. But both religion and science have changed over the course of centuries. Some of those changes—in both religion and science— lie at the root our of current complexities in relating the two enter- prises. (This is elaborated upon in Chapter 1, "Exposing the 'Warfare' Myth.")

In contrast with warfare imagery, which does not suggest inner growth in the very human enterprises of religion and science, the wrestling-brothers metaphor invites it. Although the Biblical narrative of Jacob and Esau does not describe any literal post-birth wrestling between those two brothers, a painting by the impressionist Paul Gauguin might suggest that boyhood wrestling could be a part of the story. (See this book's cover.) Gauguin, who sometimes depicted Biblical themes in contemporary settings, made a colorful oil painting titled "Young Wrestlers." Gauguin seems to have been more focused on the color arrangements than on the identities of the boys in his painting.[8] But in it, two pre- adolescent boys, wet-haired, have just gotten out of the neighborhood swimming hole, and are having a tussle. There is no suggestion that either brother is trying to destroy the other. Instead, what is conveyed is closeness and possible growth into a still far- off adulthood.

That open-endedness suggested by Gauguin's painting is also relevant. We do not know what the future holds for either religion or science.

The Jacob-Esau narrative also conveys how the lives of sometimes wrestling brothers can have periods in which the two separate, do their own thing, and sometimes later re-connect. On many levels, that dynamic is also true of religion and science in both the past and the present. This book reflects and draws upon the renewed discussions between theologians, philosophers, and scientists over the past few decades. It grapples with science's implications for religion and spirituality.

Besides the broad problem of the prevalent but misleading "warfare" metaphor, there are two other ways today's general media oversimplify the matter of religion-science relationships. One simplification has to do with a superficial use of the word "religion." The other has to do with the plurality of faith-traditions. It might prove helpful if I here speak to each of these matters in turn.

"Religion" Not So Simple a Word

Rarely recognized in our contemporary society's discussion about the relationship of religion and science is how the word "**religion**" covers an immense range of components, even within a single faith-tradition. Sometimes the issue of religion-science relationships is even reduced to just the question of whether God exists. But any single faith-tradition can include:[9]

- rituals
- experience and emotions
- narratives
- doctrines
- ethics
- social organizations
- art and architecture

As the word "Rethinking" in the subtitle of this book indicates, this book covers in large degree the reflective dimension of religious traditions and a person's religious life. But that reflective dimension has ramifications radiating into all of those other components of religion. Although the reflective dimension encompasses the more formal thinking called **theology**, it is by no means confined to it (as readers of this book will discover). For example, the "rethinking" dimension of a person's life can be at work when that person struggles with how to cope emotionally with the illness of a loved one, grappling with how to retain meaningfulness— even though formal theological analysis has not been engaged in.

Religion is deeply intertwined with our view of the world. And our view of the world is interwoven with how our individual personalities engage with the world. Religions are tied in with what we understand the world to be like, and who we understand ourselves to be. Religions thus encompass understanding.

Because of the widespread influence of science on our modern Western societies, we often think of understanding as receiving information about something and having mentally grasped that information. For example, chemistry class teaches me that water is composed of two atoms of hydrogen and one atom of oxygen (H_2O). I understand water chemically as I understand that formula, along with knowing what a molecule is.

Religion, however, emphasizes another form of understanding that is revealed in the derivation of the word itself: To "understand" is to stand-under. Religions do not see their forms of knowledge as being simply information that needs to be grasped mentally. Instead, religions hope that people will grow into a deeper, heart-felt type of understanding as they engage in song and ritual, listen to and re-tell stories, and practice disciplines such as prayer and meditation. As a Christian, I understand religiously what water is by attending baptisms, singing hymns and hearing scriptures containing the word "thirst," and joining with other people of faith to see that homeless people are provided water.

Religion is thus in part submission to a process. Nevertheless, the thinking (and "rethinking") dimension of religion is *also* in ways a form of submission. It takes as one of its premises the belief that all of us can come to better understandings as we listen to the voices of people—both past and present—who have struggled with religion's issues and questions. It is for that reason that the chapters of this book include many quotations from people who have thought, rethought, and wrestled with fundamental concerns of human existence.

(I have preserved the integrity of quotations from before our era of inclusive English. I trust that readers will recognize from the context when even women writers were employing the word "man" to mean humans, not just males.)

A Plurality of Faith-Traditions

A second oversimplification in the media's discussion of the religion-science issue is that it often lacks any recognition that the word "religion" can refer to more than one of our different faith-traditions. That is an unfortunate omission. The U.S. is composed of Christians, practicing Jews,[10] Muslims, Buddhists, Hindus, Sikhs, Taoists, and more. From its inception, there have been non-Christians in the nation, even beyond native Americans (some of the first Muslim-Americans having been slaves from Africa).[11] And the non-Christian population has increased with the growth in the number of people from non-European backgrounds. Similarly, Britain and Europe have a greater variety of faith-traditions than they did in their predominantly Christian past when modern science arose.

With such plurality in the West, the religion-science discussion could be improved by recognizing how different issues shift in relevance depending upon a person's particular faith-tradition. So let me speak some to that matter now, explaining its relevance to this book in particular.

Of course, when there is a religiously-influenced dispute over the choice of science textbooks for public schools, any person might be concerned, regardless of faith-tradition. And even if a person holds to no faith-tradition. Similarly, the technologies that have spun off of scientific knowledge can affect almost any person. (Even the Amish, who do not use motorized vehicles, have to take automobiles into account when their horse-carriages venture onto public roads.)

People who are of a minority faith-tradition within a society that is primarily Christian can be concerned about preserving their religious traditions in a modern, primarily Christian culture. That is also a concern in non-Western nations that first experienced modern scientific technologies hand-in-hand with the spread of Christian colonialism. Even though non-Christians can have these special concerns, they bear a rough resemblance to one challenge to Christianity today, even where it is the majority faith-tradition. That is because modern science has transformed patterns of thought in ways that can make some traditional religious ideas feel less relevant, obscure, or even alien. All faith-traditions can be challenged in this way.

There are, however, some issues regarding the relationships of religion and science that are of greater significance to Western

Christianity. Our modern form of science arose in a predominantly Christian culture beginning in the 17th century. In this book's first chapter, which is a broad historical overview, I explain some of the reasons why the relationship between religion and science became of particular concern for Western Christianity. However, even readers who consider themselves neither devout nor practicing Christians will be able to gain perspective from that chapter's clarifications about Christian history and its implications for current religion-science issues.

Particular theological issues, such as God's existence, are of greater concern to people of **theistic** faiths (that is, those that sometimes depict the Ultimate as a personal being). Nevertheless, people of non-theistic faiths (such as many Buddhists) can also be concerned about science's effects upon how we act and what we value. Questions about values, meaning, and our purpose in life— which will be spoken to in many places in this book—lie at the heart of many religion-science relationships. Although often unnoticed, of great importance are the ways in which the ever-increasing predominance of scientific knowledge in our modern culture has affected our sensibilities and ways of thinking. It has affected our approach toward thought and life. That matter is the unspoken issue behind many topics in this book.

The interactions of religion and science thus possess nearly universal significance. And for that reason, this book in many ways holds a widespread relevance. Even when it deals with topics of greater importance to the Judeo-Christian traditions (such as Chapter 17, "A Lost Dimension of the Bible"), it aims for the wider relevance (such as our culture's awareness of animals and plants). This book as a whole can also provide enlightenment on modern science's knowledge about the stupendous universe we live in, and what that might mean for our human condition.

Even though this book has been written out of my own Christian background, it will time and again be seeking depths that might speak to readers regardless of their faith-tradition. And might speak to readers even if they consider themselves to be more spiritual than religious.

Clarifying Some Basic Words

IN THIS BOOK I use the word "**faith-traditions**" to refer to those heritages (Christianity, Buddhism, etc.) through which people develop and give expression to religious sentiments, beliefs, and practices.

The English word "**science**" is used today in may ways. In this book, when speaking about present times, I use the word "science" to refer primarily to the natural sciences (such as physics, chemistry, biology, geology, and astronomy) rather than to such fields as political science.[12] Although the character and methods of science have changed over the course of many centuries, when speaking about pre-modern times, I will still employ the words "science" and "scientist" to refer to the rough equivalents of what those words mean today.[13] Whenever necessary, I will differentiate between *science's methods* (or "tools"), *scientists* (with their own worldviews), and *the enterprise of science* (i.e., as a component of society).

Throughout this book, I capitalize the word "**Nature**" when I am using it in our everyday sense of referring to the *non*-human world: animals, plants, and the inanimate. I recognize that, in another sense, we humans are part of the natural world. But our ordinary use of the word "Nature" demonstrates our need at times to distinguish the non-human sphere from our human sphere. By capitalizing "Nature," I am *not* personifying it. I am simply trying to differentiate that use of the word from other uses, such as when we talk about the nature or character of some entity.

Using this Book

EACH CHAPTER in this book stands on its own as much as possible. That construction will make it easier for book-discussion groups and for any reader who prefers to zero in on particular areas of interest. Each chapter opens with a historical incident. Not too far into the text that follows is an explanation about the contents of that particular chapter. Occasionally throughout each chapter are references letting the reader know about related material in other chapters.

This book, however, is *not* a mere collection of essays. The chapters are arranged so that earlier chapters provide background for later chapters. Some issues first examined in one chapter are explored more deeply from a different angle in a later chapter. As the book progresses, it will lead readers into a wider sense of interactions between religion and science.

The chapters are grouped into five large Parts, whose titles reflect the book's over-arching movement. That progression is from past history, to ongoing challenges, to a forward-looking sense of our place in the cosmos.

Because some people gain understanding more easily by learning about people than thinking about concepts, this book includes not just theological ideas but also examples of how various people have addressed religion-science relationships. Interspersed in the book are three chapters focusing upon the ever-fascinating life of Charles Darwin and the context of his 19th-century England, with it its pivotal implications for today.

Although throughout this book I have avoided using technical words as much as possible, a Glossary of Conflicting Usages is provided as an additional avenue for clarifying certain religion-science misunderstandings. If the reader requires the meanings of other words, they can be found by following the appropriate entries in the Index. Throughout the book, key words are in **bold** where they are first defined or clarified; the index does likewise for those key words

♦

THIS BOOK does not aim to provide you all the "answers." (As if there could be such a pre-packaged commodity on so broad a subject—one that impinges upon values, faith, and sense of meaning.) But this book will reveal to you the lay of the land. It will tell you about paths some travelers before you have taken. It will warn you of stumbling blocks. It will suggest some more productive routes. And it will raise questions for you to explore with your own thoughts, feelings, and life.

PART ONE
Historical Clarifications

"A dialogue on science and religion? Must be a short conversation!" quipped a British customs officer at Heathrow Airport to one of us on her way to attend a monthlong seminar on science and religion at Oxford University. The customs officer's surprise and skepticism reflects a widespread myth that science and religion are antagonistic, or at best unrelated ways of viewing the world.
— Heidi A. Campbell & Heather Looy
(contemporary professors)

The history of science has often been regarded as a series of conflicts between science and religion (usually Christianity)....
[But] the conflict thesis engenders a distorted view of disputes resulting from other causes than those of religion versus science.
— Colin A. Russell
(historian of science)

Life can only be understood backwards....
— Soren Kierkegaard
(19th-century religious philosopher)

Chapter 1
Exposing the "Warfare" Myth

W hen I was of elementary-school age (long before the invention of CD's or cassette tapes), my parents bought me and my sister a small 45-rpm record player. That parental thoughtfulness was soon followed by the occasional purchase of 45-rpm records aimed at children, many of them with an educational twist. One record I especially remember was the narrated story of Christopher Columbus interspersed with catchy songs. I can still hear in my head Columbus's frightened sailors imploring him to turn their ship around and head back to Spain lest they sail over the edge of the Earth. In chorus, the sailors sang to the tune of Santa Lucia:

Turn back, Co-lum-bus,
Turn back, Co-lum-bus!

Thus it was that I was initiated into one of the U.S.'s founding narratives, prepared to learn in school how an enlightened Christopher Columbus led the way, overthrowing medieval Europe's ignorant belief that the Earth was flat.

Except for one major difficulty: None of the modern, widely circulated story about Columbus's proving the Earth was round is true. It is simply a myth that in medieval times, everyone or virtually everyone thought that the Earth was flat. As Figure 1 from a 13th-century book demonstrates, students were taught that the Earth was a sphere, even though that required people on opposite sides of the Earth to be upside down in relation to each other.

Mathematical skills would not have been required to observe that the Earth was not flat. That observation was probably first made among ancient seafaring cultures, because when a boat with a sail travels far enough from shore, people on land can observe how the lower part of the boat vanishes from sight below the Earth's curvature, while the top of the mast remains in sight. The ancient Greeks had studied this matter. And in the 3rd century B.C.E, a man named Eratosthenes calculated the circumference of the Earth fairly well given the tools of the time.

*Figure 1: Later copy of
a 13th century original
by Gautier de Metz. (Note in
circular diagrams the
two depictions of people
standing on tiny globes.)*

In the first few centuries of Western Christianity, the most influential church fathers, such as Clement of Alexandria, Origen, Ambrose, Jerome, and Augustine, accepted the Earth's sphericity, some of them even directly endorsing that idea.[1] From the 7th to the 14th century, every important medieval thinker concerned about the natural world made a reference to or stated explicitly that the world was a round globe. Figure 2, an illustration from the main astronomy textbook of the 13th century, again demonstrates that such knowledge was not lost in medieval times. Christian leaders shared in and supported this knowledge. As just one example, the leading theologian Thomas Aquinas cited the ancient Greek philosopher Aristotle's evidence that as we shift our "position ... southward or northward" on the Earth's surface, the "stars above our heads change their position."[2]

Recognition of the Earth's sphericity shows up not just in the writings of scientists and theologians, but also in literary works.[3]

*Figure 2: From later edition of
13th-century astronomy textbook
"De sphaera mundi" (On the Sphere of the World)*

In the 14th century, both Dante's *Divine Comedy* and one tale in Chaucer's *Canterbury Tales* make reference to the Earth being a sphere.[4]

As for Columbus, his argument with those who had reservations about his voyage was not over whether the Earth was round, but over its size and, therefore, the time it would take to make the journey. In fact, the traditional calculation of its size was correct, and his was vastly small. If the unknown America had not unexpectedly gotten in Columbus's way, he and his sailors would have perished at sea when their provisions ran out.[5]

The myth that medieval people believed the Earth was flat (with or without the Columbus add-on) is significant for today's religion-science relationships. That is because the myth is usually presented as a story of open-minded scientific knowledge overcoming the superstitious and religiously-minded past.[6] When, in 1828, the author Washington Irving became one of the originators of the fictional story, he depicted Columbus before an array of "professors, friars and dignitaries of the church; maintaining his theory with natural eloquence," but "assailed by monastic bigotry ... with citations from the Bible."[7] A 1979 play by Joseph Chiari perpetuated that religion-science motif, despite all the historical evidence to the contrary.[8]

The flat-Earth myth is one of many myths frequently repeated today (even by devoted Christians) that sustain the widespread impression that religion and science have primarily been at war during their joint histories. If we are going to get a better handle on how to properly interrelate the two fields, we need a better understanding of what have truly been their relationships down through history.

In this Chapter, we will focus on Western Christianity because it is that part of Christian thought whose forms have been most impacted by the rise of modern science. And also because it was in primarily Christian Western Europe that the Scientific Revolution of the 17th century occurred.

Any telling of history has to be selective. And so for this Chapter's overview, material has been selected that fulfills two aims: First, to provide examples demonstrating that the relationship between science and Christianity has most often been one of *compatibility*, not warfare. Leading Christian figures whose approach is indicative of Christianity's general relationship have been selected. (See Figure 3, timeline.) Second, we will begin to draw out a few challenges that science presents to Christianity today because of this historical legacy.

In the same way that Christianity is not the same today as it was centuries ago, so also has science changed down through history in its character and constitution. There will, however, be two matters we will need to keep our eyes on as we try to understand historically the relation between Christianity and what we now call "science":

- First, Christianity's attitudes toward the natural world,
- And second, Christianity's attitude toward reason because of its role in gaining knowledge.

Early Christianity

For most of the 2,000 years of Christian history, there was no such thing as the separation of church and state. Studying much of that history thus requires that we try to discern whether a leading person was taking a certain stand for theological reasons or more from political reasons. Therefore, an important period to examine is the first four centuries of Christianity, before the Christian emperor Theodosius closed non-Christian temples.[9]

Today, many fundamentalists who hold to a literal, historical interpretation of the Bible claim that using figurative readings is a betrayal of the Christian tradition, which (they claim) believed that the Bible was true without such supposed evasions. Quite to the contrary, even in the ancient world it was recognized that we humans communicate and gain knowledge and understanding about the world through two different means: through factual-analytical means, and through stories and poetry. And so, early Christian leaders laid out a variety of ways of interpreting Biblical passages—ways that we today would describe as spiritual, allegorical, and mystical—rather than being literal in our strict, modern sense.

One of the most significant Christian theologians in this regard was Origen, who lived in the third century. Origen explored multiple ways that Scripture could be interpreted, including an allegorical method.[10] Some of Origen's interpretations of particular passages would strike us today as being too far from the passage's original context. Nevertheless, Origen did develop a lasting idea that would come to be called the principle of **accommodation**. It is the idea that parts of the Bible are not describing some things as they actually are, but are instead written so as to make accommodation for a limited, human understanding. Conspicuous examples of such accommodation are those Bible passages in which God is depicted as having hands (ex.: 1 Peter 5:6), or as walking in a garden (Gen. 3:8).[11] Besides addressing such Biblical passages, the principle of accommodation would prove of lasting value in recognizing that the Bible in many places is not trying to provide a literal description of the world based on the science of the day, but is instead for the purpose of leading the reader into a deeper relationship with God. One example was ancient Christians' accepting that the Earth is a sphere, even though that was not the Bible's picture of the world.

Of special importance are the interrelationships between Christian theology and the ideas of ancient Greek philosophers from the 6th through the 3rd centuries B.C.E, who are the precursors of Western science. Particularly Pythagoras, Plato, and

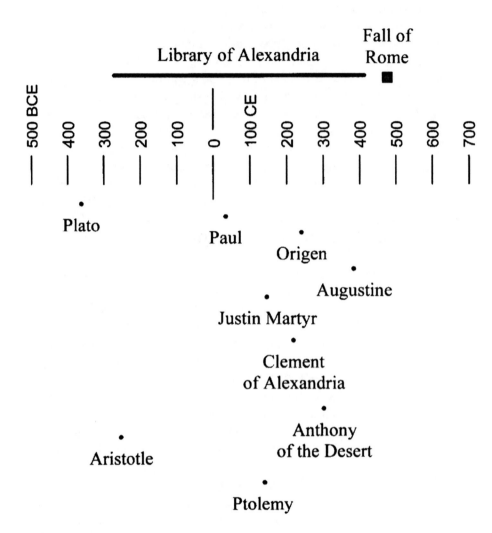

Figure 3:
Timeline of Christianity and Science

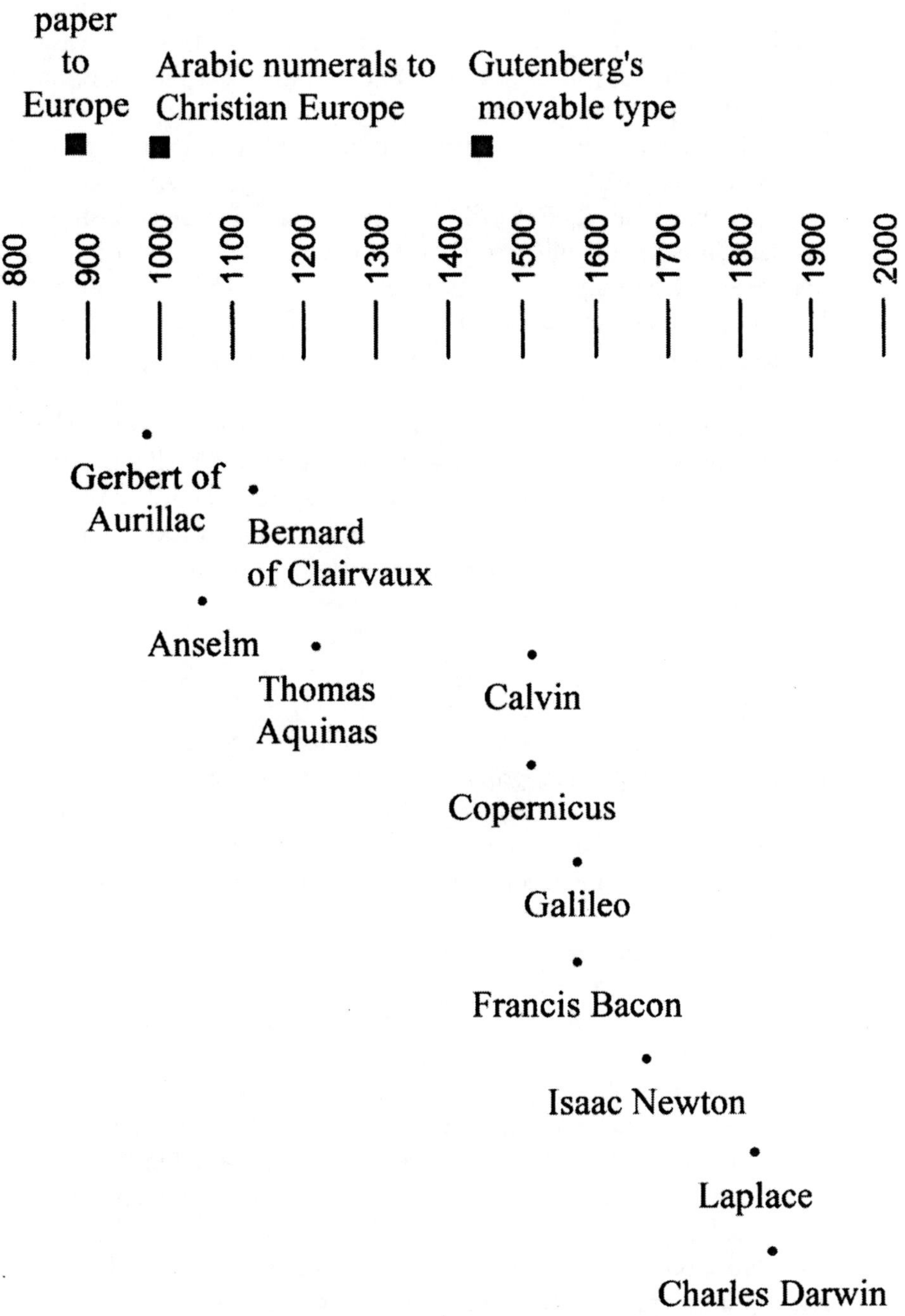

paper
to　　Arabic numerals to　　Gutenberg's
Europe　Christian Europe　　movable type
■　　　■　　　　　　　　　■

800　900　1000　1100　1200　1300　1400　1500　1600　1700　1800　1900　2000
|　|　|　|　|　|　|　|　|　|　|　|　|

•

Gerbert of　•
Aurillac　　Bernard
　　　　of Clairvaux

•

Anselm　　•
　　Thomas　　Calvin
　　Aquinas

•

Copernicus

•

Galileo

•

Francis Bacon

•

Isaac Newton

•

Laplace

•

Charles Darwin

Aristotle. One geographic hub for the circulation of such ancient thinking was the great Library of Alexandria in Egypt, which was in existence for several centuries before and after the time-period of the Bible's New Testament. The cosmopolitan city of Alexandria was a center for interaction between cultures, and was also where some early Christian theologians worked. Particularly, Origen, Athanasius, and Cyril of Alexandria. The relationship between Christian thought and ancient Greek thinkers is important because contemporary perpetuators of the "warfare" myth often claim that Christianity suppressed the body of intellectual thought of those ancient Greeks who emphasized the power of human investigation and reason.

Contemporary historians of science reject such a distortion. Instead, they see Christianity engaging with ancient Greek thought in a variety of ways, wrestling with it, analyzing it, and weighing it.[12] The general approach of Christian thinkers was to accept what could be true knowledge even if its original source was non-Christian. For, as the 2nd-century Christian theologian Justin Martyr put it:

> Whatever things were rightly said among all men, are
> the property of us Christians.[13]

Moreover, for the most part, leading Christian thinkers elevated knowledge, recognizing that Christians should not be misguided by ignorance about core Christian thought or about the world God created. For example, the widely influential Augustine, who was a bishop in northwest Africa in the early 4th century, wrote:

> Even a non-Christian knows something about the
> earth, the heavens ... animals, shrubs, stones, and so
> forth, and this knowledge he holds to ... from reason
> and experience.... Now, it is a disgraceful and
> dangerous thing for a [non-believer] to hear a Christian
> ... talking nonsense on these topics; and we should take
> all means to prevent such an embarrassing situation.[14]

Influenced by the ancient Greek philosopher Plato and his followers, Western Christianity wrestled out ways its theology could talk about God in terms of concepts (in contrast with the story-telling approach the Bible was inclined to, with its Judaic orientation). Perhaps one of the most enduring ideas a Plato-inspired Christianity developed is that the Divine—God—is revealed to humans through three qualities that humans can perceive: the Good, the True, and the Beautiful.[15]

Of greater relevance to the development of the sciences in Europe would be the works of Aristotle, who was less philosophical in his approach than Plato. Virtually all of Aristotle's scientific thought that was available became integrated into Christian culture. Among Aristotle's immense teachings were works in biology, zoology, meteorology, and an older kind of physics.[16] European Christian culture also assimilated a model of the universe that fused the physics of Aristotle with the detailed mathematical calculations of the 2nd-century Claudius Ptolemy, an astronomer who lived in Alexandria, Egypt.

Given that Christians (following the advice of Augustine) were not to display ignorance regarding science's knowledge of the natural world, what was to be the relationship between science and theology? To that question, Augustine also provided an answer, one that had been initiated in the first century by Clement of Alexandria, founder of an important earlier movement of Christian theology. Clement's and Augustine's idea was that science would be the "handmaiden" of theology, meaning that knowledge was not to be elevated for its own sake but was to serve the good of Christian society.[17] The "handmaiden" formula would remain the prevalent approach not only for early Christianity but also throughout the Middle Ages, sometimes even being employed into the beginnings of modern science.[18] "Handmaiden," being a metaphor, did not provide a precise blueprint delineating how science and theology should interact. But it provided a handy defense for preserving the scientific discoveries and knowledge of the ancient Greeks—particularly because those people were non-Christians.

Throughout the 2,000 years of Christianity's life, there have been two areas of scientific knowledge that have been of greatest interest to the Church: medicine and astronomy. Christianity's interest in medicine is perhaps obvious. Even though for most of Christian history the field of medicine possessed nowhere its capability of today, caring for the ill has always been one of the Christian concerns.

As for the interest in astronomy, the connections to religion may not be as obvious. One reason was so that the Church could properly set the date for religious holidays such as Easter (a complex matter because it is based on both the solar and lunar calendars). The second reason astronomy has been of interest to the Church has been to differentiate astronomy from astrology, particularly a belief that our lives are determined by the movements of stars, rather than by our own actions. That Christian moral emphasis could be summed up in a line extracted from Shakespeare many centuries later: "The fault, dear Brutus, is not in our stars, But in ourselves."[19]

In this regard, parts of Augustine's book *The City of God* are illuminating. Following a line of thinking that can be traced back to the Bible's Old Testament, Augustine objects to astrology because it can reduce peoples' sense of free will and responsibility. But significantly, Augustine also pulls up observational evidence against astrology: namely, that twins can have quite different outcomes in their lives despite their being born at virtually the same moment.[20] Although Augustine's evidence based on twins is not a modern, scientifically controlled study, it stands as an example that religious thinking encompassed both observation of the natural world and reason.

Historians of science, when they tell the story of Christianity's first centuries, usually identify some theological attitudes of Christianity that made it compatible with science (attitudes that will eventually be conducive to the emergence of modern science in a Christian culture). One Christian attitude in particular stands out during this early period of history. Specifically, the Judeo-Christian belief that all the universe is made by one God who had declared it to "very good" (Genesis 1:31a). Such an attitude might seem obvious to many today, but it was not a given in the cultures into which Christianity first spread. Early Christian theologians repeatedly fought against various forms of Gnosticism that saw the physical world as being bad, and saw a person's spiritual aim as being to escape from this world unscathed. If you believe the natural world is that bad, you will not think there is value in learning more about it. But early Christianity strongly rejected such beliefs that demeaned the natural world.[21]

It was not merely for any practical knowledge science might provide that most of Christianity has upheld Christians' turning their attention to the natural world. Even in its Biblical roots, most of Christianity (at least before contemporary times), has held that experience of and reflection about the natural world can lead not only to scientific knowledge but also to revelation about God. And down through the centuries, on numerous occasions, a variety of Christian thinkers would use the metaphor of the "Book of Nature" to express that theological and spiritual idea. As a 3rd-century example, the early desert father St. Anthony of the Desert wrote:

> My book is the nature of created things, and any time I wish to read the words of God, the book is before me.[22]

Into the Medieval Period

The end of the Roman Empire is dated at 476 C.E., when Rome collapsed to invaders. In the century before and two centuries following Rome's fall, there were marked changes in the possibilities for learning and scientific investigation. Political control became broken apart under many different identities in western Europe as people struggled and fought over who would rule where.

The final collapse of the Roman Empire invariably provides warfare-myth proponents an opportunity to claim that Europe thereafter entered a time of intellectual darkness, in which (supposedly) the Church suppressed learning, particularly that ancient Greek learning that had been transmitted under Roman rule. For example, one contemporary book on the history of science written for laymen states:

> In the year 529 ... the first Benedictine abbey was
> founded at Monte Cassino, Italy.... The abbey was on a
> mountaintop. Intellectual life was being sent off to
> tucked-away, cloistered monasteries.[23]

This is, however, a misreading of events. The protection of books within the monasteries was a way of preserving accumulated knowledge during the shiftings of secular power and political structures, which continued over the course of what we have come to call the Middle Ages.

Simplified timelines of prominent figures in the story of Christianity's relation to science (such as Figure 3) do not show any people of key importance in the several centuries following the fall of Rome, which are called the medieval period. As a result, portrayals of those Middle Ages often depict it as a period in which there was no inventiveness or discovery. According to warfare-myth advocates, it was a time of religious suppression and darkness.

It is true that compared to the science of the ancient Greeks, there was less work on theoretical science in the Middle Ages. However there was significant practical inventiveness in applying the science of the times. The list of medieval inventions include: The blast furnace. The iron plow. The horse collar. The windmill. The water-mill. The mechanical clock. And spectacles.[24] Such significant inventions demonstrate that this was *not* a time in which the Church held everybody in a standstill of ignorance.

There is another important matter regarding those Christian monasteries that developed in the centuries following the fall of the Roman Empire. As one historian succinctly states, "The Church and the monasteries set the stage for universities."[25] Between the years 1200 and 1419, (the latter part of the Middle Ages), twenty-nine universities were begun across mainland Europe and England. They included such now notable ones as those of Paris, Oxford, Cambridge, and Heidelberg.

Nor was the education the medieval universities provided solely religious indoctrination (as the "warfare" myth would have it). Instead, as one historian of science explains:

> Most students had no theological or biblical studies at all.... About 30 percent of the medieval university curriculum covered subjects and texts concerned with the natural world.... Dozens of universities introduced large numbers of students to Euclidean geometry, optics, the problems of generation and reproduction, the rudiments of astronomy... and the mathematical sciences.[26]

Although in this overview we have been concentrating on the relationship between Christianity and scientific knowledge about the natural world, an additional matter deserving attention is the relationship between faith and human reason. Today, in our society's debates about religion and science, a strong contrast is frequently drawn between religious faith and science's power of reason. With such a black-and-white contrast drawn, conflict between religion and science appears to be inevitable.

However, the suggestion that Christian faith and reason are mutually exclusive, or even at odds, would have seemed especially ludicrous to the 11th-century and 13th-century theologians Anselm and Thomas Aquinas.

Anselm believed that faith in God's trustworthiness could be the very thing that could allow us to be drawn forward, using human reason, into more and more understanding and knowledge. It is from him that our contemporary theological parlance inherited the formula "faith seeking understanding." It was a phrase that opened one of his major theological works.[27]

The artistic flowering we call "the Renaissance," which was to develop its strength in the 1400's, was inspired by sculptors and painters in Europe drawing on a re-appreciation of the art of the ancient Greek and Roman world. A century-and-a-half before that Renaissance, there was another way that knowledge about the ancient Greeks inspired a revival. The background was that over the preceding several centuries, Islamic culture had spread over northern Africa. And beginning in the 9th century, a massive trans-lation movement developed, during which, for over 200 years, an enormous number of ancient Greek manuscripts were translated into Arabic. Commentaries on them were also developed. It was through this Islamic avenue that even more ancient Greek scien-tific work—including more of the philosophical and scientific teachings of Aristotle—made their way into Christian culture.

Just as with most Christian thinkers in the first few centuries of Christianity, the 13th-century Roman Catholic theologian Thomas Aquinas did not reject that new influx of works of Aris-totle just because that ancient Greek was neither a theologian nor a Christian. Instead, Aquinas developed an immense system of theo-logical thought aimed at demonstrating the *compatibility* of Chris-tian belief with the learning from Aristotle. Aquinas's system also strongly emphasized reason.

15th- through 17th-Century

Following the medieval period, many changes in society occurred in Europe during the 15th, 16th, and early 17th centuries. In the way we today tend to categorize time-periods, the medieval period was followed by the Renaissance and then by the Protestant

Reformation.

Some perpetuators of the "warfare" myth try to garner additional evidence for their "warfare" claim from the increase in the number of books after the beginning of the Protestant Reformation (compared to the number of books in the centuries before the reformer Martin Luther posted his landmark theses in 1517). It is claimed that the increase in books was caused by scientific knowledge and education breaking free from the Roman Catholic Church (which supposedly suppressed most learning).

Apart from the falseness of that stereotype about the Roman Catholic Church, the better explanation for the increase in the number of books is simply the invention by Gutenberg of a printing press with repositionable type in about 1450. The books that came from those presses would not have been anywhere as numerous if it had not been for a second contribution from Islamic culture. Namely, making paper. It was a technique Muslims had gotten from China and introduced to the Mideast by the 8th century, with the first paper entering Europe through Spain in the 10th century.[28] That serves as still another example that Europe was not sealed off in darkness before the Scientific Revolution that was still to come.

The Protestant Reformation beginning in the 16th century would eventually bring more complexities into the story of Christianity. But at first it created no major problems regarding science. John Calvin, a leading reformer, developed further the idea that parts of the Bible were written in accommodation to the understanding of ordinary people, and not meant to be science.[29] Calvin, at one point in interpreting the Bible, wrote that, "The Holy Spirit had no intention to teach astronomy."[30]

The Protestant Reformation was closely followed by what is called the Scientific Revolution. The latter is usually dated from the work of Galileo in the 1600's, or sometimes from that of the Polish astronomer Copernicus, who lived a half-century earlier. Galileo promoted Copernicus's mathematical system by which the Earth could orbit around the sun, rather than the Earth being at the center of the planetary system (as was the case with the traditional system that had been inherited from the ancient astronomer Ptolemy). Today, the Galileo story is so often used as an icon supposedly demonstrating a fundamental historical conflict between religion and science, and there are so many myths regarding that affair, that it is dealt with fully in the upcoming Chapter 2. Suffice it to say at this point simply that the science was not clear-cut, and the conflict had more to do with individual personalities and circumstances than with religious thought.

The form of science we have today has strong roots in the Scientific Revolution of the 1600's, but that "revolution," was not a single event. It was a long process extending even beyond the 1600's.

In popular books and media today, that Scientific Revolution is often depicted as being a shift from unquestioning reliance on authority to a reliance on empirical observations. Or depicted as a shift from sheer speculation to scientific experimentation. But such black-and-white caricatures—in which religion is often cast as being on the losing side—are highly misleading. One historian of science, Reijer Hooykaas, after listing four elements of modern science (such as the use of observations, experiments, and mathematics), then adds, "It should be stressed that these characteristics are not wholly absent from *ancient* science."[31]

What did occur beginning in the period we call "the Scientific Revolution" was in part a rearranging of the weight given to those elements so that less emphasis was laid on deductive reasoning from prior principles, and greater emphasis was placed on inductive reasoning tested mathematically with experiments. That gradual shift in methodology became linked with economic and other social changes, in which the value of new technology in turn propelled more abstract scientific investigation. Technology and knowledge together, each feeding the other.

The Book-of-Nature tradition (mentioned above) was still a part of a lot of Christian thought during both the time of the Scientific Revolution and the following century. For example, the man who laid out principles by which modern science would operate, Francis Bacon, wrote:

> Let no man ... think or maintain that a man can search
> too far, or be too well studied in the book of God's
> word [i.e., the Bible], or in the book of God's works.[32]

Despite the possibility for harmony that Bacon expressed in that two-books statement, significant changes were beginning to occur during the Scientific Revolution that would progressively make it harder to harmonize science's and religion's ways of knowing. For one thing, modern science began to emphasize the value of an abstract kind of knowing of the world obtainable through mathematics. Galileo, who is sometimes called the pioneer of modern science, was so ecstatic about the power of mathematics that he wrote:

> This grand book the universe ... is written in the
> language of mathematics ... without which it is
> humanly impossible to understand a single word of it.[33]

Notice how that viewpoint makes it sound as if mathematical equations about the world are the *ultimate* form of knowledge.

But is the firsthand religious experience of God something that can be mathematically measured? Thus, there lie ahead some difficulties for the role of religion in a world in which science will eventually come to dominate. Thirteen centuries earlier, Anthony of the Desert had spoken of the natural world as being like a book by which, "any time I wish to read the words of God, the book is before me."[34] As Anthony saw it, any Christian could read that "Book of Nature." In contrast, this emerging modern science was beginning to make the claim that it was the only one who knew how to read that "Book" of the natural world accurately.

During this period in which a more mathematical and empirical kind of science was emerging, one of the most significant discoveries was Isaac Newton's laying out mathematical laws by which one force, gravity, could be understood as guiding both the fall of an apple on the Earth and the movements of the planets in the heavens. How could Newton have imagined that the entire universe could follow the same physical "laws" as those here on Earth, given that he had no way to send scientific instruments into outer space? Some current writers who examine the history of science suggest that his assumption was made easier because of the Judeo-Christian heritage, which emphasized that there was one Creator of the entire universe, who was also a law-giving God.

However, because of the revolutionary character of Newton's discovery, purveyors of the "warfare" myth sometimes present Newton as a man who did away with God by depicting a mechanical universe that could run itself, just like a clock. God was viewed as the Grand Clockmaker who created and wound up the clock of the universe long ago but was no longer needed.[35] But

Newton did not in his own mind do away with God, nor with religion. In fact, Newton (who actually wrote more on religious topics than on scientific ones) could not imagine how the force of gravity could permeate space properly without God continuing to make that possible.[36]

Nevertheless, the stage was being set for problems for Christian theology. In the century following Newton's discovery (that is, in the 18th-century "Enlightenment" period), some scientists *would* imagine that this clockwork-like universe could run without requiring God to do anything more than establish it with natural laws. An example of this slowly emerging religious challenge is an often-told (even if apocryphal) story about the French astronomer Laplace. When Laplace presented his book to Napoleon with its hypothesis of how the solar system could have begun, Napoleon asked him why there was no mention of God in the book. To which, Laplace, even though he was not against religion, is said to have replied, "Sir, I have no need for that hypothesis."[37] Whether or not that story is historically true, it is used to illustrate how a mental line was beginning to be drawn walling off intellectual scientific thought from religious thought.

We might also notice that even though these early modern scientists had preserved a place for God as initial Creator in their picture of the world, that God is a far cry from the God of the Bible. A God who merely set up the natural laws by which the universe operates is quite different than the God in the Bible who promised Jacob that, "I am *with* you and will keep you wherever you go."[38] Thus, there was beginning to be a lot of wrestling with where to place God within one's mental picture of this world—a world being more and more learned about through science. A few intellectuals would entertain eliminating God altogether.[39]

Political Revolutions and the Revolutionary 1800's

Where real conflict did appear during the Enlightenment period, it usually involved political struggles, not just such conceptual matters. In the second-half of the 1700's, in the British colonies of America and in France, some leading thinkers cultivated the idea that Reason, as inspired by science, could transform society. And where the institutionalized Church was viewed as being in league with oppressive monarchies, science and reason became pitted against religion in the revolutionary rhetoric of the times. The American firebrand revolutionary Thomas Paine, attacking the established powers, thus made the greatly exaggerated claim that there was, "continual persecution carried on by the Church, for several hundred years, against the sciences and against the professors of science."[40] And in France, the satirist Voltaire turned his biting tongue against both the monarchy and the Church.

However, given the context of the times, most people heard such statements as being primarily political attacks, and not a belief that science necessarily meant the end of religion or the end of belief in God's existence. This is demonstrated by the fact that writings of Paine envisioned a new kind of religion based on God as revealed through the natural world, rather than through institutionalized Christianity's Bible. Voltaire also believed in God, and even made fun of atheists.

Evidence that the verbal attacks by Paine and Voltaire were mostly aimed at the institution of the Church (rather than demonstrating for most people an insurmountable opposition between religion and science) can also be found if we simply cross over the English Channel from France and look at the situation in Britain during the very same time. There, especially in England, the social role of a parson-naturalist had developed. That is, a parson who also devoted time to collecting and studying samples of flora and insects. Some of the species found in Nature could even provide ready-made examples of the wonders of God's creation when it was time to write next Sunday's sermon. Thus, scientific observations and religious lessons were viewed as being in harmony.

Of course, the most significant event during the 1800's was the groundbreaking publication of *Origin of Species* by Charles Darwin (who actually imagined that he might become such a country parson before his journey on HMS *Beagle* set him on a different course). The "warfare" myth depicts the reaction to Darwin's theory of evolution as people being strongly divided over the theory, with scientists supporting it and the religious community opposing it.

The truth, however, is that in the first decade after *Origin of Species*, both the scientific and religious communities were divided, with supporters and opponents in both fields. Many religious people soon found ways to adjust to, and sometimes even embrace an evolutionary history for life on Earth. Moreover, during the following 20th century, most mainline Protestant denominations, as well as Roman Catholicism and branches of Judaism, would come to adopt official statements expressing the acceptability of the scientific theory of evolution. (Chapters 3 and 4 deal with these matters further.)

Today, most discussion about tensions between Christianity and science depicts the difficulties as being simply that some Christians have not wanted to accept particular scientific discoveries, such as Darwin's theory of evolution. It is not generally understood (not even by some scientists) that there are broader challenges involving modern science's methodology. That is because, beginning in the 1600's, what we call "modern science" progressively made changes in the way it gave explanations for things.

The background is that before the Scientific Revolution, Western science had followed the lead of the ancient thinker Aristotle in how it described the causes for anything. Aristotle believed that in order to adequately explain something, you needed to identify four types of causes.[41] The easiest way to understand this is to think of something made by humans, such as a house:

- The first type of cause is the **matter** out of which the house is made (that is, the building materials).
- The second type of cause is the **actions** upon those materials (in this case, the actions of the construction workers).
- The third type of cause is the **guiding idea** that shapes the construction (in this case, the plan or idea in the mind of the architect).
- And the fourth type of cause is the **purpose** or goal that has brought the whole process about (in this case, we might say the purpose is so that there will be a home in which some people can live).[42]

For over nineteen-hundred years, Western science followed this four-cause approach.

Beginning in the 1600's, however, scientists began to more and more *eliminate* the 3rd and 4th types of causes from their explanations.[43] The reason they did so was because they gradually came to realize that trying to identify those types of causes—the ideas and purpose that might lie behind things—entailed making evaluative judgments. In the case of something made by humans, such as a house, it may not be so obvious how identifying its purpose is making an evaluative judgment. It might be easier to see how an evaluative judgment is involved the case of a natural object. For example, if we try to answer questions such as "What is the purpose for birds existing?" Or, "What is purpose for there being flowers?" The motivations for eliminating the 3rd and 4th causes were thus primarily practical. Having to make evaluative statements (such as about the overall purpose of things) slowed down the identification of mechanical causes and effects. And knowing mechanical causes and effects enabled science to gain greater technological power.[44]

The often unrecognized consequences of this change in scientific methodology come from those 3rd and 4th types of causes being so highly important to religion. It is in those types of causes that lie the significance and meaning of things—the very things religion and theology try to identify. Concerns about value, meaning, and purpose are not required for modern science, but they are critical for religion.

Modern science's beginning to set aside questions about the underlying idea or purpose behind causes and effects did not pose too many problems when it was first applied to inanimate objects. For example, it was not too much of a challenge for science to shed Aristotle's explanation that objects fall to the Earth because they were following the purpose of seeking their natural level. However, it was much harder to set aside questions about the shaping idea and purpose when it came to animate things. In the 19th century, after *Origin of Species* was published, it was not just closed-minded theologians but also some scientists who had a hard time accepting a scientific explanation for how the variety of species had come about without there being some guiding idea and purpose directing the overall course of evolution. But Darwin was following the approach modern science had already been taking when he gave an explanation for evolution that did not require those 3rd and 4th types of causes.

Emergence of "Warfare" Rhetoric

With the rise of modern science, there have thus been changing methodological and philosophical boundaries between the fields of religion and science. During the 1800's, there were also shifting *social* boundaries between them.

We have seen in this overview of Western Christian history that even though there have been points at which Christians have wrestled with how to interrelate Christian faith, reason, and scientific knowledge, there has not been much of a notion that religion and science have always been at "war" historically (except perhaps in the rhetoric of some politically-motivated Enlightenment writers such as Paine and a few French revolutionaries).

In the latter half of the 1800's, however, two books appeared: In 1874, *History of the Conflict between Religion and Science* by John Draper; and in 1896, *A History of the Warfare of Science with Theology in Christendom* by Andrew Dickson White. The very titles of these two books might reveal that we would not expect to find in them a balanced, objective treatment of Christianity's historical relationship with the sciences. And indeed, both books have been totally discredited by contemporary historians of science. As one leading historian, Ronald L. Numbers, explains:

> Historians of science have known for years that White's and Draper's accounts are more propaganda than history.[45]

So, after 1,800 years of Christian history—in which science and Western religion for the most part led compatible lives—we come at last to the origin of our contemporary myth that the religion-science relationship has been predominantly one of "conflict" and "warfare." The notion is not as old as the hills. It is a quite modern myth.

So what lies behind these latter 19th-century books? John Draper, who was a chemist, was personally incensed by actions of the Roman Catholic Church during his lifetime, his anger being compounded by his sister converting to Catholicism. More significant is the background behind White's book. He was president of Cornell University, and was trying to establish it as a school without any religious affiliation at a time when most universities had been established by Christian denominations. He drew criticism for doing so, and was incensed by that criticism. He also had to make a case that his non-religious university should receive funds that might have otherwise gone to religiously affiliated schools.

Behind those academic conflicts lay larger societal changes in which scientists in both the U.S. and Britain were seeking to separate and professionalize their fields (in contrast to those parson-naturalists of a half-century earlier).[46] And what better way to elevate your own cause in a turf battle fighting for funds and professorships than to depict a competing academic field—religion —as ever in the wrong, and even as a threat to academic freedom! Thus, for example, the biologist Thomas Henry Huxley, campaigning for a dominance of scientists in the university and in British society, floridly claimed that:

> Extinguished theologians lie about the cradle of every
> science as the strangled snakes beside that of
> Hercules.[47]

The lasting difficulty with Draper's and White's late 19th-century books (besides their introducing the strident and now commonplace metaphors "conflict" and "warfare") has been that those books were filled with many incorrect or misleading statements about Christian history and the history of science.[48] Many myths. (Such as the myth about belief in a flat Earth.)

Despite being error-filled, Draper's and White's books were widely read and believed, even translated into several languages. And their myths regarding history worked their way into Western culture and popular books on science. That process was accelerated by some of the myths even being put into public-school textbooks—presented there as being history.[49]

Today's Legacy of Changes in Science

As science and Christianity both moved into the 20th century, like brothers who had long known each other, so also did other Western religions such as Judaism and Islam. But life-experiences that had changed both science and Christianity made them unclear about their relationship to each other.

Nevertheless, Western Christianity's long-standing tradition of thinking that science could be a handmaiden to religion was sustained through Catholicism's and mainline Protestantism's constructing many new hospitals in the U.S. Those institutions took advantage of the accelerating knowledge in medicine that the scientific method was bringing.

But scientific technology also brought great challenges to Christianity and Western culture, especially over the question of whether the use of human reason, even if coupled with religious tradition, could sufficiently control human destiny. The 18th-century Enlightenment's idea that Reason would bring inevitable progress was shattered when World War I brought instead the deaths of more than 16 million people.[50] Nor did the massive warfare made possible by new scientific technology end there, for in less than three decades, there was a second World War, which in turn ushered in atomic and nuclear weapons.

There also continued to be conceptual problems in how to understand the Bible and traditional Christian concepts in a scientifically-minded age. We, of course, see such struggles most prominently in the kind of anti-evolutionism that developed in parts of Christianity in the middle of the 20th century. That anti-evolutionism, which attracts so much media attention, can distract us from the challenges science truly poses to a Christianity that does accept the findings of science. Such as:

- Where do we mentally place God in a universe that seems to be able to operate on its own through natural laws?
- And, with so much of our understanding of the world coming from a form of science that excludes questions of meaning and purpose from its methods, does meaning and purpose become something we simply make up or impose upon the world?

(These questions are laid out in more detail in Chapter 6, "Ancient Wisdom Raises Her Head.")

Over such challenges hangs the stubbornly persistent myth that religion and science have usually been at war. One fairly recent survey in Britain of university students revealed that 72 per cent of them agreed with the statement that "There has been continual conflict between religion and science throughout history."[51] That myth has in the West tarnished even the good in Christianity's reputation, at a time in which it already has so many other challenges.

The fact that there have been and still are real-life struggles should not deafen us to the voices of Christian leaders who have not seen religion as fundamentally in conflict with science. Such moderate voices are in touch with a long chain of Judeo-Christian thought reaching back even into the Bible—a chain affirming that the natural world is good and orderly. And deserving of our attention, thought, and contemplation.

Chapter 2

The Galileo Story:
Great Drama, Mostly False

I t is scene seemingly perfect for the opening frames of a Holly-
wood movie. A 70-year-old man lies on his deathbed, two
close friends at his side. And when one of the friends refers to the
dying man as "Copernicus," we know we are watching the death
of the revolutionary 16th-century astronomer Nicolaus Copernicus. In case we do not know, a few lines of dialogue establish the
importance of the dying man, as well as setting up the conflict that
will be at the center of the movie:

"Did you get it printed?" asks a nearly desperate Copernicus.

"Yes, yes we did," they reassure him, and place on his chest a
heavy book, which he clutches with his, gnarled fingers.

"So many years I worked on it!" Copernicus tells his friends,
and they nod in acknowledgment. "So many years it took me to
establish proof that the sun doesn't really revolve around the
Earth. It is our planet, the Earth, that revolves around the sun!"

The friends instantly hush him, looking about to make sure no
one else has heard. "Yes, we believe you, Nicolaus. We know
science proves it, but the Church must not hear you say such a
thing, or we will all be charged with heresy and be condemned to
death."

"But at least you have put my calculations into print. I can die
knowing that my idea will not be lost. And I pray that centuries
from now, the Church will no longer dictate what scientists can
and cannot write, as has always been in the past."

Of course, this dramatic opening scene ends with Copernicus
exhaling his final, dying breath.[1]

A Dramatic Scene, But...

Copernicus always affords purveyors of the "warfare" myth an
opportunity to perpetuate the misconception that religion and
science have usually been in conflict historically. For example, one

contemporary book on science for general readers states:

> Copernicus dared not publish his radical idea during
> his lifetime ... for fear that it would clash with the
> doctrine of the church.... [He was] suggesting that the
> Earth was not the center of the universe, implying that
> humans were not the most important beings in it, as
> favored by an anthropocentric [i.e., human-centered]
> god.[2]

The truth is that Copernicus (who held an official church position as canon at Frauenburg Cathedral) was more concerned about
the response of *scientists*.[3] And the hesitant Copernicus was urged
to publish his book *On the Revolutions of the Heavenly Spheres* by
a cardinal (Nicolas von Schönberg) and by bishops. Moreover,
even after Copernicus circulated a preliminary work thirty years
earlier outlining the idea that the Earth could orbit around the sun,
he was among those asked by Pope Leo X to come to Rome in an
effort to revise the calendar.[4] And Copernicus's work was received
favorably by the papal court of another Pope, Clement VII.

In Chapter 1, an overview of Western Christianity was
presented exposing many "warfare" myths of this type. It was
shown that for the most part, Christianity has been open to science,
reason, and knowledge about the natural world. There still
remains, however, the matter of Galileo, only mentioned in
passing in Chapter 1.

Today, in any discussion of the relation between religion and
science, the story of Galileo and the Church is almost invariably
brought up, as if to demonstrate a fundamental conflict between
Christianity and science. For example, one youth-level book states
that, "Galileo's life shows the age-old conflict between science
and faith."[5] The Galileo story has become iconic. And so, this
chapter will uncover the real nature of the Galileo affair. We will
also see some of the complexities of arriving at truth through
science.

Let us first look at how the Galileo story is commonly
portrayed. Although the narrative I am now going to give is a
composite, every main point in it is either explicitly stated or
strongly implied in more than one book about Galileo, science, or
history. Here is the way the Galileo story is often presented:

In medieval Europe, the Church had come to suppress learning, indoctrinating people instead with religious beliefs. In those Dark Ages, most people thought the Earth was at the center of the planetary system, with the sun circling around the Earth. The Church taught that doctrine, which was based on such passages in the Bible as the statement in Joshua 10:13 that, miraculously, "the sun stood still" during a pivotal battle.

But then, Galileo invented the modern telescope, and using it discovered proof of Copernicus's idea that the Earth circled around the sun. Not only did Galileo's discovery pose great difficulty for the Church with its traditional literal interpretation of the Bible, his discovery was hard for people to accept because it deposed the Earth from its privileged place at the center of the planetary system. The Church had become so adverse to evidence that one leading Church official would not even look through Galileo's telescope to see with his own eyes that what Galileo said was true.

Galileo did nothing wrong other than put forward the idea that the sun was at the center of the solar system. Nevertheless, Galileo was immediately arrested by the Pope, tortured on the rack, tried, and convicted of teaching the heresy that the Earth circled around the sun. He was sentenced and put in prison for the rest of his life, where he died, prevented from ever again publishing any scientific knowledge.

Misleads and Falsehoods

Great drama! Except for one major problem—it's mostly false. There are at least sixteen points at which this common way of telling the Galileo story states outright falsehoods or severely misleads us as to what actually occurred. The remainder of this chapter will go through the Galileo narrative again, correcting the falsehoods. The explication is based on the work of historians of science, astronomers, and historians of religion.

Chapter 1 ("Exposing the 'Warfare' Myth") already explained how it is a modern myth that people in the Middle Ages were ignorant about many things, in the way we frequently portray it, sometimes giving all or part of that period the derogatory label "the Dark Ages." Nor, for the most part, did the medieval Church suppress learning. In the centuries of political strife in Europe following the fall of Rome in 476 C.E., monasteries were in fact the primary means of preserving accumulated knowledge, including scientific knowledge. And, between the years 1200 and 1419 (the latter part of the Middle Ages), twenty-nine universities were begun across mainland Europe and England, drawing upon that knowledge.

Anyway, it is chronologically incorrect to mentally place Galileo in the medieval times. That is because when Galileo was born in Italy in 1564, that flowering of art and culture we call the Renaissance—which followed the medieval period—had been going on for a century-and-a-half.

In order to understand the actual Galileo affair, it is critical to understand that Europe had inherited a body of knowledge about biology, physics and other sciences from the ancient teacher Aristotle. It was that Aristotelian teaching that Galileo primarily came in conflict with, *not* theological doctrines of the Church.[6] Although Aristotle predated the Church, Western Christianity, using reason, had over the course of centuries found ways to reconcile Christian ideas with much of that ancient Greek thought.

Of particular relevance is that predominantly Christian Europe had assimilated a model of the universe that fused the physics of Aristotle with the detailed mathematical calculations of the 2nd-century Ptolemy, an astronomer who lived in Alexandria, Egypt. The Ptolemaic teaching that the planetary system had the Earth at its center did *not* come out of any church doctrine nor even from the Bible. It came from ancient science. And that system for the planets had worked quite well for navigation for over fourteen centuries—and continued to work quite well.

So, if Galileo did not get into trouble because the Church suppressed learning, nor because the Ptolemaic system was official Church doctrine, why did Galileo's troubles occur? Even Galileo thought they began not with the Roman Catholic Church but instead with some of his fellow scientists and academic colleagues (and rivals). So, let us begin the true chronology of events by concentrating on Galileo's academic life.

Conflicts and Complexities

Galileo studied medicine at the University of Pisa, but did not complete his degree. At the age of twenty-one, he began giving private lessons, and four years later began teaching mathematics at the University of Pisa. After only three years, he moved to the University of Padua, getting a higher-paying position as the chair of mathematics.

Even those current writers who are sympathetic to Galileo admit that from his first years in universities, even as a student, Galileo offended other intellectuals, not just orally, but also in his scientific papers. As the 20th-century science-historian and writer Isaac Asimov puts it:

> Galileo wrote articles about his discoveries. In them,
> he defended himself against his attackers with sarcastic
> anger.... Galileo had a knack for making his opponents
> look ridiculous, and they rarely forgave him.[7]

The first disagreements Galileo had with some other scientists were not over astronomy, but over other points of Aristotelian science (such as the speed of falling objects). He did not begin investigations using a telescope until he was middle-aged. Galileo did not actually invent the telescope, even though he seems to have given that impression to the leaders of Venice to whom he demonstrated it, and in his later writings spoke of it as if it were his own invention.

Many people today who have at one time seen a play dramatizing the Galileo affair (such as the play by Bertolt Brecht) feel they have some memory of a scene in which a leading figure refuses to even look through Galileo's telescope to see what Galileo has seen. Wasn't that person one of those Church leaders who, according to our stereotyped Galileo story, opposed science with blind dogmatism?

In fact, the persons we know to have refused at some point to look through Galileo's telescope were not Church officials but professors of science at the universities in Pisa and Padua.[8] To be fair, we know from one professor's own writing that he declined to look because on previous occasions he had looked, but he (as well as others) had *not* seen those things Galileo claimed to have seen. The difficulty probably had to do with the limitations of even Galileo's improved telescope. It had not much more magnification than a modern pair of binoculars, and also had a narrower field of view, making it difficult to see much through it.[9] Also, its being a small refracting telescope would have caused color aberrations, as well as posing difficulty in trying to see clearly pinpoints of light such as stars.

Figure 4: Ptolemaic Model (simplified schematic of the sun, Venus, and the Earth)

The two planetary models that would become a central part of Galileo's latter life were the traditional Ptolemaic model, in which planets and the sun circle around the Earth, and the Copernican model, in which the Earth and other planets circle around the sun. (See simplified Figures 4 & 5.) The Copernican model, which Galileo came to prefer, was named after Nicolaus Copernicus, who had developed the mathematical formulations for it over half-a-century before Galileo aimed his telescope at the sky.

It is essential to realize that even if people did accept that Galileo saw what he thought he saw through his telescope, it still did *not* prove that the Earth circulated around the sun, rather than vice versa. For example, Galileo discovered that some moons circled around the planet Jupiter, whereas Aristotle had thought all moving bodies circulated around the Earth. However, it only takes a bit of reflection to realize that Jupiter's having moons does not necessarily lead to the conclusion that the Earth revolves around the sun.[10]

Figure 5: Copernican Model (simplified schematic of the Earth, the sun, and Venus)

As the contemporary astronomer Owen Gingerich states, "when [Galileo] presented his ideas, there was as yet no observational proof" that the Copernican model was a true picture of how the universe was structured.[11] Of all the fundamental points for understanding the Galileo affair, this one is critical, even though it is the one most often omitted from stereotyped versions of the Galileo story. And in Galileo's time, given the instruments of the day, *both* models—even the older Ptolemaic model—remained workable systems for predicting the positions of the planets, moon, and sun.[12] Despite the fact that Galileo could not deduce from the evidence he possessed that the Earth moves around the sun, numerous books today make it sound as if Galileo's telescopic evidence provided proof. The implication thus becomes that those who did not follow Galileo's conclusion were simply being closed-minded.

Today, the most widespread way of characterizing objections to the sun-centered Copernican system is saying it dethroned the Earth from a privileged position. For example:

> Galileo's advocacy of the Copernican theory,
> displacing man from the center of the universe,
> brought him the enmity of the Inquisition.[13]

However, a close examination of 16th-and 17th-century documents reveals that a supposed demotion of the Earth was not really a concern of that time. When we today assume that removing the Earth from the physical center of the planetary system must have implied a reduction in the Earth's status, we are making a totally modern equation between the two. The fact is that in Galileo's time, repositioning the Earth implied either no change in the Earth's status or, if anything, an elevation in its status. That is because the Aristotelian model envisioned the heavy, earthly world here below as being inferior to the ethereal world of the planets and stars above. And so, shifting the Earth upward into the realm of other planets was actually perceived by some people as elevating the Earth toward the superior, heavenly realm.[14]

Interlude: Some Scientific Matters Clarified

So, if the primary objections to the Copernican model were not that the Ptolemaic system was Church doctrine, and not that the Copernican model diminished the importance of the Earth, what was the problem with it? As prosaic as it might seem, the major difficulties with the Copernican model during Galileo's lifetime (and for many decades afterward) were *scientific* problems. The idea that the Earth moved fit neither the evidence of the senses nor the scientific reasoning of the time.

In the Copernican model, the Earth's motion would not be merely a single, smooth movement that we might not feel, but instead multiple motions as the Earth revolved around the sun and rotated on its own axis. Wouldn't we notice such shifts, in the way when riding in a cart, we feel any change in its speed or direction? The only way this problem could be resolved would have been if major presuppositions in the field of physics were thrown out the window.[15] (We might try to imagine what would be the response from physicists today if some astronomer said he had figured out how to rearrange the planets, and all it required was to throw away our knowledge of the laws of physics.)

The idea that the Earth revolved around the sun also did not jive with observational evidence regarding the stars. Scientists who disagreed with Galileo were able to point out that if the Earth did move, the relative positions of a near object and distant stars would change as the Earth moved. This would be what is called "stellar parallax." The effect would be similar to the way that if you hold out your finger at arm's length and view it with first one eye and then the other, your finger's position shifts in relation to the distant background. Most importantly, throughout Galileo's lifetime and for a long time afterward, scientists could not see such a change in the relative position of stars. This is still another instance of how Galileo's support of the Copernican hypothesis did not fit the observed evidence—despite our myth-filled Galileo story portraying Galileo as the person who followed the evidence of his senses.[16] Stellar parallax would not actually be observed until two centuries after Galileo's death.[17]

There was one other thing Galileo sighted through his telescope that made him a believer in the Copernican system. In 1610, he observed how the planet Venus went through phases of light and dark (the way the Earth's moon goes through phases from light to dark). The specific contours of Venus's phases were something the traditional Ptolemaic model could not explain accurately.

However, the observations about Venus's phases still did not constitute proof that the Copernican model was truly the way the universe was constructed. That is because there was actually a third model developed by the eminent astronomer Tycho Brahe, which myth-filled stories presenting a black-and-white stereotype never tell us about.[18] (See Figure 6.) In Brahe's model, Venus and other planets did revolve around the sun, thus creating Venus's phases, but the sun in turn revolved around a stable Earth—thus not requiring scientists' knowledge of physics to be thrown out the window.[19] During Galileo's lifetime, and for over a century afterward, it was Brahe's model—not the Copernican model Galileo liked—that best fit all the scientific evidence regarding moving bodies, absence of stellar parallax, and the phases of Venus.[20]

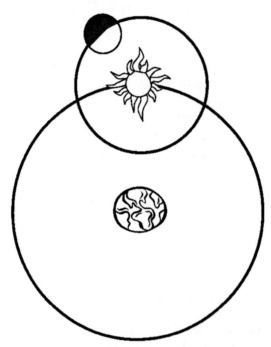

Figure 6: Brahe's Model (simplified schematic of Venus, the sun, and the Earth)

More Historical Developments

By 1611, a middle-aged Galileo had begun to challenge the traditional Aristotelian base of knowledge and picture of the cosmos that had been employed by both scientists and theologians for centuries. But was he punished by the Church for his discoveries? No. In fact, for his work Galileo was received warmly in Rome by Pope Paul V and was honored by Jesuits at the Collegio Romano (Roman College).[21] Galileo was also made a member of the scientific Lyncean Academy, having at this point personally offended only a modest number of scientists. That number, however, would soon increase.

The warm glow from both religious leaders and scientists Galileo basked in during his visit to Rome was clouded during the next two years when Galileo got into a dispute with still another scientist, this time about sunspots. This argument, over what the dark spots were and over who had spotted them first, gained him more enemies among fellow astronomers. Particularly that of the Jesuit astronomer Christopher Scheiner. One historian explains that:

> This dispute alienated Galileo from a group who might otherwise have been willing to offer him support—up until 1613, the Jesuit astronomers in Rome had been among Galileo's strongest advocates.[22]

There was another feature of Galileo's publication *Letters on the Sunspots* that is even more significant: In it, Galileo explicitly endorsed the Copernican model for the first time in public writing. However—contrary to our myth-filled Galileo story, which portrays the Copernican model as so heretical that any advocacy of it would have been immediately snuffed out—no action was taken against Galileo for his endorsement of that idea.

The Bible Enters the Picture

It would be another matter, a Biblical matter, that would become the focus of his writing for the next two years. It began when Galileo heard from a friend, Benedetto Castelli, a professor of math at Pisa, about a breakfast party in which Castelli had engaged in discussion about whether Copernicus's idea that the Earth moved conflicted with a few passages in the Bible that seemed to say that the Earth did not move or that the sun did. Galileo's friend wrote Galileo that a sound case had been made for there not being any conflict with the Bible.

Galileo might have left the matter at that. Nevertheless, he decided he would take matters into his own hands. Over the course of the next two years, Galileo produced two letters, knowing their arguments would probably be circulated to others (as was the custom with letters arguing academic points). First was a letter to his friend; and then a longer letter to another person who had been in that breakfast-party discussion. The latter is what we now know

as the *Letter to the Grand Duchess Christina* (1615). Thus it was
that the first major step of placing into writing questions about
possible conflict between the Bible and Galileo's support of
Copernicanism was not undertaken by any Church official, but by
Galileo himself.

Because today countless popular accounts of the Galileo affair
claim that the problem was that the Copernican model conflicted
with the Church's having traditionally interpreted the Bible literally, there is something that deserves reiterating from Chapter 1:
Christianity had *not* traditionally limited itself to a literal interpretation of the Bible. Although some Bible passages do express a
perspective imagining the sun revolving around the Earth, with the
Earth being stable, those passages alone would not have posed an
obstacle.[23] When dealing with Bible passages that would seem to
contradict our knowledge of the world, an important principle
developed early in Christianity was that of **accommodation**. That
principle recognized that certain Bible passages were viewing the
world not from the perspective of sophisticated scientific knowledge but from a common person's way of experiencing the world.

In the Galileo affair, however, the challenge was in part
deciding whether a particular Bible passage was written in accommodation to a common person's way of experiencing the world, or
whether it was to be taken as a statement of fact. How would such
a question be determined in this controversy in which astronomers
had three workable planetary models, and could not be sure which
one best described factual reality, if any of them did at all?

In his lengthy *Letter to the Grand Duchess Christina*, Galileo
first drew upon Christianity's traditional principle of accommodation so that the Copernican model would not be bound to the problematic Biblical passages if read literally. Peculiarly though, after
making room for science to have a freedom beyond the Bible,
Galileo then went on to employ Bible passages to try to *support*
the Copernican model that he favored.[24] Those scientists who
disagreed with Galileo were able to point out that Galileo was
trying to eat his cake and have it too: Galileo was on the one hand
trying to separate a possible scientific discovery from Biblical
interpretation, and on the other hand trying to use the Bible to
support a scientific concept he favored.

Even beyond these snarls Galileo got himself into with his

venture into Biblical interpretation, Galileo was moving onto risky ground because of the context of his times. In 1517, the priest and professor Martin Luther had posted his defiant theses on the door of a church in Wittenberg, and the Protestant Reformation had begun. Christian Europe found itself divided in religious wars, Protestant versus Roman Catholic. For the Pope, this warfare was made more complicated by his being also the secular ruler over part of Italy. Rome had even been attacked in 1527.

Moreover, many Protestants were saying that each person had the right to interpret the Bible his own way. In response, the Roman Catholic Church had convened the Council of Trent beginning in 1545, and had taken a much more conservative approach toward interpreting the Bible, with the Dominicans being especially cautious. The Council of Trent had issued an edict against people "distorting the Holy Scriptures ... contrary to" the Roman Catholic Church's authority to interpret it.[25]

Our myth-filled Galileo story depicts Galileo as being almost immediately punished once he expressed support for the Copernican system. But it has been over a year now since Galileo publicly expressed support for the Copernican system. And Galileo has even openly circulated a letter supporting the Copernican system with his own analysis of how to apply Biblical passages— and yet no action has been taken by the Church against him.

Nevertheless, the circulation of letters such as *Letter to the Grand Duchess* by a public figure like Galileo, debating the relevance of Biblical passages to a new scientific hypothesis, compounded social and political anxieties. The year after Galileo wrote his earlier letter, a young Dominican priest, Tommaso Caccini, denounced the Copernican idea in a sermon at the main church in Florence, where Galileo now lived. The priest had been encouraged by one of those professors of Aristotelian science whom Galileo had previously offended. But that priest received a rebuke from his Dominican superior in Rome, who also wrote a deeply apologetic letter to Galileo.[26] Now, however, the controversy was spreading beyond Florence.

At this point, in 1615, Cardinal Roberto Bellarmine, the Roman Catholic Church's leading person for investigating such disputes, sent a letter that is critical in disproving the myth that the Church's problem was (supposedly) rigid Biblical literalism.

Bellarmine wrote a letter to a supporter of Galileo, knowing that it would be shared with Galileo. Bellarmine wrote that it was proper to treat the Copernican model as a hypothesis, for, after all, Copernicus's own book *On the Revolutions* had included an introduction by the editor presenting the Copernican model as just that.[27] The key line in Bellarmine's letter reads:

> If there were a real proof that the Sun is in the center
> of the universe ... and does not go round the Earth, but
> the Earth round the Sun, then we would have to
> proceed with great circumspection in explaining
> passages of Scripture which *seem* to teach the
> contrary.[28]

We should note that Bellarmine stated that the Bible passages under discussion could and "would" have to be re-interpreted "if there were a real proof" that the Earth did move. Biblical interpretation would have to yield to new scientific ideas—but only if there were proof, which Bellarmine, along with most scientists, did not believe there was.

Galileo agreed with Cardinal Bellarmine's key point.[29] One reason Galileo could have been agreeable is that even though he had not yet revealed it, he was working on what he thought would be real proof. Galileo had come to think that the regular movements of tides could constitute real proof that the Earth moved. Galileo's notion was that the regular tidal movements of oceans upon the shores were caused by the combination of the Earth's movements. Galileo's analogy was to the way water in a bowl sloshes as we move the bowl about.

The very next year, Galileo published his "Discourse on the Tides." Today, we know that Galileo was quite wrong: It is primarily the gravitational pull of the moon that causes tides. Even though neither Galileo nor any of his adversaries knew about that cause, scientists in Galileo's day were able to see that there was a major flaw in Galileo's supposed explanation for the tides. Namely, that Galileo's idea would have resulted in only a single daily spring tide, whereas actual observations had been of two tides at spring.[30] Thus, Galileo's supposed explanation could not really solve the puzzle of why there were tides, and therefore could not prove that the Earth moved. But Galileo was counting on the tides because he knew his earlier observations about Jupiter and Venus had not constituted proof.[31]

The Critical Year 1616, and Following

Although Galileo had hoped the 1616 publication of his book on tides would prove pivotal, the year 1616 turned out to be critical in a quite different way. The preceding year, Galileo, concerned about recent events, had gone to Rome even against the advice of the Tuscan ambassador, who cautioned that there was in-fighting there between Dominicans and Jesuits. Galileo's talking-up the Copernican model while in Rome led to Pope Paul submitting the Copernican question to a panel of theological consultants. Those consultants did take into account the scientific knowledge as it then stood, but their specialties were theological. They published a decree saying that the view that the sun truly stands motionless is heretical, and the view that the earth is not the center of the planetary system is philosophically false.[32] But it is important to understand that these theological consultants had no final power to say what was officially a heresy. As one leading historian explains:

> Only a pope or a church council could establish
> anything as a heresy in the Catholic faith.... Nothing
> was officially made heretical, then or later, in the
> Copernican matter.[33]

The theologians' decree of 1616 did not mention Galileo by name. Nevertheless, immediately after their decision, Cardinal Bellarmine, in his official capacity, spoke with Galileo and explained what, in the Church's view, could and could not be properly expressed in regard to the Copernican idea. Galileo requested and received from Bellarmine a document putting the instructions in writing. That document would prove critical seventeen years later when Galileo's trial would occur.

For the next seven years, Galileo concentrated on other matters related to astronomy, such as observations of comets, about which he was also wrong. And his combative style gained him even more adversaries.

A new stage in the Galileo saga begin in 1623 when someone Galileo knew, Cardinal Maffeo Barberini, became Pope Urban VIII. Galileo had met that man back in 1611, when Galileo had been so warmly received in Rome. When he was a cardinal, Urban had written sonnets praising Galileo and his discoveries.[34]

Nevertheless, the new Pope Urban had much more on his mind than maintaining his friendship with Galileo. Over the preceding century, the Protestant Reformation had spread across the northern and central countries of Europe like a domino effect. In the summer of 1632, Pope Urban would be so worried about Spanish assassins that he would leave the Vatican and move to a summer house outside Rome.

Galileo was nevertheless hopeful that having someone in the papacy who had shown him special friendship might mean he could revive his maneuvering for the Copernican model. Galileo requested and received six visitations with Pope Urban. The Pope told Galileo he could write a book that compared the different models, treating them as working hypotheses, and laying out their differences. For several years, Galileo worked on the book.

The Book and the Trial

Finally published in 1632, it was titled *Dialogue on the Two Great World Systems*. The two "world systems" Galileo compared in that book were the old Ptolemaic model (along with many ideas from Aristotle) and the newer Copernican model, which Galileo had long favored. With that choice, Galileo was behind the times scientifically because, as one historian explains:

> By that time the Ptolemaic system had been largely
> abandoned by believers in a central Earth, and
> astronomers who could not accept the Sun-centered
> system of Copernicus—the great majority—were
> opting for [Brahe's] Tychonic or one of the other
> Earth-centered compromises.[35]

Another scientific weakness was that the book included Galileo's erroneous idea that tides provided evidence of the Earth's move-ment. But scientists could again see that the number of tides Galileo's formulation predicted did not match what had been observed.[36]

Galileo's greatest mistake, however, involved the character of the book itself. It was written as a classic-style dialogue between three contrived characters: One weakly defending traditional Aristotelianism and the Ptolemaic model, one skillfully defending the Copernican model, and the third an interested third party. Today, virtually all writers agree that, as the scientist Francis

Collins puts it:

> The narrative frame fooled nobody. Galileo's
> preference for the [Copernican] heliocentric point of
> view was obvious by the end of the book.[37]

Moreover, in the dialogue, the character who argued for the Ptolemaic model (which Galileo opposed) was named "Simplicio," which was somewhat like naming him "the Simpleton," or "the Simple-minded One."[38] Even worse, near the climax of the book, Galileo had placed on the lips of Simplicio almost word for word one of the very arguments for Aristotelianism that had been put forward by Pope Urban himself—with Simplicio saying that argument had come from "an eminent personage." Even those writers today who are most sympathetic toward Galileo have to admit that this was not good judgment on Galileo's part.

Accounts from the Tuscan ambassador and others who talked with Pope Urban in the following months describe Urban as being truly outraged.[39] Not only because he felt he had been made an object of satire, but also because he felt Galileo had broken their agreement that Galileo could write about Copernicanism if it were made part of a balanced comparison. And all of this from a scientist Urban knew personally, and had even dedicated a book of sonnets to! It was not just Pope Urban who was upset. Some scientists were too. Various complaints were filed.[40]

Nevertheless, Galileo was not immediately arrested by the Pope, as myth-filled accounts state or imply. Instead, the Pope set up a committee to make a preliminary examination of the matter, which in turn led to the Pope's decision to have Galileo summoned before the Roman Inquisition for fuller investigation. Galileo arrived in Rome in February of 1633. The trial was held from mid-April to mid-June of that year. Even though it had once been commonplace to assume that Galileo was tortured, extensive research indicates that he never was.[41]

Even though one book today on science states that, "the records of the Inquisition are never revealed,"[42] we do have them, including their summary of the questions put to Galileo, and his responses. Early in the trial, the matter of the restrictions that had been placed upon Galileo in 1616 were raised.[43] But Galileo produced his document from Cardinal Bellarmine (who was no longer alive). The wording of that document allowed Galileo to teach about the Copernican model as long as he did not "defend" it. Asked why he did not make that restriction known when he was getting approval for publication of his book, Galileo stated:

> I did not say anything [about the 1616 ruling]... since with the said book I had neither held nor defended the [Copernican] opinion.[44]

Galileo even claimed that his book had *refuted* the Copernican model,[45] something that (to the best of my knowledge) no one has ever believed. Given the very contents of *Dialogue*, the judges of the Inquisition's court were not convinced by Galileo's claim that he had not "defended" the Copernican model in his book. As one historian succinctly puts it, "It was for disobeying the Church, rather than for seeking to understand the natural world through observation and reasoning, that Galileo was condemned."[46]

As the trial continued over many days, Galileo did concede that perhaps the exuberance of some of the characters' arguments in *Dialogue* could have led to the *impression* among readers that he was trying to defend the Copernican model.[47] Galileo yielded to the court's judgment, signing a statement accepting the authority of the Church, and relenting from holding the Copernican idea.

The nature of the sentence against Galileo is also misrepresented in virtually all brief accounts of the Galileo affair. Countless books state that he was found guilty of the "heresy" that the Earth moved around the sun. As has already been explained by one leading historian, "Nothing was officially made heretical, then or later, in the Copernican matter."[48] Technically, the charge upon which Galileo was found guilty was not heresy itself, but was a second-level offense.[49] (Similar to the way that today a person's killing someone can be judged to be either murder or manslaughter based upon considerations about the defendant's intentions.)

Most importantly for evaluating whether or not the Galileo affair was a religion-vs.-science conflict, even after his conviction, Galileo did not see the culprit as having been fundamentally religion. Instead, he especially blamed those scientists who disagreed with him.[50] As he later wrote to a correspondent in France who had read his scientific work:

> You have read my writings and from them you have certainly understood which was the true and real

motive that caused, under the lying *mask of religion*, this war against me.[51]

After Galileo's Conviction

The Inquisition court's sentence of indefinite imprisonment was almost immediately suspended by the Pope. Numerous myth-filled accounts of the Galileo story leave the impression that Galileo was put in jail, perhaps even for the rest of his life. This is not a new notion, having long been a part of our modern science-religion "warfare" myth. The 18th-century philosopher Voltaire wrote that Galileo, "groaned away his days in the dungeons."[52] Again, this is simply not true. During the time of the trial, Galileo was housed sometimes in the Tuscan embassy and sometimes in a six-room apartment (with servant) in the palace of the Office of the Inquisition.[53]

Even after he was found guilty, Galileo was *not* put in prison. A good number of contemporary science books do now try to correct that falsehood by stating that Galileo was put under "house arrest." However, even that phrase, which usually suggests being totally confined within a house, does not adequately describe the remainder of his life. Only two days after signing a confession, Galileo was placed in the custody of a close friend, the Grand Duke of Tuscany, whose villa and gardens in Rome Galileo had enjoyed in the past. Galileo was allowed to leave Rome, which he did twelve days later, traveling to Siena, where he again stayed with a close friend, a church leader, the Archbishop of Siena. He spent five months there, where he received many distinguished visitors in a room described as being "richly furnished and its walls hung with silk tapestries."[54]

Galileo then received permission from the Pope to return to his own home in Arcetri. Even there he was not totally confined to his house. He was able to visit his daughter, Sister Maria Celeste, who was in a nearby convent. Although his movements into the larger public were restricted, he was allowed to go to Mass on Feast Days, as well as spend a brief time with his family in nearby Florence when he needed to see a doctor there.[55] When at his own home, he received visitors, including the noted English philosopher Thomas Hobbes and the great English poet John Milton.

Nor was Galileo in those last years prevented from doing

further scientific writing. Working in his own house with an assistant, he completed a book titled *Discourse on Two New Sciences*, which was sent to a printer in Holland, where it was published in 1638. Galileo died a natural death at home in 1642.

Conclusions

How far-removed this actual history is from the way our modern Galileo myth has come to portray the Galileo affair as a black-and-white conflict between religion and science! Most historians of science today concur with the opinion of the contemporary theologian Alister McGrath, who writes:

> Tensions and conflicts [between religion and science],
> such as the Galileo controversy, often turn out on
> closer examination to have more to do with papal
> politics, ecclesiastical power struggles, and personality
> issues than with any fundamental tensions between
> faith and science.[56]

Ironically, sometimes even Christians who are open to scientific discoveries perpetuate the misleading Galileo myth. For, after all, one quick and easy way to try to elevate one's own modern, religious advancement is to portray ourselves as so much more enlightened than the (supposedly) ignorant Christians of the past.

A second point about which we might draw conclusions involves the nature of scientific discovery itself. Gaining scientific knowledge is virtually never a matter of a simple, direct line from observation to conclusion without any presuppositions. We today can understand even better than people in Galileo's day could how modern science is a complex process, with assumptions influencing what evidence is collected, and with observations in turn influencing assumptions. And some matters, to a greater or lesser degree, being still up in the air. Moreover, science is always an open-ended process. And all of this complexity is handled within a scientific community in which persuasion plays a role.

The histories of both science and religion are complex. And the processes of modern science are complex. These are some of the challenges religion faces today in a world in which so much of our knowledge comes from science.

Pulling up a black-and-white version of the Galileo story as an icon implies that the only challenge Christianity faces from science is simply for Christians not to be closed-minded toward scientific discoveries. But the matter is much more complicated—especially if we want to try to bring together scientific knowledge and religious understanding to form one worldview.

Chapter 3
Tempest in a British Teapot

In the mid-1800's, the British poet Alfred, Lord Tennyson published a long poem that struggled with issues of belief and trust in God at a time when the emerging discoveries of science had compounded intellectuals' faith-struggles. Tennyson described a predatory Nature as "red in tooth and claw."[1] Voicing the concerns of many in the Victorian age about suffering and the natural world, Tennyson pointedly asked:

Are God and Nature then at strife ...?[2]

Today, that phrase describing predatory nature as "red in tooth and claw" is frequently quoted as a way of portraying the shock many Victorians experienced upon being confronted by Charles Darwin's theory of evolution by natural selection following the publication of *Origin of Species*. Darwin's idea about evolution is understood by many people to be a competitive "survival of the fittest," in which the competition sometimes even leads to the death of the unfit.

There is, however, a problem with using Tennyson's now-famous phrase in that fashion. Tennyson's poem, titled "In Memoriam," was published almost a decade *before* Darwin's 1859 *Origin of Species*. And Tennyson began writing his poem in 1833 prompted not by the death of any dinosaur, but instead by the death of one of his closest human friends.[3]

This myth that Tennyson's phrase "red in tooth and claw" was inspired by the publication of *Origin of Species*—which had actually not occurred yet—is but one of many myths in the way our culture today talks about the theory of evolution, even when we accept that theory. Typically, summaries of how Darwin's groundbreaking book was received depict it as opening a fissure in Victorian society, dividing narrow-minded Christian leaders who were creationists from scientists who were evolutionists. The truth is that in the first decade after *Origin* was published, the religious and scientific communities were both divided over the new theory.

And what disturbances did occur were by no means a tsunami sweeping religion aside.

In the U.S. today, partly because of our contemporary school-textbook controversies over evolution, many religious people (even liberals and progressives) think that the theological challenge the theory of evolution brings is merely whether to accept it or not. It is also frequently stated that the issue is simply whether or not to read literally the creation account in the Bible's first chapter of Genesis. In fact, even before Darwin's *Origin of Species* was published, many Christian intellectuals had developed non-literal and figurative readings of Genesis that allowed for the acceptance of new science.[4] And even in Darwin's day, there were more issues—both religious and scientific—than just whether or not to accept his theory.

Such simplifications only reinforce the myth that the struggle regarding evolution is a black-and-white conflict of religion vs. science. The stereotype is often that of dogmatic religious people wearing the metaphorical black hats and scientists open to truth wearing the white hats. This is a much larger concern than that of getting history right. That is because when we get pulled into a black-and white stereotype about the reception of Darwin's theory, we easily overlook the genuine theological challenges the theory poses even to a Christianity that accepts it.

And so, in this chapter, we will first briefly profile the reactions of a number of Victorians, both religious leaders and scientists, to demonstrate the variety of responses in *both* fields. The second part of this chapter will pinpoint some genuine theological issues that deserve being addressed but which can become obscured by over-simplified depictions about Darwin's theory and its reception.

Myths about the Wilberforce Debate

Because today in the U.S. a common question is whether one can accept evolution and also believe God created us, accounts of Darwin's scientific discovery are often molded around the story of a debate that occurred in 1860, the year after *Origin of Species* was published. That debate between Samuel Wilberforce and Thomas Henry Huxley occurred as part of the proceedings of the British Association for the Advancement of Science. As the story is usually told, Bishop Samuel Wilberforce, mocking the theory of evolution, asked the biologist Thomas Henry Huxley on which side of his family he was descended from a monkey. And Huxley responded that he would rather be descended from such an animal than from someone who was being contemptuous of new learning the way Wilberforce was. Thus it was—at least as the myth goes—that the biologist Huxley famously trounced Wilberforce, winning most of the audience to the side of accepting Darwin's new theory of evolution.

The truth is that this widespread characterization of the debate actually came from Huxley's own laudatory description of himself, writing from memory two decades after the event. In fact, newspaper and other written accounts immediately after the debate vary immensely about who "won" the debate, if anyone spoke in a way that was decisive at all. Accounts immediately afterward even vary about what the two men actually said during the debate.[5]

Besides all these difficulties with knowing what precisely occurred during that 1860 debate, there are problems in using that incident as evidence of a clear-cut battle between religion and science. To start with, if we get beyond the caricature, even though the real Samuel Wilberforce was a religious leader (a bishop), he was by no means unfamiliar with science. He himself had considerable knowledge in the field of ornithology, and had been a Fellow of the Royal Society of scientists for fifteen years. Moreover, Wilberforce would have been able to point out that most of the scientists assembled at the British Association meeting were on his side as far as *not* accepting Darwin's new theory. As one journal at the time reported: "The most eminent naturalists assembled at Oxford were on Wilberforce's side."[6]

It is also probable that during the debate, (except for any punch-line about animal ancestors) Wilberforce had presented mostly scientific arguments against the theory of evolution by natural selection. That is because he had done just that previously in writing a review of Darwin's book for a publication called *The Quarterly Review*.[7] In that essay, Wilberforce did express some theological concerns, but he emphasized science. He even made a point of saying that he was rejecting Darwin's theory of evolution because of its scientific difficulties, not for religious reasons.

Indeed, Charles Darwin himself admitted that Wilberforce had spotted the scientific difficulties with the theory of evolution by natural selection as it stood at that time. Darwin wrote that Wilberforce's review "picks out with skill all the most conjectural parts [of my theory] and brings forward well all the difficulties."[8]

There are more complexities going on here in British society, complexities which the black-and-white battle stereotype conceals. We need to understand some of them if we are going to extract from this history the genuine challenges religion needs to wrestle with.

Other Religious Responses

Although the story of the usually stereotyped Wilberforce-Huxley debate has become a staple of accounts about the reception of Darwin's book, what is rarely told is the story of a sermon given the very next day to those same participants at the meetings of the British Association for the Advancement of Science. On that Sunday, a church leader named Frederick Temple, who would later become the Archbishop of Canterbury, gave a sermon distancing himself from Wilberforce's religious conservatism, and welcoming the possibility of new scientific discoveries. Moreover, addressing how the Bible should be studied as a spiritual guide, rather than being put in opposition to science, Frederick Temple said:

> The more the Bible is [properly] studied and the more nature is studied, the deeper will be found the harmony between them.[9]

Nor was Frederick Temple the only prominent voice within the religious community who was quite open to the theory of evolution from the beginning. After the first edition of *Origin of Species* brought charges by some of eliminating God, Darwin asked the writer of a favorable letter praising the book if some of that religious leader's comments might be included in the next edition. That person consented, and so subsequent editions of *Origin* have included the comment of the Rev. Charles Kingsley, a noted Anglican minister and author. Kingsley wrote that he had:

> gradually learnt to see that it is just as noble a conception of the Deity to believe that He created a few original forms capable of self-development ... as to believe that He required a fresh act of creation [for each separate species].[10]

Today there are a few outspoken atheists, such as the biologist Richard Dawkins, who claim that the theory of evolution, if accepted, must end any belief in God.[11] Such authors do not tell you that the text of *Origin of Species* has for almost a century-and-a-half contained an endorsement of evolution by Kingsley—a clergyman so notable that he was chaplain to Queen Victoria, and later became the minister of Westminster Abbey.

Nor, generally speaking, was a courtesy by religious people toward Darwin and his book confined to religious leaders who were more educated. The leading lending library in London, Mudie's Circulating Library, was usually sensitive about buying books that might offend moral or religious sensibilities. Nevertheless, Mudie's Library purchased over 500 copies of *Origin of Species*, a significantly large quantify for a nonfiction book.

The Mixed Response of Scientists

These are just some of many examples of how the religious reception of Darwin's *Origin of Species* was far from today's stereotype of nothing but narrow-minded Christian leaders opposing science. Similarly, the reception of the new theory by scientists was not merely a matter of open-minded scientists who readily accepted the theory of evolution through natural selection. In fact, even leading scientists were themselves divided over many legitimate scientific issues. Such as the estimation of the Earth's time-span. Even though science had previously stretched it back greatly, it was still not long enough to allow for the diversity of life-forms that existed to have evolved solely through Darwin's mechanism of natural selection.

Let us briefly look at some of those scientists' responses as a way of getting further beyond the stereotype, and getting closer to understanding the real issues that remain relevant to religion.

The prime example of scientific opposition to Darwin's theory was the British zoologist Richard Owen, who specialized in comparative anatomy. Richard Owen was the man standing in the wings, so to speak, unseen during the Wilberforce-Huxley debate. That is because Owen had helped prepare Wilberforce with scientific arguments to counter the new evolutionary theory of Darwin. For the rest of his life, Richard Owen remained the most prominent British scientific voice against Darwin's theory of evolution.

We can get no better example of the truly mixed scientific reaction to *Origin of Species* than if we turn to the other side of the Atlantic and look at the American scene. Chapter 4 ("An Awkward History") explores in depth the U.S. controversies after 1900, but here we might note one American debate before 1900 that very much paralleled these British debates.

In the U.S., there were two prominent scientists, both of whom taught at Harvard, who were very outspoken about the theory of evolution. One was Louis Agassiz, a zoologist who was celebrated for his studies regarding fossils of the ice ages. The other outspoken scientist was Asa Gray, a botanist who concentrated on North American flora. The two were polar opposites when it came to evolution.

Knowing that Asa Gray was much more concerned about the *religious* implications of evolution, our black-and-white stereotype about religion and science would lead us to believe that Gray was the one who opposed evolution, and Agassiz the one who supported it. In fact the opposite was true: Agassiz, the one less concerned with evolution's religious implications, remained an implacable foe of evolution. In contrast, the quite religious Asa Gray became the most important American advocate for evolution. Not only to the scientific community but also the general reading public.

So, what is going on here with this diversity of views, even among scientists? Some of this looks completely backward from our common "warfare" stereotype!

Obscured Theological Issues

To understand these British responses and their implications. a bit of clarification about the theory evolution itself is needed. By the early 1870's (a dozen years after *Origin*), most scientists, despite some early resistance, had come to accept that all species had evolved out of other species. But even then, scientists were still greatly conflicted over whether natural selection—which was Darwin's key idea—could have been the primary mechanism. Many scientists legitimately wondered if other unknown mechanisms could be at work. Because in the 1800's scientists did not yet know about chromosomes and mutations, how and why variations appeared in species in the first place remained a great unknown.

The consequence of those gaps in scientific knowledge was that even into the early 1900's, religious responses to the idea of evolution could come up with many different ideas about the import of evolution as regards God. If we get beyond today's stereotype, we can better see in that variety of late 19th-century responses the real theological issues evolution raises.

In order to do that, we need to look at the process which Darwin said was the primary means for new species evolving. There are basically three steps for evolution through **natural selection**:

- Step 1: Variations appear within a species.
- Step 2: Some of those variations become greater in number within a species because of the survival and reproductive advantages they provide.
- Step 3: When enough variation occurs within a segment of a species, a new species can develop from that segment.

The possibility that new species might have evolved out of existing species was actually under some scientific consideration for decades before *Origin* was published. What was new in Darwin's book was his proposal that Nature would "select" those features in organisms that could become part of new species because those features provided a survival or reproductive advantage. Darwin's key idea was that "natural selection," a culling process, is the primary shaping force—rather than the variations appearing in Step 1 in some guided fashion.

It was because of the new theory's claim that variations did not first appear in any guided way that the scientist John Herschel derided Darwin's theory as "the law of higgledy-piggledy."[12]

The religious consequence of scientific uncertainty was that it was easier in Darwin's day to still reasonably think that God remained in the shadows, so to speak, behind the appearance of variations in Step 1, guiding the process in favor of beneficial variations. It was not only the religious person but also the scientist who could think that way.

Benefits and Challenges of the Theory

Despite that limitation in scientific knowledge during the 19th century, a good number of religious leaders who accepted evolution were able to recognize several points at which acceptance of the theory of evolution called for thoughtful theological engagement. In fact, there are three genuine theological matters that emerged during Darwin's lifetime and which still deserve being addressed today, even by people who accept the theory of evolution by natural selection.

Even during Darwin's lifetime, some religious people, as well as Darwin himself, recognized that it was a benefit to moral thought to *not* think of all the details of the natural world as being expressly designed by God, but instead to have evolved naturally. Today, with our knowledge about chromosomes that Darwin never possessed, people are generally more aware that many deformities in living beings are attributable to something that is essentially random: genetic mutations.

It is for this reason that the contemporary biologist Francisco Ayala—who is also educated in theology—describes Darwin's theory as a "gift" not just to science but also to religion. Ayala explains it this way:

> When I was studying theology, ... Darwin was a much-welcomed friend .... Theologians in the past struggled with the issue of dysfunction [i.e., abnormalities] because they thought it had to be attributed to God's design. Science, much to the relief of theologians, provides an explanation that convincingly attributes defects, deformities, and dysfunctions to *natural* causes.[13]

Those mainline Christian theologians today who not only accept evolution but also try to address the genuine theological issues it raises have thus identified at least one way our contemporary scientific understanding of evolution can be considered a bonus to theology and religion, not an enemy to them. Those theologians have, however, also identified some ways our contemporary scientific understanding presents a greater challenge to envisioning the role of God.

It is fascinating that both an additional key benefit and a key challenge regarding evolution were identified in 1888, even though neither have been seized upon by most of Christianity today. That additional key benefit and key challenge were expressed well over a century ago by Anglican theologians in a set of essays titled *Lux Mundi*.

The benefit has to do with the overall effects of the Scientific Revolution that had begun in the 17th century. As science became increasingly able to describe the processes of the universe in terms of natural laws that acted somewhat mechanically, God became more and more like a clock-maker who had made the "clock" of the universe, but had then walked away from it, God's presence no longer being needed. (A half-century before Darwin's *Origin*, a leading British theologian, William Paley, produced a book in which he used the very analogy of an intricate watch for the order-liness that could be found in living beings.)[14] Today, in religious circles, the depiction of God as being involved only at the initial creation of the world is called **deism**. The hazard of such an approach is that God becomes an absentee god—somewhat like an absentee landlord who doesn't care enough about the universe to remain involved with it.

One Anglican writer in *Lux Mundi*, Aubrey Moore, recognized that Darwin's explanation for how all creatures were not created at one point at the beginning of time could possibly resolve that tendency by which God the Creator had been shoved back to the beginning of time. Moore put it this way:

> The one absolutely impossible conception of God, in
> the present day, is that which represents him as an
> occasional visitor. Science has pushed the deist's God
> further and further away,... [but] at the moment when it
> seemed as if he would be thrust out all together
> Darwinism appeared, and, under the disguise of a foe,
> did the work of a friend. It has conferred upon ...
> religion an inestimable benefit, by showing us that we
> must choose between two alternatives. Either God is
> everywhere present in nature, or he is nowhere.[15]

However, an essay by another Anglican theologian in the book *Lux Mundi* spotted a challenge to any theology that attempts to address the implications of our contemporary knowledge about evolution—even though the full weight of this challenge was not appreciated in Darwin's day.

Let us say we do seize hold of this benefit Moore pointed out. Let us say we resist the temptation of letting God's creative role be simply establishing the laws of nature at the first appearance of life but then letting everything run on its own. If we do that, we have a new challenge posed by contemporary evolutionary biology's knowledge about the primary means by which new species have emerged. It is a challenge even greater today than in Darwin's day. In the 19th century, because people did not yet know that variations in species first appear because of random mutations in chromosomes, even scientists could still imagine that some unknown process might be guiding the appearance of variations (in Step 1) in ways that would be primarily beneficial for creatures.

We now know that such is not the case: New genetic variations do not appear in a fashion that necessarily addresses the current needs of a species. The classic example is that offspring of giraffes do not have longer necks because the parent giraffes have been stretching their necks to reach leaves high in trees. Instead, variations in offspring appear randomly—higgledy-piggledy—with some members of a species benefiting and some not.

Even though there are some lesser forces (such as sexual selection), Darwin was correct in seeing the primary shaping force of evolution to be in natural selection. He called it "the struggle for existence."[16]

As one contemporary philosopher of religion, Holmes Rolston, so vividly puts it regarding predatory animals and prey:

> The cougar's fang has carved the limbs of the fleet-
> footed deer, and vice versa.[17]

Here is the theological upshot if we speak of God as a "Creator" who remains in ongoing relationship with all of life: The shaping of new species lies not in any predetermined beneficial design, but instead in part through the living struggles and even suffering of the creatures.

In *Lux Mund*i, a second Anglican theologian, J.R. Illingworth, recognized the challenge to Christian theology caused by this arrangement, stating:

> The universality of pain throughout the range of the
> animal world, reaching back into the distant ages of
> geology, and involved in the very structure of the
> animal organism, is without doubt among the most
> serious [theological] problems ... to face.[18]

These theologians in *Lux Mundi* were onto some very significant points. If God is to be understood as the caring Creator of *all* of life, it is hard to explain why, after the first appearance of life on this planet, God would have an ongoing relationship only with humans but not with other species of life. Our contemporary knowledge of the creation of new species through an ongoing evolutionary process can help rescue us from the kind of deism that a lot of Christianity succumbed to over the past several centuries. But it can do so only if we let God's ongoing role extend beyond the human sphere.

However, with Darwin having discovered that the primary means for new species coming into being has been to a great deal through the struggles—and even the extinction—of species, theology needs to explain how such a difficult means for creation can be consistent with a picture of God as loving and caring. (Approaches to this challenge that some contemporary theologians have taken are explained in Chapter 9, "Opening Darwin's Gift.")

Brewing Lessons out of the British Teapot

Even beyond further debunking the black-and-white "warfare" myth, the responses of these 19th-century religious thinkers have pointed to lessons and issues we can wrestle with. In *Lux Mundi*, Aubrey Moore recognized that the implications of evolution for Christian theology had to do not just with Darwin's theory but also with the rise of modern science. Moore pointed to the way that Christian theology had let science reduce God to a god of deism. We need to get God as Creator out of the remote past.[19]

Although a good part of modern Western Christianity has gotten rid of deism in the human realm by having God impinge upon the inner lives of humans, most of Western Christianity has narrowed its focus for God's ongoing involvement with the world to human psychology or human society. The result is a kind of de facto deism as regards the non-human realm, with it being depicted as having been created at some beginning point but no longer being a place where God is involved. As part of our restoring Christian theology in an age of science, we do not want God's acts of creation to be just the Big Bang at the beginning of the universe or just the first appearance of life on this planet. We also need to keep God from being "an occasional visitor" to the natural world, as the Moore put it.

As J.R. Illingworth pointed out in *Lux Mundi*, the creation of the diversity of species on this planet has been very much in the living struggles of beings, stretching back over an unimaginable number of years even before humans were around. And the complex forces that underlie and make up the evolutionary process are still in existence today. The challenge is how to depict God as involved in an ongoing creative relationship with all of the living world—but not in such a way as to have God designing every dysfunction in the world.

I can quickly demonstrate this challenge by sharing two comments that were made when I presented the core of this chapter to an adult church-school class. In the discussion, a mother of a child with Down's syndrome said she greatly appreciated the quotation I read by Francisco Ayala saying it was a benefit to Christian thought to not see dysfunctions as coming from God's design, but instead from a natural cause. She identified with that sentiment strongly because after her son with Down's syndrome was born, some people tried to suggest that "God had done that" to her son for some reason.

However, a second woman in the class discussion, who herself has dwarfism (entailing medical complications), responded that she had a different perspective. She said she saw herself—with her dysfunction—as being part of that diversity of creation that is intrinsic to the evolutionary process.

So, how do we draw a picture of God's role as Creator in such a way as to not be telling the mother of child with a dysfunction that "God did that"—but also make a person born with a major dysfunction still feel that they have been created by God? There in a nutshell is the challenge if we depict God as being in an ongoing creative relationship with all of our evolutionary natural world.

Chapter 4
An Awkward History:
The U.S. and Evolution

Fifty dollars. It was not an enormous amount, not even in 1927. Nevertheless, fifty dollars made a gigantic difference when the Tennessee Supreme Court overthrew a lower court's decision on a face-saving technicality. The year before, the judge in the lower court had imposed a fine of $100, whereas state law required any fine above $50 to be imposed by a jury. In overthrowing the lower-court decision, the Tennessee Supreme Court exhorted prosecutors in the state to never again bring a case on the particular state law at issue. The Supreme Court even labeled the lower court's 1925 trial, "a bizarre case."[1] And indeed, there had been many bizarre features to it. The most bizarre was that the lower-court trial had climaxed with the leading defense attorney putting the leading prosecutor on the witness stand.[2]

That trial was the now historic Scopes trial over the teaching of evolution (sometimes called "The Monkey Trial"). Many people think they know about it from having read the play *Inherit the Wind* or seen the movie version starring Spencer Tracy. However, the play and movie are at critical points highly misleading about the trial. And thus they are misleading about the history of relationships between religion and science. More specifically, myths and stereotypes about the Scopes trial can deceive us as to what lay behind the religious resistance to evolution that had emerged in the U.S. This chapter, therefore, will correct those myths and stereotypes—and in the process uncover some challenges to religion that *accepts* the theory of evolution.

Fundamentalism and Anti-Evolutionism
Today, the majority of Christians who oppose the teaching of evolution are usually categorized as being a part of "fundamentalism" because of their anti-evolutionist beliefs. However, that was *not* the case with Christian fundamentalism at its origins. That movement takes its name from a series of

pamphlets, *The Fundamentals*, published between 1910 and 1915. When the Christian leaders who started that movement decided which fundamental principles were to them essential for their very conservative form of Christianity, opposing evolution did not rank among their list of top five beliefs.[3] The theory of evolution was even acceptable to some early fundamentalist leaders. For example, Benjamin B. Warfield, one author of articles for the *Fundamentals* pamphlets, and one of the strongest defenders of Biblical "inerrancy"[4] at that time, had previously written, "I do not think that there is any general statement in the Bible or any part of the [Bible's] account of creation ... that need be opposed to evolution."[5]

Where then did American anti-evolutionism originate? To answer that question, we have to look back to the first decade of the 1900's and look at a then obscure sect of Christianity: the Seventh-day Adventists. That sect had been established in 1863 by Ellen Harmon White. She had said that in a vision God had told her that Christians should be holding their Sabbath on Saturdays because that was the original seventh day God rested on in the creation narrative in the first chapter of the Bible's book of Genesis.

The matter might not have gone much further as regards evolution had it not been for one particular Seventh-day Adventist, George McCready Price. He took upon himself the mission of fusing the stories in the first part of Genesis with his own particular interpretations of geology, first published in 1906. Price's so-called "flood geology" (which most geologists dismissed as not being good science) claimed that the diversity of fossils had not come about over immense time, but instead in a short time because of a single catastrophic flood, as told in the Bible's story of Noah.[6] Price's particular version of geology, called young-Earth creationism, was incorporated into the anti-evolutionist teaching of Seventh-day Adventism. But its full effect would not come into play until half-a-century later. That was because Seventh-day Adventism was a very small sect.

Anti-evolutionism might not have developed much further in the U.S. if it had not been for matters that had nothing to do with seven days, the Sabbath, fossils, or geology. It was primarily for other reasons that the anti-evolutionism movement become strong during the 1920's, climaxing in the Scopes "Monkey" trial in 1925 in Dayton, Tennessee.

Falsehoods about the Famous Trial

Many liberal, progressive, and moderate Christians think they know about the Scopes trial from having seen the 1960 movie *Inherit the Wind*. The movie opens with a group of angry towns-people, led by a fire-and-brimstone preacher, marching into a school classroom, arresting the teacher during his lecture on evolution, and then taking him off to prison.

The truth of the matter is that the real John Scopes, who was tried in the famous 1925 trial, was never imprisoned. He had actually agreed to stand trial on behalf of the American Civil Liberties Union (ACLU), which had been wanting to legally challenge a new Tennessee law prohibiting the teaching of human evolution so as to deny the Biblical account of creation.[7] And there was no such preacher among the town leaders of Dayton who arranged for the trial to occur in their town.

The trial gained much public attention, primarily because the legal teams had already famous figures on both sides: On the defense's side was the outspoken lawyer Clarence Darrow; and on the prosecution's side was the former political figure and gifted orator William Jennings Bryan.

Because William Jennings Bryan was the leading spokesperson for U.S. anti-evolutionism during its formative period of the 1920's, Bryan can be one of the best lenses for understanding the motivations behind that movement. However, in order to do that, we have to get beyond the caricature of Bryan that the play and movie have instilled in so many people's minds, because they grossly distort the beliefs of Bryan (as well as some other anti-evolutionists of the time).

For example, the *Inherit the Wind* character representing Bryan, when examined on the witness stand by Darrow, maintains that the world was literally created in a mere six days, based on a literal reading of the Bible's first chapter of Genesis. In fact, although Bryan was religiously very conservative, several years prior to the trial, he had publicly expressed his belief in a non-literal reading of Genesis 1 in a way that allowed for a long time-span for creation.[8] And when on the witness stand, Bryan showed that same flexibility on the six-day matter. In so doing, Bryan was following one of the non-literal ways of interpreting Genesis that had developed within conservative Christianity after early modern geology had vastly extended the timeline of the Earth.[9]

Bryan's Real Objections

If Bryan's objection to the theory of evolution was *not* literalism on the length of time of creation or the Earth's age, why did William Jennings Bryan oppose evolution? Bryan's greatest concern about evolution was that it would cause people to abandon religious morality. Bryan thought that the theory of evolution endorsed the idea of "might makes right." As Bryan had put it in one of his speeches, "The Darwinian theory represents man as reaching his present perfection by the operation of the law of hate —the merciless law by which the strong crowd out and kill off the weak."[10]

Where did Bryan get such a notion? Actually, it was a quite widespread idea in the latter 1800's and early 1900's. Moreover, the idea that might makes right (especially economic might) was being employed by those who had enormous economic wealth during a period of great economic inequality.

For example, the oil tycoon John D. Rockefeller Sr., in his Sunday-school address that became famous said, "The growth of a large business is merely a survival of the fittest.... It is merely the working-out of a law of nature and a law of God."[11]

In a similar vein, the wealthy industrialist Andrew Carnegie maintained in an essay titled *The Gospel of Wealth* that we must "accept and welcome ... great inequality [and] the concentration of business, industrial and commercial, in the hands of a few; and the law of competition between these, as being not only beneficial, but *essential* to the future progress of the race."[12] That is because in capitalism, "A struggle is inevitable and it is a question of the survival of the fittest."[13] Carnegie even claimed that, "The gospel of wealth but echoes Christ's words."[14]

Therefore, Bryan had good evidence for his belief that Darwin's evolution as applied to humans was rooting up and replacing the Christian value of love with a predatory "survival of the fittest."

To better understand Bryan's anti-evolutionism, we also need to understand his core values as developed through his political stance. Although Bryan's religious views were conservative (and not particularly sophisticated), politically he was a progressive, believing, in his words, that "God made all men, and he did not make some to crawl on hands and knees and others to ride upon their back."[15] Therefore, in his political positions he was usually on the side of the weak or the powerless. He was for women's suffrage years before women were allowed to vote in national elections. And he was for the publication of campaign contributions.

And so, opposing evolution—perceived as the endorsement of "might makes right"—was a natural extension of his political convictions.

Skeletons in Science's Closet

Even though in the U.S. Darwin's theory of biological evolution had gotten swirled in with these sorts of social concerns, it was a Britisher who first applied the idea of evolution to human society. And that man, Herbert Spencer, did so eight years before Darwin ever published *Origin of Species*. In 1851, Spencer published the book *Social Statics*, in which he depicted societies and social institutions as changing and improving under the pressures of competition. It was actually Spencer—not Darwin—who coined the phrase "survival of the fittest" in his own 1864 book *Principles of Biology*. (Years later, Darwin went along with others who suggested that he apply the phrase to the concept of biological evolution by natural selection that he had developed.)[16]

Spencer thought that evolution was inherently progressive, and that the concept could be applied to human societies. Therefore, Spencer claimed, it would be wrong to interfere with this built-in evolutionary progress in society. It was with that kind of thinking that he wrote regarding the poor, the "unfit":

> The whole effort of nature is to get rid of such, to clear
> the world of them, and make room for better.... If they
> are sufficiently complete to live, they *do* live, and it is
> well they should live. If they are not sufficiently
> complete to live, they die, and it is best they should
> die.[17]

Today, this kind of thinking is called **social Darwinism**, even though many writers have commented that it would be more appropriately called "social Spencerism" because it owes its origins to Herbert Spencer, not to Darwin.

In the decades leading up to the Scopes trial, there was yet another way that many people tried to apply the idea of evolution to human societies, along with the belief that we should tailor our social polices to give evolution a helping hand. This is a part of U.S. history that is so embarrassing that it is not even mentioned in some contemporary books about the struggles between evolution and religion. And yet it is most relevant to the concerns of William Jennings Bryan. It is the **eugenics** movement.

The idea of eugenics and the name for it (from the Greek "well-born") originated with the 19th-century Britisher Francis Galton. His writings promoted the idea that people should take a hand in evolution by ensuring that proportionally more humans with good qualities are born, even to the point of reducing the number of humans with bad qualities who are born.

The eugenics movement believed that "unfit" humans had to be bred out of the human species through strict immigration policies, selective breeding of "superior" individuals, and sterilization of people with particular mental and physical weaknesses. In the U.S., the idea of promoting eugenics took hold in the first several decades of the 20th century and steadily grew in influence. In 1906, a founding committee had been formed, and it included the president of Stanford University, David Starr Jordan, and a sociologist at the University of Chicago, Charles Henderson. That committee lead to the creation of the Eugenics Record Office at Cold Spring Harbor in New York in 1910. Other eugenics organizations then formed in many other parts of the U.S. and in several other countries of Europe, such as England and Germany.

Out of this movement, the first law to permit legal, forced sterilization was passed in Indiana in 1907. That law stated that even against their will, sterilization could be performed on, "confirmed criminals, idiots, imbeciles, and rapists."[18] By 1915 (ten years before the Scopes trial), thirteen states had passed such laws, giving their governments authority to sterilize certain criminals and mentally deficient people who were in public institutions. And seventeen additional states followed suit over the next decade-and-a-half.[19]

The eugenics movement gained so much support—even among many scientists—that by the time a case involving a sterilization law reached the Supreme Court of the U.S. in 1927, that state law of Virginia was upheld by the Supreme Court with only one dissenting vote. With that Supreme-Court permission to sterilize a mother whose child had also been sterilized, even more states would enact such laws. By the beginning of the 1930's, a total of over 12,000 forced sterilizations had been performed in the U.S.

Despite the expanding popularity of the eugenics movement during the 1920's, William Jennings Bryan viewed it as but one more example of how the notion of evolution (that is, the law of the "survival of the fittest") was a "merciless law by which the strong crowd out and kill off the weak."[20]

In the movie *Inherit the Wind* (which portrays Bryan as primarily a buffoon), the textbook which Scopes is accused of teaching from is depicted as being problematic simply because it taught that higher animals and humans evolved from lower animals. The truth is that the textbook involved in the real Scopes case, written by the prominent biologist George W. Hunter, contained an *endorsement* of eugenics. That bestselling textbook, *A Civic Biology*, contained the following statement about the mentally ill, the retarded, and other people who were subject to the eugenics sterilization laws:

> If such people were lower animals, we would probably
> kill them off to prevent them from spreading....
> Humanity will not allow this, but we do have the
> remedy ... in various ways of preventing ... the
> possibility of perpetuating such a low and degenerate
> race.[21]

Thus, there was no need for William Jennings Bryan to have made a leap from Darwin's theory to the forced sterilizations of the eugenics movement, which he deplored. Scopes's biology text-book explicitly endorsed that link.

Whether he looked at business monopolists, at the eugenics movement (or at German World-War-I militarists who swore by Darwin), Bryan saw the doctrine of an evolutionary "survival of the fittest" as going against his core values for humankind. And so did many others who joined the early anti-evolutionist cause in the

United States.

Anti-Evolutionism following the 1920's

Bryan died less than a week after the Scopes trial ended, but even after his death, his reputation serves as a lens for understanding anti-evolutionism within the U.S.

Most people who accepted evolution came over time to think of him as nothing but a ranting, ignorant buffoon. That caricature was reinforced by Frederick Lewis Allen's best-selling 1931 book *Only Yesterday.*[22] The caricature was passed on to another generation of Americans by the 1955 play and 1960 movie *Inherit the Wind*, with their strategic distortions of the historical record. In the climax of the movie, the babbling Bryan character collapses, abandoned by the townspeople.

The truth is that the three-times-presidential-candidate William Jennings Bryan was given a funeral worthy of a state hero, with thousands of people lining the railroad tracks, and with cabinet members and senators serving as pallbearers.

John Scopes was convicted under Tennessee's law against teaching evolution, but the law itself could not be tested on appeal because the fine was overturned on a technicality. Therefore, Tennessee's law prohibiting teaching evolution remained in effect for forty years. Only a few other states passed laws similar to Tennessee's.[23] Nevertheless, as a result of that early-20th-century wave of anti-evolutionism, textbook makers adjusted the text of their science books to make the topic of evolution less conspicuous or less offensive. Resistance to science textbooks thus declined. To many liberals, therefore, it seemed as if the issue had gone away.

What liberals were not so aware of was that the anti-evolutionists within conservative America had just gone out of sight, creating their own subculture. With Bryan's anti-evolutionist campaign having so heavily spotlighted the seeming moral impacts of teaching evolution, especially to young people, it was perhaps inevitable that the issue of evolution grew in importance within fundamentalism, which had initially not been too concerned about it. Which moral issues were of particular concern changed over time, but the theory of evolution retained its taint of immorality among anti-evolutionist Christians in the U.S.

Today, those who accept evolution, upon hearing about anti-evolutionist Christians, often try to point to biological evidence of our physical links with other primates in the past. However, for the conservative wing of U.S. Christians who have rejected evolution, it is a moral or theological link that is of concern. Frequently, to the Christian who opposes evolution, Darwin's theory either breaks down the moral line between humans and "brute" animals, or it breaks down a link between humans and God.

During the 20th century, most mainline Protestant denominations, as well as Roman Catholicism and Judaism, issued official statements expressing that to them evolution is acceptable. (See inset "Official Religious Statements Accepting Evolution."[24])

However, after the Scopes trial, anti-evolutionism expanded into Southern Baptists and various forms of conservative evangelical Christianity, becoming part of the package along with other fundamentalist ideas. As anti-evolutionism spread, there was an increased tendency in a new generation of conservative Christians to read literally more parts of the Bible, including Genesis 1—in contrast to the earlier fundamentalism that had been represented by Warfield and Bryan. Nevertheless, the over-arching concern has been that the evolutionary explanation eliminates God from the picture.

Resurgence of Anti-Evolutionism

If liberal Americans thought anti-evolutionism had gone away, they found out otherwise following the Soviet Union's launch in 1957 of Sputnik, the first satellite. That Soviet coup prompted the U.S. to beef up its science textbooks, all the way down to including more evolutionary biology. As evolution became more prominent in textbooks, there came an increased resistance to how science was being taught in public schools.

A 1961 de facto handbook for the resurgence of anti-evolutionism was co-authored by Henry Morris, who was neither a geologist nor a biologist, but instead a hydraulic engineer. Morris, a nominal Southern Baptist, got to thinking about how remarkable animals such as butterflies could not have developed "just by chance." (Evolutionary biologists keep trying to explain that evolution is *not* merely a random process, but that idea persists.) And so, Morris dusted off an old "flood-geology" book of the

Official Religious Statements Accepting Evolution

It is a widespread misconception that most Christians do not accept the theory of evolution. Mainline Protestantism, Catholicism, and branches of Judaism even have official pronouncements expressing its acceptability. Here are brief excerpts from some of those statements.

Roman Catholic Church:

"Evolution is more than a hypothesis.... The convergence, neither sought nor fabricated, of the results of [scientific] work that was concluded independently is in itself a significant argument in favor of this theory."

— *Pope John Paul II (1996)*

Episcopal Church:

"The theory of evolution provides a fruitful and unifying scientific explanation for the emergence of life on earth."

— *Statement from 75th General Convention (2006)*

United Methodist Church:

"We find that as science expands human understanding of the natural world, our understanding of the mysteries of God's creation and word are enhanced."

— *Resolution of UMC General Conference (2008)*

Presbyterian Church, USA:

"There is no contradiction between an evolutionary theory of human origins and the doctrine of God as Creator."

— *Statement by 214th General Assembly (2002)*

United Church of Christ:

"We acknowledge modern evolutionary theory as the best present-day scientific explanation of the existence of life on earth ... in no way at odds with our belief in a Creator God."

— *Statement by United Church Board for Homeland Ministries (1992)*

Judaism:

"The principles and concepts of biological evolution are basic to understanding science.... Students who are not taught these principles.... will not be receiving an education based on modern scientific knowledge."

— *Statement of 95th Annual Convention of American Rabbis (1984)*

Seventh-day Adventist George McCready Price written a half-century early. Henry Morris, along with John Whitcomb, co-authored the book *The Genesis Flood*, which stimulated the resurgence of anti-evolutionism during the 1960's.

Moreover, with Morris's spin upon geology supposedly proving that the Earth was very young, there was no need for those flexible readings of Genesis 1 that Warfield, Bryan, and early fundamentalism had employed. Although God and religious values remained the central concerns, a young-Earth literalism in reading Genesis was made easier by believing Morris's book.

From 1961 onward, the history of anti-evolutionism in the U.S. can be seen as a series of court cases, each court decision halting an attempt to introduce some form of anti-evolutionism into public-school science classrooms. In all of these cases, the legal challenge to anti-evolutionism was based on the U.S. Constitution's First Amendment, specifically its Establishment Clause, which prohibits the government's establishing religion. The key court decisions are:

- The landmark 1968 case "Epperson vs. Arkansas," in which the U. S. Supreme Court invalidated an Arkansas law prohibiting the teaching of evolution.
- In 1987, in the case of Edwards vs. Aguillard, the U. S. Supreme Court invalidated a Louisiana law requiring teaching "creation science" along with evolution.[25] "Creation science" was held by the court to not in fact be science.
- In 2005, in the "Dover Case,"[26] a District Court judge in Pennsylvania prohibited a move to introduce "intelligent design" into science class, holding that such a move had the force of introducing religion. And the judge held that "Intelligent Design" was not science. (Although the idea of "intelligent design" remains popular among some people within the anti-evolutionist camp, mainstream theologians point to many theological difficulties with it—as explained in Chapter 9, "Opening Darwin's Gift.")

Extracting Lessons from the Controversies

We have now covered one-hundred years of the history of anti-evolutionism in the U.S.—that part most relevant to our school-textbook battles today. With this perspective, we who accept evolution might be better able to step back and extract some lessons.

One over-arching lesson is that many people who accept evolution, including many religious people, have myths about what has been behind religious resistance to evolution. Frequently, such myths obscure the challenge of addressing some of the real objections to evolution, whether founded or unfounded. And they frequently obscure the theological challenges the theory of evolution really does pose.

A second lesson that might be drawn is the need for addressing all those troublesome matters related to Rockefeller, Carnegie, Herbert Spencer, the eugenics movement (and even German militarists). That is, those instances in which somebody claims that Darwin's theory of evolution endorses a certain type of social behavior because it is following a natural law of "the survival of the fittest." Which is to say, if we are going to better relate religion to science, we need to address social Darwinism (using that phrase loosely to cover all those sorts of claims).

There is a big problem with trying to draw conclusions about how we should behave socially based upon biological evolution, even as prevalent as that leap has been. And even as prevalent as it still is today. Whenever any kind of social behavior is said to be endorsed because it is said to be copying a feature of our natural, biological makeup, three leaps are being made. They are:

• **Biological to Social:** The first leap being made is from biological characteristics to social behavior. Even though Darwin did also later write a book (*The Descent of Man*[27]) in which he wrote about how our being social animals roots us in our evolutionary past, the theory of evolution is primarily about biology. It is about how biological species have branched out of earlier species.

But we humans are bio-cultural beings. Compared with other animals, much of our behavior and abilities are shaped by cultural factors, not just by instinct. And it is often very problematic to claim that any specific behavior is *caused* by biological makeup rather than involving some cultural influences. (This matter is addressed more in Chapter 11, "Problems with a Problematic Species.")

• **Inheritable and Determined?:** The second leap being made with the various forms of social Darwinism is the assumption that the qualities being endorsed by favoring such people as the wealthy, or the qualities being disfavored by sterilizing a criminal, are qualities that are genetically inheritable.

But we should ask: Are there genetically inheritable—and genetically determined—characteristics that make one person more successful in, say, the business world? Or does the success of such people more likely owe itself to things such as benefits of upbringing, education, and being given assistance socially in becoming a successful adult?

• **Is-Ought Fallacy:** The third leap is a much wider error. It is a logical fallacy called the "**is-ought fallacy.**"[28] That fallacy is the error of thinking that because something *is*, therefore that is how I *ought* to behave. The various forms of social Darwinism look at something that exists in the realm of Nature (such as competition for existence between different species), and then conclude that is how we ought to behave.

But that is simply not proven logically. Just because something exists in the natural world does not mean that we human beings should aim to imitate it. There might be some interconnections between Nature and our moral behavior, but the connection is not automatically a simple leap from one to the other. (This complex issue is addressed further in Chapter 16, "When All the World's Not a Stage.")

Today, science is becoming more frequently the avenue through which we learn what the natural word *is* like. And faith-traditions have always had *ought's* as one of their concerns. Therefore, the danger of leaping from "is" to "ought," even if it is commonplace, remains an important issue in religion-science relationships.

Facing the Past

The U.S. eugenics movement faded out in the 1940's as Hitler's atrocities led to second thoughts about having governments reduce the population level of a nation's "unfit" people. Making estimates in this instance is difficult because of irregularities in record-keeping, but one careful calculation places at 64,000 the number of people in the U.S. who were by that time involuntarily sterilized as part of the eugenics movement.[29]

Numbers are the forte of modern science. Religion demands more. The best voices of our faith-traditions call us to listen to our hearts as well as using our heads.

And so, we close this awkward history with a closer look at the 1927 Supreme Court case that upheld Virginia's sterilization law, thus giving the go-ahead to other states in the U.S., a total of 30 states in all. That Court decision was made with only one dissenting vote. Both the liberal justice Louis Brandeis and the conservative justice Oliver Wendell Holmes, Jr. voted to uphold the Virginia law. Supreme Court Justice Holmes, a most celebrated justice, wrote the majority opinion in that case of Buck v. Bell. It supported the forced sterilization of a woman, Carrie Buck. Part of the Court's decision read:

> Instead of waiting to execute degenerate offspring for
> crime or to let them starve for their imbecility, society
> can prevent those who are manifestly unfit from
> continuing their kind.... Three generations of imbeciles
> are enough.[30]

What needs to be told is the story that lies behind the phrase "three generations." What needs to be told is the story of Carrie Buck herself. She had been declared to be "feebleminded," and was a patient at the Virginia State colony for Epileptics and Feebleminded. Her mother, Emma, had also been said to be "feebleminded," as had Carrie's daughter, Vivian, who had been sterilized as a child.

Eventually paroled, the "feebleminded" Carrie Buck was an avid reader. Although she had been forcefully sterilized, the case against her supposed mental deficiency was undermined when it was uncovered that she had been committed to Virginia's state institution to cover up the fact that she had been raped. She had been institutionalized to protect the reputation of the rapist's family.

Carrie's daughter Vivian, also sterilized because she too was supposedly "feebleminded," only lived to the age of eight (dying of an intestinal disease). But Vivian had credible success in school, even making it onto the school's honor roll.[31]

PART TWO
Theological Challenges

A God who 'exists' but does nothing in the world, who in no way affects the outcome of events, is simply a God who does not matter. Of course most people do not say things like this, do not even think them in their minds. But this modern world-picture ... is nevertheless the unconscious background of modern life.... [Science has not] resulted in people saying 'there is no God,' but in the draining of all life out of the assertion that there is.
— *W.T. Stace*
(20th-century philosopher)

It is customary to blame secular science and anti-religious philosophy for the eclipse of religion in modern society. It would be more honest to blame religion for its own defeats. Religion declined not because it was refuted, but because it became irrelevant, dull, oppressive, insipid.... Religion is an answer to man's ultimate questions. The moment we become oblivious to ultimate questions, religion becomes irrelevant.
— *Abraham Joshua Heschel*
(20th-century Jewish theologian)

Chapter 5

Two Windows onto the World

In medieval Europe, ten centuries ago, a momentous change occurred in science: Arabic numerals, familiar today to any schoolchild, were introduced into the European continent, coming by way of Islamic Arabia (as the name "Arabic" attests). That imported set of numerals (1 through 9) replaced Roman numerals (the characters I, V, X, etc.).[1] Although this was hundreds of years before the Scientific Revolution, the effect the new Arabic numerals had upon mathematics, and in turn upon theoretical science, was profound. To appreciate why, first try multiplying these two numbers expressed in Roman numerals:

XLIX

times VII

And now, multiply the identical numbers rendered with Arabic numerals:

49

times 7

The Arabic numerals by themselves could not have proved consequential had there not been someone to teach and promote them (so strange they at first seemed even to the educated). But the revolutionary numerals did have such a promoter—the mathematician and leading astronomer of the day, Gerbert of Aurillac. The intriguing part of this often overlooked page in the history of science is that Gerbert of Aurillac became a Pope. Specifically, Pope Sylvester II, sometimes called "the Scientist Pope."[2]

Of course, it can be tempting to imagine that people in past times led simpler, less challenged lives than we do today. Nevertheless, there is something appealing in this picture of revolutionary scientific knowledge being comfortably integrated into the thought and life of a premier religious leader (especially if we have just finished reading a newspaper article about the latest fight over evolution in science textbooks).

However, there have been changes in the methods of science since Pope Sylvester's day (as was explained in the latter part of

Chapter 1). So how can we today not merely accept science but also properly interrelate religious statements with science's statements about the world? That will be the subject of this chapter.

The Metaphor of Windows

As Huston Smith, an authority on the world's faith-traditions once put it, reality is one world, but religion and science offer different "windows" onto reality.[3] They give different perspectives. If we use that metaphor of windows, the question at hand would be: How do we make sense of or make connections between what we "see" through the window of religion and through the window of science? Is there a partial overlap between the two windows? Or do we have to be content with simply shifting our position back and forth to look first through one and then through the other, without making any connections between the two?

In the movie *The Captain's Paradise*, Alec Guinness portrays a sea captain whose ship shuttles back and forth between both sides of the Strait of Gibraltar. The captain has a wife on one side of the Strait and a mistress on the other side, the two quite different women bringing out contrasting sides of his own personality. The only way he can pull it off is to keep his two worlds isolated as he switches back and forth between the two. (A comic collision inevitably ensues.) Guinness's dilemma can illustrate metaphorically the drawback of believing we can shift back and forth between the "windows" of religion and science without ever making connections between the two. So, how do we interrelate them without the results turning out to be comic, or even tragic?

Many religious people have found ways to successfully interrelate them. But contemporary philosophers and theologians repeatedly remind us that doing so requires that we properly *distinguish between* science and religion.[4] The National Academy of Sciences (NAS) agrees, having stated:

> At the root of the apparent conflict between some religions and evolution is a misunderstanding of the critical difference between religious and scientific ways of knowing. Religions and science answer different questions about the world.[5]

Levels of Understanding

There will probably be no good resolution of today's struggles involving science and religion until we realize that one reality can be known through different levels of understanding—all of which can be true. Unnecessary conflicts over religious and scientific statements often result from a failure to realize how different types of explanations—all valid—can be offered as an answer to the same question. This is not just so as regards science and religion. It is also true about everyday experience as well.

In order to appreciate this better, let us look at a demonstration that expands upon an example the theologian John Haught presented in one of his books.[6] Imagine that several people have simultaneously witnessed a car going down a street. All of them know who the driver was. They also know all the same information about the driver and related circumstances. So there is no difference in their knowledge about the incident. Nonetheless, look at the different answers they might give to the single question, "Why was the car with Bill in it going down the road?":

- Because the car's wheels were turning on the pavement.
- Because the spark plugs were igniting the gasoline-air mixture, thus forcing the pistons in the internal combustion engine to move, turning the drive-shaft.
- Because Bill was driving to the drug store.
- Because Bill needed to get some medicine for his mother, who was ill.
- Because Bill cared about his mother, even though he had been angry with her in the past, and even though he was frightened by her being so ill; but he didn't want her to die.
- Because love is so powerful it can cast out anger and fear.

Notice that all of these answers can be equally true simultaneously —each true on its own level. But also notice how extraordinarily different are the pictures of reality each one gives. The range of pictures the levels provide represents in a rough way our academic areas of knowledge, which are diagrammed in Figure 7. (The exact name placed on each level is not significant. What is important is remaining aware that one reality is open to multiple levels of understanding.)

The diagram also has one more level, the one diagrammed with dotted lines. Imagine that we go a step beyond the last

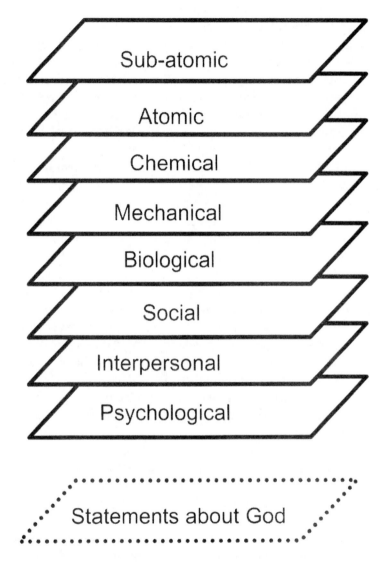

Figure 7: Levels of understanding

witness's answer ("Because love is so powerful it can cast out anger and fear") and make an *ultimate* assertion by saying, "Love is ultimately more powerful than anger and fear." Such an assertion, unlike the other answers, goes beyond our direct knowledge.

For how could I know about all situations, past and present, measure the amount of love in each, and know about their ultimate outcomes? But we might recognize such an ultimate assertion as being the kind we make in religion when we talk about God, the Ultimate Reality. (There will be further analysis of the concept of God later in this chapter.)

It is at this point, therefore, that religious **faith** enters in—as a kind of trust that holding to love as a higher value will ultimately turn out to be the best path. But we should notice that faith is not sheerly holding to some idea totally in the absence of evidence. The circumstances surrounding Bill and his mother provide some evidence. Other instances, past and present, in which the power of love has been experienced would also be evidence. This point is critical because perpetuators of the "warfare" myth frequently portray religious faith as blindly holding to a belief without any evidence, in contrast to modern science's basing its theories on observed facts. The contrast, instead, is the type of evidence and how it is obtained and cultivated.[7]

This demonstration, besides showing how even everyday experience opens itself up to different levels of understanding, can also help us see how problems in the relationship between science and religion occur when we erroneously move answers from one category of understanding into a different category of understanding. Giving an answer in one category that really belongs in another category is called a **category mistake**, or sometimes a category fault. Like a tennis player, you have stepped over the line, giving a response that belongs in a different category than the category in which you are working. When I have my car towed into a repair garage and ask the mechanic why my car won't move, I don't want the mechanic to reply, "Your car won't move because God isn't pushing it." If the mechanic insists on a theological answer in the area of mechanics, such a reply stands in the way of gaining further knowledge about my car's mechanical operation (or not operating in this case).

Moreover, notice how the mechanic's answer that my "car won't move because God isn't pushing it" reduces God to something like an invisible person who will sit beside me in my car and get out and push my car when it won't go. The mechanic's answer flattens the richness of language about God—with all its power and depth of symbol—down into that much more literal, descriptive level of language necessary in the study of mechanics.

Contrasts of Science & Religion

Even though this example of the mechanic might seem contrived, it helps demonstrate the NAS's key point that, "Religion and science answer different questions about the world."[8] Ian Barbour, a professor of physics and of religion, points to a way out of contemporary confusions:

> The dominance of either science or religion and the
> assumption that one must exclude the other have been
> in part products of the failure to analyze adequately the
> characteristics of diverse ways of knowing. What are
> the functions of differing types of explanations, and
> what are the appropriate processes of inquiry?[9]

The rise of modern science has been a process of sectoring off a certain region for scientific knowledge. Modern science excludes questions of value, meaning, purpose, and God.[10] Religion in contrast emphasizes value, meaning, purpose, and the Ultimate, which is most often called "God" in theistic faith-traditions. These limitations of science are examined in the following Chapter 6 ("Ancient Wisdom Raises Her Head"). In the current chapter, we will step back from the real world of particular struggles, and look at the nature of scientific and religious language in general—as a way of grasping the differences between those two contemporary enterprises.

The languages of science and religion help reveal how they are very different enterprises. Stating the contrasts briefly:

> • Science prefers an objectiveness that makes possible
> repeatability, regardless of which scientist is doing the
> experiment or making the observations. Modern science
> prefers precise statements and precise observations. It
> makes observations from the "outside," so to speak (this
> being what is called its **empirical** method). An example
> would be a scientist monitoring movements in the body as
> another person dreams.
> • Religion in contrast prefers metaphors, images, even
> hyperbole. It prefers symbols and stories. Also, religious
> stories are "lived into" so that they might be experienced

from the "inside." For example, a person's own immediate experience of their dream. Religion seeks with its statements to engage people existentially.

In order to appreciate the way these differences in language facilitate both enterprises, let us examine some examples.

Let us begin with the matter of religion's use of hyperboles, which are exaggerations intentionally used to create some effect upon the listener. This approach is so different from the one-pointedness of description demanded in scientific observations. Imagine if a physician were referring a patient to a specialist, and wrote on the referral slip that the patient had swallowed a camel. Not exactly a scientific medical observation or report! But that is the kind of metaphor and hyperbole so commonly used by religious speakers, as by Jesus when he warns, "You strain out a gnat but swallow a camel!" (Matthew 23:24). Jesus is employing an exaggerated, impossible image to wake people up to how we can be critical of the least flaw in other people while overlooking our own larger flaws.

With the beginning of the modern Scientific Revolution (beginning in the 17th century), it was decided that one of science's methods would be to hold to a one-pointedness of language for a precision of meaning. René Descartes, one of the promoters of the new methodology for science, expressed the need for this kind of scientific clarity of understanding:

> If we give assent only to those things which we *clearly and distinctly* perceive, we will never accept anything false as being true.... We always judge badly when we assent to things which are not clearly perceived.[11]

This is quite a contrast with metaphors and symbols, which can suggest multiple, even ambiguous meanings. That multilayered, somewhat unresolved character of symbols (whether in religion, literature, or art) allows us to be drawn forward in life, discovering more depth of meanings as we employ them in different circumstances.

(This use of the word "symbol" is different than the way the word is sometimes used in science or mathematics to refer to a letter of the alphabet that is assigned a specific meaning in a particular situation. In contrast, religious symbols have many layers of interrelated meanings radiating outward.)[12]

Not that the enterprise of science is completely devoid of metaphors. Sometimes scientists will use a metaphor as an aid to visualizing a scientific idea; but it is the scientific idea that will be pursued, even if it would result in dropping the metaphor along the way. When some contemporary scientists talk of string theory, they are using the analogy to a piece of string as an aid to visualization. But whether string theory or the theory that preceded it are correct about the arrangement of elementary microscopic particles will depend upon other matters than whether or not "string" is the best aid for visualization. It is because metaphors in science are discardable (contrasted with their being essential in religion) that James R. Moore states that, "Particular metaphors *are* always dispensable, if not in literature,... then in science."[13] In science, the metaphor will be readily dropped. In religion, the central metaphors and symbols will be pursued, explored, and elaborated upon in various ways.

The contrasts between science's uses of numbers to gain mathematical precision and religion's use of numbers primarily in a symbolic way are explored using Biblical examples in Chapter 7 ("Rescuing the Bible from Science").

Religion also prefers stories. And a story is most powerful when the person hearing or reading it does not observe the characters in the story objectively, but instead is pulled into the story, experiencing internally what the characters might be feeling. Religion is thus concerned with experiences from the "inside." That is to say, a person's own internal, subjective experience, or the experience of being within a social group.[14] Religion seeks in its statements to engage listeners existentially, making them feel immediately their personal engagement with the world around them on a deep level.

Another related difference is between what might be called science's "zooming in" and religion's "zooming out." Science "zooms in," so to speak. Science analyzes the smaller parts of the natural world before assembling those pieces of knowledge into a larger theory. Religion, in contrast, "zooms out," trying to help a person experience their current situation within a wider, meaningful perspective.

For example, imagine a botany teacher talking about a certain classification of flowers and saying, "Consider the genus *Lilium*."

The teacher might then show a diagram representing a cross-section of one of that type of flower, focusing on each small part of the flower, and naming each part. That's an example of science "zooming in."

Jesus said something almost identical to "Consider the genus *Lilium*," but he used the everyday name for the flowers, saying, "Consider the lilies" (Matthew 6:28). However, by saying, "Consider the lilies of the field," Jesus was "zooming out." He was encouraging his anxious disciples to widen their perspective to encompass the world around them in such a way that the disciples could let go of their anxiousness, resting themselves within God's wider care.

"God-Talk"

Our modern mindsets, so influenced by the expansion of scientific ways of thinking, have made it harder for many people in modern Western society to comprehend theistic religions' use of language about God.[15] Therefore, Christian theologians in the second half of the 20th century spent a lot of time analyzing the nature of our language about God—what came to be called "God-talk."

Paul Tillich, a towering theologian of that period, repeatedly reminded Christians of the principle that **God** is not a being alongside other beings.[16] It is true that theistic faith-traditions frequently employ language that on the surface can make it sound as if God is another kind of living being. But we need to be careful not to treat God as if God were a finite being among other beings, or a finite cause in a chain of finite causes.

Religious people can become so familiar with the language their faith-tradition employs that they can sometimes forget that all of our language for God has to be in some sense metaphorical. (How, after all, could our finite human language talk about the Infinite without employing metaphors?) This limitation of God-talk was recognized even in the early centuries of Christianity, and was generally expressed in two ways:[17]
- By describing the words used for God as God's "names."
- By saying that whenever we affirm something about God to be the case, we also need to affirm that, in another sense, it is not true about God.

So what is it that our God-talk, our God-metaphors, are trying to point to? To answer that question, many mainstream theologians today refer to Paul Tillich's work. Tillich used a number of approaches, but one of his most valuable formulas was to say that the word "God" expressed "ultimate concern."[18]

There is more to that phrase than meets the eye. It holds a double meaning: That is because, at their best, Christians have used the word "God" to express both their highest (or deepest) values and also their subtlest (or deepest) discernment of the nature of reality. Here, however, is where it gets more intricate. What I value the most can be out of touch with reality. As Tillich so skillfully put it, what is my "ultimate concern" might not be what is truly *the* Ultimate Concern because of the actual nature of reality. To use classic religious language, what I consider to be god might be an idol. Or to put it another way, what we humans might want to call "sacred" might not be what really deserves being treated as sacred.

The philosopher Troy Wilson Organ, drawing strongly upon Tillich, elaborates:

When a modern man uses the term "god" he is
symbolizing his assumption that the cosmic
environment is one in which reality and value are
integrated, that the higher one penetrates into reality
the deeper one penetrates into value, that goodness and
beauty are not subjective human assessments pinned
on an indifferent world, [and] that values are
discovered as well as created.... God-talk is poetic talk
[expressing] "reality-value integration."[19]

It is because of this hope for finding a convergence of value and reality in our use of the word "God" that Tillich states that "the term 'ultimate concern' unites the subjective and the objective side of the act of faith."[20]

Most interestingly, a statement by the American Association for the Advancement of Science (AAAS) at one point combines Tillich's word "ultimate" with another word—"ground"—which Tillich also employed by describing God as the "ground of being."[21] The scientists' statement did so when it described the classic rule of thumb that science answers questions of "how," whereas religion answers questions of "why":

Science deals with how things happen in nature,

religion with why there is anything rather than nothing. Science answers specific questions about the workings of nature, religion addresses the *ultimate ground* of nature.[22]

What is truly God is that untouchable, unreachable point where the deepest truths and the greatest good *do* converge. And so the word "God" is a dynamic symbol that should help me in trying to continuously stay tuned to the widest horizon, the most important truths, the deepest values.

But how do I stay in touch with such a dynamic thing on a cosmic scale amid all the flux of the multitude of things I encounter in life? How can I even envision such a thing as this invisible convergence "God"? Only by using metaphors, symbols, and stories.

Our modern Western mindsets, so heavily influenced by science's ways of thinking, can make it particularly difficult to comprehend traditional religious language that speaks of God as if God were a *person*. Here again, the insights of Paul Tillich can be helpful, especially in an often overlooked exchange Tillich had with the famous physicist Albert Einstein. In a presentation for a 1940 conference on "Science, Philosophy, and Religion," Einstein outlined several arguments against religion, including the religious concept of a Personal God. Paul Tillich responded courteously in a manner aimed at clarifying theology, rather than being disputatious.

As part of his careful response, Tillich first emphasized the metaphorical nature of God-talk:

Religion lives and tries to maintain the presence of, and community with [the] divine depth of our existence. But ... it must be expressed in symbols. One of these symbols is Personal God. It is the common opinion of classical theology, practically in all periods of Church history, that the predicate "personal" can be said of the Divine only symbolically ... or if affirmed and negated at the same time.[23]

Being metaphors, person-language for God is therefore cultivating a depth of relationship with God similar to the relationships between persons. It is not saying that God is literally a person, nor literally a being:

> Why must the symbol of the personal be used at all?...
> The depth of being cannot be symbolized by objects
> taken from a realm which is lower than the personal,
> from the realm of things or sub-personal living
> beings.... This is the reason that the symbol of the
> Personal God is indispensable for living religion.... It
> is one symbol beside others indicating that *our*
> *personal center* is grasped by the manifestation of the
> inaccessible ground and abyss of being.[24]

Ending the Absentee God

The overview of history in Chapter 1 explained how the rise and expansion of modern science did not lead directly to atheism, but did lead to a reduction of God's role in many intellectuals' mental pictures of the world. God became mostly just the Creator of the universe and its natural laws at the beginning of time, which then operated itself without much further need for God. This is what is referred to today as **deism**.

In the first centuries of modern science (the 1600's and 1700's), this arrangement actually seemed good for both science and Christian theology. Scientists could continue to identify in more detail the orderly "laws" governing the world without God interfering and making the natural world unpredictable. Scientists could even be seen as people who could adjudicate when there was a "supernatural" disruption, thus ensuring a protected role for scientists at a time when religion still held sway.[25] (Evidence of this development in thought is that the use of the word "supernatural" to describe external events did not appear in the English language until the 1600's.[26]) At first, many theologians also thought this arrangement was beneficial: The orderliness revealed in the natural laws could be proof that a Divine Designer existed, and supernatural events could be proof of God still intervening.

Over the course of a couple centuries, however, it seemed that supernatural events defined in this fashion were fewer and farther between. God had thus become an absentee god to many intellectuals in the West. This theological malaise is evidenced in how far our modern, commonplace Western conception of miracles has diverged from that of the Bible and early Christianity. Ever since the 18th-century Scottish philosopher David Hume wrote a classic essay about it, modern debate has considered a miracle to be a disruption of natural laws.[27] But, as the contemporary professor of science and religion Peter Harrison points out:

> The authors of the Gospels were not working with a
> formal conception of "miracle" ... in the Humean [i.e.,
> Hume's] sense of a "contravention of the laws of
> nature," familiar to modern readers.... This is barely
> surprising, but is frequently overlooked in modern
> philosophical discussions of miracles.[28]

Thus it is that along with the rise of modern science there arose a "dichotomy between the natural and supernatural, along with the familiar notion of miracles as violations of the laws of nature."[29]

In contrast, when we look, for example, at the 5th-century Saint Augustine's *City of God*, we see that "for Augustine, the whole of nature was a miraculous work of God. Accordingly, miracles ([Latin:] *miraculum*) were to be understood primarily in terms of their impact on the observer."[30] The Bible also expresses that subjective dimension by using words such as "signs" (Greek: *semeia*) and "wonders" (Greek: *terrata*), and not actually employing the word "miracle."[31] Augustine expressively wrote:

> Isn't the daily course of nature itself a miracle,
> something to be wondered at? Everything is full of
> marvels and miracles, but they are so common that we
> regard them as cheap and of no account.[32]

With this perspective upon the drawback of our modern concept of "supernatural intervention," we may understand better why metaphors and symbols are crucial for speaking about God. That is because God is not an object, nor a finite cause, nor a being that can be objectively observed with the external senses. Instead, God is the meaningful Ultimate Depth in the world and in our experience of it. Our God-talk aims at keeping us in touch with that Ultimate Depth that works through the natural world. Again, the theologian Paul Tillich:

> It is an old, and always emphasized, theological
> doctrine that God acts *in* all beings according to their
> special nature; in man according to his rational nature,
> in animals and plants according to their organic nature,
> in stones according to their inorganic nature.[33]

Tillich's statement might sound like a novel theological idea for those who have not encountered it. But it was expressed poetically nineteen centuries ago by the major Christian theologian Irenaeus:

God sleeps in a stone, dreams in a flower, moves in an animal, and wakes in a human.[34]

Relating Science and Religion

So, given their great differences, where do science and religion meet? Having now explored their very different languages, we might return to our earlier question: How do we make sense of or make connections between what we see through the "window" of science and the "window" of religion. Is there a way to properly connect them?

It is at this point that we need to remember our mechanic giving the quite inappropriate answer of "God" to an engineering question. We must not make the category mistake of giving a theological answer to a scientific question. Nor try to claim that science by itself can answer religious questions that lie beyond the bounds of science.

The late science-writer Stephen Jay Gould made a valiant effort to keep science and religion from stepping on each other's toes by outlining two non-overlapping spheres (or "magisteria"), calling his plan "NOMA."[35] Although Gould allowed for discussion between the two spheres,[36] his scheme was much criticized for a couple of reasons—even by those who wanted peaceful relationships. One reason was because it did not provide space for people to integrate aspects of science and religion. A two-part mental diagram is not adequate for explaining where such integration can occur. That is why I suggest adding a third compartment to the diagram. The third compartment is each person's *worldview*. (See Figure 8.)

Despite the major caution against making category mistakes, aspects of science's and religion's two different forms of talking about the world can be brought together into a way of viewing the world. Each person's worldview will vary depending on how much they take into it from science or from religion or from other part's of their experience and culture. (Other areas of life from which we gain knowledge and understanding include history, art, and everyday experience.) And each person's worldview will vary

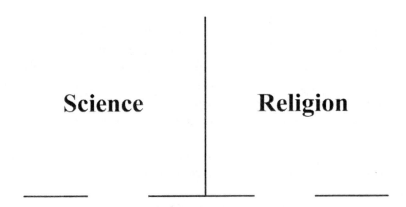

Science   **Religion**

Each person's Worldview

*Figure 8: Diagram of how to relate
science and religion properly*

depending upon how that person interrelates what they take in from science and religion and other areas.

That each person's worldview is a key locus for interrelating science and religion accounts for the great variability of interactions, as each person wrestles with how to relate a particular statement from the field of science with a particular religious affirmation, idea, or story. That variety of interrelationships is why historians of science prefer the idea of *complexity* as a thesis for understanding religion-science history, rather than the discredited "warfare" or "conflict" thesis.

Comparing the languages of science and of religion in abstract, as has been done in this chapter, can be a big step in distinguishing between them. But it can have a disadvantage. It can make it seem as if religious language consists of stated propositions about the world, such as science's statements. But in context, religious language often has a *performative* character. That is, it seeks to accomplish things with its language's effects upon people. Religious language aims to comfort, to encourage, to inspire, to motivate, to guide, and much more.

Religion is not merely a "window" through which religious people look out at the world. Neither is the enterprise of science. In both cases, the "window" metaphor needs to be stretched. Both science's and religion's windows are more like glass patio-doors, through which we do see and learn about things in the world. But, in a sense, we also open those sliding doors and step out into the world, interacting with it.

Contemporary science's most widespread form of interaction is through the technologies we have developed by applying scientific knowledge.

And what about religion? How is it performative? It what way does it use its language to seek to comfort? Who does it try to encourage? What does it hold up as inspiring? What actions does it try to motivate people to? It what direction does it try to guide groups of people? These questions demonstrate how the issue of religion cannot escape the issue of values.

Chapter 6

Ancient Wisdom
Raises Her Head

W e begin this chapter with a modern-day parable adapted from the contemporary spiritual writer Diane Karay Tripp:[1]

Once upon a time, there lived a man who had 3 sons and 17 camels. In his will, the man said that upon his death his camels should be divided between his sons in the following manner: One-half of the 17 camels to his eldest son, one-third of them to his middle son, and one-ninth to his youngest son. When the father died, there were obvious problems. None of the portions he had designated could divide up the 17 camels without destroying them. Conflict broke out among the 3 sons over what to do.

Fortunately, Wisdom arrived on the scene, riding a camel. She said to the troubled sons, "Please take my camel, add it to yours, and then try again." Having now 18 camels, the sons followed their father's instructions, and easily allotted one-half (9 camels) to the eldest son, one-third (6 camels) to the middle son, and one-ninth (2 camels) to the youngest. Amazingly, when they were done, the sons discovered that they had used only 17 of the 18 camels, thus allowing Wisdom to ride on her way again on her own camel—she having lost nothing, and they having gained much!

This parable reminds us of something known since ancient times, even though it is frequently forgotten: Wisdom, although encompassing knowledge, provides something of even greater value. In the parable, Wisdom used the knowledge of arithmetic the sons already possessed, but provided essential extras. Compared to the word "knowledge," the word "wisdom" implies extras such as insight, good judgment, and even a better spirit in approaching life. For example, when Wisdom speaks in the Bible's book of Proverbs, saying, "I, wisdom, live with *prudence*, and I attain knowledge and *discretion*."[2]

We might adapt this parable to ask what are the essential extras that religion can add to science and scientific knowledge. The Biblical scholar Lawrence Richards has described the concept of wisdom in the Christian Old Testament (the Hebrew Bible/*Tanakh*) as expressing an "approach to life."[3] As an approach to life, wisdom has reminded people that for life to be good, something more is required than knowledge and power. Traditionally, faith-traditions have been vehicles for that voice of Wisdom. How then might we today proceed toward interrelating religion and science so that the call of Wisdom will be heeded? That will be the subject of this chapter.

Science in Society, and Prophets of Wisdom

The modern Christian theologian Langdon Gilkey repeatedly emphasized that in any society, an enterprise that provides both power and knowledge will be held in high esteem.[4] Especially during the past century-and-a-half, modern science has given humans increasing technological power along with more and more knowledge. Consequently, science has gained esteem—one of the reasons religion needs to consciously address the interrelationships between religion and science if it wants to remain relevant.

Our general news media, when they occasionally look at religion-science issues beyond debates over teaching evolution, primarily raise the matter of using particular scientific technologies. Even though which technologies are at issue has changed over the course of time, there is nothing new in general about that concern. When today's news media do look beyond the matter of technologies and look at the knowledge science provides, the general media's scope is again limited. They deal mostly with a few specific issues, such as whether evolution really occurred and whether God exists. Here again, the media are not adequate in helping us get a solid understanding of what is required of religion in an age of science. That is because a broader and deeper matter involves the very *nature* of the knowledge science provides.

As science in its modern form began to increasingly influence Western society during the 1700's, there were alarm calls, often from poets. They expressed an awareness that this modern form of science could not by itself provide an adequate way of apprehending and approaching the world.

For one thing, some promoters of modern science's methods, rather than cultivating an integration of science's knowing with other ways of knowing, had begun to talk as if modern scientific knowing *superseded* other ways of gaining knowledge about the world.[5] And science's new approach was that of treating the world as if it were a machine that could be observed objectively, analyzed, and manipulated, taking power over it. Modern science also increasingly emphasized the value of an abstract kind of knowing of the world, especially what was obtainable through mathematics. Thus, over time, scientific knowledge moved further and further away from people's everyday knowledge about the world.

Some people did raise alarms about the limitations of modern science's approach to knowledge of the world. Most notable of the early cautionary voices were poets of the Romantic movement in the latter 1700's, such as Wordsworth, Keats, and Coleridge. Even though today those men are mostly remembered dismissively and incorrectly as just writers of flowery poetry, central to their thinking was the conviction that there were limits to scientific knowledge, and that there also was another way of knowing. This alternative way was one of communion and empathy with Nature —being receptive to it, rather than acting upon Nature as it were a passive object, dead matter. As the contemporary writer Charlene Spretnak explains:

> The founding fathers of modern science ... [had] prided themselves in having devised a method of impersonal knowing that was impeccably objective ... a machine-like regulation of thought.... [In contrast,] the Romantics ... sought to resuscitate the relationship between humans and the rest of the natural world.... Wordsworth for example cultivated a receptive attitude toward the natural world, regarding his sensory perceptions, particularly seeing and hearing, with an open heart.[6]

Perhaps the clearest poetic expression of this kind of caution about science is a poem by the 19th-century American Walt Whitman, part of which reads:

> When I heard the learn'd astronomer;

> When the proofs, the figures, were ranged in columns
>   before me,
> When I was shown the charts and the diagrams, to add,
>   divide, and measure them,...
> How soon unaccountable I became tired and sick,
> Till rising and gliding out, I wander'd off by myself,
> In the mystical moist night-air, and from time to time,
> Look'd up in perfect silence at the stars.[7]

It would be wrong to dismiss Walt Whitman as a Luddite, someone opposed to any new technology. In other poems Whitman celebrated the energy and creativity of Americans during an era of rapid industrialization. But here, Whitman has laid his finger on the fact that scientific knowledge, as powerful as it can be, is nevertheless an abstraction—a separating and isolating of particular information from our overall, living experience of the world.[8]

Modern Science's Self-Limitations

If those cautionary Romantic poets were correct in sounding an alarm, what then is it that modern science by itself cannot provide? Fortunately, we have the work of many philosophers of science over the past several decades who, with the help of historians of science, have sorted through these matters, including how they relate to religion.

As our modern form of science arose, the borderline between religion and science shifted, with science placing major limitations upon itself. Most introductory books on the religion-science relationship will explain that science as it is presently constituted *excludes* from its toolbox four major things. By its own ground-rules, the tools and methods of science have nothing to say, good or bad, about:[9]

- value
- meaning
- purpose (in most senses of the word)
- God.

(By this is not meant that scientists as people do not have values, meaning, or purposes in their lives, or that they necessarily do not believe in God. What is being referred to are the methods of scientific investigation.)

Let me very briefly add a bit of clarification about each of these major limitations.

Value: The first limitation is that even though scientific bodies might develop codes of conduct, the tools of science by themselves cannot make decisions about values. Even the contemporary atheist biologist Richard Dawkins, who sees science as a conqueror of religion, has stated in one of his books:

Science has no methods for deciding what is ethical.[10]

Meaning: A second limitation is that science's methods by themselves do not ask nor answer questions about meaning. As a statement by the American Association for the Advancement of Science states:

Science is about causes, religion about meaning.[11]

Purpose: The third major limitation is science's inability to deal with questions of purpose. Science can explain how things in the world function in relation to each other (such as when we might talk about the purpose a bird's tail-feathers serve). But when we ask questions of purpose or meaning in a larger sense, the way religion does, we are moving beyond modern science's own self-imposed limits. We are not talking about functions but instead about purpose when we wonder such things as, "Why should there be birds, or any animals at all?" Or, "Why am I here?" Or, "What is my purpose in life?"

Chapter 1 explained how, beginning in the 1600's, scientists began to more and more eliminate from their toolbox explanations of purpose as a cause, to the point that no scientist for the past century-and-a-half has considered purpose (in this sense) to be within the sphere of scientific explanations.[12]

God: Nor are questions about God in modern science's toolbox. As the evolutionary biologist Stephen Jay Gould, echoing similar statements by Niles Eldredge[13] and other evolutionists, emphasizes:

Science simply cannot (by its legitimate methods)
adjudicate the issue of God's possible superintendence
of nature. We neither affirm nor deny it; we simply
can't comment on it as scientists.[14]

The exclusion of the categories of value, meaning, purpose, and God is done for good scientific reason. As it developed into its modern form, science discovered that dealing with such "why" questions could stand in the way of answering the "how" questions about how the world operates. And thus stand in the way of obtaining the power such knowledge provides.

Unfortunately, we still have a lot of confusion in our contemporary U. S. culture about how to properly interrelate religion and science. And one of the major culprits is the way the news media frequently handle this matter of science's self-limitations. For example, a 2006 *Time* magazine cover exclaimed, "Science Finds God."[15] That cover—especially with its drawings of one person looking through a telescope and another person looking through a microscope—strongly suggests that God is an object that might be located by science using the tools of science. But can we really experience God by setting aside questions of meaning, purpose, and value—as modern science does?

Our culture's ongoing confusion about these major limitations of science is also perpetuated by a slew of books that have hit the marketplace over the past several decades. But consider the opposite claims of these two titles: One book is subtitled *How Science Is Discovering God in Everything, Including Us*,[16] and the other is titled *God, The Failed Hypothesis: How Science Shows That God Does Not Exist*.[17] So which is true? The answer is that both titles go beyond what modern science by itself can claim. And most mainstream Christian theologians agree that science can neither prove nor disprove the existence of God.[18]

Some of the recent books that cause confusion have even been written by scientists—who many people turn to hoping that modern science can answer some of life's deepest questions. (Examples of such statements by some scientists are examined in Chapter 19, "Belonging to Earth and Cosmos.")

Besides these four major exclusions that are usually mentioned in introductory books about the differences between religion and science, there are additional subtler things modern science excludes because of its methods. The contemporary theologian John Haught has been adept at spotting these subtler things that lie beyond the bounds of science. And he argues that they provide us additional knowledge and understanding about the world we live in.[19]

Subjectivity: One of the additional things science cannot deal with directly is our inner subjective experiences. Scientists can ask you or me to try to describe how it feels to experience something, or they can chart what happens in our brains during that experience. But such scientific data is not the same as your or my subjective experience as we know it directly.

Intersubjectivity: Similarly, scientific knowledge, which is based on observation of external objects, cannot directly include intersubjectivity. That is, the way that I can sometimes empathize with other people, thus experiencing within myself what other people are experiencing subjectively. That too is a type of knowledge, but it lies beyond the bounds of what modern science can know directly.

Aesthetic affect: Another subtle matter lying beyond the tools of modern science is the aesthetic affect of something I see or hear. I can feel it, for example, when I experience a sunset. Or a bird's song. Or the shape of a tree's branches silhouetted against the sky. Or a piece of music. Part of what I know about such things is through the aesthetic affect they have, inducing an experience within me. Scientific observation, being from the outside, cannot encompass directly that aspect of knowing reality.

Laying Out Science's Major Challenges

Much too frequently today, in popular books written by scientists will be found the phrase "the scientific worldview" without a solid analysis of what such a thing would be. (Whatever it might mean, the scientist using the phrase "scientific worldview" is in favor of it.) Usually what is meant is the adopting of modern science's explanation of the Big Bang, the evolution of the universe, and the evolution of species on this planet—all as a replacement for traditional religion's faith-stories.

However, what is often overlooked in such appeals for the predominance of a "scientific worldview" is that science itself can only provide what we commonly call the "facts" about the history of the universe and living species. We might well ask how adequate a worldview could be without possessing the tools of values, meaning, and purpose, and without including subjective experience, intersubjectivity, and the aesthetic affects this world has upon us.

The overall problem is not so much that science has these limitations, but instead that our culture does not usually understand these limitations, even as we more and more turn to science hoping it will provide us guidance. Most people (even quite a number of scientists) do not comprehend what are the aspects of reality that modern science places outside its working boundaries. This then, is the first challenge science poses to contemporary religion that accepts scientific knowledge: that of understanding, and helping other people understand, science's inherent limitations, and dealing with those limitations.

A second challenge is that over the past several centuries, most modern Western Christianity has become narrowed down to the human realm, turning the non-human realm over to science. Most of modern Western Christianity concentrates on either the interior spiritual life of the individual person or on human societies. In contrast to this narrowing of modern Christianity to the human sphere, the contemporary theologian Elizabeth Johnson explains:

> Such amnesia about the cosmic world has not always
> been the case. In fact, for three-quarters of this history,
> creation [i.e., the created world] was actively present
> as an *intrinsic* part of theological reflection.[20]

Here then is how the situation stands: Most of modern Western Christianity (except for some of it occasionally visiting environmental problems) has its focus narrowed to the human sphere, having turned the non-human realm over to science. Our modern culture expects science to give us deep understanding and guidance about Nature and the cosmos. But modern science is incapable of answering questions about value, meaning, or purpose. This is not a good setup.

One way God became mostly exiled from the non-human realm in the present is that, as science became increasingly able to describe the processes of the universe in terms of natural laws that acted somewhat mechanically like a clock, God became the giant Clockmaker whose presence was no longer necessary. How and where do we mentally locate God in a universe that seems to be able to operate on its own through natural laws?

Another challenge is thus that of theology, religion, and spirituality needing to recover an awareness of the presence and role of the Divine everywhere.

Simplifications Resulting from Science

Still another challenge contemporary religion needs to deal with is to counter three simplifications that can result because of an over-confidence in science: scientism, reductionism, and determinism. Let us look at each in turn.

Scientism: This simplification is that of overstating science's power. There are various form of it. And it has become more frequent in scientists' writing over the past half-century. One form of scientism is the claim that scientific knowledge replaces all previously held knowledge. With science being such a powerful tool today, it is sometimes easy to forget that science is not our only way of knowing the natural world.

Scientism can also show up in a belief that scientific knowledge with its technology can be the solution to all of the world's problems. It was a claim frequently made in the 20th century. As one example, Nehru, who became prime minister of India, proclaimed:

> It is science alone that can solve the problems of
> hunger and poverty, of insanitation and illiteracy ... of
> a rich country inhabited by starving people. [21]

However, the 20th-century philosopher Mary Midgley raises a skeptical, penetrating question:

> Science alone? No decent laws needed, no honest
> politicians and administrators, no common sense, no
> congenial way of life...? [22]

Reductionism: This second type of simplification can occur either between scientific fields or between science and non-science. The best way to understand the problem of reductionism is to recognize that each of the various physical, biological, and social sciences slices through reality at a particular level. (See Figure 7 in the preceding chapter.) Starting with the most elementary level, we can slice into reality at the sub-atomic and atomic levels. Moving toward levels of more complexity, we can slice through reality at the chemical level, then at a mechanical level of larger interacting objects, and with more complexity, at the biological level. And we can continue in that fashion into the even more complex levels of social understanding and psychological understanding.

Reductionism occurs when a more complex level of reality is thought to be no more than something at a simpler level. As examples, take these statements: "The human body is merely a network of complex molecules, interacting and changing continuously." Or, "Human beings are nothing but objects moving about interacting with each other." The words "nothing but," "only," or "merely" are often indicators that reductionism is at work, although sometimes those words are not used explicitly.

One reason scientists today so easily fall into reductionism in their writings (usually without realizing it) is that all fields of science have become so highly specialized. People majoring at college level in any science quickly become immersed in their own field as it becomes more detailed and complicated. Thus, it becomes easy to see the world as fundamentally *consisting of* one's own specialized area of concentration.

Indeed, if one's specialty has become particle physics, it does become easy to believe that one has reached the ultimate explanation for anything once something has been described as subatomic particles in motion. Or, if one's specialty is brain scans, it can become easy to believe that one has reached the ultimate explanation for any human thought or feeling when an accompanying brain activity is located. But the world is much more than particles in motion, and we are more than our brains.

Reductionism sometimes appears combined with an attitude of scientism when some scientists claim that what we know through the humanities—such as the fields of history, religious studies, and theology—will eventually be reduced to knowledge of biological and atomic processes. (This is dealt with in Chapter 20, "Scientists and Mystics in Dialogue.")

Determinism: This third type of simplification can occur because of an overconfidence in science's ability to predict. Determinism is the idea that events or behaviors *inevitably* turned out the way they did—they had to turn out the particular way they did.

One ancient form of determinism was the idea of fate, the idea that gods controlled events, turning humans into puppets. Today, however, the most frequent form of determinism is genetic determinism. That is, the idea that certain behaviors are "hard-wired" because such behavior among early humans 100,000 years ago supposedly provided a reproductive or survival advantage, and that is why such behavior inevitably occurs today.

On radio and TV every month there will be a news story about some scientific researcher having (supposedly) figured out the evolutionary explanation for some particular behavior. Such as why men are promiscuous. Or why women are less adventurous. Or why stepfathers abuse their stepchildren. (All these are actual examples of claims by scientific researchers.[23])

There is one big problem with all these claims, which the radio or TV announcers virtually never mention. Namely, that there is no simple, direct cause-and-effect link between any gene and a physical feature of human beings—much less any direct cause-and-effect link between any gene and a human behavior. The effects of any one gene are complex, working their way through interactions with other genes, through embryonic processes, and through development after birth, all involving interactions with the environment. As the late evolutionary biologist Stephen Jay Gould cautioned:

> There is no gene "for" such unambiguous bits of
> morphology [i.e., bodily structure] as your left kneecap
> or your fingernail.... Hundreds of genes contribute to
> the building of most body parts and their action is
> channeled through a kaleidoscopic series of
> environmental influences.[24]

Even more complex is the development of behaviors, because we humans are complex intertwinings of biological potential and cultural influences. We are not genetically "hard-wired" machines, either in our physical development or our behavior. (Even if the evolutionary biologist Richard Dawkins did call us "robot vehicles blindly programmed to preserve the selfish molecules known as genes.")[25]

How does this tendency of scientists to overstate supposed links between human behaviors and genetic makeup apply to religion? Simply this: Overstatements of connections between biological makeup and behavior—especially to the point of determinism—lessen society's and individuals' desires to make changes that can reduce levels of bad behavior. Why try to make changes in ourselves or in society if bad behavior is inevitable because it is "hard-wired"?

A contemporary of Charles Darwin, the philosopher, John Stuart Mill, writing in an age of classism and racism, was aware of the danger of attributing too much to biological causes, and therefore overlooking the ways society could be changed. Mill wrote:

> Of all the vulgar modes of escaping from the
> consideration of the social and moral influences on the
> human mind, the most vulgar is that of attributing the
> diversities of conduct and character to inherent natural
> differences.[26]

Christianity has not been alone among the world's faith-traditions in resisting determinism by emphasizing the importance of individual's making decisions employing their will. And by emphasizing the improvement of social environments that affect behavioral patterns.

Additional Challenges from Science

Still another challenge for Western religion in our age of science involves finding a basis for religious assertions. This problem is especially pronounced in Western Christianity. As it narrowed its focus over the past few centuries more and more to the human realm, it has tried to ground its religious claims primarily in the inner life of the person. We see the consequence of this change in our tendency in the U.S. today to see religious beliefs as being one's individual opinions or chosen values (in contrast to science's dealing with factual truths about the world). But we might well ask if such an arrangement is theologically adequate: Is there not some need for Christianity to find ways to ground Christian assertions in our knowledge of the world, rather than leaving them "suspended somewhat perilously in mid-air," as the theologian John Macquarrie so beautifully put it.[27] Otherwise, religious claims can become whatever opinion an individual chooses to make them.

Yet another challenge to add to our list is that of integrating our scientific knowledge with the best emotional aspects of ourselves as human beings. In the early decades of modern science, scientific thinkers were motivated by the approach of such people as René Descartes, a philosopher and mathematician who promoted the emerging science. Descartes had said that human *reasoning* was the sure way to knowing. He looked down upon human emotions as vague and misleading. As the contemporary writer Spretnak puts it, Descartes "regarded feelings as corruptions of pure perception."[28]

In contrast, those 18th-century Romantic poets who were sensitive to the limits of modern science's form of knowledge held up the value of our emotions to sensitize ourselves to aspects of reality. Such as the German Romantic writer Johann Herder, who reminded us that, "Love is the noblest form of knowing, as it is the noblest feeling."[29] Herder's statement resonates with the theologian John Haught's pointing out that intersubjectivity is one way of knowing the world. A way that extends beyond science's method of gaining knowledge.

The Need for Vision

A final challenge is that of developing a good vision. A vision that discerns the depth and value of this world and the possibilities of a good future for it as a whole. A vision that integrates scientific knowledge and our best religiously-grounded beliefs. Providing visions of the good has always been one of the roles of faith-traditions. Quoting again the philosopher Mary Midgley:

> Imaginative vision isn't a luxury, an extra, an
> irrelevance, a childish taste that adult scientific heroes
> can dispense with.... If [science] isn't furnished with a
> sensible vision, it cannot fail to gather a wild one
> instead.[30]

And, indeed, we might be skeptical about some of the visions of the future that have been put forward by those scientists who see ever-advancing scientific knowledge and technology as being the very thing that will save the human race.

For example, a *New York Times* article in the winter of 2014 reported that a considerable number of people would be willing to be among those sent to the planet Mars—even knowing they would die there within a few weeks because that planet could not sustain life.[31] We might wonder how scientifically grounded inter-planetary scenarios for the future of humankind are when we remember that there is no other planet in our solar system that is naturally able to sustain the life of any human being. And when we remember that the natural resources to sustain the physical needs of human beings in their journey to settlement on another planet would have to be taken from this already-overstrained planet Earth.

Strangely, while on the one hand we have confidence in technology to conquer other planets, when we turn on the TV, we also see a growing number of movies with dark, dystopian visions of a highly technologized world. That there are such opposite visions of a future heavily influenced by scientific technology strongly implies that at least one vision is not grounded in facts.

Either type of vision of an increasingly technological world raises a basic question: What is science for? More than science's tools are required here. That is because, as the historian of science John Hedley Brooke reminds us, "As soon as one asks why science should be pursued at all, questions of value immediately arise."[32]

What Can Faith-Traditions Provide?

Many of these challenges, especially as they impinge upon questions of values, are relevant for people of all faith-traditions, not just Christianity. Faith-traditions have been humankind's primary vehicles for carrying reminders about the need for wisdom, as well as providing understandings of what wisdom consists of.

With this outline of challenges before us, we might return now to a question that was left open at the close of the preceding chapter: Broadly speaking, what kind of direction, guidance, and assistance does religion provide to people? Ian Barbour, having dealt extensively with religion-science relationships, recognizes that religion is variegated, but he points to this core role:

> A religious tradition is not just a set of intellectual
> beliefs or abstract ideas.... Above all, religion aims at
> the transformation of personal life, particularly by
> liberation from self-centeredness.[33]

There are differences in emphases between faith-traditions (as well as diversity within each tradition). However, because in this chapter we have heard the figure of Wisdom speaking out of the Judeo-Christian tradition (through the Bible's book of Proverbs), we might close by touching upon something considered to be a vital part of faith-traditions influenced by the Bible. Charlene Spretnak, in her book *States of Grace,* identifies elements from various faith-traditions that she sees as being highly relevant in our modern world. When she focuses upon the Judeo-Christian tradition, she echoes Barbour's concern about the danger of self-centeredness:

> For the narcissistic "I," the only valued collective is
> the tightly proscribed "we." People outside the "we"

group are seen as deserving of less concern, or no
concern at all.[34]

To offset that human weakness, the Abrahamic traditions influenced by the Bible (Judaism, Christianity, and Islam)[35] repeatedly remind their followers of the need to embody concern for those who are less fortunate.[36] As Spretnak explains:

A central focus in the development of Judaism was the
understanding that the divine is manifested not only in
nature, but also in the dynamics of human history....
The manifestation of the divine in Hebrew scriptures
[shared by Christianity] responds especially to the poor
and disadvantaged.... Hence in the evolution of
Judaism, as well as those religions that grew from its
foundation, Christianity and Islam, active social
concern is an imperative.[37]

This is but one ancient concern out of our wisdom-traditions that can factor into our seeking ways to employ science wisely, and understand our world more deeply.

Chapter 7

Rescuing the Bible
from Science

In the very early 1800's, Thomas Jefferson began removing pages from his Bible and discarding them. Jefferson retained only a tiny fraction of the Bible's contents in his customized version (sometimes called "The Jefferson Bible").[1] He left out things he could not believe happened, and things he simply did not agree with or like. Although Jefferson still considered himself a Christian, he wrote to a friend how he considered the discarded parts of the Bible to be, "Vulgar ignorance,... things impossible,... superstitions, fanaticisms, and fabrication."[2]

The distress Jefferson was having can be traced back to the rise of modern science beginning in the 1700's. The powers of modern science gradually led to its methods being expanded into other areas of life. As the historian Karen Armstrong explains, "Increasingly, truth had to be demonstrated empirically [i.e., through observations using the external senses] and objectively, assessed by its ... fidelity to the external world. Consequently, the more intuitive modes of thought became suspect."[3] This expansion of science's requirements for truth into other fields was a significant feature of the movement called the Enlightenment, which penetrated 18th-century thought in Western Europe, England, and the U.S.

> Changes associated with the American Revolution led to the establishment of a Christianized form of the Enlightenment as the dominant intellectual force in the country. Almost all Americans, to be sure, repudiated ... the sneers at religion from the French savant Voltaire.... [But American intellectuals] were convinced that [Isaac] Newton's scientific triumphs could be repeated in ... ethics, jurisprudence, and other spheres, if only practitioners in those fields were as rigorous and dispassionate as Newton had been in scientific work.[4]

This description by historian Mark Noll of the Enlightenment's approach to knowledge helps explain Jefferson's problems with the Bible. Jefferson was a child of the Enlightenment. He could not accept anything in the Bible that did not meet science's type of test for truth, or did not express his own sense of morality. And so, his troubles can be a springboard into the question of how we might preserve any truth that might be in the Bible in our contemporary age of science. That is the subject we will wrestle with in this chapter.

Some of the material Jefferson expunged from the Bible did not seem to him to encourage proper moral behavior. Whether or not that is the case depends in part upon what we consider the Biblical material to be. For example, any narrative in which a person acts immorally can still be aimed at inspiring moral behavior. Cautionary tales often contain characters thinking and acting badly. Therefore, the larger question in discovering whether or not the Bible contains truth is what type (or types) of literary material the Bible consists of. And it is here that the question of the Bible's relation to science comes into play.

Christianity actually has a long history of saying that material in the Bible was *not* intended to be treated like scientific descriptions or explanations. As an example: In the 16th century, when Copernicus was laying out mathematical calculations that placed the sun at the center of the planetary system, the Protestant leader John Calvin wrote commentaries on the Bible, which he viewed as being Scriptures inspired by God's Spirit. In commenting upon part of Psalm 136, in which it is said that God created sun, moon, and stars, Calvin was able to say of the Bible's intent that "the Holy Spirit had no intention to teach astronomy."[5] In the 20th century, mainline Protestant denominations and Roman Catholicism have echoed that sentiment in official statements. As just one example, in 1969 the nation-wide Presbyterian Church succinctly stated, "The Bible is not a book of science."[6]

Nonetheless, science today is such a predominant way of obtaining knowledge that it can be very tempting to try to affirm the truth of the Bible by asserting that it aligns with what modern science has discovered. Bookstore shelves contain any number of books making such claims. One Christian minister of evangelism, who has degrees in physics and astronomy, claims in one of his books the following about the Bible's opening account of the creation of the universe:

> Moses, the probable author, penned this account more than thirty-four centuries ago. Somehow he managed to get it right—the right initial conditions, the right events accurately described and correctly sequenced ... to align with the still-accumulating evidence from multiple scientific disciplines equipped with space-age technological tools.[7]

But is that really so? Even if the Bible is not science, it could at least conceivably contain some pieces of science within it. Let us explore that question.

The most debated piece of the Bible in this regard is this very creation account in Genesis 1, which opens the Old Testament (the Hebrew Bible/*Tanakh*). But does that account meet the test of the best modern science, as the physicist and astronomer just quoted claims? More pointedly—and more importantly—does that account meet the test of being anything resembling science so that we should treat it using science's standards?

Putting the Genesis Accounts to the "Science" Test

Although many Christians today do not realize it, the Bible's book of Genesis in fact contains *two* creation accounts, one right after the other (a fact that was noticed by some ancient Christian Biblical interpreters such as Augustine[8]). The first account, which runs from Gen. 1:1 to Gen. 2:4a, is recognizable to many people from God's actions being arranged on a seven-day framework. The second creation account is the first part of the famous "Adam and Eve" story, which runs from Gen. 2:4b to Gen. 3:22.

So, as an exploration, let us pretend that we are scientists involved in some scientific research. Let's say we have two different research teams, each team collecting its own data so as to double-check each other. Each team has already been out getting observational data, and the teams are now back together, reviewing their data.

The first team of scientists, using Genesis's chapter 1 as its "data" for its "observations," will come up with the following list of the order in which "events" occurred. That is, the order in which things were created by God:

- light
- bodies of water, air, and sky
- dry land and plants
- sun, moon, and stars
- fishes and birds
- land animals
- humans (male and female together)

The second team of mock scientists, using as their "data" chapter 2 of Genesis, would come up with a different list in which "events" occurred. According to their "data," God created things in this order:

- earth
- human (male)
- plants and trees
- land animals and birds
- woman

Notice in particular the different order of the man-plants-woman sequence in the second list.

That these accounts are significantly different in the order of the "events" of God's creation would be a real problem if the two accounts were supposed to be scientific statements. But it is *not* a problem if Genesis 1 and Genesis 2 are each accepted as being what they are: *religious* material. In fact, these two narratives (from different strands of tradition) were carefully placed side by side and considered complementary when the book of Genesis was assembled by Jewish scribes centuries before Jesus.

Moreover, even in ancient Christianity, people such as the 3rd-century theologian Origen recognized that Genesis 1 was manifestly not a literal, historical record of events. Origen pointed out that it could not be such because in it the writer has God creating light—as well as days and nights—even before God creates the sun, which anyone knows is the source of light.[9]

Modern Biblical scholarship, dating back over a century, has labeled the two ancient religious strands (not actually written by Moses himself) as being the Priestly and the Yahwist strands. The first account is considered to be part of the Priestly tradition because it includes matters of special concern to the priests, such as the Sabbath. It is something like a psalm of praise. The second account is considered to be part of what is called the Yahwist tradition because it uses the name "Yahweh" for God. It is actually just the first part of the "Adam and Eve" story, which is something like an extended moral parable.[10] For our purposes in this Chapter, we will focus on some critical differences between scientific and religious writings that can be demonstrated by these Genesis accounts.

If these two creation accounts *were* meant to be scientific observations, we would be in real trouble. That is because the primary way modern science gains information is by observing and recording sequences of events. Think, for example of lab experiments you may have done in high school, and how you were instructed to record step-by-step what actions you took and what you observed. (Such as: "We put 10 milliliters of chemical A in the beaker. Then we added 3 milliliters of chemical B. We stirred it. Nothing happened. Then we put a piece of white litmus paper into the mixture. The paper immediately turned blue.")

In contrast, literary narratives (religious or otherwise), have different purposes and follow different rules than scientific obser- vations. Within a story, parable, or poem, the elements are frequently arranged for reasons *other* than that of recording a string of causes and effects. For example, one element within a narrative might be postponed to the climax near the end of the narrative to elevate its importance—not because it has to occur in that position in time. For example, in the story of Cinderella, all the ugly sisters try on the glass slipper before Cinderella, and Cinderella tries it on last, for the purpose of heightening the reader's suspense and concern about what happens to Cinderella, not because logically they had to have all tried it on it any partic- ular order. Whatever order they tried the slipper on, the results would have been the same.

But that flexibility in sequence is not the case with science.

If we do a literary analysis of that first creation narrative in Genesis 1, we can uncover the probable reason for its particular arrangement. On the first three days, God creates places in which things in the natural world can exist (such as water and land). And in the following three days, God creates things (such as fishes and land animals), putting them in the corresponding places that have been provided in advance. This message of God's gracious providing appropriate places to sustain life gains poignancy when we draw upon knowledge from modern Biblical scholarship about when this account was most probably written: It was in the 6th century B.C.E. during the Babylonian exile. It was a time when the audience for this creation narrative had been *dis-placed* by war and captivity.[11] What a wonderful vision of God providing places for living things! A vision developed even in the midst of destruction. A vision of the ultimate goodness of the world (as God repeatedly says in the narrative while creating the world).

But that wonderful message is obscured or lost altogether if we approach the Genesis 1 account with a mindset that tries to see if Genesis 1 aligns with modern scientific knowledge about sequences of events billions of years ago.

Character and Meanings of Creation Narratives

As expressed by Ian G. Barbour (who should know because he is fully trained in both physics and religion):

Creation stories serve functions in human life that are very different from those of scientific theories.[12]

It might prove helpful to think of creation narratives, such as our two creation accounts in Genesis, as being *root* stories. Creation stories in ancient cultures were not so much going back in historical time, as they were trying to get to the root of things. Creation or "root" stories are getting to the bottom of things, down to enduring religious truths about existence. Getting down to a deeper understanding beneath the flux of events.

The contrast between religious and scientific statements about creation can also be demonstrated by opening up the theological meanings the statement "God is **Creator**" has held in the Judeo-Christian tradition. These meanings can also be found in the Islamic faith-tradition. To begin with, saying that God created something is a way of reminding ourselves that *we* did not bring that thing about. When we say, for example, that God made a tree, we remind ourselves that we did not make that tree. Similarly, by saying God made humans, we remind ourselves that none of us has brought ourselves into existence. Nor has anything else that exists brought itself into existence.

Furthermore, in saying that God created not just us but everything, we emphasize our *commonality* with all of the natural world. Not just with other forms of life, but also with the inanimate parts of the natural world.

The statement "God is Creator" emphasizes not only our commonality but also our dependence. That is, we express that our continuing to exist is also more than something of our own doing. In the Bible, God's actions as Creator continue beyond the initial creation, sustaining and renewing life. As the physicist and theologian John Polkinghorne says:

> God is as much the Creator today as at the instant of
> the big bang, fifteen billion years ago.... God's role is
> not merely initiation but sustaining.[13]

This is not a novel theological idea. It is expressed, for example, in the Bible's Psalm 104, in which the writer says to God, using the present tense:

> You cause the grass to grow for the cattle, and plants
> for people to use, to bring forth food from the earth....
> When you send forth your spirit, they are created; and
> you renew the face of the ground.[14]

Moreover, when expressed as a religious affirmation, the statement "God is Creator" can be a way of turning ultimate matters of our lives over to God, of being grasped by something greater than ourselves, and yielding to the power of that experience.

Saying that the world is God's creation is also a way of expressing that the world, rather than necessarily existing, is an expression of God's *giving* nature—God's grace. And so we can experience existence as a gift from God, thus changing our orientation toward life.

Because God is a continuing Creator, and because God's creative activity is an outpouring of grace, we can wake to each new day receiving it as a gift. Not just each new day, but each new spring, and each new season of life, as all of creation is renewed by the Creator.

Feeling the weight of this whole constellation of meanings for the theological statement that "God is Creator of all," we might now recall the scientific question of what happened molecularly at some point in time about 15 billion years ago at the Big Bang. Feeling the immense contrast, we might see how comparing religious and scientific statements is not even equivalent to comparing apples and oranges. It's more like comparing apples and orangutans! Both types of statements have their own value in their own way. But there is vastly more contrast than similarity.

Overcoming Our Modern Mindset

Preserving the distinction between religion and science is extremely important so that religious statements, such as those in the Bible, are not flattened into supposedly scientific-like observations. Trying to flatten them into quasi-scientific statements removes from them the depth of meaning that symbols and stories can carry. It removes the depth of meaning that we experience existentially when we live into stories and participate in symbolic rituals.

Among many moderate and liberal Americans today, there is, quite rightfully, concern about rescuing science education from those who would want to introduce non-scientific claims into the public-school science classrooms. However, as the examples provided in this chapter demonstrate, there is also a great need to rescue the Bible from science.

There are three aspects of our modern mindset that can easily be impediments to our trying to understand the Bible, it being from an era with a quite different way of thinking. The three aspects are that we today tend to think in terms that are:
- mathematical
- physical and spatial
- historical

Each of these will be elaborated upon in turn.

Getting Beyond Mathematical Terms

One aspect is that we are inclined to think of numbers as expressing quantities or measurements rather than being symbolic, which they frequently are in the Bible.

An example can be provided from the book of Genesis's narrative of Noah and the flood. If that narrative is read carefully, the reader might discover that at one point God tells Noah to take "two" of every animal into the ark (Gen. 9:19), while at another point God instructs Noah to take "seven pairs" of certain animals into the ark (Gen. 7:2-3). If we treat such instructions on how to load the ark as if they were scientific instructions, we will run into real difficulties, even disaster. In scientific measurements, the number 2 is critically different from 14. If we employ a scientific mindset, we might try to reason the difference away or reject the narrative as being a "fabrication" (to borrow Thomas Jefferson's word.).

So what is the explanation for the different numbers? It is simply that the Noah narrative as it stands in the Bible can tolerate both numbers because it is expressing religious and theological ideas in story form.[15] And the numbers 2 and 7 both have symbolic meanings. In this instance, 2 expresses the fecundity of life, male and female. And 7 symbolizes perfection, completion. Both numbers express particular types of wholeness. By instructing Noah on what animals to preserve on the ark, God is bringing about a new, cleansed creation—a wholeness to re-populate the Earth.

Contrast this ability of a religious narrative to tolerate either the number 2 or the number 7 with an example of Charles Darwin's use of numbers in his scientific studies of animal populations. Darwin was providing data showing that seeds can travel on ocean currents from one island to another, and thus be able to evolve into new species once they are separated from the original population. First, Darwin has calculated that the Atlantic current moved at 33 nautical miles a day, and so a seed travels more than 1,300 miles in 42 days. Then Darwin adds the observation that "an asparagus plant with ripe berries floated for 23 days, when dried it floated for 85 days, and the seeds afterwards germinated."[16]

How different is this exacting, mathematical use of numbers from the Bible's approach, in which numbers virtually always have symbolic overtones. The depth of meanings lying within those symbolic uses would be lost if we treat the Bible as if it were anything like scientific data.

We might also look at a Biblical example related to issues regarding the theory of evolution, one of the more contested areas of religion-science relationships in the U.S. As shown in Chapter 4 ("An Awkward History"), it is a myth that anti-evolutionists' main problem with evolution has been that they have always read the Bible's Genesis 1 account literally, as if creation occurred in only six days. Even before Darwin's book, when geologists began stretching back the Earth's life span immensely, even conservative Christians developed ways to read that Biblical account figuratively.[17] One way was to understand the word "day" in it to mean a period of time. And so, there has continued to be a good bit of debate between conservative and liberal Christians over whether those "days" in Genesis 1 should be considered to be long periods of time, or considered to be 24-hour days but without the account being taken as straight history. Notice, however, how the question —if framed in that fashion—is still a debate about two mathematically measurable lengths of time: long periods or 24-hour days.

Remembering how our modern mindset inclines us to think of numbers as units of measurement, we might ask whether that debate over long lengths of time or 24-hour periods might be misguided from the outset. Especially once we learn that in the Bible the number seven usually symbolizes completion. Could it be that the Biblical writer is not thinking primarily about any lengths of measurable time? Could it be that the Biblical writer is primarily thinking about some kinds of relationships? About some kind of completeness and completion of relationships? Evidence that this is the probable theme is that the final day of creation is followed by the seventh-day Sabbath. That is the day on which the ancient Hebrews completed their week, rested from their work, and aimed to bask in the goodness of God's created world.

Getting Beyond Physical and Spatial Terms

A second aspect of our modern mindset is that we tend to think in terms that are physical and spatial.

Here is one example of that effect of our modern mindset upon reading the Bible: When we hear it said that something "ascended," we tend to think of it as physically rising up from the Earth's surface, in the way that a rocket ascends into outer space. That physical way of thinking, however, can be an impediment when we he hear the New Testament's statements that Jesus, following his resurrection, ascended into heaven.[18] Today, we can think of such statements as meaning that Jesus somehow physically rose upward from the Earth's surface.

But the Biblical writers meant something different, and in this case we can clearly know so because the writer of Ephesians asks directly the rhetorical question, "When it says, 'He ascended,' what does it mean...?" (Eph. 4:9). And the writer answers his own question by saying it means that Jesus "ascended far above all the heavens, so that he might fill all things."[19]

With our modern, physical and spatial mindset, we are not likely to think of the language of "ascent" as meaning something is somehow *in* all things. It can require effort to hear the Bible's use of seemingly physical and spatial language to describe spiritual and theological relationships. The Bible scholar Marcus Borg clarifies the meanings of Jesus's ascension:

> Its foundational meaning is that Jesus is now with God ... [which] has a number of nuances. First, Jesus is no longer "here"—that is, no longer here as a flesh-and-blood reality.... Rather, Jesus is now with God, and God is everywhere—and so Jesus is *everywhere*.[20]

Borg's statement that "Jesus is everywhere" coincides with the Ephesians clarification that ascent into heaven means that Jesus now "fill[s] all things."

Statements regarding God usually have a value-component (as was explained in Chapter 5, "Two Windows onto the World"). Remembering that, we can better understand an additional nuance that, according to Borg, "ascension is associated with the lordship of Jesus, that is, with his authority."[21] The values that Jesus's disciples have seen in Jesus are now to be the ruling values in "all things."

Getting Beyond Historical Terms

A third aspect from our scientific inheritance is that we moderns are inclined to think about truth in historical terms. As one character in an 1888 novel expressed that mindset, "If the Gospels [in the Bible] are not true as fact, as history, I cannot see that they are true at all, or of any value."[22]

Modern Western science cultivated a method of explaining things primarily in terms of series of causes and effects that can be observed. The Enlightenment period of the 1700's, much influenced by science, developed a way of thinking of the past as similarly being a series of events that could be uncovered. But this is a very modern way of thinking.

Ancient writers never thought the way we do about historical events. And so, as the contemporary Biblical scholar Lawrence Boadt explains, ancient writers "as a result did not record the events of their time with such neutral objectivity, nor did they ever believe in telling the past as a simple and objective search for exactly what happened." Therefore, there is "a fundamental problem that plagues most modern believers who read the Bible."[23] We can mistakenly try to read the Bible as if it were supposed to be observations of external events as if they were videotaped. The consequence is that we easily dismiss or discard parts of the Bible when they do not meet that scientific test.

Conclusion (and a Couple Matters More)

Our modern mindset, influenced so much by science, can thus be an obstacle to religion in a number of ways. Biblical writers were not concerned with recording any objective events as such. They were interested instead in expressing what was the meaning and *significance* of events—particularly the ultimate significance. Which is to say, their significance as regards God. And the meaning and significance of events is never anything that can be seen with the physical senses. Nor is meaning and significance anything that is physically spatial. Nor anything mathematically measurable.

Ever since the 17th-century Scientific Revolution, science has expanded immensely, giving us more and more of science's kind of knowledge about the world. So much so that we can easily get to treating *all* types of knowledge and statements (such as religious statements) by science's standards. But the complex and variegated material of the Bible needs to be rescued from that modern tendency. Frank Burch Brown, a seminary professor, describes well the rich variety of material in the Bible. (In this quotation, Brown uses the word "myth" not in the sense of a falsehood, but in the sense of a mythology, a particular genre for expressing enduring truths about life):

> As theologians have realized more and more, the language of art (in the broadest sense) is native to religion.... Christian ideas and practices are unavoidably rooted in aesthetically rich forms: myth, metaphor, parable, song, ritual, image, edifice. With regard to scriptures, moreover, it is now clearer than ever that literary strategies are intrinsic to the biblical texts and their religious import.[24]

One additional thing we can do to offset our modern handicap of a historical mindset is, paradoxically, to take advantage of it.

We can do that by coming to understand better the historical context that influenced each piece of the Bible. As the Presbyterian Church reminded its congregants about the Scriptures:

> They reflect views of life, history, and the cosmos
> which were *then* current. The church, therefore, has an
> obligation to approach the Scriptures with literary and
> historical understanding.[25]

But even as we use our historical knowledge to learn about the Bible, we need to remember that the Bible itself is not history in our novel, modern sense.

In all our contemporary religion-science debates about whether or not the Bible is true, and about the technicalities of how its statements should be related to science, there is one element that usually gets overlooked. Namely, the spirit in which we interpret the Bible. The methods of science cannot by themselves answer questions about values. But our faith-traditions can. And one principle of the Reformed tradition of Christianity for interpreting the Bible has been the overriding principle called "the rule of love." As the Christian teacher Shirley Guthrie summarizes so beautifully:

> The rule of love ... an often forgotten rule,... is based
> on the fact that the fundamental expression of God's
> will is the twofold commandment to love God and
> neighbor. Any interpretation of scripture is wrong that
> shows indifference toward or contempt for any
> individual or group inside or outside the church. All
> right interpretations reflect the love of God and the
> love of God's people for all kinds of people
> everywhere, everyone included and no one excluded.[26]

Chapter 8
Unfinished Odysseys, Darwin's and Ours

In 1882, amid much pomp and splendor, a body was laid to rest in London's Westminster Abbey. Although Queen Victoria and Prime Minister Gladstone did not attend (if out of political discretion is not known), there were numerous people of high status in British society at the funeral to make up for it. Among the pall-bearers were two dukes, an earl, and the American ambassador J. Russell Lowell.

The now dead man had left directions for a simple rough-hewn coffin to be made by his neighborhood carpenter, but that coffin had not been deemed appropriate for Westminster Abbey, Britain's most hallowed ground. And so the wood coffin had been rejected, replaced with a coffin so shiny it was said you could see yourself in it to shave.

With all the pomp they could muster, the deceased was laid to rest where monarchs such as William the Conqueror, scientists such as Sir Isaac Newton, and poets such as Geoffrey Chaucer had been laid to rest centuries before. It was the very kind of social excitement the man being buried had often excused himself from attending in his old age. And he would have excused himself from attending this time as well, had he been alive to have any say in the matter.

He had even wanted to be buried in an unpretentious village graveyard near where he had lived. But he did not get to have his way because the man being buried was Charles Darwin—the man whose theory explaining how all species of life evolved from one origin revolutionized scientific thinking. The theory of evolution by natural selection is still disturbing to a good number of non-scientists today, even though it is recognized by biologists as being perhaps the most important scientific theory ever discovered.

A Myth about Darwin and Religion

Just as with many other religion-science relationships in Christian history, myths have grown up around the telling of Charles Darwin's life story. One myth goes like this: Before he came up with his theory of evolution by natural selection, Charles Darwin believed in God, and felt called to be ordained in the Church of England. However, his coming to believe in evolution shattered his faith, turning him into an atheist. That atheism in turn lead him into a despairing view of life.

This myth is especially popular among those who oppose teaching evolution and want to characterize that scientific idea as atheistic and dangerous. Therefore, sorting out the truth about Darwin's life, as this chapter will do, can prove valuable for clarifying religion-science relationships. And maybe prove valuable for reflecting upon our own spiritual lives.

The truth about Darwin, science, and religion is complex. Before his round-the-world voyage on H.M.S. *Beagle*, the 22-year old, undeveloped Charles Darwin had been as sincere about becoming a clergyman as he could have been at that point in his life—but not out of any sense of call or any ingrained religious temperament. The simple truth is that Charles Darwin was never in his life inclined toward being religious, in the sense of being inclined to turn toward institutional religion, or theology, or prayer for guidance and comfort. The decision of studying for the clergy had been his father's decision, and the young Charles Darwin seems to have resigned himself to it because the other avenues he had explored had fallen apart. For example, he had abandoned studying to become a physician because he could not endure again watching an operation being performed on a child without benefit of anesthesia.

Even when he had been a young student studying for the clergy at Cambridge, Charles had loved the collecting of beetles and walking with a professor discussing botany more than he had been interested in theology. And so, it was really the opportunity to voyage around the world on the *Beagle* (becoming its de facto naturalist) that provided his true calling.[1] That voyage would, however, also prove to be the beginning of the lifelong religious odyssey of Darwin.

Odyssey Unfinished?

Charles Darwin's religious beliefs did change over the course of his lifetime, but not so simply and starkly as the myth claims. Nevertheless, it is an engaging question as to what degree Darwin's religious odyssey remained unfinished—to what degree his religious thoughts and feelings found new ground or remained adrift when his life came to an end. Exploring that question journeys us into spiritual questions still being asked today.

It was not just Darwin whose religious beliefs changed during the turbulent 1800's in England. Many educated people were making adjustments in their beliefs. The thousands of observations about plant and animal species Darwin made during the dockings of H.M.S. *Beagle* had pulled him intensely into scientific questions. Darwin always considered himself a scientist, not a theologian. Nevertheless, after his book *Origin of Species* was published many years later, presenting a new way of answering those scientific questions, Darwin found himself the recipient of letter after letter asking religious questions that his theory had raised.

Darwin had been aware during his two decades of research leading up to the book that those theological issues would be raised. And he had thought about them to some degree himself. But he had tried to keep most of his religious thoughts to himself. Now, however, out of his courteously trying to reply to every letter he received, whether from friend or stranger, Darwin was challenged to express his own personal theological views in a way that his truncated studies for becoming a clergyman had never demanded of him.

Against those who charged that his theory of evolution was atheistic, Darwin always maintained that he did not believe accepting evolution prevented belief in God. After the first edition of *Origin* was published, Darwin even inserted into the second edition a statement from the Rev. Charles Kingsley, a noted Anglican minister. Kingsley expressed how he had come to see that evolution did not diminish God's nobility.[2] With that employment of someone else's theological formulation, Darwin was able to keep his own reflections about God to himself. He thus maintained the role of a modern scientist, who makes explanations of natural processes without recourse to the concept of God.

Lingering Questions

Nevertheless, questions about God—perplexing questions—remained for many readers of Darwin's book, and even for people who just heard about the theory of evolution.

In the latter 1700's and the 1800's, a good many educated Christians in Europe and the U.S. had come to no longer believe the Church's claim that Christianity was a special revealed religion, as had also Darwin. However, that did not mean they had abandoned belief in the existence of God.

But the Church, especially in Britain, had gotten itself into some problematic theological positions in the century before *Origin* was published. Natural science and theology had become co-joined in a particular type of what is called **natural theology**. That general strand of theology (which can be found in some form down through Christian history and even in the Bible) finds evidence for God in the natural world, not just in scriptures. However, the particular natural theology that developed in the century before *Origin* increasingly maintained that every detail about the natural world was specially designed by and demonstrated the existence of an omnipotent, beneficent God.

Even though Darwin never considered himself a theologian, this claim of church theology about the natural world became challenged by Darwin's explanation of how features of species came about by evolution, rather than by a designing, controlling Intelligence—God. Although Darwin did not during his lifetime publish overt statements about theology, his skepticism shows up in a letter to a fellow biologist Asa Gray. In that letter, Darwin provides the example of a species of wasp that lays its eggs within the body of caterpillars so that the wasp's larvae might feed on the caterpillars' inner organs. Darwin wrote:

> I had no intention to write atheistically, but ... I cannot see as plainly as others do ... evidence of design and beneficence on all sides of us. There seems to me too much misery in the world. I cannot persuade myself that a beneficent and omnipotent God would have designedly created [that wasp] with the express intention of their feeding within the living bodies of caterpillars.[3]

One theological solution some educated people at that time

had come to was to retain a belief that God had been the initial Creator of the world and of natural laws that could then operate on their own. This view was the one Darwin had come to at the time he wrote *Origin of Species*, and he describes that view in his letter to Asa Gray:

> I cannot anyhow be contented to view this wonderful universe, and especially the nature of man, and to conclude that everything is the result of brute force. I am inclined to look at everything as resulting from designed laws, with the details, whether good or bad, left to the working out of what we may call chance.[4]

Today, we can see more clearly than many theologians in Darwin's day did that attempts to preserve God's existence by turning God into the Maker of mechanical, natural laws at the beginning of the universe was pushing God back to the beginning of time—with God's presence no longer being required.

And what about that desire which was so much a part of the religious temperament of the time, to establish proof of God as Divine Intelligence? Here, Charles Darwin confessed the limits of his thinking:

> [There is] the extreme difficulty or rather impossibility of conceiving this immense and wonderful universe ... as the result of blind chance or necessity. When thus reflecting I feel compelled to look at a first cause having an intelligent mind in some degree analogous to that of man; and I deserve to be called a theist.... But then arises the doubt—can the mind of man, which has, as I fully believe, been developed from a mind as low as possessed by the lowest animal, be trusted when it draws such a grand conclusion? ... I cannot pretend to throw the least light on such abstruse problems. The mystery of the beginning of all things is insoluble to us; and I for one must be content to remain an Agnostic.[5]

We see here Charles Darwin's frank admission of the limits of his own mind in such theological matters—"a simple muddle," as he put it at one point.[6]

Mind, but Feelings Too

Thus had Charles Darwin's theological reflections led him on a journey from being mostly an unquestioning, perfunctory Christian when he embarked on the *Beagle*, to classifying himself most often as an agnostic at the end of his life.

The story of Charles Darwin's religious journey might end here, and a very short story it would be, if it were not for one thing: Charles Darwin was not just a man with a mind (a brilliant scientific mind). He was also a man with a heart. He was not just a man with thoughts about God. He was also a man with feelings. Feelings as well as values. And it is this aspect that makes his religious journey a real odyssey.

The story cannot be told without mentioning Annie, one of ten children Charles's wife Emma gave birth to. Their third child, Mary, had died only three weeks after birth. And their tenth child, Charles Jr., would die at the age of two.

Annie would live longer. The photograph we have of her can scarcely capture the liveliness Charles Darwin enjoyed so much about her. Like so many daguerreotypes of that time, the long exposure times forced subjects to sit awkwardly in a nearly lifeless manner. But visitors to the Darwin home agreed with Charles's assessment of her:

> Her dear face bright all the time with the sweetest of smiles.[7]

The age Darwin lived in was not only an age of shifting religious opinions. It was also an age before an understanding of the transmission of disease by microscopic germs. It was a time before oral or injected antibiotics, and before most childhood vaccinations. It was before anesthetics strong enough to provide any substantial relief from pain. It was also an age in which one out of every five children died within only the first year of life. And even a child who had reached early adolescence was still twenty-five times more likely to die of illness than in Britain today.[8]

Charles and Emma Darwin would not be exempt, losing two of their children at the age of two or younger. Annie lived longer.

With all of Charles Darwin's children, there was no sharp line between his life with the children and his scientific exploration of animals and of humankind's evolutionary roots. Darwin did most of his research in a room at their home, Down House, as it was named. And Darwin would engage his children in some of his experiments. Such as soaking seeds of different species of plants in seawater, then watching to see if they could sprout.

Together, the children and their father would look through animal pictures (some of them colored) in his scientific books, making up games about the animals. Charles Darwin would let the children put their hands inside his shirt to feel his hairy chest while, as the son put it, "He would growl like a bear at us."[9]

Unlike their two children who Charles and Emma Darwin lost before the age of two, Annie lived longer. But only to the age of ten.

The death of Annie—that child whose face Charles Darwin had described as "bright all the time"—solidified those doubts that had already been growing in him for several years about many of the claims the Church made about God.[10] Specifically, about the existence of a God with a particular kind of power, who acted in particular ways. The church, in claiming the existence of that particular kind of God would quote Biblical passages such as the verse in the book of Proverbs that read:

There shall no evil happen to the just.[11]

But how could no evil happen to the just when one so good as Annie had not been protected from death at so early an age? Charles Darwin could not believe the Church's claim about such a protective God in this world that seemed instead so filled with chance. Nor for a moment could he question that Annie had not been good. The gravestone they placed upon her grave, with dates of birth and death, held only the simple inscription:

ANNIE ELIZABETH DARWIN
A DEAR AND GOOD CHILD [12]

The Rationalization of Suffering

Over the course of several years, Charles Darwin's desolating grief over the death of Annie did pass. But what would remain would be Darwin's inability to accept some of the theological explanations for suffering that were commonly provided by the Church of his day. The Church was unable to adjust its theology, which had often been saying that *every* detail of the natural world was designed by a benevolent God for human good, and that God brought about specific details of people's lives, good and bad. Unable to adjust its understanding of the character of God's power, the Church instead rationalized suffering. One such rationalization shows up in a letter Charles's own wife Emma had written him soon after their marriage. The letter displays Emma's genuine religious devotion, as she explains what she believes to be God's providence in suffering:

> Suffering & illness is meant to help us exalt our minds
> & to look forward with hope to a future state.[13]

But Charles Darwin could not accept the explanation that suffering has been imposed by God to build moral character (much less as punishment, which was another explanation of the times). Darwin could not accept trying to account for suffering by saying it exists to build moral character because Darwin's awareness ranged wider than the human sphere. Darwin thought about the sufferings other animals endured as well. Charles Darwin's ability to be aware of the similarities between humans and other animals —to a degree that in the early 1800's many Victorians were not— was key to Darwin's seeing the flaw in the moral argument for rationalizing suffering. He would later write:

> That there is much suffering in he world no one
> disputes. Some have attempted to explain this in
> reference to man by imagining that it serves for his
> moral improvement. But the number of men in the
> world is as nothing compared with that of all other
> sentient beings, and these often suffer greatly without
> any moral improvement .... For what advantage can
> there be in the suffering of millions of the lower
> animals throughout almost endless time?[14]

To Darwin, the theory of evolution explained the presence of such suffering much better than the Church's attempts. Darwin wrote:

> The presence of much suffering agrees well with the
> view that all organic beings have been developed
> through variation and natural selection.[15]

Sharing Consolations and Hopes

Charles Darwin was, of course, not the only father to lose a beloved child to early death. The scientific colleague who was closest to Darwin was the botanist Joseph Hooker, who became almost like a close brother to Darwin. The correspondence between these two men more than that of any of Darwin's other colleagues speaks to matters of the heart.

Only an hour after Hooker's daughter died, Hooker was writing to Darwin to tell of his grief. Darwin wrote back at once. Less than two months later, even though Darwin was struggling through one of the worst periods of his own chronic illness, he responded when Hooker wrote to say that now Hooker's son had become afflicted with scarlet fever. Darwin, writing back, expressing concern and sympathy, commented at one point:

Much love, much trial.[16]

In Darwin's day, the Church, as another theological response to suffering, also held up the hope for an afterlife. Especially given that it was a time in which there were so many deaths before old age, many Christians held onto the hope of seeing loved ones again after death.

It was a hope Charles Darwin's own wife Emma held in her religious devotion. But by the official teaching of the Anglican Church, the prospect of an afterlife in heaven seemed to require belief in Jesus Christ.[17] At one point, early in their marriage, Emma wrote her husband, having detected that he had doubts about some religious doctrines in a way that she did not. We see in her words her concern about the possible implications of his doubts. She wrote to him:

Everything that concerns you concerns me and I
should be most unhappy if I thought we did not belong
to each other *for ever.*[18]

The Church had apparently not taken into consideration that the prospect of an afterlife for believers might not be so appealing if a person's closest loved ones would not be with them in heaven. Or worse, might be somewhere else after death.

Emma wished that her husband would become able to tell her that he had come to share the same strong religious beliefs she held. But he never could. And he could never lie to her. But we also know that, in loving devotion, Charles Darwin had more than once returned to re-read that very letter from his wife. We know because on the outer fold of the letter, found among his belongings, he had written.

When I am dead, know that many times I have kissed

and cried over this.[19]

Such open expressions of Charles Darwin's heart (in contrast to the sometimes theological "muddle" he found his mind in) characterize the *Autobiography* he wrote late in his life. During his lifetime, he had always stepped gingerly around other people's religious views, having the deepest consideration for good religious people such his wife and the American biologist Asa Gray. Darwin had never lost his respect for those people, nor his love for his wife. However, working on his *Autobiography* toward the end of his life, and apparently believing it would not be published until after his and Emma's deaths, he was more open about his views regarding a number of the Church's doctrines. In his *Autobiography* Darwin's compassionate heart vents its strongest indictment upon that Church doctrine about the afterlife:

> I can indeed hardly see how anyone ought to wish
> Christianity to be true; for if so the plain language of
> the text seems to show that the men who do not
> believe, and this would include my Father, Brother and
> almost all of my friends, will be everlasting punished.
> And this is a damnable doctrine.[20]

Thirteen years before working on his *Autobiography*, Charles Darwin had written to his friend Joseph Hooker:

> Much love, much trial....[21]

That combination of love and trial would continue to characterize Darwin's life in its final six years. Darwin's daughter-in-law gave birth to Charles's and Emma's first grandchild—but then died after giving birth. That loss, however, became offset by a new joy: Charles's new grandson and the baby's father moved in with grandparents Charles and Emma, bringing young life into their house, which had not experienced it in many years. By the time the grandson was five, he was joining granddad Darwin in the latest scientific experiment by blowing a metal whistle to test whether earthworms could hear. (They could not.)

How could a person weigh such suffering and such happiness against each other? In his *Autobiography*, Darwin attempted an evolutionary biologist's evaluation:

> Whether there is more of misery or of happiness;—
> whether the world as a whole is a good or a bad one.
> According to my judgement happiness decidedly

prevails,... [Such a conclusion] harmonises well with the effects which we might expect from natural selection.... Pain or suffering of any kind, if long continued, causes depression and lessens the power of action.... Pleasurable sensations, on the other hand ... stimulate the whole system to increase action.... This lead[s] to the belief that all sentient beings have been formed so as to enjoy, as a general rule, happiness.[22]

The Church's Gate, and Strolls in Nature

Charles Darwin continued to give financial aid to charities related to the Church. But after Annie's death, the contrast in Charles' and Emma's orientations toward religion became intensified. In the latter decades of their loving marriage, that contrast could be seen in their Sunday morning routine. From around the time of Annie's death, Charles no longer went into the village church to worship. But he would still walk with Emma, accompanying her to the church yard. But then he would separate his path from hers at the outside gate, letting her go inside for the worship that remained meaningful to her, but which could not provide comfort to him. Although his sense of duty and morality remained strong, he had shed any possibility that the Church's official teachings would guide his way of viewing the world.

Today, anti-evolutionists who believe the theory of evolution is atheistic make much of Charles Darwin's choice to no longer accompany his wife into church. But to get a better sense of Charles Darwin, we need to follow his Sunday-morning routine a bit further in order to see what Charles did after his and Emma's paths diverged. Charles did not just sit and wait for his wife, but instead went for a walk—a walk in Nature, just as he had done so often in his days at Down House when weather and his chronic illness allowed. Walking, looking, as he had once put it, at "beautiful adaptations everywhere and in every part of the organic world."[23]

He turned his attention—as he had countless times before—to all the features of the natural world he found so fascinating. On countless occasions, during years of chronic illness and years of grief over Annie, this ritual of focusing closely upon Nature, and frequently turning his scientific mind to its complexities, had given him satisfaction. That practice, along with the invaluable mutual love between him and Emma, had sustained him most.

In the very last months of his life, he received another of the type of letters he got after becoming famous. But this was different than those with religious questions; this letter offered bits of information about the natural world. The letter-writer told about a curious finding: a water-beetle with a small freshwater clam clamped onto its leg. As a result, the clam had been transported far beyond the powers of its own locomotion. Darwin responded promptly and had the tiny living specimen—beetle with clam attached—sent to him by post.

To the uninitiated, this specimen would appear to be an inconsequential oddity. But to Darwin, it was still another piece of evidence of how species can diverge. As part of supporting his arguments in *Origin of Species*, he had to show how land-animals could have been transported to separated pieces of land, and water-creatures transported to separated bodies of water, thus becoming isolated from their relatives and evolving into new species. So here, by luck and by post was one such voyager.

Darwin examined the tiny animals. And then, making one of the very last reportings of his long scientific career, Darwin recorded:

As the wretched beetle was still feebly alive, I have put
it in a bottle with chopped laurel leaves....

This detail about laurel leaves bears interpretation. Laurel leaves when crushed release hydrogen cyanide. Darwin had not thrown out the beetle with the garbage, but had instead anesthetized the little creature, put it to sleep, laid it to rest. As Darwin explained his actions:

... that it may die an easy and quicker death.[24]

There had been little the medicine of the day could do to relieve the suffering of Darwin's daughter Annie in her final weeks. After her death, her grieving father could only hope she had not suffered too badly. "Much love, much trial," Darwin had written to his friend Joseph Hooker when Hooker's daughter died. But for this little beetle, shipped far from its home because it had unwittingly become part of one of those chance circumstances that are part of evolution, there would be relief from further trials. Having traveled by post to a great scientist's home, it would be put to sleep with laurel leaves.

There had, after all, been enough suffering already. No need for more. And so the little beetle, the little voyager was laid to rest, not with the pomp and splendor of Westminster Abbey. But with a reverent scientist's humane care.

Chapter 9

Opening Darwin's Gift

In 1876, a passenger ship from Britain approached the New York harbor. On board was a man on a missionary journey of sorts: He was spreading a message, only seventeen years old, about Darwin's theory of evolution. The ship's passenger, so noteworthy that he was accompanied by the *New York Tribune's* London correspondent, was Thomas Henry Huxley, a man so feisty that he was sometimes called "Darwin's bulldog." Huxley devoted himself to fighting academic turf wars for the dominance of science (a legacy of which is our contemporary myth that religion and science have usually been at war). When told by the reporter that the prominent buildings seen at a distance were the Tribune and Western Union buildings, Huxley replied, "Ah, that is interesting; that is American. In the Old World the first things you see as you approach a great city are steeples; here you see, first, centers of intelligence."[1]

If Thomas Huxley visited New York City today, he would find the place much changed. As in other U.S. cities, there would be more secular buildings for him to interpret as symbols of the advance of science. If he ventured into the U.S. beyond the New York harbor, hopefully he would notice many new churches, synagogues, and mosques that had been erected as well. Those buildings would suggest the diversity of modern Western religion, with their architectures ranging from traditional to avant-garde.

Much has also changed in both religious and scientific thinking in the past century-and-a-half. And it has not been the retreat of religion under threat from science, as Huxley simplistically portrayed it.[2] One reason is that, "a majority of Americans would comfortably accept separate spheres of influence for science and religion," as the contemporary writer Susan Jacoby puts it.[3] Another reason is that beginning even during Huxley's lifetime, many religious thinkers began exploring ways that a religious framework could incorporate Darwin's idea that human beings and all other species of life had come about through evolution. (Some of the early religious efforts in that direction were presented in Chapter 3, "Tempest in a British Teapot.")

Allies for Evolution

From the very first decades after *Origin of Species* was published, some Christian leaders even welcomed Darwin's discovery because of the ways it could refine and improve religious thinking. Such theological appreciation has continued to this day. Arthur Peacocke of the Church of England has written a book titled *Evolution: The Disguised Friend of Faith?* with suggestions of ways it can be a friend.[4] John Haught, arguably the leading Christian theologian in the area of evolution, has more than once referred to Darwin's "gift" to theology.[5] In the two most important U.S. court cases over teaching evolution in public schools, a leading theologian served as expert witness not against but *for* evolution: Langdon Gilkey in the 1981 trial in Little Rock,[6] and John Haught in the 2005 Dover case.[7]

If evolution and theology are to be friends, how do we bring them together for at least a potential companionship? This chapter will make a preliminary approach to answering that question. We will unwrap Darwin's gift.

I remember a woman pastor who, if asked by any of her parishioners whether she believed God created us or if we evolved, would reply, "I believe God created us, and evolution was how God did it." I liked the ingenuity of that response in the way that it brought religious belief and an acceptance of science together into a single sentence. So why is it so difficult today for many people to bring the theory of evolution and religion into some sort of harmony?

Getting Rid of the "Shrink-Wrapping"

The contemporary theologian Ted Peters and his co-author, the biologist Martinez Hewlett, have hit the nail on the head about one major obstacle:

> What makes our present situation difficult is [that] good science frequently comes *shrink-wrapped* in nonscientific ideologies.[8]

And it is the shrink-wrapping that is unpalatable to many religious believers.

One of the most famous of such statements is that of the outspoken atheist biologist Richard Dawkins, who in writing about DNA and evolution stated that, "We are survival machines, robot vehicles blindly programmed to preserve the selfish molecules known as genes."[9] That characterization of evolution has disturbed many religious writers because it seems to attribute more consciousness to genes than to human beings. But as the writer Marilynne Robinson observes, "Finding selfishness in a gene ... resembles finding wrath in thunder."[10] (Something Dawkins would in all probability deride as being superstitious if he heard such an idea voiced by a religious believer.)

The biologist Edward O. Wilson, known for his eloquence and enthusiasm, similarly wrote:

> No species, ours included, possesses a purpose beyond
> the imperatives created by its own genetic history....
> We have no particular place to go. The species lacks
> any goal external to its own biological nature.[11]

Echoing criticisms of quite a number of philosophers and theologians, the scientist John Polkinghorne and his co-author Nicholas Beale comment:

> Wilson is a distinguished scientist, but statements
> about "purpose" and "goals" immediately take you
> beyond the realms of science into metaphysical,
> philosophical, or theological territories: such
> statements are not susceptible to scientific
> investigation and are thus beyond his specific
> competence.[12]

Such "shrink-wrapped" depictions of the evolutionary world as being a world without purpose, in which other species and even humans are "robots," understandably trouble many religious believers. So also do statements by scientists claiming that evolution and God are not compatible. Dawkins wrote that, "Darwin made it possible to be an intellectually fulfilled atheist."[13] And the science promoter William Provine has made the extravagant but misguided claim:

> Let me summarize my views on what modern
> evolutionary biology tells us loud and clear.... There
> are no gods, no purposes, no goal-directed forces of
> any kind.... There is no ultimate foundation for ethics,
> no ultimate meaning to life, and no free will for
> humans, either.[14]

Once we remove all the "shrink-wrapping" that is not of

Darwin's making, we find that the process of evolution is fairly straightforward. Although the diversity of species on this planet has come about through multiple natural forces (one being sexual selection in some species), the most important force remains the process of natural selection that Darwin identified. It consists of three basic steps:

- Step 1: Variations appear within a species.
- Step 2: Some of those variations become greater in number within a species because of the survival and reproductive advantages they provide.
- Step 3: When enough variation occurs within a segment of a species, a new species can develop from that segment.

This three-step process is not one of mere chance. As a biologist explained in an introduction to one edition of *Origin of Species*, evolution is the *"non-random* survival of randomly varying hereditary elements [i.e., genetically based characteristics].["][15] Nevertheless, what is counter-intuitive about evolution is that the variations that appear in step 1 are not guided according to the needs of the current members of the species. That is to say, the variations that appear are not pre-designed.

The Not-so-new Idea of "Design"

Many people in the U.S. may have first heard about the notion that species are "designed" with the appearance of the anti-evolutionist Intelligent Design Movement during the past few decades. But it is an old idea, having been most famously put forward by the late 18th-century philosopher William Paley, who compared the physical structures of living creatures to the intricate workings of a watch, with God being the watchmaker. The idea of "intelligent design," can seem appealing. After all, doesn't the living world display a lot of orderliness? Of course it does; evolutionary science does not deny that. What we need to realize is that the recent Intelligent Design Movement has been saying that some things in nature are so complex that science must explain such things as *not* having evolved but instead having been designed. Because the Intelligent Design Movement wanted to get its idea into public-school science classrooms, it avoided saying who the implied designer might be. Sometimes, however, the religious motivations did slip out. For example, in 2003, on the conservative

American Family Radio, the leader of the movement, the lawyer Phillip Johnson (author of *Darwin on Trial*[16]), said of the Intelligent Design Movement:

> Our strategy has been to change the subject a bit so that we can get the issue of intelligent design, which really means the reality of God, before the academic world and into the schools.[17]

Despite the Intelligent Design Movement's attempt at subterfuge, in the 2005 "Dover Case," a District Court judge prohibited an attempt to introduce "intelligent design" into science classes, holding that it was not science.[18] One of the many pieces of evidence to that fact was that the American Association for the Advancement of Science had previously stated:

> [Intelligent-design] is characterized by significant conceptual flaws in its formulation, a lack of credible scientific evidence, and misrepresentation of scientific facts.... [It is] in fact religious, not scientific.[19]

Our focus in this chapter, however, will not be science, but instead that of learning from the Intelligent Design Movement's *theological* mistakes.[20] Because the idea of "design" dates back centuries, the problems with their approach are quite well known. Even before Darwin's discovery, the problems with the idea of "design" were beginning to show. In this chapter, we will focus on the matter of God because that is the heart of the matter for many religious believers who have a hard time combining evolution with their beliefs. Our doing so will provide us valuable techniques for talking about God in our scientific age. And not just in regard to evolution.

Avoiding the Shrinking God

One major problem with the Intelligent-Design approach is that it is one form of the worst possible mistake theology can make in an age of advancing science. Namely, the mistake of turning God into a **god of the gaps**.[21] That is to say, the mistake of putting the explanation of "God did it" into a gap in scientific knowledge for which science does not yet have an explanation. But what happens when modern science later uncovers the natural causes to explain something it previously could not explain? God has to be yanked out of the picture as science fills in that gap with new knowledge.

If we let God be turned into a god of the gaps, whenever science fills in a gap in scientific knowledge, we have to remove another duty from God's job description. With a god of the gaps, as science continues to advance, God's role in the world shrinks and shrinks and shrinks.

And indeed, an instance of that very thing did occur with what had become the Intelligent Design Movement's poster child for their idea. In his 1996 book *Darwin's Black Box*,[22] Michael Behe claimed that the rotary flagellum (a sort of rotary tail) of a particular bacteria could not have evolved because it was too complex. Therefore, Behe maintained, that bacteria could have gotten its rotary flagellum only by some intelligent force intervening into the evolutionary process to make that flagellum all at once. But only several years after the publication of Behe's book, that gap in scientific knowledge was filled in when evolutionary biologists explained how the parts of the rotary flagellum *could* have evolved gradually from virtually identical parts in a syringe-like projection in a different species of bacteria. Gaps in scientific knowledge get filled in continually in that way.

This is why Paul Tillich, a monumental figure in 20th-century theology, said of the god-of-the-gaps approach:

> That was an unworthy idea of God.... Theology does not need to put God to work to fill an empty space in our scientific knowledge.[23]

Remembering the Core Value

There is an even more severe theological problem with the Intelligent Design Movement's approach. Once you claim that an "intelligent designer" ("God" being implied) has intervened into natural evolutionary processes a billion years ago in order to specially design a rotary tail for a particular bacteria, how do you explain to a parent today whose child is suffering from an illness that God is *not* intervening to re-structure that child's immune system so that the child might live? Or even worse, if you do maintain that God intervenes so minutely as to purposefully design every feature of the living world, how do you explain to a parent God's reason for (supposedly) giving their newborn child a severe birth deformity? These two questions show how asserting that God intervenes so specifically to interrupt natural processes can lead to a theological position that is morally repugnant. This is why the biologist Francisco Ayala—who is also educated in theology—is among those who describe Darwin's theory as a "gift" to religion. As he expresses it, the science of evolution "much to the relief of theologians, provides an explanation that convincingly attributes defects, deformities, and dysfunctions to *natural* causes."[24]

Stepping back a little further, mainstream theologians point to a more fundamental problem with Intelligent Design: The proponents of that idea have gotten the essential character of God fundamentally wrong. This can be expressed best by testing the Intelligent Design Movement's treatment of God as an intelligent designer against two Bible passages that have been considered pivotal to Christians for understanding God (the movement's leaders being from Christian backgrounds, some having been forthright in their Christian beliefs). Notice what is being conveyed in these two Biblical verses from the New Testament— in which an *alteration* has been made in each passage:

> John 3:16 *modified*: For God was such an intelligent designer that he gave his only Son, so that everyone who believes in him may not perish but may have eternal life.
>
> 1 John 4:8 *modified*: Whoever does not know how to design intelligently does not know God, for God is an intelligent designer.

In these altered passages "intelligent designer" or "design" has been substituted for the New Testament's word "love." Here is what the Bible actually says:

> John 3:16 (NRSV): For God so loved the world that he gave his only Son, so that everyone who believes in him may not perish but may have eternal life.
>
> 1 John 4:8 (NRSV): Whoever does not love does not know God, for God is love.

The immense contrast between the modified forms and the originals demonstrates how the very frame of reference from which the proponents of Intelligent Design are operating is off-center theologically. They treat God's character as being like that of a designing engineer.

This marked contrast is significant not just as regards Christianity. The theologian James Wiseman points out:

> Within the Judeo-Christian tradition [i.e. Judaism and

Christianity] the love of God for creatures is especially prominent.... [Also,] granting important differences in nuance, all of the world's major theistic religions regularly speak of God in terms of love and compassion. In the *Bhagavad Gita*, Lord Krishna reveals himself to Arjuna as..."the one true friend" (9:18). In the *Qur'an* every sura [i.e., chapter] except one begins with a prayer of invocation: "in the name of God, the Merciful, the Compassionate."[25]

The Important "en" in "Panentheism"

So how do we find a way to describe God's *continuing* presence in the natural world (with evolution being a part of those natural processes)? Most useful has turned out to be the concept of **panentheism**. It is the idea that God is greater than and encompassing everything, but is also in some fashion immanent in everything. Thus, pan*en*theism—with the syllable "en" at its center—is quite different from pantheism, which is the concept that everything actually is God. The word "panentheism" was created by K.C.F. Krause in the early 1800's for his own purposes, but came into wide use in the latter 20th century because of Christian theology's immense need to recover a sense of the presence of God everywhere.[26] (Modern science having been a major cause for that loss.)

Although the word "panentheism" itself is fairly new, the concept is ancient, as shown by the following sample of quotations that convey similar ideas. In the Bible's New Testament, the writer of Ephesians describes God as:

one God and Father of all, who is above all and through all and in all.[27]

The leading Roman Catholic theologian of the Middle Ages, Thomas Aquinas, wrote:

God is in things as containing them: nevertheless by a certain similitude to corporeal [i.e., material] things, it is said that all things are in God; inasmuch as they are contained by him.[28]

And Martin Luther, one of the leading figures of the Protestant Reformation, which broke away from the Roman Catholic Church, wrote:

> God is substantially present everywhere, in and
> through all creatures, in all their parts and places, so
> that the world is full of God and He fills all, but
> without His being encompassed and surrounded by it.[29]

Some religious people, upon first encountering this concept of panentheism, might wonder if it does not diminish God's transcendence. If it seems to, that might be because we today—being so influenced by scientific ways of thinking—are inclined to think of transcendence and immanence in physical and spatial terms. Making God in some way "in" all things can, therefore, seem to reduce transcendence if it is conceptualized in terms of spatial distance. But before the rise of modern science, God's imminence and God's transcendence were *not* thought of by major theologians as being alternative choices. "On the contrary, the wholly other God, precisely because of a radical transcendence, could also be most present to all of creation."[30] So states the theologian William Placher. Moreover, Kallistros Ware has pointed out that even in Islam, which emphasizes God's transcendence, it is taught that God is nearer to the believer than his or her own jugular vein.[31]

We might see here how the advantages of this concept of panentheism and the problems with the Intelligent Design Movement's theology converge. Michael Behe had been looking for proof of a Designer (God being implied) in some out-of-the-ordinary feature in the natural world he was studying as a biologist. The religious scholar William E. Phipps pinpoints the religious and spiritual difficulty with that general approach, even if it is so common:

> Many people persist in thinking that the clearest proofs
> of God's existence are when the Deity allegedly breaks
> the accustomed natural order. Correspondingly, when
> everything is rolling smoothly, little thought is given to
> God's greatness.[32]

Phipps' perceptive observation shows how this caution about looking for God in spots that cannot be explained in scientific terms is relevant to much more than the theory of evolution.[33] It is relevant to our entire spiritual lives. If I go about my ordinary day waiting for an indication of God's presence in some event that science cannot explain, I will go day after day without a sense of God being present. That is because every detail of my everyday experiences can be described in natural terms by science.

Panentheism—with its paradoxical assertion that the world is in God but God is also in the world—obviously demands that we think of relationships in a different sense than the way we use the word "in" for physical relationships. Perhaps metaphors can best stretch our imaginations in this regard. Hans Kung is just one modern theologian who has gone back to a metaphor used by Augustine in the 4th century. Kung writes:

> God is in this universe and this universe is in God....
> We could follow Augustine in comparing the world
> with a sponge, supported and swimming in the eternal,
> infinite sea of the deity.[34]

And yet, the sea permeates the porous sponge!

Sketches of God's Character

So, if we do try to mentally picture God as "something far more deeply interfused,"[35] (to use the apt phrase of William Wordsworth), what type of mental picture would it be? Any attempt to paint a picture of God would do well to remember a caution that has long been a part of all three Abrahamic faith-traditions (Judaism, Christianity, and Islam): All imaging of God, whether visual or in words, is in some sense metaphorical.[36] What we create are, therefore, rough sketches from different angles, but never any final detailed portrait. Nevertheless, is there some guidance for those who want to visualize God in a way that will be consistent with scientific knowledge about evolution? Especially if we stay in touch with the understanding of all three Abrahamic traditions that God is the Ultimate Creator of everything?

One matter which demands being addressed is that evolution is *not* a totally controlled process in the way that an engineer's designing an object might be. Even though evolution by natural selection is neither a totally directed process nor pure chance, it does depend upon a substantial amount of chance (such as in genetic mutations, but also in other ways). Philosophers and theologians discuss this matter using the word "**contingency**." We rarely use that word in everyday English, and so it deserves a bit of thought. When I was growing up, and my family was loading the car for a day's outing, my cautious mother would say we needed to "be prepared for all contingencies." Contingencies are possible but not likely events, given the uncertainties of existence. The biological evolution that has brought us and all other species to the present moment on this planet Earth has been a *contingent* process. Every little event could not have been predicted.

A little over a decade ago, a bit of a public verbal scuffle occurred among some theological thinkers in the Roman Catholic Church. It was precipitated by some of those shrink-wrapped depictions of evolution as being so chance-filled that it (supposedly) showed there is no God. The outcome of the scuffle was a joint op-ed by three scientists who were also faithful Roman Catholics: Francisco Ayala, Lawrence M. Kraus, and Kenneth R. Miller. In their open letter, they quoted from an official Commission chaired by the quite conservative Joseph Ratzinger (later Pope Benedict XVI), which had affirmed that even though evolution is a "radically contingent ... process driven by natural selection and random genetic variation, ... even the outcome of a truly contingent natural process can nonetheless fall within God's providential plan for creation."[37]

There is another matter related to contingency that cannot be avoided in any adequate picture of biological evolution. That is how much the power of physical creativity has been embedded into living beings themselves, a bit similar to the way human beings experience a freedom to make choices. (Here is where the depiction of God as a controlling, designing engineer met its downfall.) Fascinatingly, a concept pulled out of the New Testament has proved useful to many theologians for sketching an appropriate picture of God: the concept of **kenosis**. It is taken from Philippians 2:7, in which it is stated that Christ Jesus—as an expression of the fundamental nature of God—"emptied himself" (NRSV). The word "kenosis" (based on the Greek *ekenosen*) thus means self-emptying.[38] Here is how the theologian Jürgen Moltmann applies that borrowed concept of *kenosis* for a sketch of God who has created through evolution by allowing freedom:

> God's determination to be Creator is linked with the *consideration for his creation* which allows it space and time and its own movement, so that it is not crushed by the divine reality.[39]

This way of thinking about God should not be misconstrued to mean that God's power is not active. A helpful analogy can be one that in Biblical thought became dominant over time—that of a parent's relationship to their child. By a certain age, a child will be allowed to go to the playground by themselves to play. At one level, someone observing the child on the playground might notice only the child's activity. But discernment to a deeper level would see the invisible power of the parent's love at work in the child's freedom to play.

Expanding upon this idea of *kenosis* turns out, however, to be a delicate balance. The theologian Ted Peters has critiqued some of the kenotic theologians because their depictions of God seem to him to "assume that for creatures to have power and hence freedom that God needs to withdraw.... [But] it is the very exertion of God's power that leads to human freedom. God's power empowers us."[40]

Remembering that talking about God requires metaphors, we will not insist on just one metaphor; each will have its limits. But some neglected metaphors in the Bible are being returned to by theologians engaged in these sorts of reflections about God and evolution. One metaphor with potential comes from the Old Testament (the Hebrew Bible/*Tanakh*), where in the book of Isaiah, God is depicted as a caring mother. (Such as in Isaiah 49:15.) That picture of a mother, even in giving birth, is drawn upon by the theologian Anne Clifford:

> My proposal is for a variation of the model of God as
> embodied in the form of the metaphor of a mother
> giving birth..... This metaphor is closer to our
> experience of life as embodied beings than [William]
> Paley's watchmaker-designer.... Isaiah's creation
> imagery focuses on God as a mother giving birth.
> Crying out like a woman in labor: gasping, and panting
> (Is. 42:14), there is anticipation. Life is emerging.[41]

Getting God Out of the Past

Quite a number of people have commented on the fact that some anti-evolutionists today, even while rejecting the theory of evolution, ironically display a mindset heavily influenced by science. This extends much further than some anti-evolutionists' mistakenly reading the Bible as if it were a book of science. Another example is the Intelligent Design Movement's emphasis on some (supposed) event in the past, such as God supposedly intervening to design a rotary tail for a bacteria. And yet, the far past is the very place that God's creative activity frequently got confined to as modern science expanded. (This was explained in Chapter 1, "Exposing the 'Warfare' Myth.")

In contrast, the weight of the spiritual focus for religious believers, even as they integrate the past and cultivate awareness in the present, has been upon what we might hope for in the future. And not necessarily just in any afterlife. Religious believers, at their best, live life forward. When I step out of my front door in the morning, I can be guided by knowledge out of the past about the ground underfoot. But it is a faith in future possibilities that draws me out the door, giving me courage.

The theologian Lonnie Kliever, in showing his appreciation of Jürgen Moltmann's theology of hope, writes, "Humankind *is* the hoping creature who dreams about the future and struggles to attain it."[42] Kliever continues, quoting in part from Moltmann:

> The God of the Bible is "ahead of us in the horizons of
> the future opened up to us in his promises."... [And,]
> humankind's projected hopes and God's... promises are
> for Moltmann by no means individualistic and
> otherworldly.[43]

Restoring to contemporary theology this spiritual and Biblical emphasis upon an orientation toward the future has also been a major concern of the theologian John Haught, such as in his book titled *The Promise of Nature*.[44]

Modern science quite rightfully concentrates on the past to analyze strings of causes that lead to subsequent events. But the Bible (including the Hebrew/*Tanakh*) repeatedly makes the bold claim that we and the world can be transformed and affected now by what has not happened yet. Future possibilities can affect the present. That is because God is seen as not just being with people but also lying ahead of people, attracting them forward into the not-yet of greater goodness. A group of contemporary theologians called "process theologians" have in particular concentrated upon God's role as a lure that lies ahead of us.

Working toward an Evolutionary Worldview

This chapter has shown why theology could benefit by befriending the theory of evolution. And it has outlined some theological resources (both old and modern) by which God could be restored to a worldview that accepts modern science.

Such theological tools, however, do not tell us which aspects of our evolved world we might consider more the work of God and which aspects we should attribute more to the freedom of living beings. Nor do the theological resources outlined here eliminate the hard task of comprehending our own human natures as evolved beings. Or comprehending the character of the evolutionary world we are a part of, with all its contingencies. Those matters—which involve not just theology but also spirituality, psychology, and society—are all explored in the three chapters of the upcoming Part Three, "Our Human Condition."

We have unwrapped Darwin's gift, shrink-wrapping and all. Now we will have to address the altered worldview it brings.

PART THREE
Our Human Condition

Caption to Victorian cartoon with husband, wife, and baby:
Husband (who had been reading passages from
Darwin's *Descent of Man*):
"So you see, Mary, Baby is descended from a Hairy Quadruped
with Pointed Ears and a Tail. We all are!"
Wife: "Speak for yourself, Jack! I'm not descended
from anything of the kind, I beg to say.
And Baby takes after me, so there!"

Biblical and related expectations envisaged
the coming of the Messiah within a cosmic frame....
The function of the bearer of the New Being [i.e., the Savior]
is not only to save individuals and to transform man's
historical existence but to renew the universe.
And the assumption is that mankind and individual men
are so dependent on the powers of the universe
that salvation of the one without the other is unthinkable.
— *Paul Tillich*
(20th-century Christian theologian)

Chapter 10
Fallen Animals
or Rising Beasts?

M any legends have grown up around Charles Darwin and how his theory of evolution was received after the publication of *Origin of Species* in 1859. Some of those legends are mostly true. Still others are outright distortions. One legend, true or not, tells about the wife of an Anglican priest upon first hearing about Darwin's theory, with its seeming implication that humans had descended from apes. That woman is reported to have said, "Descended from the apes? My dear, we will hope it is not true. But if it is, let us pray that it may not become generally known."[1]

Despite that woman's wishes, the name of Charles Darwin and the association of his name with the theory of evolution have become widely known. Show any adult in the U.S. a picture of a queue of primates or other animals with a human at the front of the line, and they will probably be able to tell you that the picture is referring to the theory of evolution's explanation of our evolutionary past.

Thousands of years ago, the writer of Psalm 8 in the Bible spoke to God, saying:

When I look at your heavens, the work of your fingers,
the moon and the stars that you have established; what
are human beings that you are mindful of them?[2]

Today, when we want answers to questions about our human nature, we are less likely to turn to psalm-writers, and more likely to turn to evolutionary *biologists*. Admittedly, the scientific theory of evolution is not universally accepted. However, most mainstream Christian denominations, as well as Roman Catholicism and Judaism, have official statements saying that it is acceptable. (Examples are provided in Chapter 4, "An Awkward History: The U.S. and Evolution.")

However, simply accepting that all species of life on Earth have evolved from one origin does not necessarily mean we have addressed the theological, spiritual, and psychological implications of the theory of evolution. Because the relationship between religion and the theory of evolution is so frequently framed in terms of religious rejection of Darwin's theory, rarely explored are the religious implications for those of us who accept the theory, along with related knowledge from evolutionary science.

We might well ask: What does our human condition appear to be like when we put the religion into dialogue with scientific knowledge about our evolutionary past? And so, in this chapter and the following one, we will bring together thoughts from both religion and science to reflect upon matters related to our human condition. We will grapple with the musings of theologians regarding human nature, mortality, suffering, and evil—all as part of an evolving web of life.

Identifying the Deeper Issues

Even more than Psalm 8 already referred to, the Biblical text most often employed by Christianity to reflect upon the human condition is the narrative commonly known as the "Adam and Eve" story. In that story in Chapters 2 and 3 of Genesis, Adam and Eve first live in a paradise-like Garden of Eden. But then they disobey God's command not to eat from the forbidden tree, guiltily try to cover up their disobedience, and receive punishment from God that includes conflict and suffering of the kind humans are all too familiar with. (Such as pain in childbirth, and strife between humans and snakes.)

As many Christians know, that frequently retold story has been part of the basis for the Christian doctrines commonly known as "the Fall" of humankind and humankind's "original sin" (even though neither the word "fall" nor the phrase "original sin" are in the Bible's narrative itself). The concepts of "the Fall" and "original sin" (which trace back to St. Augustine in the 4th century, and earlier) have been interpreted in a number of ways. They have also at times proved troublesome for Western Christianity in a number of ways. In the worst distortions, original sin has been simplistically interpreted to say that I suffer today as a punishment by God for what Adam and Eve did eons ago.

With such a distasteful distortion on the loose, it should be no surprise that many liberal and moderate 20th-century theologians worked to address the matter of sin, trying to see what meanings of "original sin" could still be reasonably maintained.[3] Those theologians developed basically two approaches:

- The first approach has been to point to how no human being is ever born into a world that is pristine, because the consequences of human sin endure, getting passed on from generation to generation. (Examples being national hatreds, or racism, or the effects of a parent's alcoholism.)
- A second approach leaned toward treating the "Adam and Eve" story, more like a parable. Adam and Eve are thus seen as archetypes. Such an approach treats the "Adam and Eve" story as teaching about our human imperfection and proclivity to act against God's wishes or will for us, without claiming any transmission of sin from one generation to the next.

Whichever general approach is used (and both can be used jointly), such reconstructed interpretations make the doctrine of original sin more palatable. But such approaches still do *not* solve the problems the theory of evolution poses to a theology that draws upon the Bible (whether Christianity or Judaism). That is because the very presence of pain and suffering in the world cannot be explained as having resulted from human actions, as traditional interpretations of the "Adam and Eve" story have maintained. Traditional interpretations in Western Christianity viewed the non-human world of animals as also "fallen"—and therefore suffering—because of Adam's and Eve's original sin. But our knowledge of evolution shows that non-human animals experienced pain, and, I might suppose, suffered in their own way for eons before humans ever emerged.

One contemporary philosopher of religion and science, Holmes Rolston III, explains this difficulty in bringing together religious concepts and the scientific theory of evolution. He writes:

> If a biologist begins reading Genesis ... the trouble is not so much the six days of creation in chapters 1 and 2 [of that Biblical book], though most of the controversy is usually thought to lie there, as in chapter 3, where, spoiling the Garden Earth, the first couple fall and Earth becomes cursed.... The real

problem is with the Fall, when a once-paradisiacal
[i.e., paradise-like] nature becomes recalcitrant as a
punishment for human sin. This does not fit into the
biological paradigm at all. Suffering in a harsh world
did not enter chronologically after sin and on account
of it. There was struggle for long epochs before the
human arrival....[4]

A number of Christian theologians have echoed Rolston's observation.[5] To put it bluntly, our scientific knowledge of the evolutionary past simply pulls the rug out from under any ability to
explain the presence of suffering in the world by resorting to the
concept of a human "fall."

It would be good to remember that the real point of re-
examination of the doctrine of original sin was not to legitimize
that doctrine itself, but instead, at least in part to address the
presence of suffering and evil in the world despite its having been
created by a good and benevolent God, as Western theistic
religions claim. (That is, Judaism, Christianity, and Islam.) This is
the problem of **theodicy**, to use the technical term Christian
theology employs. Theologies that accept and address evolution
have to reconcile the presence of random, uncontrollable suffering
that is a part of evolution with the claim that God is both
benevolent and the Creator of the entire universe.

The theologian John Haught, who has grappled with matters
relating theology to evolution more than anyone else, sets forth the
task of theodicy—the task of addressing the matter of suffering—
for any theology that incorporates evolution. John Haught writes:

The task of theodicy henceforth should not be to fit the
fact of suffering onto the grid of guilt and punishment.
Instead, ... it might ask why an all-good and all-
powerful God would create an *unfinished, imperfect,
evolutionary* universe in the first place rather than one
that is complete and perfect from the beginning.[6]

Different Causes of Suffering

At this point, it might help if we recall something in general about
how the matter of evil and suffering has been treated by most
traditional Christian theology. In its analysis of those things in this
world that we experience as being in some way "bad," Christian

theology has always made a distinction between:
- "moral evil," which is clearly caused by human actions, and,
- suffering not caused by human actions, but by natural events such as lightning, earthquakes, and disease.

Making that traditional distinction immediately proves helpful in sorting through the suffering that is present in the natural world that has evolved. Nevertheless, making that distinction by no means eliminates the *moral* dimension with its questions regarding suffering. There are two reasons why.

For one thing, human sins, whether wrongdoings or short-comings, can compound the suffering caused by natural events, For example the greed of a landlord and a bribed building inspector might result in the use of substandard materials that are less likely to resist natural forces, thus leading to someone's death. We can make a distinction between the two types of suffering, but we cannot construct an absolute wall between them.

The second reason the moral dimension of suffering cannot be eliminated as far as theology is concerned is because a funda-mental premise of Biblical theology, and almost all Christian theology, has been that God, even as Creator of the universe, is not morally neutral, but is instead just. "Righteous," is the word often employed. Nor can we, with any integrity, stay within the Biblical tradition and try to maintain that God simply does not care about non-human animals. As one example, part of Psalm 145 states, "The LORD is good to all, and his compassion is over all that he has made."[7]

The role our human makeup plays in leading to moral evil is addressed in the following Chapter 11, "Problems with a Problem-atic Species." The remainder of the current chapter will explore the challenge of addressing the second category of suffering listed above—that *not* caused by human actions.

If I am a religious believer who accepts evolution, when I hear someone claim that religion and science are not compatible, I can take solace in knowing that scientists down through Western Euro-pean history believed in the existence of God.[8] I can even remember that one of the pivotal discoveries of modern evolu-tionary biology about the patterns of inheritance was first made by the 19th-century Christian friar Gregor Mendel.[9] But the gardens in which Mendel grew his varieties of pea plants seem idyllic compared to the plains of Africa, in which predator chases prey, and is in turn devoured by an even larger predator. How do I integrate my knowledge about the struggles and suffering of living beings with my belief that there is an Unseen Power making possible and lending purpose to all of life, even all of existence?

When violent weather causes tragedy, I can console myself in knowing that inanimate forces do not have minds nor act purposefully. My mind, as it engages in theological reflection, can even recognize that other species of living beings have been endowed with a kind of freedom, somewhat similar to the way that human beings have freedom and wills to act. But even when my mind knows that, my heart can be troubled by the way animals cause suffering in other animals.

Obviously, the presence of suffering that has not been caused by human failures is for theology the more challenging matter. Most modern Christian theology, however, avoids the full extent of that challenge because most of modern Western Christianity has narrowed its focus to the human sphere. As a result, most its of its theodicy—its reflections on suffering—has concentrated upon the suffering endured by people, forgetting about the suffering endured by other animals.

Additional Challenges from Evolution

Thus it is that any Christian theology that widens its focus to include the *non*-human realm has a basic challenge to begin with. To this, however, we need to add two other challenging aspects brought by Darwin with his theory of evolution primarily through natural selection.

First of all, there is the realization of the vast stretches of time before the arrival of humans, filled with the struggles of animals with disease, pain, and death. This difficulty was recognized even before Darwin's *Origin* was published in 1859, because geology had already been stretching back the Earth's timeline further into the past. One historian, James Turner explains:

> The Victorians were hardly the first to notice the
> suffering blindly inflicted by nature.... But they saw
> the agony on a wider canvas than earlier generations.
> The time-scale of life, previously compressed within a

> few thousand years ... suddenly shot backwards....
> Geology unburied the grim fossil memorabilia of the
> bloody competition for survival, eons of individual
> deaths and ... extinction: a natural history of pain.[10]

Today, with our contemporary scientific knowledge, we know that those vast stretches of time in which there has been animal suffering are even longer than Darwin imagined. Not something like 100,000 years, but hundreds of millions of years!

Even more than that challenge, there is a second matter: Namely, that such suffering, according to Darwin, is not some side effect, but has instead been *intrinsic* to the very process by which unfit creatures and unfit species have died off and new creatures and species have evolved. Again, the historian Turner:

> Darwin made pain not a byproduct of creation but the
> very mechanism by which life developed.[11]

We might wonder theologically how that can be reconciled with God, in the first chapter of Genesis, declaring all of the created world "very good" (Gen. 1:31). It is no surprise to theologians who have struggled with these matters that a collection of essays published by Anglican writers back in 1888—less than three decades after *Origin of Species* was published—contained a recognition of this very theological challenge.[12]

Because I am a human, and am the result of a long evolutionary process that led to beings with sophisticated levels of consciousness, I might want to say that the reason for all the suffering of creatures for many millions of years before me was to make *me* possible. But such a maneuver raises a red flag theologically. If the purpose of animals' suffering in the past was just to get to me, wouldn't that mean that God was simply using those animals as a means to an end? Such a picture of God is not very compatible with the belief that God is a God of justice and compassion (as Bible passages such as the one already cited maintain). Such a means-to-an-end explanation is not a fully satisfactory theodicy to most of the theologians who try to address the implications of evolution. After all, whenever modern Christian theology has tried to address the problem of suffering, one of the most troubling matters—not just intellectually but emotionally—has been that of instances in which the innocent suffer.

One of the most poignant expressions of such anguish over the suffering of the innocent was expressed by the character Ivan in Dostoyevsky's *Brothers Karamazov*. Expressing his anguish, and his dissatisfaction with some explanations for such suffering, Ivan says:

> Listen: if everyone has to suffer in order to bring about eternal harmony through that suffering, tell me, please, what have children to do with this? ...Why should they be the grist to someone else's mill, the means of ensuring [someone else's] future harmony? ... I absolutely reject that higher harmony. It's not worth one little tear from one single little tortured child.[13]

One contemporary theologian, Christopher Southgate, quotes this very passage from Dostoyevsky's novel, and points out the even greater challenge the theory of evolution brings regarding the suffering of the innocent. Namely, that animals without any moral culpability have to be considered the most innocent ones of all when they suffer. Have all such animals, to use Dostoyevsky's phrase, been just grist for someone else's mill—merely a means to lead to human evolution?[14]

The Broader Issue of Perishability

These issues related to animal suffering can be seen to part of a broader matter: the vulnerability and perishability of all of life, not just human life. Such concerns about perishability and vulnerability raise two kinds of theological questions:

- First, they raise questions about to what degree the world God has created is an orderly world, or to what degree it is a chaotic world. One of the basic things biology students are taught about evolution is that mutations in chromosomes, often described as "random," bring about changes in offspring. "Random" can sound pretty close to "chaotic." Even though evolution is not totally chance, it is a mixture of order and chance and does depend upon a substantial amount of chance, such as in mutations (as was explained in the preceding Chapter 9). How do I deal with the strange mixture of order and chance that makes up all of the larger natural world, not just the evolutionary process?
- Second, perishability and vulnerability raise questions

about God's ongoing care. That is, about to what degree and in what way it can be said that God is *involved* in the natural world (of which we are a part) in a helpful or protective ongoing way. For, after all, one enduring idea within the Christian tradition has been that the created world in some way reveals something about the mind of God, the Creator.

The evolutionary theologian John Haught writes poignantly of this inner human concern about perishability, a concern so often left unspoken. Haught writes:

The things we treasure the most such as life, consciousness, personality, moral goodness, heroism, culture and peace all abide only tenuously.... The fact that cells degenerate, that organisms decay, that our own lives ebb toward death, that civilizations eventually fall and that noble deeds and ideals fade into oblivion—all this makes us wonder how the universe could conceivably have any abiding seal of purpose.[15]

Moreover, as Haught has expressed, it is often those things of deepest value to us that are the most vulnerable, the most subject to perishing. Life is more precious than a rock, but a rock is able to endure longer. Isn't that somehow backward? We might wonder what kind of divine values, as it were, are displayed by that kind of arrangement.

Today in the 21st-century United States, and in a good number of other highly developed countries in the world, we are extraordinarily blessed by usually being able to live quite long lives (thanks mostly to vaccinations and modern antibiotics). And, because of modern anesthetics, we have been freed from physical pain in circumstances where human beings usually had to endure excruciating pain. Those blessed changes in our way of living that have come out of modern science can result in a distancing of ourselves from the reality of death. Thus it is easy for us to avoid fully addressing this theological challenge of perishability.

Some liberal Christian writers today dismiss much of past Christianity by saying that it was too often concentrated on promising people an afterlife. Such writers today say we should instead concentrate on the present life. For, after all, our medical technology today enables us to provide the healing, whereas in the past religion had to provide solace instead. But I would submit that such writers have only sidestepped the major religious issue. The hard fact remains that we will all die. Nor does such sidestepping address the anguish of parents who have a child who *cannot* be saved by modern technology. Such parents can experience much agony. Moreover, as Haught has insightfully pointed out, death is just the tip of the iceberg: Beneath it is that immense iceberg of perishability.

Concerns about disorder, purposelessness, and unnecessary suffering have always been deeply religious concerns, not just a matter of developing some abstract theology. Modern science is a self-limiting enterprise. And so, by its own ground rules, the methods and research techniques of science can say nothing about value, meaning, purpose, or God. (This was explained in Chapter 6, "Ancient Wisdom Raises Her Head.") People who work as scientists may have values and meaning in their own lives, but the methods of modern science exclude questions of meaning and overall purpose.

That is not so with religion! In fact, addressing matters of meaning and purpose is one of religion's specialties. One professor of theology, Lonnie Kliever, explains this link between suffering and religion's customary role. Commenting on the actual experience of a man who suffered severe pain and disfigurement from an accident that was in no way that man's fault, Kliever writes:

> Invasions of chaos into everyday life cannot be
> repelled or redressed apart from some way of locating
> the beleaguered individual within a larger universe of
> meaning and purpose.... Religions are built to carry the
> "peak load" of human bafflement, suffering, and
> perversity.[16]

Issues that Have Come into Focus

Our having placed some traditional religious ideas in dialogue with scientific knowledge about evolution has brought a number of issues into the foreground. Such as:

- That suffering is intrinsic to evolution.
- The vast time animals have endured suffering before humans were around to have caused any of it.

- The problem that life is so perishable and vulnerable.
- The way these kinds of issues challenge our sense of existence being meaningful.

These issues are relevant to the concerns of all faith-traditions. There are additional issues that are more pertinent to theistic faith-traditions (those that often depict the Ultimate as a personal being). Christianity, Judaism, and Islam, can ask additional questions such as:

- Whether or not we can still claim—with evolution having been the means by which living species were created—that a righteous, compassionate God can be called the Creator of that means of creation.
- The question of God's ongoing care. How is the Divine present through these life-struggles?

In order to address these religious challenges the theory of evolution poses for the matter of suffering, it looks as though one thing required of religion is to have at least some general understanding of the evolutionary process, how it occurs, and what it fundamentally involves. In a nutshell, it might be said that just as living as a human is a complicated mixture of order and chance, so also is evolution. Thus we can add another issues to our list:

- The element of chance cannot be eliminated from the processes that have brought about life's diversity.

We might notice something that has occurred in this chapter by bringing into dialogue thoughts from both religion and science. Generally speaking, for the past several centuries, there have been two primary foci for Christian theology: God and *human* nature. Notice that those two foci do not include the nature of the rest of the natural world. As was already mentioned in regard to theodicy, most modern Western Christianity has become narrowed down to addressing suffering only in the human sphere. However, merely by bringing our theological reflections into dialogue with the theory of evolution and its implications, we have been forced to expand our awareness beyond the human sphere. We began these explorations with musings regarding the "Adam and Eve" story— a story employed by the Christian tradition primarily to talk about *human* nature. However, by putting religion in dialogue with evolutionary science, we have been forced to add a third area of focus to our reflections: the *non*-human realm. When Christian theology does accept evolution and examine its implications, it is forced to expand its thinking beyond the human sphere, as the explorations in this chapter have demonstrated. Science can thus prove to be a gift to religion, challenging it to expand and deepen its worldview.

Our musings have forced us to ask about the character of this evolutionary world we are a part of. We have not been able to explore the question of who we are as humans apart from the wider question of animal suffering. Nor apart from the question of our own evolutionary makeup as creatures who share in suffering.

Religious people expand their worldviews not only with their minds but also with their hearts. A more expansive vision can come not only with increased scientific knowledge but in other ways. One widespread method in the world's faith-traditions is that of being inspired by the example of religious believers who exemplify an expansion of mind and heart.

In Christianity, one such person was the theologian, medical doctor, and missionary Albert Schweitzer. He was renowned for medical work in Africa helping humans. But he was also greatly concerned about the fate of non-human animals. Writing as an adult, Schweitzer told of an experience he had as a child when saying aloud his prayers at bedtime. He recalled.

> It was quite incomprehensible to me—this was before I began going to school—why in my evening prayers I should pray for human beings only. So when my mother had prayed with me and had kissed me good night, I used to add silently a prayer that I had composed myself for all living creatures. It ran thus: "O, heavenly Father, protect and bless all things that have breath; guard them from all evil, and let them sleep in peace."[17]

Chapter 11
Problems with a Problematic Species

In 1864, five years into the controversy that resulted from the publication of *Origin of Species*, the leader of the Tory party in England, Benjamin Disraeli, welcomed the opportunity to speak to the moral concerns of his time before an audience at Oxford. The most memorable moment of Disraeli's speech came when he focused pointedly upon the threat that new scientific ideas such as Charles Darwin's seemed to pose. Disraeli famously said, "Is man an ape or an angel? I, my lord, I am on the side of the angels."[1] (Thus prompting a cartoonist for *Punch* magazine to depict an effeminate Disraeli, adorned with large wings, donning an angelic gown for a masked ball, and admiring himself before a mirror.)

Fast-forward 140 years: Arthur Peacocke, a biochemist and ordained Anglican priest, makes an observation that echoes Disraeli's phrasing. Peacocke, who accepts the theory of evolution, writes regarding one of its implications for humans:

> Human beings seem to be "rising beasts" rather than "fallen angels."[2]

Disraeli did not accept human evolution; Peacocke did. But both realized that human evolution bore implications about human nature. And about humans' acting morally (or not). And with their use of the world "angels," both drew upon a symbol in their Judeo-Christian culture.

In the preceding Chapter 10, we saw that in an evolutionary world, it is difficult to consider the human condition without also reflecting upon the struggles and suffering of other animals. In the current chapter, we will zero in on an element that can compound suffering—the moral evil committed by humans. In the first part of this chapter, we will look more closely at our human makeup in light of evolutionary science. Then, in the second part of this chapter, we will juxtapose that knowledge from evolutionary biology with some key ideas from the Judeo-Christian tradition.

We will try to bring the science and the religion together.

Our Evolutionary Uniqueness

The famous "Adam and Eve" story[3] in the Bible suggests that something that differentiates humans from other primates is our moral capacity and our reflective moral consciousness. But the moral problem with humans is certainly greater than our ability to know moral right from wrong. There is also the problem of *acting* morally. The humorist Mark Twain quipped over a century ago, "Man is the only animal that blushes. Or needs to."[4]

Despite Twain's humorous separation of humans from other animals, many people have been concerned that humans might act immorally if we consider ourselves to be too much like the "beasts." That is, if we think of man, as Gilbert and Sullivan humorously put it, as being "at best ... only a monkey shaved!"[5] That concern was Disraeli's in part. He was not alone among Victorians in voicing it.

In the following 20th century, the catalog of human atrocities and consequent suffering became so large that some Christian theologians today feel it necessary to begin their discussions of evil not with abstract questions but with sobering reminders. For example, the first chapter of a book on God and suffering written by one theologian, Gloria Schaab, opens with the following litany:

> The horrors of nationalistic genocide and terroristic
> suicide; the ravages of poverty, starvation, and AIDS;
> the prevalence of global, urban, and domestic violence;
> and the insidiousness of racism, sexism, and classism.[6]

The suffering during the 20th century cannot be dismissed as being entirely the result of superior modern technology that enables us to kill people in greater numbers even faster. That is because many of the miseries Schaab lists—such as domestic violence, racism, and classism—preceded the rise of modern science. And even preceded ancient Greek science.

Therefore, the matter we will focus on in this chapter is: What, in a most fundamental way, lies behind human-caused suffering—particularly given what illumination we might get from scientific knowledge about evolution?

Today, all around us, we have information enlightening us about the behavior of our non-human primate ancestors. From articles in popular magazines to TV shows on PBS and the Discovery Channel. Over the past few decades, as biologists have been more carefully observing and testing the behavior of other primates, there has been considerable interest in trying to identify in our primate cousins any characteristics we humans might have inherited that might explain our human violence. I remember one cartoonist who found amusement in such interest in our primate cousins. The cartoonist had drawn a human and a monkey sitting side-by-side. The human was reading a book on chimp behavior. Meanwhile, the monkey was reading a book on ethics, apparently seeking enlightenment about his human relatives.

But what if it should really be the other way around? What if we should be reading the book the monkey is reading—the book about human beings? That is to say, what if the better explanation for human anguish, violence, and evil is to be found in our distinctly *human* characteristics, not in those characteristics we share with our primate cousins? True, we do now know more than ever that there is no absolute break between humans and animals in regard to such abilities as tool-making and language. Nevertheless, if we are going to better comprehend the presence of suffering caused by humans, we have to understand the ways human beings are *different* from our primate cousins.

The Dirty Secret about Evolution

Here is the dirty secret about evolution: Evolution does *not* always lead to features or characteristics that are the best for individuals or even for the species. This is more easily seen when we look at physical features that have come about through evolution but which do not seem to have evolved well enough. One example is that in the human eye, the light-receptors are on the backside of the retina, thus requiring light to pass through the retina to get to them. Other examples of physical imperfections in humans are revealed in our back problems and in a twenty percent miscarriage rate.[7]

Such imperfection also holds true for humans' mental, emotional, and social capabilities. One writer, Timothy Anders, examining the roots of our evolutionary past, explained in 1994 how evolutionary biologists, trying to gain acceptance for the often unpopular theory of evolution, had downplayed this dirty

secret that evolution does not always lead to features or characteristics that are the best:

> Most Darwinian scholars have repeatedly denied that
> there is any connection between human evolution and
> human suffering.... At times they ... have gone to great
> lengths to convince the public that evolution is
> essentially a benign process which is ultimately
> responsible for our strengths but not our weaknesses.[8]

Sometimes religious leaders who accept evolution have been
partners in this cover-up of evolution's dirty secret. Many Christian writers today, if they do make a reference to evolution, will
usually do so by pointing to humans' superior qualities compared
to other primates. The problematic characteristics that evolution
has given humans will usually go unmentioned.

What distinguishes us humans is a set of capabilities involving
conceptual thinking, language, and learning that allow us to extend
our biological heritage with cultural heritages. Here swirls the
debate over nature versus nurture.

The Nature-Nurture Nexus

When we try to sort out whether a particular behavior by an individual was the result of inherent human weakness or because of
that person's bad upbringing, we weigh human nature against that
person's being nurtured improperly. Our common formula for
debating this question is to mentally categorize some human
behaviors as having resulted from human nature and other behaviors as having resulted from nurture. (See Figure 9.) The juxtaposi-
tion of the two words dates back at least to a line from
Shakespeare that the half-human monster Caliban was "a devil, a
born devil, on whose nature / Nurture can never stick."[9]

Because of contemporary science's discoveries about genes,
the body, and especially the brain, we today are inclined to give
those causes more weight than we do our being cultivated socially.
We lean toward attributing more to "nature." As an example, when
we see a person being slid into a brain-scanning machine, because
we are getting a picture of electrochemical activity within the
brain, we can easily get the impression that we are peeking into
human nature by itself. But that is not so. That person's brain had
been constructing connections between its nerve cells ever since

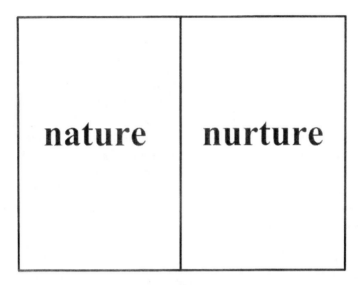

*Figure 9: The mental picture evoked by our
nature-nurture debates*

that person was born—affected in part by the nurturing of family, educational institutions, and other elements of human culture. There is in real life no pure isolated "human nature."

Although musings about nature and nurture have been going on for a long time, the most impassioned debates over the past several decades have resulted from the rise of two new movements, sociobiology and evolutionary psychology. Both movements have attempted to give evolutionary explanations for the way we humans are today, although sociobiology focused more on human behavior, and evolutionary psychology (which morphed out of sociobiology) focuses more on human cognitive faculties. One key issue is whether our genes keep us on a "short leash" or allow us a "long leash." The professor of psychology Heather Looy summarizes the uncertain character of this area of investigation:

> Within EP [evolutionary psychology] there is a range of perspectives on how to theorize and how to gather and interpret evidence about human psychological evolution. The most prominent in the popular media

(Pinker ... and others) have been criticized by other scholars for presenting an oversimplified view that is not empirically well supported.[10]

Part of the problem is that our nature-nurture formula presents a misleading either-or choice. Just to start with, even when we behave in a way that has been strongly influenced by our cultural conditioning, we are still biological beings. As the evolutionary scientist Stephen Jay Gould puts it, "Humans are animals and everything we do lies within our biological potential."[11] Taking a lead from Gould, we might re-draw our mental picture as I have done in Figure 10, positioning our natural biological potential as the *foundation* for everything we do. Human nurturing is built on the ever-present foundation of biological nature.

However Stephen Jay Gould was also among those who thought that sociobiologists were speculatively attributing too much of human behavior and cognition to our evolutionary human makeup, and not enough to the effects of culture. We are, after all, affected by our environment since before we are born. The amount

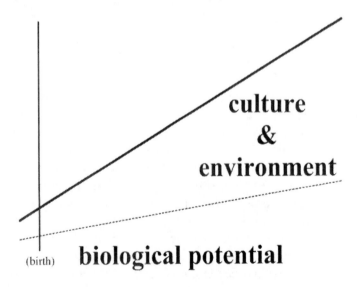

Figure 10: An alternative mental picture based on Gould's lead (The vertical line on the left indicates the individual human's birth)

of cultural nurturing increases as a child grows, but is never zero (as also shown in Figure 10). As Gould emphasizes, "Children are socialized from their earliest memories."[12]

Diagnosing the Human Problem

Compared with other animals, the most basic problems with humans beings derive from the way our behavior and abilities come much more from our individual development and culturing, and much less from instinct. No doubt a whole book could be written on the problems with even normal human beings. Here I will simply outline the matter to show how, ironically, these problems are tied in with our distinctly human abilities—and not so much with our continuity with other animals.

In terms of the whole package of what makes up human beings, we are, comparatively, an unusually underdeveloped species biologically. We are heavily dependent on cultural extensions to assist and guide us. And so, compared to other animals, our instinctive behaviors are relatively under-evolved. An example: The offspring of some live-bearing fish (such as guppies) can be on their own, leaving their mother within only 2 or 3 minutes after being born. In contrast, many human children, after 21 years of being helped by their parents, can still have a hard time getting their feet on the ground.

Human abilities that enable us to develop elaborate cultures and learn from them do make possible more plasticity in human behavior than purely instinctive behavior would allow. But with plasticity comes a price: In other animals, disadvantageous instinctive behaviors will, over the course of time, usually become expunged through natural selection. In contrast, we humans can sometimes behave in ways that are dangerous to ourselves. Or dangerous to other people. Or to both. Timothy Anders explains the problem pointedly:

> At birth the human infant possesses virtually no innate
> knowledge at all, and none of the skills it will
> eventually need to survive. Rather it must learn as it
> goes along, taking advantage of whatever ... is
> provided by its personal experience and by its social
> milieu.... What it actually learns, however, is by no
> means always beneficial.... The *need* to learn is

inextricably tied up with the vulnerability to improper learning.[13]

We humans have unparalleled conceptual and imaginative powers. But that ability also means that we can construct cultural concepts and ideas that are out of touch with reality. As the 20th-century philosopher and theologian Charles Hartshorne puts it:

> We human beings, naked apes, featherless bipeds, who
> enjoy the privileges of conscious thought, must also
> bear its burdens.... We may, much of the time, be living
> in some little scheme of our own imagining.[14]

Certainly another characteristic of humans is our faculty of reason. One neurologist, Donald B. Caine, who has examined that aspect of human beings, has written a book titled *Within Reason*. A rhetorical question on the book's back cover expresses the book's main point:

> We have believed that reason is the centerpiece of our
> decision-making process. Yet if reason directs what we
> do, why is human behavior so often violent, irrational,
> and disastrous?[15]

Yes, emotion can sometimes be a detriment to reasoning clearly. But despite the perceptiveness of Caine's question, we should be on guard against characterizing human reason and conceptual abilities as being our most preferred characteristics, while characterizing human emotions, in contrast, as being bad. Some emotions can serve very valuable purposes; and our idea-making can sometimes blind us.

Some contemporary research on the human brain by Lasan Harris and by David Eagleman confirms this complexity, which can also be seen by studying violence and genocide in modern history. Specifically, the way that propagandistic ideas and categorizing of other people can override our natural tendency to feel within ourselves the pain of other people. One experiment detected a lessened internal reaction to photographs of a hand being pierced by a needle when the hand was labeled as belonging to a person of a different belief-system than of the experimental subject being measured. Interestingly, atheists showed the same pattern: They had a greater physiological response when a hand being pierced was labeled "atheist," and less response when the hand was labeled with the name of one of the world's religions.[16]

We need not turn to such extreme examples as genocide to see human turmoil resulting from human conditioning. The philosopher and theologian Charles Hartshorne previously quoted also explains how humans' having to learn behavior, along with our earliest learning usually coming from our parents, can lead to emotional difficulties perpetuated generation after generation. Hartshorne writes:

> In [our] species (for good reasons) the young are born
> radically helpless and immature.... If their parents or
> caretakers are themselves suffering severe
> frustrations ... then the offspring are likely to be badly
> treated.... How then will the offspring react to the bad
> treatment they receive? Because of their immaturity ...
> they cannot react in an ethically noble way.... Thus
> their emotional development begins badly.[17]

Given these tangled difficulties with human beings, it is fortunate that we have the ability to develop ethical standards and be self-reflective about our behavior. But here again, there is a price. Our ability to be reflective about ourselves can result not only in benefits but also in damage to ourselves. Self-evaluation can turn into a lack of confidence or even self-hate. That self-damage can lead in turn into damage to other people.

The psychological suffering traceable to the human shortcomings I have outlined can also create a feedback loop, with personal psychological anguish causing conflict with other people, and with that conflict then causing more anguish. Round and round. This is why actively cultivating periods of social peace, and actively healing traumatized psyches, is so crucial.

Charles Hartshorne sums up the problem with our species:

> We are, then, a species of animal whose members ...
> are peculiarly sensitive and capable of suffering in a
> far greater variety of ways than other sorts of animals,
> with complex mental as well as merely physical forms
> of suffering or frustration.[18]

Reconciling Religious Concepts with Science

Knowledge from evolutionary science can thus give us insights into why the level of human suffering can be so high. That's our "science" side of the dialogue. But what about the "religion" side regarding human nature? We will now address that side, drawing upon the Judeo-Christian tradition, and then explore a way of reconciling the two sides.

Disraeli's jibe regarding "apes" and "angels" is merely one example of how evolutionary science's discovery of our humble human origins has sometimes been viewed as a threat to Christian teaching about the unique status of human beings. Today, that teaching is frequently expressed by saying that we humans have been made "in the image of God." That phrase is often employed to stress the sanctity and dignity of each person. And Christian writers using that phrase usually stress that humans hold a very high and special status.

Admittedly, the "image-of-God" concept has frequently been employed to assert an extreme difference between humans and other animals (whom, it is implied, were not created in the "image of God"). If presented in that fashion, the concept of the image-of-God can, for some people, seem to be contradicted by evolutionary science's explanation of how *Homo sapiens* are an extension of other evolutionary lineages, with humans having so much continuity with other life-forms.

However, if the Christian theological tradition down through centuries is examined, one will find that "image-of-God" has, in fact, been a multifaceted highly *flexible*, symbolic concept. Bringing together scientific knowledge and this major religious concept of the "image of God" may not be as difficult as it seems once we realize that there has been a great variety of thinking regarding that phrase, even in mainstream theology. Like so many other vibrant symbols within religions, there has been no single correct way to use that "image-of-God" symbol.

As an example, in early Western Christianity and in Eastern Christianity, it has not been at all uncommon to speak of *all* creatures as partaking of the image of God. A typical example of this broader use of the symbol is found in the writing of Athanasius, who was a bishop and towering theologian in the 4th century. Drawing also upon the Biblical theme that God created through divine Wisdom, Athanasius wrote:

> God placed in each and every creature and in the
> totality of creation a certain imprint [Greek: *typon*] and
> reflection of the Image of [divine] Wisdom.[19]

Employed in that fashion, the "image-of-God" idea stresses the way all creatures, being created by God, share in the ability of the created world to be revelatory. That is, the ability of the totality of creation to in some way show us something about God's power and character. As the great medieval theologian Thomas Aquinas wrote:

> Each creature is a witness to God's power and
> omnipotence; and its beauty is a witness to the divine
> wisdom.... Every creature participates in some way in
> the likeness of the Divine Essence.[20]

Used in that way, the image-of-God concept expresses primarily a relationship of all of life to God, rather than being anything analogous to physical genetic material that *Homo sapiens* carries and other species do not.

Such flexibility has been possible with the image-of-God symbol because there is actually so little within the Bible laying out the meaning of that phrase. In the entire Bible, there are merely *four* occasions, mostly in the book of Genesis, in which anything is said about humans using the image-of-God phrase, particularly two verses in the opening chapter of that book (Gen. 1:26 & 1:27).[21]

Today, the phrase "image of God" is frequently tossed about by Christians without really examining the context in which it originated. So, what did that phrase mean in its original Biblical setting? Its origins are a bit obscure. But the consensus of Biblical scholars today is, as W. Sibley Towner explains, that it is drawing upon "the practice of ancient kings of placing statues of themselves in every corner of their dominion" to symbolize the ruler's supervision over that region.[22] The suggestion of those Genesis passages would then be, as Bernhard Anderson expresses it, that "Human beings, male and female, are designed to be God's representative.... To be made in the image of God is to be endowed with a special task."[23]

What might this mean for Christian theology in regard to our relationships with other animals? Over a century ago (about forty years after Darwin's *Origin of Species* provoked questions about humans' status), one pastor in the Church of Scotland gave a possible implication for image-of-God in this sense of our representing God. George Matheson wrote:

God never gives dominion to any creature which has
not received his image. His image is love.[24]

During the twentieth century, much time was spent by field
biologists and laboratory experimenters trying to identify a quality
of human beings that was absolutely unique. That is, a quality no
other animals possessed, not even primates. All sorts of possibilities were explored. Are humans unique in that only they make
tools? Are humans unique in that only they have language? As it
turned out, each of the qualities once considered to be unique to
humans has been found in some rudimentary fashion in some other
species.

The Christian eco-theologian Thomas Berry proposed one
human quality that has not usually been on the list of scientists'
possibilities. Thomas Berry pointed out that humans are unique in
that only we have the ability to feel compassion for *all* other
species. Although some instances have been observed in which
some mammals have shown distress when an animal of another
species was in anguish, to the best of our knowledge, only we
humans can try to identify with what all other species experience.
Even if Berry's suggestion does not hold universally, it resonates
with Matheson's reminder that God's "image is love."[25]

Thus, there is nothing that prevents us from still using the
image-of-God symbol to remind us of the sanctity and dignity of
each person, or to remind us of our special responsibilities as
human beings, while at the same time accepting science's knowledge about the human race's being one branch of the evolutionary
tree of life.

Biblical Perspective on Human-Animal Commonality

There is another dimension to the Biblical approach toward human
beings that needs to be mentioned—a dimension that demonstrates
even more clearly the compatibility of the Bible with evolutionary
science. In contrast with those very few occasions in which the
Bible states that humans were created in "the image of God," the
Bible on numerous occasions reminds us of the *commonality*
between humans and other creatures. One of the most frequent
ways the Bible does so is through the use of the phrase "all flesh"
(occurring 35 times in the NRSV translation) and the word
"mortals" (occurring 88 times in NRSV). This is a notable contrast

to the minuscule number of times the phrase "image of God" appears in regard to humans. Both the phrase "all flesh" and the word "mortals" (in English translation) often emphasize how *both* humans and animals are mortal, limited beings created by God.

This explication has presented separately two Biblical themes: that of humans' being made in "the image of God," and humans' being "mortals," part of "all flesh." Frequently, those two seemingly contrasting ideas are seen as being in tension, even in opposition. However, if we truly explore those ideas by drawing upon their original context in the Bible (as has been done here), we find instead that the two theological ideas are complementary. We might ask: Who can better experience and show compassion (that is, better image God's love) toward other mortal creatures? Someone who elevates himself inordinately above other creatures, or someone who feels a commonality with them as fellow mortal creatures? If we answer that a person is better served by feeling a commonality, we can recognize that our scientific knowledge about evolution can contribute to the Biblical call for compassion.

Chapter 13 ("Finding a Broad Place") will bring back into discussion the suffering of *non*-human animals, given that Judeo-Christian teachings and various Bible passages tell us that God is compassionate toward animals too. That chapter will show one way of bringing the Biblical concept of salvation into the array of matters raised in the current chapter. Perhaps it will be none too soon, given the numerous human vulnerabilities that have been outlined in this chapter. A concept of salvation will need to address our human vulnerability to anguish and mental suffering that Charles Hartshorne and the other writers quoted in this chapter have spoken of.

Our Place, Humility, and Humor

We cannot escape the fact that our evolutionary heritage as human beings has left us with biological complexities and social challenges that other species do not have to deal with. Fortunately, we have also been given the ability to have a sense of humor. And humor can be wonderful for reminding ourselves that we can benefit from some humility about our place in the long evolutionary history of life on planet Earth.

When Victorians in England grappled with the implications of

Charles Darwin's theory of evolution, they often relied upon their humorists. The following excerpt is from a poem written in 1887, in which the poet muses about fossils of an extinct group of species called trilobites. Such extinct trilobites lived in the ocean in what is called the Silurian period of ancient geologic times. The witty poem ends with the poet's humorous lament:

> I wish our brains were not so good,
> I wish our skulls were thicker,
> I wish that Evolution could
> Have stopped a little quicker;
> For oh, it was a happy plight,
> Of liberty and ease,
> To be a simple Trilobite
> In the Silurian seas![26]

Chapter 12
Darwin, Race, Slavery, Science, and the Tree of Life

In 1826, a young medical student at Edinburgh University began to be tutored in a craft that was not a required part of his formal education. He began to learn the craft of stuffing dead birds. Little did he know that five years later his knowing how to preserve specimens of dead animals would prove invaluable. That was because that young medical student was none other than Charles Darwin, who would become the de facto naturalist on HMS *Beagle* on its landmark voyage around the world.[1] The unexpected opportunity to travel to other continents, studying biological life-forms, would provide the groundwork for his revolutionary book *Origin of Species*, which would be published three decades later.

There was another detail about Darwin's being tutored in taxidermy that would also turn out to have a connection with the theory of evolution, although in a less obvious way. Namely, that the man who tutored the seventeen-year-old Darwin was black. More specifically, the man who tutored Darwin for a modest fee was a black freed slave, John Edmonston. At that time, it was not that uncommon for some blacks to be seen in the large cities of England. But for someone of a wealthy family (as this medical student was) to sit at length with and submit himself to the tutelage of a black man *was* uncommon in England's class-based society. Thus, Charles's being tutored was a learning experience not just about dead animals, but also about a living person of another race.

Moreover, as strange as it might seem, the issue of black enslavement would play a role in the publication of Charles Darwin's second major book, published a dozen years after the more famous *Origin of Species*. Charles Darwin always emphasized that he was a scientist, not a social reformer. But his theory of evolution quickly threw him into the midst of the hottest social and moral controversies of his day. Such as the issues of slavery and race. And also the ethical treatment of animals. Today, most history is told with Nature as just the backdrop for the human drama. But ironically, it was partly through Darwin's connecting the tree of human ancestry to animals that non-white races were integrated into the human family tree. How that occurred requires some explaining. That will be the subject of this chapter. The explanation will reveal many subtle interfaces between religion and science. And reveal much about our human condition, both in society and in the natural world.

Background: Slavery & Race

In 1807, only two years before Charles Darwin was born, Britain had outlawed the slave trade with the British West Indies, a slave-trade hub. But neither slavery nor the slave trade had ended. People who had been slaves of the British before 1807 usually remained slaves. Illicit trade continued. And other nations such as the U.S. still allowed slavery.

Although slavery had existed in the ancient world (such as in the Bible), in the ancient world, someone became a slave usually from having become a prisoner of war or as a way of paying off a debt.[2] In contrast, the modern form of slavery that developed during European colonization was a commercial enterprise, with a person subject to being turned into a slave simply because of that person's racial ancestry. Virtually always, this new commercial slavery was along the lines of race: white over non-white, most often white over black.[3] And the expansion of that commercial slavery was achieved through the colonizing countries' possessing a superiority in scientific technology.

As accounts filtered back to Britain from other countries about experiences with people of so many different skin colors and features, the puzzle of such differences did provoke disagreement. Nevertheless, it was widely believed that a person's different character and morality were *tied in with* the innate, biological differences between people of different races.[4]

Even though Britain had ended its West-Indies slave trade a quarter-century before Darwin embarked on the *Beagle*, slavery itself had not yet been abolished in the British Empire as a whole, nor in many other countries. The main mission of the *Beagle* had in fact been to map the coastlines of South America as part of maintaining the power of the British navy. In port after port of South America where the *Beagle* landed, Charles Darwin witnessed slavery and what he called its "heart-sickening atrocities."[5] Darwin wrote:

> Near Rio de Janeiro I lived opposite to an old lady, who kept [thumb]screws to crush the fingers of her female slaves.... I have seen a little boy, six or seven years old, struck thrice with a horse-whip (before I could interfere) on his naked head, for having handed me a glass of water not quite clean.[6]

Charles Darwin seems to have always been sensitive toward the pain of other humans. And so, given the atrocities of slavery he observed, it is no surprise that he exclaimed later in a letter to a friend:

> Great God how I should like to see that greatest curse on Earth slavery abolished.[7]

When the *Beagle's* voyage ended in 1836, Darwin returned to an England that had at last abolished slavery throughout the entire British Empire. The greatest credit had to go to William Wilberforce, leader of the anti-slavery movement in Parliament. William Wilberforce, an evangelical Christian, was, in the eyes of many supporters of abolition, a giant oak of a man, having, according to legend, taken a pledge in 1787 under a giant oak tree that he would not rest until Britain brought an end to slavery. Wilberforce's decision to fight slavery had come out of an ecumenical action: Quakers opposed slavery but were considered religious "Dissenters," and so were not allowed to run for Parliament. They persuaded the evangelical Wilberforce, a reformist member of Parliament, to work to make slavery illegal.

Charles Darwin and his siblings had grown up during the campaigns to abolish slavery. They also grew up learning that their family had an anti-slavery heritage. Charles Darwin's grandfather, Josiah Wedgwood, had his pottery factory produce small medallions that were distributed to cultivate support for the abolitionist cause. The medallions, using the powerful New Testament word "brothers,"[8] depicted a kneeling, shackled Negro imploring, "Am I not a man and a brother?[9]

Of course, even centuries before the modern slave trade, travelers from Europe had encountered non-whites, most famously beginning in 1492 with Christopher Columbus's landing in the "New World." But when Columbus and other Spanish explorers sent back to Europe the question of whether the human-like beings they had encountered—with strange features—were of the same kind as themselves, the Roman Catholic Church's clear answer was "Yes!" The church's answer, based on theological grounds was fairly straightforward: Yes, because all humans, no matter their appearance, are descendants of Adam and Eve. And in 1537, Pope Paul III made that traditional view official.[10] He declared that the Indians were "truly men," and said that on no account should they be reduced to slavery.[11]

Thus it was that even though Darwin's theory (at least in the eyes of some people today) seems to make the Biblical story of Adam and Eve antiquated, the official position of the Roman Catholic church regarding the common origin of all races was in alignment with the conclusion Darwin would come to about the single origin of humankind.

Despite that long Christian tradition, during the century-and-a-half before Darwin, the English had come to think of themselves as being descendants of the Anglo-Saxons who had inhabited the British Isles in the 5th and 6th centuries. Those 18th- and 19th-century British also came to think of those Anglo-Saxons as being separate from and superior to the mid-Eastern descendants of Adam and Eve. That Anglo-Saxonism easily supported the view that the slavery of blacks was natural because of the supposedly inferior character of the separate black race.

Background: Evolution

For Charles Darwin, slavery and race were indeed ethical issues. But they were for him also related to scientific problems.

Before Darwin developed an explanation for how one species could have evolved out of another species, even most scientists thought that all species had come down through history as separate lineages, somewhat like parallel lines. Substantive differences between living organisms today were considered to be not only separate endpoints but also separate beginning points—separate origins.

In the same fashion, some scientists maintained that the different racial types of human beings were different biological

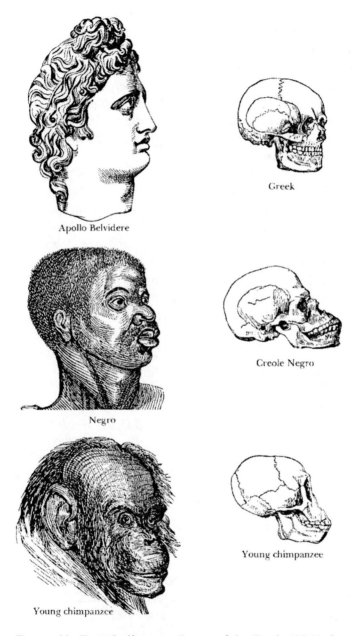

Figure 11: From Indigenous Races of the Earth *(1868) by Josiah Nott and George Gliddon. (Notice the falsely extended jaw of the Negro skull and the falsely enlarged forehead of the chimpanzee skull—thus making them appear more alike.)*

species—also separate from their beginnings.[12] Such scientists were called "polygenists," meaning they supported the idea of multiple, separate origins for the races. This was sometimes even represented by diagramming the different races of people as being in watertight compartments, in the same way that different species of animals were diagrammed as being compartmentalized one from another. A not untypical diagram from 1855 represented the white and Negro races as being as separate and compartmentalized as antelopes and elephants.[13]

This *non-evolutionary* approach to explaining biological variety was readily used by those scientists who had biased views about non-white races. An example can be seen in one drawing that developed out of that racially biased anthropology. (See Figure 11.) Although to our eyes today, the Negro man's face and skull have obviously been drawn to make him more like the chimpanzee than the white man, this seemingly scientific approach was used to justify beliefs in the inherent inferiority of blacks. Such racially biased conclusions by some scientists was given additional credibility by its being supported by one of the leading 19th-century zoologists in the U.S., Louis Agassiz of Harvard, a polygenist who indisputably had racial prejudices.[14]

But what if this whole approach was flawed from the very start? What if not only the human races but *all* species of animals had originated not as separate beginning points but instead from a common point?

Within two years after returning to England, Charles Darwin did something critically important for the history of science. He began a set of secret notebooks in which he jotted down his private thoughts about how it might have been possible for all species of life to have come about through evolution. On one of those secret pages, Darwin sketched a tree-like diagram of branchings out from a single trunk. (Figure 12.)

Other details in those notebooks reveal that Darwin was aware of the implications his theory of evolution held for the hottest social controversies of his day.

Controversies, Scientific and Political

Darwin's notebook drawing of a tree-like arrangement for how the diversity of species came about eventually lead to a passage in his

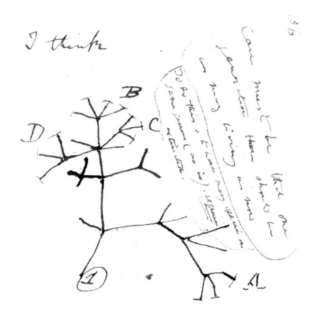

*Figure 12: Figure 12: Darwin's early tree-like
diagram for evolution (with
his comment "I think")*

revolutionary 1859 book *Origin of Species*. There, he drew upon
an ancient religious symbol for the perpetuation of life—the tree
of life. It was a symbol that stretched back through Christianity
and the Bible into the ancient Near East. Darwin, in *Origin*,
described it as:

> The great Tree of Life, which fills with its dead and
> broken branches the crust of the earth, and covers the
> surface with its ever-branching and beautiful
> ramifications.[15]

However, because he did not feel he had enough scientific
evidence to support the idea of human evolution, Darwin dropped
the subject of human origins from his book, making only a passing
comment that in the future, "Light will be thrown on the origin of
man and his history."[16]

Despite Darwin's scientific caution, after the publication of

Origin, most people's minds did turn to evolution's implications about humans, particularly about human ancestry. And about race. One satirical cartoon revealed how people detected that Darwin's theory describing other species had implications regarding humankind and the races. Echoing that abolitionist slogan of "Am I not a man and a brother?," the cartoon depicted an ape walking upright like a human being and wearing a placard that read, "Am I a man and brother?"[17]

The theory of natural selection Darwin presented in his book explained how characteristics within a species that were superior in their reproductive or survival value could come to be more widespread over time, thus leading to the branching out of new species. Left by itself, that theory could be misinterpreted to claim that the features of any group of people who were dominant in the world, such as British imperialists, must (supposedly) be superior to the characteristics of the non-whites they ruled over. And indeed, some tried to interpret Darwin's theory in that very way.

Thus it was that the publication of *Origin of Species* landed Darwin in the midst of continuing, swirling controversies about race and slavery.

Meanwhile, as scientists remained polarized over the question of the origin of the races, unexpected experiences pressed in upon their attempts to decide what was the truth about humankind. In 1865, tensions regarding relationships between whites and blacks came to a head in Jamaica, one of Britain's territorial possessions, igniting all the passions of British scientists and non-scientists over matters related to race. The British governor of Jamaica, Edward John Eyre, suppressed an uprising of blacks with immense force, killing over 400 blacks and flogging hundreds more. Although the British governor was called back to England, the British population quickly became divided over whether or not he should be prosecuted. And opinions—not just facts—about the races of humankind, and how much the character of blacks was intrinsic to their race, quickly swirled into legal and political arguments.

The link between the Jamaican controversy and scientists' debate over race, and even the link to Darwin himself, was made explicit only days after the Jamaican governor returned to England. At a meeting of the British Association for the

Advancement of Science, an anthropologist named James Hunt attacked Darwin's key supporter, Thomas Huxley for suggesting (through the theory of evolution) that all humankind came from a single origin. When Darwin received a copy of that anthropologist's paper, he realized how much the paper was a challenge not only to the traditional Christian position that all races were a single species, but also a challenge to the ability of his theory of evolution to explain human diversity. The anthropologist's paper even contained an explicit challenge to the man Darwin, stating:

> I beg to express a wish that, in consideration of the conflicting views held on this subject, Mr. Darwin himself may be induced to come forward, and tell us if the application of his theory leads to unity of origin as contended ... by Professor Huxley.[18]

Charles Darwin realized he could remain silent no longer. Especially because he was quite sure he *did* have a scientific explanation showing that so many of the differences between the races were not a matter of biological superiority of one race over another. But he would have to accumulate still more evidence to make a scientific case for his explanation.

Explaining The Races

Darwin had pulled the topic of human evolution out of his manuscript of *Origin of Species* because he did not yet feel he had sufficient scientific evidence to make a solid case for it. But for years now, besides his own research, he had been accumulating correspondence with people around the world, bringing him information about humans, primates, and numerous other species of life. (All the way down to the observation that baboons are similar to humans in that they like beer, get drunk on it, and have a hangover.)

Finally published in 1871, Darwin's second major book is usually referred to by its shortened title *Descent of Man*. (Because the use of words has changed since Darwin's day, it should be explained that "descent" does not mean a lowering, but instead a lineage from ancestors to descendants.) The key to the main idea in *Descent of Man* is represented by the book's full title: *The Descent of Man, and Selection in Relation to Sex*. Darwin laid out the evidence for humans' having descended from other primates, summarizing the evidence with the statement that, "Man still bears in his bodily frame the indelible stamp of his lowly origin."[19]

In the second part of the book, Darwin seems to shift to other animals, especially birds. He raises the question, for example of how something such as the peacock's elaborate fantail could have come about through evolution, because it has no survival benefit. The peacock's enormous tail could even make the bird more vulnerable to predators. Darwin's explanation for these kinds of features is that of **sexual selection**. The peacock's tail has evolved as the result of a choice for sexual partners. As the female peahens have allowed themselves to be mated by males with larger, more elaborate tails, the size and extravagance of the tails has increased over the course of many generations.

The recognition of sexual selection in humans is critical to Darwin's attempt to debunk the racism among scientists that had been gaining influence even after the publication of *Origin*. Darwin made the critical link between the book's two parts as expressed in its title: Human evolution has also been in part the result of sexual choices. As Darwin explains, all those seemingly strange differences between the races, such as in facial features, should not be considered to be evidence of differences in superiority. Instead, such differences have simply developed as separated groups of people developed different senses of what is sexually beautiful. In the book's second edition of 1874, Charles Darwin put it bluntly in a remarkably egalitarian manner:

Each race has its own style of beauty.[20]

Darwin also provided evidence to counter the widespread belief that people of African descent were innately inferior in intellect and character. And here is where Darwin's experience with and attitude toward that black former slave who had tutored him in taxidermy forty-four years earlier proved valuable in yet another way. In the text of *Descent of Man*, Darwin gives firsthand testimony of his close acquaintance with someone of another race, writing:

How similar their minds ... to ours; and so it was with
a full-blooded negro with whom I happened once to be
intimate.[21]

More Than an Explanation of Origins Needed

As strange as it may seem to us today, even accepting the traditional Christian belief, supported by Darwin, that blacks and whites had both evolved from one common origin did not resolve the question of how close the different races were. Nor did it even resolve whether they constituted a single species. During Darwin's lifetime, no one knew about chromosomes or genes, so there was no way to measure the amount of inheritable commonality between peoples of different racial backgrounds. And so, what knowledge people did have—even scientific knowledge—was especially vulnerable to being misinterpreted or misused because of a person's attitudes.

One idea in Darwin's time was that although the human races were of one origin, whites had evolved vastly beyond non-whites, especially beyond blacks. One tree-like diagram published by some scientists in 1878 positioned Anglo-Saxons at the very top of the white races, thus portraying them as having evolved far beyond Mongolian races positioned at the middle level, and even more beyond Negro races positioned at the bottom.[22] It did so even though it diagrammed all humans as having come from one origin.

And so, despite all of Darwin's scientific research, something else was needed to open the door toward 19th-century Britishers thinking of blacks more as brothers. And this additional element would not come exclusively from either the field of science or the field of religion. That critical additional element, ironically, was changing attitudes toward animals.

The traditional hierarchy of Western culture placed humans in a separate category from animals, similar to the way animals were in a separate category from plants. Western Christianity had come to think of human moral consciousness as being something in a quite different category than the material body. And a greater emphasis on the role of human reasoning in 13th-century Christian theology and in 18th-century Enlightenment thought magnified the separation of humans from animals. Also, Western scientific thinking following the 16th-century Scientific Revolution had been strongly influenced by the philosopher René Descartes, who had drawn an extreme contrast between body and mind, saying that only humans had minds.[23] Thus, Western religious, scientific, and intellectual thought had come to treat humans as being in a different category of beings from other animals. In developing such a sharp line, Christianity had lost touch with its roots in the Bible, in which the commonality of humans and other animals is repeatedly emphasized, such as by referring to both as "all flesh."[24]

Nevertheless, despite Descartes' extreme body-mind dualism, by the 19th century, science had revealed more and more biological similarities between humans and animals.[25] And whereas much of Western Christian theology had come to heavily emphasize the human ability to reason, beginning in the preceding 18th century, there began to grow an emphasis on the capacity to feel.[26] In 1780, the British social reformer Jeremy Bentham, even though he was somewhat ahead of his time, was able to write of animals, "The question is not, Can they *reason*? nor, Can they *talk*? but, Can they *suffer*?"[27]

That emphasis on the feelings of animals expanded even more in Britain in the 1800's. It is no coincidence that the SPCA was created in England in that century, the Christian abolitionist William Wilberforce being one of its founders.

Previously, animals were mostly either wild animals hidden in the woods or laboring domesticated animals forced into servitude. But in the 1800's, the movement of people into cities and the emergence of a middle class with some leisure hours meant that more people kept pets. That dog or cat, rather than being a working animal in the barn, would be kept right beside a person, even on the person's lap, making it easier for the person to experience the animal's emotions as being like their own.

Charles Darwin included in his 1871 book *Descent of Man* observations he had made of his own pet dogs. And he was by that time able to write:

> The fact that the lower animals are excited by the same emotions as ourselves is so well established.... The lower animals, like man, manifestly feel pleasure and pain, happiness and misery.[28]

The change in attitudes was not just an expanding recognition of animals' feelings. It was also a higher evaluation of the human feeling of sympathy. There was thus an expanding emphasis on the importance of compassion itself—toward animals and humans alike. For, after all, if we were to open our hearts toward the suffering of animals, how even more we should open our hearts toward humans. Even humans of other races, who were even closer to our own kind!

For Darwin, with his evolutionary view of the world, the ability to both feel pain and recognize the expression of pain by another living being was not an elevated moral sense unique to humans, but was instead a quality also possessed by other higher vertebrates. And so, in *Descent of Man*, Darwin explained how the highest moral qualities of humans were not totally different from emotions, but had instead developed out of social instincts that humans share with some other animals. The irony was that Darwin was calling people to a display a higher moral behavior by responding to something within themselves that they shared with the "lower" animals.

Moreover, in *Descent of Man*, in describing humankind's evolutionary past, Darwin wrote that in the development of humans' "social instincts..., his sympathies became more tender and widely diffused, *extending to men of all races.*"[29] There it was at last: The link between our sympathy toward animals, which also have feelings, and people of other races.

Darwin had been aware of the interrelationship between all those interwoven matters—animal feelings, human origins, race, and slavery—even in his earliest jottings in those secret notebooks over three decades earlier, in which he sketched his tree-like diagram. We can see all those matters swirling together in one notebook passage in particular. With an employment of that powerful Christian word "brethren," he had written:

> Animals—whom we have made our slaves we do not
> like to consider our equals.—Do not slave holders
> wish to make the black man other kind? ... Animals our
> fellow brethren in pain, disease death & suffering ...
> our slaves in the most laborious work, our companions
> in our amusements, they may partake, from our origin
> in one common ancestor .... we may be all netted
> together.[30]

Even though Darwin thought the normal expansion of sympathy was first to other humans and then to animals, there were thus ways that connecting the human evolutionary tree first to animals helped open the door toward 19th-century Britishers thinking of blacks more as brothers. Darwin's elevation of animals

*Figure 13: Members of the Church Missionary Society beneath
the "Wilberforce oak" (1873)*

and animal feelings indirectly endorsed the similar feelings that
were a part of human nature. That elevation formed a foundation
for the call to sympathize on a gut level with the suffering of other
human beings, regardless of their race.

An Emerging Vision

In a way, the entire controversy had been a dispute over the question, "What does it mean that a creature is a human?" That is an
important question for both religion and science, even though, by
the nature of the two enterprises, they approach it differently.
Charles Darwin was showing that the question could not be
adequately answered biologically—nor even historically—without
understanding our human connection with animals.

In 1873, two years after *Descent of Man* was published,

members of the Church Missionary Society—both white and black, both British and African—posed for a group photograph beneath the famous oak tree under which a century earlier, the Christian evangelist William Wilberforce had made his pledge to abolish slavery. (Figure 13.) Even though it would take half-a-century before it could really be appreciated even by most scientists (because racism in science would retain a grip on the field of anthropology for decades),[31] Darwin had at the time the picture was taken planted another type of tree. Not a physical tree, but a virtual tree planted in people's minds, by which people could define themselves. Darwin had planted in people's minds a mental picture that could at least begin to take root. That mental picture was an elaboration of the ancient religious symbol of the tree of life. It was a picture of a living, growing tree of life, deeply rooted in an ancient past, growing all of life out of one common origin: plants, animals, and people of all races.

With all of them more closely bound at their root than their different appearances would have ever revealed.

Chapter 13
Finding a Broad Place

Sometimes in studying the history of religious thinkers and scientists, we can gain insight from an event in the life of an ordinary citizen. Such is the case with what might be called The Puzzling Case of the Pet-Avoider.

In Britain in 1842, a not unordinary gentleman, John Dunlop, writes in his diary that earlier in the day he became uncomfortable after "the landlady's black cat [was brought] into the room, and played with." We might wonder why Mr. Dunlop became so uncomfortable. Did he look down upon such animals? No. Was he allergic to cats? No. Instead, he became depressed because he was seeing the cat through the lens of a belief that had developed in Western Christian culture. As he confided to his diary:

> I always get morbid on coming into close quarters with one of the lower animals—it is inexpressibly mournful to me to think that its soul dies and enjoys existence no more.[1]

Here we have an example of a tenderhearted individual who was torn between his natural empathy for another mammal, but whose scientifically-influenced Christian culture had placed animals in a quite different category than humankind—a category beyond God's possible eternal compassion. And so, a Christian doctrine that had been intended to provide comfort, the idea of the soul, had instead caused additional malaise regarding the perishability of life.

The truth of the matter is that down through centuries of Christianity, there has never been any single understanding about animals in regard to an afterlife. Nor any single understanding about the soul.[2]

Also, as many mainline theologians today will point out, the idea of an eternal soul that dwells within the human body derives more from the ancient Greek philosopher Plato's thought than from the Bible. The Biblical perspective is that of understanding the human to be an integration of body and the depth-within that we experience as soulness.[3] That perspective is more appealing to many religious people today in the West, especially given our growing knowledge from science about the inseparability of bodily, emotional, and thought processes.

Mainline Christian theologians today also try to remind Christians that their faith-tradition has a long legacy of being cautious about any approach to talking about the soul that removes value from our earthly, bodily human struggles. In the first few centuries of Christianity, the Church fought off one idea after another that maintained that Jesus was not a real human being.[4] The early Church, in expressing that God's fullness was present in Jesus, even resorted to a paradox rather than abandon its conviction that Jesus was a real, earthly human being.[5] The commanding basis for that belief was that Christians had experienced how deeply Jesus spoke to and touched their earthly struggles and sorrows.

The Larger Issues

In the preceding three chapters, we have been focusing upon matters related to our human condition in a world shaped by scientific knowledge about evolution. We found in Chapter 10 ("Fallen Animals or Rising Beasts?"), that the major challenge the theory of evolution poses to theology is not if Earth and the life on it were created in six days. Instead, we have come up with an array of interrelated issues involving vulnerability, the suffering, and perishability of all forms of life. In Chapter 11 ("Problems with a Problematic Species"), when we focused more specifically upon our human makeup, we found, ironically, that the more fundamental causes of our suffering are tied in with our distinctively *human* features. Because we humans are able to develop complex cultures and be self-reflective, we suffer anguish in a number of ways other animals do not. But in Chapter 12, ("Darwin, Race, Slavery, Science, and the Tree of Life"), we followed a saga in which our sense of human identity was intertangled with the struggles of animals other than ourselves.

It thus seems that we cannot gain enlightenment about our human condition without remembering other animals. And our Puzzling Case of the Pet-Avoider reminds us that we cannot develop a religious approach for lifting the weight of human malaise without also remembering animals. That is because distressed people like Mr. Dunlop will quite rightfully think about them. Can we speak to the lifting of suffering in a way that brings scientific knowledge into our religious framework? That will be the goal of this chapter. Although we will draw upon the Christian heritage, we will aim to strike chords that resonate more widely—touching upon the entire human condition.

Working toward a Comprehensive Worldview

A first step in trying to encompass both scientific knowledge and religious insights when trying to address such complex matters, will be to remember the basic differences between religion and science. As the philosopher Mary Midgley so aptly puts it:

There are two points of view—inside and outside, subjective and objective, the patient's point of view on his toothache and that of the dentist who studies him.[6]

The two views in her example roughly correspond to science's external observation and the knowing of life "from the inside," so to speak, which is so important to religion.

In order to draw upon both angles of vision, and apply both to the evolved life on this planet, we are going to use as an entrypoint a single feature of life. Our doing so will demonstrate how to properly integrate scientific knowledge into a larger religious awareness. The feature of life we will use is water. The connection between life and water is important for both science and religion. But it is important to remember that the way in which the two disciplines handle it could hardly be more different.

If you have heard about scientists' speculations about whether there exist or have existed forms of life on other planets, you may know that, to the best of our knowledge, water is essential for any life. On Earth or elsewhere.[7] Modern chemists doing experiments and observing the properties of water, know what water is chemically in order to identify it. Biochemists employ chemistry to look at water as two atoms of hydrogen and one atom of oxygen combined into a molecule: H_2O. Water as a chemical formula.

Let's now shift our perspective to reflect upon water in a way that lends itself to religion's way of knowing. The hot summer days we experience might enable us to recall some of the ways we have known water, but in a way quite different than as a chemical formula. Recall some occasion in the summer when you might have been walking or working outdoors, or were away from home, and had no water handy. Recall how it felt to be thirsty, wanting to find a way to get something to drink. Remember how it felt to take that first drink when you were so thirsty.

Writers of the Bible also knew those immediate ways of knowing water. They also knew how these ways of knowing water are not confined to the human race but are also experienced by other animals. The writers of the Bible also knew how such ways of experiencing water's life-giving properties could open a person to remembering and re-encountering God. As a typical psalm of creation, Psalm 104, puts it, speaking to God:

> You make springs gush forth in the valleys;
>> they flow between the hills,
> giving drink to every wild animal.[8]

Experiencing that inner yearning for the goodness of something that sustained life was so close to knowing God that at times in the Bible it is even a symbol for wanting to know God. For example, as part of Psalm 42 puts it:

> As a deer longs for flowing streams,
>> so my soul longs for you, O God.
> My soul thirsts for God, for the living God.[9]

Our everyday experience as living beings enables us to know what water is as we experience within ourselves a thirsting, yearning, and striving for water. That is quite a different way from science's knowing water as two atoms of hydrogen and one atom of oxygen combined into a molecule. But if we preserve the integrity of both religion and science, the two ways of knowing are quite compatible.

Knowing Life as Striving

These two ways of knowing are not just the ways we know what water is. These are also the ways we know the presence of life. For astronomers and astrophysicists who want to know if there might be life on other planets, their identifier might be a spectrographic analysis of light from the planet, analyzing the chemical elements on that planet. In contrast, for any living being, life is known "from the inside" as *striving*. Through our subjective experiences of striving, each of us knows part of what it means for us to be alive.

Moreover, it is through a recognition of types of striving in

other kinds of living beings (animals and plants) that we intuit that
they are alive too. Even all the way down to creatures that can be
seen only with the aid of a microscope. The theologian John
Haught suggests that it is the very recognition of an interior
striving by which humans ordinarily identify what is a living being
and what is not. (In this quotation, Haught uses the word
"sentient," which means being able to have sensations.)

> We humans can identify living beings and distinguish
> them from inanimate ones only because ... we
> personally intuit in them a striving and struggling, as
> well as a capacity to suffer, at least to some degree....
> We do not speak except poetically of a river, mountain
> or thunderstorm straining to accomplish some goal,
> whereas we do speak quite literally of sentient animals
> grubbing for food or trying to avoid predators, and
> therefore of their succeeding or failing in such
> exertions.[10]

In the early decades of the 20th century, animals and plants
tended to be depicted by evolutionists as being either lucky
survivors or unlucky victims of their environment. It was almost
as if some invisible hand of fate pointed at each individual being
or each species, and then declared "You shall survive," or "You
shall not survive." Over the past few decades, however, as biologists and animal-behaviorists have discovered more details about
living systems, animals (and even plants) have come to be viewed
as being more active, and certainly not passive. Evolutionary biologists are discovering more about how the evolution of animal
species has been influenced through individual animals within the
species seeking out and exploring new territory and new possibilities in how to live.[11] Striving!

A theology that draws upon knowledge from evolutionary
science can, therefore, include a recognition of a *commonality of
life in striving*. Striving, yearning, and longing in many forms. All
the way down to the microscopic, single-celled amoeba pushing
part of it's body out like a foot, striving to explore new territory.
And including our many human yearnings of body, mind, and
heart.

Over ten centuries ago, the medieval visionary and mystic
theologian Hildegard of Bingen discerned a commonality in terms

of the Holy Spirit—the Spirit of God—which the 4th-century Nicene Creed had called "the Giver of Life." Hildegard wrote:

[God says,]
I am the one whose praise echoes on high.
I adorn all the earth.
I am the breeze that nurtures all things green.
I encourage blossoms to flourish with ripening fruits....
I am the rain coming from the dew
that causes the grasses to laugh with the joy of life.
I call forth tears, the aroma of holy work.
I am the yearning for good.[12]

This quotation by Hildegard of Bingen suggests that God is to be discovered as we experience deeply within ourselves our best yearnings—and as we widen our vision to feel our commonality with the striving of all forms of life. Each living being, no matter its species, has its own interests and endeavors, but each one is striving out of a past and into the future.

Hildegard's suggestion that the Spirit of God is known as we experience our inner yearning for life and goodness (just as all of the living world yearns in its own way), echoes the thought of the writer Goethe seven centuries later: "What kind of God would push only from outside.... He likes to drive the world from inside."[13]

If that is one place God is to be found, a good theological assumption might be that it is in that commonality in striving that we might also come to a way of understanding salvation in an evolutionary and ecological context. That is to say, understanding salvation in a way that is not narrowed down to the human sphere and human needs. So let us now draw that topic of salvation into this religious picture that includes scientific knowledge.

Yearning, Perishability, and Salvation

What we humans strive for, what we yearn for, is not always achieved. And we can have conflicting yearnings as well. Also, as was explained in Chapter 10, behind concerns about suffering and death lies the wider, compelling problem of perishability. Death is just the tip of the iceberg, the unpleasant reminder of our human concern that amid all the flux of time, that which is valuable to us will not endure. Ironically, it is often that which we feel to have the deepest value that is most vulnerable and most subject to perishing. The blossoming but soon wilting rose feels more precious to us than the thorny, drab plant itself.

Many contemporary Christian theologians who integrate religion and science have drawn upon the work of the early 20th-century British philosopher Alfred North Whitehead. Although Whitehead's thinking is at times dense, his description of the heart of religion is so lucid that it is often quoted:

> Religion is the vision of something which stands
> beyond, behind, and within, the passing flux of
> immediate things, something which is real, and yet
> waiting to be realised [realized] ... something that
> gives meaning to all that passes and yet eludes
> apprehension.[14]

However, it is in regard to God's enduring relationship to the *non*-human sphere that most of modern Western Christianity finds itself handicapped. The formulas most modern Western Christianity employs to address this perennial concern about perishability are either narrowed to human matters or are too human-focused to allow for any picture of God redeeming the non-human world.

Fortunately, if we return to the Bible, we will find that it does not have such a narrow or human-centered picture of God's saving and redemptive concern. Even though in the Bible **salvation** can include forgiveness of human sins, the Bible does *not* see salvation solely in terms of forgiving sins. Even much less does the Bible see salvation as being primarily about an afterlife.

Instead, in the Bible, God's saving is understood to cover a wide range of activities through which God supports, strengthens, and empowers the world. Activities such as delivering people out of slavery (Exodus 14-15). Or providing people a new well of water when they were torn by dispute over a single well (Gen. 26:19-22). **Salvation** in the Bible covers almost any kind of deliverance from danger, or freeing from a confined situation. One image the Bible employs to express this sweeping understanding of salvation is that of being placed by God into "a broad place." As just one example, the writer of Psalm 118 declares, "Out of my distress I called on the LORD; the LORD answered me and set me in a broad place."[15] It is because of the Bible's wide understanding of salvation that Psalm 36 is able to say, in speaking to God:

> Your righteousness is like the mighty mountains,
> your judgments are like the great deep;
> *you save humans and animals alike*, O LORD.[16]

In other Bible verses, we get some additional glimpses of ways God is understood to be providing for forms of life other than the human species. For example, another part of Psalm 104, again in speaking to God, reads:

> O LORD, how manifold are your works!
> In wisdom you have made them all;
> the earth is full of your creatures....
> These all look to you
> to give them their food in due season;
> when you give to them, they gather it up;
> when you open your hand, they are filled with good
>   things.[17]

Moreover, several Biblical books in the New Testament repeatedly proclaim that God's great work of redemption through Jesus Christ is a gathering-up into salvation of "all things"—all things "in heaven and on earth." (The key Greek phrase is *ta panta*, with *"panta"* meaning "all.")[18] Examples can be found in Colossians 1:15-20, Ephesians 1:9-10, Hebrews 1:1-3, and 1 Corinthians 15:25-28.

Perhaps we can get a feel for this all-embracing meaning for salvation if we recall our theological definition of life as striving. In these Nature-related psalms in the Bible, we have the suggestion that the psalm-writers were doing the same thing. That is, observing animals striving to find water in the often austere terrain of the Mideast, or striving to escape from predators.

Also, there is in the New Testament one passage that seems to have captured the attention of virtually all contemporary Christian theologians who are trying to address the implications of the theory of evolution. It is the passage in the book of Romans in which the writer Paul describes all of God's created world as "groaning in labor pains."[19] That is certainly an image of an inward striving! And it is all of the created world that is seen as experiencing it. A commonality of humans and all of the rest of the natural world.

One 20th-century theologian, Roger Hazelton, has provided a description of salvation that is broad enough to encompass all of creation in its inner striving, in its groaning:

> The saved life means the human life dynamically
> transformed from within; this happens when man
> experiences in himself *the same drive toward
> wholeness which moves throughout all levels of
> creation.*[20]

Hazelton's word "wholeness" can be a key aid in bringing science
—particularly biological science—and religion together to develop
one worldview. That is because one scientific concept that has
emerged over the past several decades as being key is "holism,"
which is seeing living systems as unified wholes, and seeing how
parts fit into those living wholes.

Modern ecology textbooks often contain diagrams depicting
the holistic cycles within ecosystems. For example, in a temperate
forest's ecosystem, bacteria and fungi in the ground transform
dead plant and animal matter into soil, which provides nourish-
ment for the trees and other plants. In turn, the trees provide a
home and food for beetles and larvae, both of which can be food
for other animals, whose waste products then return to the soil to
be recycled. Many cycles of dependency creating wholes.

Such ecosystems, whether in forests or deserts or on beaches,
are examples of how chemical molecules and elements that make
up life are not lost, but are instead folded back into living systems.
A good number of religious writers have found in such systems an
inspiring vision of how the *value of life* is not lost—does not
perish—but is enfolded and folded back into new life. That vision
has been expressed by people of many faith-traditions, perhaps
one of the most eloquent examples coming from the Hindu
Gandhi, who wrote:

> I do dimly perceive that whilst everything around me
> is ever changing, ever dying, there is underlying all
> that change a living power that is changeless, that
> holds all together, that creates, dissolves, and
> re-creates.... And is this power benevolent or
> malevolent? I see it as purely benevolent. For I can see
> that in the midst of death life persists, in the midst of
> untruth truth persists, in the midst of darkness light
> persists. Hence I gather that God is Life, Truth, Light.[21]

Modern science has given us a new twist on this ancient way

of seeing the value of life being recycled back into new life. We ourselves here today might have within us right now some of the very atoms that were part of dinosaurs who walked this planet over 65 million years ago.[22]

Taking an evolutionary approach, we can see that such ecosystems are not frozen in one place in one period of time. Various ecosystems (themselves interacting with each other) stretch back in evolutionary time, and also embody strivings reaching out into the future. Groaning at times, but also bringing an emergence of new life.

Evolution and Emergence

Despite the challenges involved in bringing together modern scientific thought and religious perspectives, there is one concept that many scientists and theologians are both finding increasingly valuable. It is the concept of **emergence**.[23] In our everyday parlance, we are in some cases describing an emergence when we say that something is greater than the sum of its parts.[24] But the concept of emergence says something more. It says that the more complex whole has emerged *out of* a less complex reality. Here is how the philosopher Steve McIntosh summarizes the scientific picture of emergence, traced from Big Bang to human beings:

> The theory of emergence has increasingly revealed a
> new picture of evolution, which shows how
> cosmological, biological, and cultural forms of
> evolution are all part of the same process of universal
> development.... From cosmological evolution there
> emerges biological evolution, and from biological
> evolution there emerges psychological evolution.[25]

One way the concept of emergence can prove useful is to counter a tendency toward **reductionism** that has accompanied so much of modern science. Because science's methods involve isolating parts of things to look at the parts separately, it is easy to jump to the conclusion that the larger wholes are nothing more than the parts they are composed of. In contemporary religion-science discussions, that reductionist viewpoint was famously expressed by the biologist Francis Crick as being the view "that 'You', your joys and your sorrows, your memories and your ambitions, your sense of identity and free will, are in fact *no more than* the behavior of a vast assembly of nerve cells and their associated molecules."[26] In contrast, the concept of emergence emphasizes that new orders of higher complexity have appeared. New types of complexity that cannot be adequately thought about according to the rules that governed the simpler parts. The scientist Stephen Jay Gould, who was a severe critic of reductionism, wrote:

> Just knowing the properties of each part as a separate
> entity (and all the laws regulating its form and action
> as well) won't give you a full explanation of the higher
> level .[27]

Modern science almost always operates by breaking reality into smaller parts (organisms into organs, chemicals into molecules, etc.). It then pieces together the knowledge accumulated about those smaller parts. But a pieced-together Humpty Dumpty, even when epoxied back together, is not the same thing as the original, whole Humpty Dumpty.

As we work to bring scientific knowledge into a religious framework, the concept of emergence can also help us deal with the way evolution seems to be so *wandering*, even having what look like dead-ends from our human perspective (such as dinosaurs). The theologian John Haught believes that a loving Creator "is not one who overpowers the world and forces it to conform to a rigid plan, [and therefore] the world must be allowed the space and time to wander about, experimenting with various possibilities."[28] Nevertheless, Haught admits that "evolution seems directionless. All the random experimentation and wild meandering ... certainly makes us wonder whether we are witnessing the unfolding of a divine plan."[29]

However, if we place biological evolution within the larger course of the history of the cosmos—out of which the Earth and life emerged—we can see more clearly the way that biological evolution has taken a direction. It has a directionality out of lifeless atoms on a lifeless planet toward the emergence of great living complexity.

Besides revealing better the direction evolution has taken, stepping back in this way to place biological evolution within the larger cosmic story might also help us see into the heart of creativity. It might help us see something about the nature of creativity itself. If we draw upon a mental image of the Big Bang, we might ask: Does not any moment of creativity stand on a knife-edge between chaos and order? If what is coming into being at any moment does not become sufficiently ordered, it will fall back into chaos. On the other hand, if what is coming into being at any moment becomes too rigid, it cannot move forward into becoming something novel. Change will not be able to occur.

Could this knife-edge perhaps account for the mysterious mixture of order and chance that characterize both biological evolution and our human lives?

The concept of emergence might even have a side-benefit pertinent to our concerns about the suffering of animals over a vast evolutionary time. When we try to weigh the amount of animal suffering down through the course of vast evolutionary time, we would do well not to think that each individual animal has suffered to the degree that each individual human is able to. There is instead a continuum of sensitivity, beginning with sensitivity to light and touch in microscopic protozoa, evolving into sentience of increasing complexity, then to a type of consciousness in vertebrates, before we get to that reflective consciousness possessed by humankind.

The concept of emergence can thus, in a number of ways, clarify and strengthen our worldview as we bring science into a religious framework.

Salvation, Participation, Belonging

One obstacle to Christian's thinking of salvation in a way that encompasses animals—as the Bible does—has been the conception of eternal life as a reward that comes with the forgiveness of human sins. Humans, therefore, being the only ones eligible (as our 19th-century Pet-Avoider anxiously lamented). However, as the Biblical scholar Marcus Borg reminds us, *"Salvation in the Bible is seldom about an afterlife."*[30] The Bible passages already quoted in this chapter help demonstrate that.

Moreover, in the New Testament, "eternal life" expresses much more than any afterlife, and much more than an extension of time into eternity. Instead, the phrase "eternal life" is used to express a depth and fullness of life.[31] And we see in the psalms quoted above a discernment of how even animals, when they find food and water, are restored to a type of fullness by God's benevolence. A reward for their strivings.

As we seek to integrate scientific knowledge about the natural world with aspects of our faith-traditions, we might also draw upon insights that lie behind the Christian theological concept of "the communion of saints," a phrase employed in the ancient Apostles' Creed and elsewhere. That phrase has been used by Christians to express the way we can feel a kind of fellowship ("communion") not only with those spiritually faithful people living around us today but also with the faithful who are no longer alive. (Here, the word "saints" refers not just to those canonized by the Roman Catholic Church, but all people whose faithfulness, struggles, and works can live on in our knowledge and our memories.)

Besides providing inspiration for us in our own struggles, the communion of the saints can be a way of cultivating gratefulness for the shoulders we stand on. Those who preceded us have made our lives possible, and can make our lives more rewarding. On countless occasions, people of faith (not just Christians) have found that cultivating gratitude can be a means to help us through times of suffering. Cultivating gratitude can also be a means to turn our hearts and minds away from emotions that can lead to evil thoughts. Or worse, actions that bring evil.

Remembering our commonality with all forms of life in striving, we might similarly consider cultivating a remembrance of how we also stand on the shoulders of an immense diversity of *non-human* life-forms that have preceded us. A communion with all forms of life. This living community extends not just all around us today, but also extends back in evolutionary time in the ancient tree of life. When I am able today to move my hand, turn my head, or see, it is because those abilities evolved through the striving of countless other non-human creatures before me.

Many people today, both religious and non-religious, already know that the presence of animals around us can be a comfort when life feels lonely. Seven centuries ago, the Christian mystic theologian Meister Eckhart wrote that if he were alone on a desert, he would want to have a child with him to make his fear disappear. Even though people in his day were less likely to have pets than we are in the West today, Meister Eckhart added:

If I could not have a child with me

> I would like to have at least a living animal
> at my side to comfort me.[32]

It is unfortunate that Mr. Dunlop, the Pet-Avoider, could not have felt likewise.

Thanks to the discovery of Charles Darwin, we can be reminded of the Bible's all-encompassing vision. We can expand our sense of commonality far beyond such animals as our pets, so as to include all animals with which we are linked through our evolutionary past. Bringing to mind grateful thoughts of the animals that have preceded us can also bring a sense of belonging. A sense of belonging within a broader place.

(The matter of our sense of belonging on an even larger cosmic scale is explored in Chapter 19, "Belonging to Earth and Cosmos.")

Science by itself cannot come to conclusions about value, purpose, or God, in the way that religion aims to. Among those who sometimes work on a borderline between science and spirituality are nature-writers. They draw upon science, but also speak to some of the same sensibilities that religion speaks to at its best. A century ago, the nature-writer John Muir discerned a spiritual message about something of supreme value as he looked at the fossil record laid in stones. Even amid the evidence of animal suffering, striving, and perishability, John Muir wrote:

> In looking through God's great stone books made of
> records reaching back millions and millions of years, it
> is a great comfort to learn that vast multitudes of
> creatures, great and small and infinite in number, lived
> and had a good time in God's love before man was
> created.[33]

PART FOUR
Recovering the Non-human Realm

Let it not suffice us to be book-learned, to read what others have
written, and to take upon trust more falsehood than truth,
but let us ourselves examine things as we have opportunity,
and converse with nature as well as books....
The treasures of nature are inexhaustible.
— *John Ray*
(17th-century biologist and philosopher)

God brought things into being in order that the divine goodness
might be communicated to creatures and be represented by them.
And because the divine goodness could not be adequately
represented by one creature alone, God produced many and
diverse creatures, that what was wanting in one in the
representation of divine goodness might be supplied by another....
Thus the whole universe together participates in
divine goodness more perfectly and represents it better
than any single creature whatever.
— *Thomas Aquinas*
(13th-century theologian)

Chapter 14
Modern Pesticides and Medieval Christian Thinkers

Among the top ten bestselling books in 1962 were the encouragingly titled *Calories Don't Count*, perhaps to offset the more fattening title *The Joy of Cooking*. Although the bestseller list did demonstrate the continuing success of Bible sales with the inclusion of *The New English Bible* translation of the New Testament, more common on the list were easygoing, heart-warming, dog-mentioning books. Such as Charles Schulz's *Happiness is a Warm Puppy* and John Steinbeck's *Travels with Charley*. Only Helen Gurley Brown's daringly titled *Sex and the Single Girl* hinted of the feminist revolution that was just emerging.

In September of 1962, however, a book would be published that would not have the appeal of those comforting books about food and dogs. Instead, it was a book that would force Americans to face unpleasant facts about dying birds, poisoned landscapes, and dangers to human health. Nevertheless, the book would make it onto the coming year's bestseller list, and would become the most talked-about book during 1963.

That book was Rachel Carson's *Silent Spring*. No matter how the story of environmentalism in the U.S. is told—whether it focuses upon science, society, or religion—any environmental history would be incomplete if it did not mention Rachel Carson's book, which alerted the American public to alarming problems with a new breed of modern pesticides.

The Pesticide Controversy

Before World War II, other chemicals had been used to reduce the numbers of certain insects. But during and after World War II, a new category of synthetic chemicals (chlorinated hydrocarbons) was employed, which never existed before. Chemicals which, as Rachel Carson put it, had "no counterparts in nature."[1] The most famous of those chemicals had the tongue-twisting name of dichloro-diphenyl-trichloroethane, better known to most of us by its abbreviation "DDT."

In the U.S. in the decade following World War II, there was a rapid acceleration in the use of these new insecticides and herbicides. Spraying for mosquitoes was often done from the air, covering wide areas of land and all the life-forms upon it. DDT had even been made available for home use. By the latter 1950's, the U.S. public had come to place a lot of faith in the petrochemical industry, which had in many ways brought "better living through chemistry," as one company's slogan put it. [2]

However, here and there, some people had noticed changes in life-forms other than in insects. Normally, robins returned every spring to the campus of Michigan State University. But by the spring of 1958, not a single living robin could be found on the campus. Elsewhere, people in separate regions of the U.S. had noticed other changes. From the northwest United States to Florida, instances of dead animals were observed, ranging from owls to rabbits to trout.

But most people had not connected those separate incidents. That would change with the 1962 publication of the biologist Rachel Carson's book *Silent Spring*. In that bestseller, Rachel Carson explained that despite the increasing number and quantity of pesticides being used, the limits to such a combative approach had already appeared. Insects had developed resistance to the pesticides (similar to the way bacteria develop resistance to antibiotics). And the pesticides were killing insects helpful to humans, such as bees, which are essential for the pollination of many crops. Also, the new pesticides traveled up food chains, killing other animals, such as those robins at Michigan State. Moreover, with natural predators thus reduced in numbers, the insect populations actually bounced back.

In this chapter, however, we will be tracing intangibles, such as attitudes and ideas. It is therefore revealing to notice how these problems with the new pesticides pointed to a picture of Nature as a living system having complex interconnections. The pesticide controversy, which went on for decades, revealed that neither science nor religion could afford to ignore our life-sustaining connections to the *non-human* realm. So much so that, as strange as it might seem, the controversy would even lead to religion's re-discovering two medieval Christian thinkers. This chapter will show how and why.

This was not the first time a voice of environmental concern had been raised to speak to the American public, reminding them of the deep interconnectedness of everything in Nature. Roughly a century before, the conservationist John Muir had reminded people how, "When we try to pick out anything by itself, we find it hitched to everything else in the universe."[3] But John Muir had been raising alarms about such things as ancient trees being cut down in forests in California, far west from where most Americans lived.

Rachel Carson, in contrast, was raising an alarm about something much closer to home. This was not a matter of trees being felled in distant California, but manufactured chemicals being sprayed, it seemed, almost everywhere, even in a baby's bedroom.[4] *This* danger was felt intimately.

The controversy over *Silent Spring* after its 1962 publication revealed that more issues were involved than just the risks of particular pesticides. The dispute that arose between Carson and her detractors revealed clashing perspectives over intangibles. Clashing perspectives over who we are in relationship to Nature. And so, rather than following the trajectory of how the public's growing concern led to landmark pieces of environmental legislation, we are going to follow the trajectory that eventually leads to our two medieval Christian thinkers.

The Connection to Religion

It is important to notice that none of this growing concern about the environment required any religious beliefs. Any person could have responded to the alarms about pesticides and other environmental problems out of a general concern for human health. Or out of a concern for the fate of robins or bald eagles. In order for our two medieval thinkers to become re-discovered, someone had to make, in an influential way, a connection between the treatment of the environment and Christianity.

When a riveting connection was made four-and-a-half years after *Silent Spring*, it was not made by a theologian in any theological journal. Instead, it was made by an historian in *Science* magazine. In 1967, Lynn White published an article titled "The

Historical Roots of Our Ecologic Crisis."[5] In that article, Lynn White laid a major part of the blame for our environmental problems on attitudes toward Nature that he saw as having been a part of Western Christianity.

Lynn White's seminal article resulted in decades of examination of his thesis by historians, theologians, and environmental writers. The majority conclusion has been that although he was right on a few points, White's thesis was much too simplified. The verdict on Lynn White's idea has been a mixed one partly because of the vastness and variety of ideas within any faith-tradition.

What turned out to be more significant than Lynn White's own ideas was how his essay became a wake-up call. In response, some Christian theologians began to examine Christianity's attitudes toward Nature down through the centuries (it having been the predominant faith-tradition in the West).[6]

As Christian writers re-explored Christian history, they did indeed often find a considerable number of statements by Christian leaders that now looked ecologically unsound, or were disturbing to most contemporary sensibilities. Frequently discovered was not so much anti-environmental attitudes per se, but a human-centeredness in thinking. An **anthropocentrism**, as it came to be called. Frequently such anthropocentrism manifested itself in the idea that the very *purpose* for the existence of plants and animals is that they provide food and other materials for sustaining human existence. For example, although the 16th-century Protestant John Calvin objected to cruelty toward animals, and criticized human greed, he had nevertheless written in his commentary on the Bible's book of Genesis:

> The end [i.e., purpose] for which all things were
> created [was] that none of the conveniences and
> necessaries of life might be wanting to men.[7]

When, in the latter 20th century a statement such as this was examined, words such as "conveniences" stood out as being problematic. Claims such as Calvin's that the reason for the world's existence is to provide for human "necessaries" and human "conveniences" seemed questionable in light of the growing environmental consciousness. In fact, the word "convenience" Calvin had used was the very word Rachel Carson also used when she criticized thinking similar to Calvin's assertion. One of the most quoted sentences from *Silent Spring* was Carson's statement:

> The "control of nature" is a phrase conceived in
> arrogance, born of the Neanderthal age of biology and
> philosophy when it was supposed that nature exists for
> the convenience of man.[8]

The late 20th-century re-examination of Christian thought revealed that there were still other types of human-centered thinking. Most common of them, especially as Christianity moved into modern times, was simply a narrowing down from the Bible's perspective encompassing all of creation to instead talking about just the human sphere. (This matter, as well as a look at the Bible itself, is addressed in Chapter 17, "A Lost Dimension of the Bible.")

Challenged by the new environmental consciousness to clean up its own house, there were basically three approaches taken by those Christian theologians who sought to mend the anthropocentric perspective that modern Christians in the West had unwittingly become accustomed to:

- One approach was to simply extend the concept of Christian stewardship, well-established in most churches, to extend beyond the human sphere so as to encompass the non-human environment. To be a good steward of the environment would mean to take good care of it.

- A second approach was to tackle those parts of the Christian tradition that now appeared either troublesome or downright dangerous from a sound environmental viewpoint. Such as Biblical passages that had been misinterpreted or misappropriated. The most common case was the passage about humans' being given "dominion" over animals (Genesis 1:26), which in Biblical context means caring stewardship, not a selfish and domineering stance. (Tellingly, historians of science and religion have discovered that it was not until the rise of modern science in the 17th century that Christianity started interpreting that Biblical verse to say that it gave humans license over Nature.)[9]

- A third approach—and this is the trajectory we are going to follow—was to find in the Christian tradition those Christian thinkers whose writings and lives displayed a more ecologically sound perspective that the growing environmental awareness called for.

St. Francis of Assisi

One such Christian had already been suggested by the historian Lynn White in his critical article in *Science* magazine. Even Lynn White saw in one medieval Christian leader a quite different orientation toward Nature than what White thought predominated in Christianity. And so White had written, "I propose Francis of Assisi as a patron saint for ecologists."[10]

Twelve years later, in 1979, Pope John Paul II would indeed proclaim St. Francis of Assisi the Patron Saint of Ecology. Of course, St. Francis of Assisi had not been entirely forgotten by Christians, especially not by Roman Catholics. Even before the alarms of the 1960's about pesticides, Saint Francis had been frequently enshrined in the form of garden statues. But the quest for Christians that demonstrated more ecologically sound perspectives led to a re-appreciation of the person of Francis—cleaning off that statue, so to speak, and taking a closer look at St. Francis's thinking.

One concept that emerged in the 1980's was **eco-justice**: the preface "eco" latched onto the word "justice." The intent of the word-combination "eco-justice" was to remind people of the interpenetration of concerns about Nature and concerns about human beings.[11] Just one of countless examples would be the way that in many cities the poor are more likely than the wealthy to be living adjacent to industrial plants that emit carcinogenic pollutants.

One way a new emphasis upon the interrelatedness of Nature and humanity was made possible was by bringing more to life that figure of St. Francis, who had to most people become associated mostly with Nature. Re-discovering and re-appreciating the man St. Francis of Assisi revealed how Francis's sense of a fraternity between humanity and animals sprung from a single source—Francis's spirited devotion to God. An eco-justice of the spirit, as it were. Because St. Francis had by the time of Rachel Carson become associated mostly with Nature, the story of Francis's preaching to birds had become more famous than the stories of his preaching to people. But both actions sprung from Francis's ecstatic sense of how all of creation praised God.

Francis's empathy with the less powerful in the world, the lowly, first appeared in unanticipated experiences that led to his religious conversion. Such as his encounter with a beggar wearing rags. And Francis's not only giving a leper alms but also kissing the man's hand, even though Francis usually had repugnance for lepers. This emerging concern about social justice blossomed when Francis renounced his own wealthy family background and formed the Franciscan Order of monks.

Today, we can easily overlook how revolutionary was Francis's founding that order. But at that time, peoples' roles in society could rarely change from the class they were born into. With such an inflexible society, privilege was power, and favoritism abounded (not to mention frequent wars between towns). By beginning a new fraternal society, Francis was undermining some of those problems of church and society. A person's family background, for example, would be obscured by all Franciscan brothers' wearing the same simple garb. Also, those who joined the order would not be allowed to swear allegiance to any of the fighting rulers.

As for the story about the birds, so often depicted in paintings: Francis had been walking home with a fellow brother of his religious order after an outing preaching, during which the human audience had not been very receptive. Noticing a flock of birds beside the path, Francis turned toward them, walked toward them slowly, and began speaking to them, finding in the birds a more receptive audience.

We see in these stories a demonstration of Francis's humble way of viewing all of creation—human and non-human—as one community of life under God. The 20th-century historian Lynn White, in proposing that Francis be designated the patron saint of ecology, had written, "The key to an understanding of Francis is his belief in the virtue of humility—not merely for the individual but for man as a species."[12]

Francis wrote very little himself. His life as a whole more than his writings represents his spirit. And yet, there is one famous piece of writing by him that expresses beautifully his spirit. It is "The Canticle (or Song) of Brother Sun." In the latter 20th century, lines from the second half of Francis's Canticle about "sin" and "pardon" sounded familiar to a Christianity that had become concentrated on human salvation and human society. But how striking was the first half of the Canticle, which seemed to survey all of non-human creation. Parts of its simple eloquence read:

Most high, all-powerful, all good, Lord!
All praise is yours, all glory, all honor
And all blessing....

All praise be yours, my Lord, through all that you have made,
And first my lord Brother Sun,
Who brings the day; and light you give to us through him.

How beautiful is he, how radiant in all his splendor,
Of you, Most High, he bears the likeness.

All praise be yours, my Lord, through Sister Moon and Stars;
In the heavens you have made them, bright
And precious and fair.

All praise be yours, my Lord, through Brothers Wind and Air,
And fair and stormy, all the weather's moods,
By which you cherish all that you have made.

All praise be yours, my Lord, through Sister Water,
So useful, lowly, precious, and pure....

All praise be yours, my Lord, through Sister Earth, our mother,
Who feeds us in her sovereignty and produces
Various fruits and colored flowers and herbs.[13]

The very natural intertwining of St. Francis's concern for vulnerable humans and vulnerable animals—lepers and birds— was thus re-discovered as inspiration for the new environmental age of the 1970's and 1980's.

The Link to Hildegard of Bingen

How would the other re-discovered medieval thinker, Hildegard of Bingen, come into play? The historian Lynn White had not mentioned her in his essay criticizing most of Christianity. It would require some parallel and overlapping currents of history to bring about the re-discovery of Hildegard of Bingen.

Those other currents came out of the women's movement,

which paralleled the emerging environmental movement of the 1960's and 1970's. Betty Friedan's groundbreaking feminist book *The Feminine Mystique* came out only one year after *Silent Spring*. In an interview with Rachel Carson the year after *Silent Spring* was published, a woman reporter for *Life* magazine broached a matter that Carson's critics frequently raised. Namely, that Carson was a woman. Carson responded by explaining that although she was unmarried, she was not a feminist, and that she was interested not in "things done by women or men, but in things done by people."[14]

Nonetheless, many women in the U.S. were interested in the fact that it was a woman who had raised the alarm about the modern pesticides. Many women had noticed the condescension toward Rachel Carson coming from her male detractors. For example, Rachel Carson had raised concerns about the possible effects of pesticides upon human reproduction. The former Secretary of Agriculture under President Eisenhower, aware that Carson was unmarried, wondered "why a spinster with no children was so concerned about genetics."[15] He was not the only man to deride her as a "spinster."

Although few women of the 1950's had defined themselves as feminists, those women had been some of the best fans of Rachel Carson's earlier books about the ocean and all the communities of life-forms in the ocean. So, in the 1960's and 1970's, that earlier generation of women were joined by a younger generation of women baby-boomers, some of whom took part in such activities as the first Earth Day in 1970. Women older and younger were looking for role models in history that generations of male historians had overlooked. And one such figure would be the exemplary medieval woman Hildegard of Bingen, most of whose writings were never even translated into English until the early 1980's.

Although Hildegard of Bingen lived three centuries before the Renaissance, she could well be called a "renaissance" woman, so diverse were her talents. The wholeness of her life—her bringing everything she touched and experienced within her sense of call—was paralleled in a wholeness of her vision of God's Spirit working in all of creation, all of the natural world.

Born to a noble family in 1098, Hildegard eventually became

the head of St. Disbod abbey. Even though a woman, she was able to have great influence because she was widely regarded as a prophetess. Ever since she was a child, Hildegard had visions. Her theological works consist in a large part of her descriptions of and interpretations of her visions.

When Hildegard's works were translated into English for the very first time in the early 1980's, some of her statements made one feel as if Hildegard were present today, observing our environmental problems, commenting upon them from a wiser vantage point. Such as:

> As often as the elements,
> are violated
> by ill-treatment,
> so God will cleanse them.
> God will cleanse them
> through the sufferings,
> through the hardships
> of humankind.[16]

Other comments of Hildegard even seemed to echo the perspective of *Silent Spring* over eight centuries later in Rachel Carson's warning that, "The 'control of nature' is a phrase conceived in arrogance."[17] How similar was Hildegard's cautionary reminder:

> All nature is at the disposal of humankind. We are to
> work *with* it. Without it we cannot survive.[18]

Such a viewpoint by Hildegard, that we ought to try to "work with" Nature, also stood in stark contrast to the view a few centuries later of Francis Bacon, who laid down the methods by which the emerging modern science should operate. Francis Bacon had declared, "Let the human race recover that right over Nature which belongs to it by divine bequest."[19]

Gaining Perspective through History

These quotations by Hildegard can help bring out more fully the intangibles that were at issue in the debate over Carson's book *Silent Spring*. Looking more closely at statements in the debate between Rachel Carson and her detractors, we can see that there was a fundamental difference in orientations toward Nature itself. There were conflicting perspectives about who we are as humankind in relationship to Nature. Simply put, the contrast of viewpoints revolved around:

- Understanding Nature as if it were something we are to master over, controlling it in the way we might control inanimate objects,
- Or, understanding Nature as if it were more like a living community, of which humankind is also a part.

This contrasting "community" view does mean that there would be no attempt to regulate Nature. Even in human communities, we regulate people's behavior (sometimes even putting some people in jail). But when we remember that we live in a community, we treat other people not as objects but as living beings, remembering that they have interests and endeavors of their own. Particularly, we remember that one's own actions can create responses from those other people—even waves of actions throughout the community. Rachel Carson emphasized that living character of Nature when she wrote, "We are dealing with life—with living populations and all their pressures and counter-pressures, their surges and recessions."[20]

Because the focal point of the 1960's dispute was over new pesticides, it might appear that it was a conflict between a pro-technology viewpoint and an anti-technology viewpoint. But that was not the case. Instead, this was a broad split over perspectives that was even dividing the scientific community.

For example, the 16th-century contributions of Francis Bacon included laying out principles of reasoning and evidence that became part of the backbone of modern science. And it was also science's tools, not just appeals to the public's heart, that Carson depended upon as she gathered scientific evidence against trying to control Nature through widespread use of the new pesticides. However, Francis Bacon (as well as some other leaders of modern science as it emerged) strongly endorsed the mastering of Nature. Bacon said that the purpose of science was, "to endeavor to establish and extend the power and dominion of the human race itself over the universe."[21] In stark contrast, Rachel Carson asserted in a television interview:

> We still talk in terms of conquest.... We still haven't
> become mature enough to think of ourselves as only a
> tiny part of a vast and incredible universe. But man is

part of nature and his war against nature is inevitably a war against himself.[22]

Even more fascinating, and even harder to have predicted, were the revealing statements feminist theologians and feminist historians discovered in their re-examination of traditional attitudes toward Nature. Before 17th-century science developed mechanical models of the universe, it was common for Nature to be depicted as a fertile and nurturing mother. Female imagery was also employed by Francis Bacon in his explanation of the orientation he thought the new science and technology should take toward Nature. But his feminine imagery was instead the language of domination. Francis Bacon, drawing upon highly suggestive domination-imagery, said that Nature should be "forced out of her natural state," and that we should "make her your slave."[23]

In the 1960's and 1970's, some feminist theologians drew attention to parallels between hierarchies that made a sharp dualism between male and female, and hierarchies that made a sharp dualism between humans and animals. In such dualistic hierarchies, as one writer explains, "The second part ... [is made] inferior to and in the service of the first.... Hence, women serve men;... animals serve humans."[24]

Some of the feminist theologians and writers who saw parallels in domineering attitudes over Nature and over women also noticed the contemptuous tone toward Rachel Carson's being a nature-writer, a woman, or both. Her critics frequently used words that were more often employed to deride women than to deride men. Besides the derision of her as a "spinster," Rachel Carson was frequently criticized as being "shrill," "irrational," and "emotional."[25]

Given the long tradition of domination of women and of Nature, what a joy it was for women in the early 1980's to discover Hildegard of Bingen—a woman who provided a vision of Nature as a community, of which human beings were a part. Most 20th-century Christians in the U.S. had experienced Christian theologies that had talked almost exclusively about God's relation to humans and about human salvation. To such Christians, it was eye-opening to hear Hildegard's many sweeping cosmic visions of the work of God's Spirit. In some of these, Hildegard points to the "verdure" of plants, meaning the lush greenness of flourishing vegetation. Such as this vision in which God's Holy Spirit says:

> I am that living and fiery essence
> of the divine substance
> that flows in the beauty of the fields,
> I shine in the water,
> I burn in the sun and the moon and the stars.
> Mine is the mysterious force of the invisible wind.
> I sustain the breath of all living.
> I breathe in the verdure,
> and in the flowers,
> and when the waters flow like living things,
> it is I.[26]

Here was a picture not of a distant God in heaven, making decisions about human salvation. This was a God present in and sustaining all of life, human and non-human alike.

Other statements of Hildegard even expressed philosophically that insight of the mutual interrelatedness of everything in the universe, of which the biologist Rachel Carson had also reminded people in the case of unsuccessful attempts to eradicate insects. Such as Hildegard of Bingen's statement:

> God has arranged all things in the world
> in consideration of everything else.[27]

Insights from Three People's Roles

Thus it was that looking back over the past half-century, we can see how the re-discovery and greater appreciation of two medieval religious thinkers was brought about in part by science's development and extensive use of modern pesticides following World War II. For a Christianity in the latter 20th century that was being challenged by the growing environmental movement's questions about its theology, St. Francis of Assisi and Hildegard of Bingen provided glimpses into an appealing vision of the community of all of God's creation. A oneness of a cosmic community.

The way this re-discovery occurred is something no theologian in the first half of the 20th century could have predicted. St. Francis and Hildegard had lived centuries before the leaders of the Scientific Revolution. And so, in the first half of the 20th century, ways of thinking such as theirs had seemed outdated to a modern mindset heavily influenced by the advancement of science. But in the latter part of that century, in light of what Rachel Carson had shown about pesticides' effects upon Nature, the perspectives of those two medieval thinkers looked new, relevant, and fresh.

The changes in thinking and sensibilities that occurred with the rise of environmental consciousness did not, however, take place through religion supplanting science, any more than science had supplanted religion in the first half of the 20th century. Nor did the changes in mindset occur through a dominance of new experience over tradition. Nor of tradition over experience. In this story of modern pesticides and medieval Christian thinkers, we see a complex interplay of science and religion. And an interplay of new experiences with ancient faith-tradition.

Chapter 15
Time, Darwin, and the Family Tree

I t was a warm June in 1877. A British family—elderly grandfather, his wife, their grown son, baby grandson, and a nurse-
maid—had all traveled on an outing to the ancient site of
Stonehenge. It was the sort of recreation a Victorian family of the
latter 1800's would engage in to enjoy being outdoors in the
warmer weather, while also appreciating their British heritage. By
that part of the 19th century, traveling farther away from home had
been made much easier by the expansion of railways. And this
particular family's trip to Stonehenge in southern England had
entailed only a two-hour train ride followed by an hour-and-a- half
coach ride.

And so, the only major anxiety during this particular family's
trip to Stonehenge involved the sixty-eight-year-old grandfather's
health problems (which had plagued him most of his adult life).
Before they had departed from home, his wife had written to their
grown daughter that she was afraid the Stonehenge outing would
"half kill" the old man.[1] Fortunately, it did not. The Stonehenge
outing went quite well. Moreover, while they were at the ancient
site of Stonehenge, consisting of a ring of megaliths (massive
standing stones) probably constructed four-thousand years ago, the
elderly grandfather got permission from the guard to do something
probably no other tourist had requested: to dig into the ground
around some of the stones. As odd as that request was, the guard
could hardly refuse it. For, after all, that bearded grandfather was
none other than Charles Darwin, who by this time, two decades
after the publication of *Origin of Species*, had become a celebrity.

If anybody had observed the old man digging into the ground,
they might have thought that he was searching for ancient artifacts
from the civilization that had erected Stonehenge's giant megaliths. But instead, of all things, he was looking in the ground for
earthworms.

Charles Darwin's interest in earthworms had begun forty years earlier, when he was a young man, and it would continue to the very end of his life, becoming the topic of his very last book published during his lifetime. Earthworms had been just one of the multitudes of types of animals Darwin examined as he accumulated evidence for his revolutionary theory about how all species on Earth had evolved from a common origin.

Time Stretching Back

Sixteen-hundred years ago, the Christian bishop St. Augustine wrote that he knew what time was as long as nobody asked him about it; but if he tried to explain time, he found that he did not know what it is.[2] Centuries later, the 20th-century theologian Paul Tillich wrote:

> The life of each of us, is permeated in every moment,
> in every experience, and in every expression, by the
> mystery of time. Time is our destiny. Time is our hope.
> Time is our despair. And time is the mirror in which
> we see eternity.[3]

Given the way that time permeates our lives, it is unfortunate that introductory Christian theologies do not focus on it at greater length. This chapter will explore the matter of time through the lens of the life of Charles Darwin and the changing society in which he lived. In so doing, it will reveal the differences between modern science's mathematical approach and our psychological and spiritual experiences, in which time varies and is mysterious. We will also uncover something about the non-human realm.

In a way, it was with the matter of digging into the ground that a 19th-century revolution in science had begun. The practice of delving into the ground had begun even before Darwin's revolutionary book *Origin* was published in 1859. And began even before Darwin as a young man had boarded H.M.S. *Beagle* for his landmark voyage of discovery around the globe. The 19th-century revolution in science had begun not with a search for earthworms, or for any other biological species. Instead, it had begun with the science of geology.

In the late 1700's, the Scottish geologist James Hutton developed the principle that geological features displayed in cliffs and landscapes—as huge as they sometimes are—had come about through the very processes we observe about us today, but over an immense amount of time. That principle was further developed by the British scientist Charles Lyell, who gathered evidence for it, which he made public in his book *Principles of Geology*, published in the early 1830's.

Most people in the world today are acquainted with Charles Darwin as a biologist, knowing something about his having developed the explanation of how biological species evolved. However, on his pivotal journey on H.M.S. *Beagle*, even before he reached the famous Galapagos Islands northwest of South America, Darwin and his fellow voyagers landed to the northeast of that continent on the Cape Verde Islands. There they saw layers of rocks that had been deposited on the seabed before being lifted up out of the sea. Darwin had brought with him on the voyage a copy of Charles Lyell's book on geology. Darwin's observations at Cape Verde, as well as at other places the *Beagle* landed in South America, helped make Darwin a believer in Lyell's theory that immense geological formations had been created through the slow accumulation of processes still going on today.

Once back in England, Darwin established his scientific reputation first as a geologist before concentrating on biology.

The real challenge the expanding geological timeline posed was that of comprehending the incomprehensibly long time-span in which humans were absent. Contrary to our contemporary "warfare" myth about religion-science relationships, it was *not* that scientists had been slavishly adhering to a short timeline based upon the Bible's genealogies read literally.[4] From its first centuries, Christians and Jews had read their Scriptures in allegorical, spiritual, and other non-literal ways.[5] That kind of adjustment that allowed for new scientific knowledge was similarly made by many people in this instance as they read the Bible's book of Genesis.[6] The major difficulty was instead that until the emergence of the science of geology in the latter 1700's, the only timelines available were human records about human civilizations and history dating back no more than several thousand years.

Now, however, with Hutton's and Lyell's geological research, a longer geological timeline was being appended to that record of human civilization. And the human timeline was looking minuscule in comparison. Today, most educated people are acquainted with the idea that scientists' calculation of the age of the Earth is incomprehensibly long, and that the Earth existed for an immensely long time before humans were around. But before Hutton's and Lyell's discoveries, the longest timeline people were accustomed to thinking in terms of was maybe back 6,000 years. The phrase "deep time" would not be coined for yet another century-and-a-half.[7]

And so, to many people in the early 1800's, hearing about the new geological timeline was like having the ground split open beneath their feet. They found themselves falling into an enormous abyss. Today, we might sense something of that falling sensation in the geologist James Hutton's startling words that the new emerging geology, in searching into the timeline carved in the rocks, could find "no vestige of a beginning, no prospect of an end."[8]

Charles Darwin, in contrast, needed time. He needed a long time-span for the Earth's history to provide enough time in which evolution could have brought about the great complexity of species in the world. He also needed time after his return from the *Beagle's* voyage in which he could gather more biological evidence to support the theory of evolution by natural selection he was developing.

Even though he needed time to do more research, Darwin did make a decision fairly quickly about another matter in his life. Only three years after returning from his voyage on the *Beagle*, he made a major, lasting change in his life: He proposed marriage to his cousin Emma Wedgwood, a religiously devout, intelligent, and trustworthy woman. She accepted, and they were married in only six months. She would give birth to ten children, of whom seven would live into adulthood (a ratio fairly typical of that age in which there were no modern antibiotics).

Tumultuous Times

Time was also a concern of the changing British society that surrounded and enfolded Charles Darwin as he worked on his scientific investigations and began raising a family. Great Britain's expanding empire during the 19th century was fueled by that nation's dominance in the production of coal and iron, which in turn fueled an expansion in industry and transportation. Just as had been the case for centuries, scientific discoveries were propelled by the technologies they could produce—but now at an ever faster pace. Industrialization in the late 1700's and into the 1800's created new kinds of jobs, bringing more people into the cities. Even though British society still showed extremes of rich and poor, it seemed as if society was also changing ever-faster during this industrial revolution.

The rapid changes in both commerce and intellectual thought during the 19th century were manifested in new words that were entering the English language: "railway," "megalith," "archaeology," and "dinosaur."

The rapid industrialization of Britain and rapid movement of people into cities had, however, turned London into a polluted, dirty, and overcrowded city. In 1819, the poet Percy Shelley had concluded that:

> Hell is a city much like London—
> A populous and smoky city.[9]

Only three years into their marriage, Charles and Emma Darwin's own house was getting crowded, just like London. Now having two children and a third one on the way, they decided to move to the village of Downe eighteen miles to the southeast of London. Living in Downe would also be more like the rural surroundings they had both grown up in. Charles enjoyed turning his attention to Nature and thinking about it. A key consideration, however, in Charles and Emma's move was that Downe, although being rural, was close enough to London for Charles to meet periodically with his scientific colleagues who lived in the city. Only a few decades earlier, Downe would not have seemed as close. But the rapid expansion of railways had already changed the pace and structure of British life.

But with change came tension over how much British society should be allowed to change. At the very time that Charles and Emma Darwin had been living in London, British troops had moved through the city on their way to put down labor riots in the city of Manchester.

Moreover, the stability of British society was widely believed to be rooted in the stability of Nature itself. British society was arranged in a hierarchy of fixed roles. And wasn't Nature also a fixed hierarchy with each species assigned a stable identity by

God?

Today, many Christians enjoy singing the hymn "All Things Bright and Beautiful," which begins by describing the order of Nature:

All things bright and beautiful,
All creatures great and small....

Few people realize that a now abandoned verse of that hymn had grounded the hierarchy of British society in that orderly, hierarchical Nature:

The rich man in his castle
The poor man at his gates
God made them, high and lowly
And ordered their estates.[10]

What would happen to the order of society if Nature, its supposed foundation, were discovered to be not permanent after all, but instead evolving?

One change in British society everybody seemed to benefit from, however, was that expansion of railways. Along with it came the expansion of the postal service, networking its way with railway and horse-coach routes. That postal service brought mail daily to the door of Darwin's home, Down House. There, Charles Darwin corresponded with literally thousands of people across the world, gathering scientific evidence in the form of observations and samples of plants and animals.

It was in that way, along with doing his own experiments at home, that Darwin was able to accumulate little by little the massive amounts of evidence that went into his revolutionary book *Origin of Species*. In total, two decades of work studying almost everything from pigeons to plumed seeds to parasites. (He even spent eight years doing microscopic research on hundreds of species of barnacles.)[11] All this research at home supplemented the scientific samples and data he had previously gathered during his voyage on the *Beagle* to such places as the Galapagos Islands, where he had observed iguanas, giant tortoises, and tiny finches, all with their clues about how species diverged.

By the time he was fifty, Darwin was both the father of seven children, and the published author of the most important theory in biology: evolution by natural selection.

Fleeting Efforts

However, in *Origin of Species*, in order to explain how species could have evolved, Darwin, had to remind his readers of that incomprehensible span of time that stretched out of sight into the past. Darwin's description of that vast time-span even evoked the melancholy many people had felt as they sensed the contrast between the countless centuries before human civilization and the relatively short time in which human civilization was known to have existed. Darwin wrote:

> How fleeting are the wishes and efforts of man! how
> short his time! and consequently how poor will his
> products be, compared with those accumulated by
> Nature during whole geological periods.[12]

Darwin's lament in *Origin* over the shortness of time echoed the words of the Christian hymn-writer Isaac Watts a century-and-a-half earlier:

> Time, like an ever rolling stream,
> Soon bears us all away;[13]

Darwin had to explain the even more dismaying message written in the fossils that over long time-spans whole species of life had gone extinct. That disturbing fossil evidence had been accumulating even before *Origin of Species* was published. But Darwin compounded the problem by explaining how the death of individuals and the death of entire species was *essential* to the very process of evolution by natural selection. Unfit species had to die—had to go extinct—to make room for the growth of those individuals and species that were more fit.

Since before written history, people knew their individual lives and the lives of individual animals came to an end. But before Darwin explained how extinction occurred, there had been the reassurance that descendants would carry on families and carry on species. Not anymore, with Darwin's explanation for life! What a shock it was to discover that God's providential care (whatever that might consist of) did not protect even a species from coming to an end.

The poet Alfred, Lord Tennyson voiced the concern of so many in the Victorian age in his poem "In Memoriam," asking:

> Are God and Nature then at strife ...?
> She [Nature] cries ...

"I care for nothing, all shall go." [14]

Even though Tennyson's poem was prompted by the death of one of his closest human friends, it actually contained references to the geologists' "quarried stone." The disturbing message the fossils carried about Nature and extinction wove its way in and out of Tennyson's grieving thoughts.

Thus it was that concerns about the perishability of life were for people of Darwin's era not abstract theological issues but heartfelt concerns, especially in a time in which some of one's family members and friends inevitably died in middle age, or in adolescence, or even in childhood. Charles and Emma Darwin were not exempt. Three of their ten children never reached adolescence.

One consolation the Church gave to people for such losses was to say that one purpose for suffering was to help us strengthen our moral character. But Charles Darwin could not accept that idea of God sending suffering to build moral character because his awareness ranged wider, remembering that other animals suffered as well. Two decades before *Origin of Species* was published, Charles Darwin had jotted in one of his notebooks the revolutionary scientific insight:

> Animals—our fellow brethren in pain, disease, death, suffering and famine,... they may partake from ... one common ancestor, we may be all *netted together*.[15]

Apes, Ancestors, and the Lowly

Darwin's groundbreaking book *Origin of Species* made only one oblique reference to the possibility of human evolution. Nevertheless, after the publication of *Origin,* most people's minds did turn to evolution's implications for humans, particularly the question of human ancestry. Darwin's theory of evolution was almost immediately dubbed "the ape theory," based on its seeming implication that humans had apes for ancestors. Cartoonists had fun depicting the very gentle man Darwin as some ape-like half-human.

The reasons for this shock can be traced back in Western culture. Despite the Bible's emphasis on commonality of humans and other mortals, Western Christian culture had generally come to think of the human moral consciousness as something in a quite different category than the brain itself. And Western scientific thought following the Scientific Revolution of the 17th century had been strongly influenced by the thinking of the 17th-century philosopher René Descartes, who had drawn an absolute contrast between body and soul. At one point, Descartes had written that:

> It is more probable that worms and flies and
> caterpillars move mechanically than that they all have
> immortal souls.[16]

Thus, both scientific and religious thought had come to treat humans as being in a different category of beings from other animals.

Only four years after the publication of *Origin of Species*, with its unspoken implication that humans and apes shared a common ancestry, two of Darwin's scientific colleagues (the geologist Charles Lyell and the more famous biologist Thomas Henry Huxley) did turn their attentions to the controversial topic of humans' having evolved from primates. And about two decades later, Darwin would publish one book on the topic of humans (*The Descent of Man* in 1871). However, for most of the remainder of his life, Darwin concentrated on other species of life with which humans are "netted together" in an even more ancient evolutionary past. Darwin studied orchids. And microscopic barnacles. And the object of his search at the ancient site of Stonehenge—earthworms.

The combined concerns that had been so much a part of Darwin's life—concerns about time and family ties—converged on that summer day in 1877 on which Charles Darwin, now an elderly grandfather, along with his wife Emma, their grown son, and baby grandson made their trip to Stonehenge. That was the outing in which Charles Darwin made his unusual request to be allowed to dig into the ground around the stone monuments so that he might dig deeper into humans' evolutionary past by investigating the soil's earthworms. As might befit such slow-moving creatures, the book Darwin would write on earthworms would be the culmination of his longest-running research project.

The year before Charles Darwin died, two outspoken and militant atheists, who mistook Darwin's religious views for being too much like their own, asked if they might meet with Darwin. After all, it seemed as if British society was changing so rapidly that it was also time to wake people up to the realization that Darwin's revolutionary theory had (supposedly) unmasked Christianity as a falsehood. They desired a meeting with Darwin even though he had never claimed to be an atheist.[17] He had even said he thought a person could accept evolution and still believe in God.[18]

In their after-dinner conversation, one of the atheists, Edward Aveling, asked Charles Darwin why he was involved in an exploration of something as "insignificant" as earthworms (to use the atheist's word). Darwin, unflustered, replied, "I have been studying their habits for forty years."[19]

Darwin's earthworm research had begun in 1842, the very first year he and his family had moved into Down House. The young Charles Darwin had spread a layer of chalk dust over the surface of a pasture near his family's house, but not to fertilize the ground, as one might expect. Instead, so that he could see how long it would take for the worms' tilling actions to lift processed soil upwards, thus burying the chalk to a measured distance below the surface of the ground. (In the same way that Stonehenge's standing stones would have thereby settled faster over time.)

Darwin did most of his research at home, and he would sometimes engage his children in the scientific experiments. That tradition of family involvement continued even once Charles' and Emma's children were grown. And, as Darwin's research on earthworms intensified toward the end of his life, the investigations became a truly multi-generational project. When it came to the matter of finding out if worms could hear, pots of worms were brought into the house, and all the family's musical abilities were called into play. For many years, Emma's piano playing had been a way to comfort her husband Charles after a day of intense work despite his chronic illness. Now, however, the piano was put to use to serenade the worms. Charles's grown son Frank played his bassoon to them. And even little grandson Bernard sounded a metal whistle.

Alas, it was discovered that worms could not hear. That earthworm disability, however, made it even more astonishing that the little creatures could accomplish so much. It was Charles Darwin who made the first detailed discoveries about matters that are commonly known today: such as that earthworms are one of the major aerators of soil and also one of its main fertilizers.

Darwin uncovered how burrowing earthworms ingested and

excreted material in the soil as they progressed forward, creating vast networks of tiny underground tunnels as much as seven feet below ground. Into these burrows the earthworms would at night pull leaves that had fallen onto the surface of the ground, using those leaves to line their burrows and sometimes plug the tops. Darwin even did experiments substituting triangular pieces of paper for the leaves to confirm that the worms had a way of identifying the narrow end of the leaf (or paper cutout) so as to pull that end in first.

Besides stating that earthworms have "some degree of intelligence," Darwin proposed that they were in some way sociable, having, as he put it, "a trace of social feeling," because, as he observed, they can be seen "crawling over each other's bodies."[20]

Earthworms' Contribution to History

Despite such recreational moments in their lives, the hardworking earthworms as Charles Darwin described them almost seemed to be models of the Protestant work ethic. Darwin explicitly made a comparison between human labor and that of worms when he wrote:

> The plough [plow] is one of the most ancient and most
> valuable of man's inventions; but long before he
> existed the land was in fact regularly ploughed, and
> still continues to be thus ploughed by earth-worms. It
> may be doubted whether there are many other animals
> which have played so important a part in the history of
> the world, as have these lowly organized creatures.[21]

Thus it was that Darwin saw in earthworms the same principle that had been discerned by the revolutionary modern geologists: namely, that immense change can result from the accumulation of small changes, given vast stretches of time.

The word "ecology" was not introduced into the biological sciences until seven years after the publication of *Origin*, and would not become an established word until after Darwin's death.[22] Nevertheless, Darwin, with his theory of evolution and with his earthworms research, was laying the foundation for the science of ecology. He did so by showing how species evolve by creating dynamic networks of relationships between themselves and other species, and between themselves and the inanimate material that surrounds them.

Even though Darwin's most famous book *Origin of Species* had sold well, Darwin's small book on earthworms, titled *The Formation of Vegetable Mould, through the Actions of Worms*, turned out to be his most popular book during his lifetime. It was something of a publishing marvel. It sold 3,500 copies in only the first two months, and 8,000 copies in its first two years.

Also, despite the more famous book *Origin* having raised outcries about humans' having possibly evolved from lower animals, this final book of Darwin's—about one of the seemingly lowest of animals—evoked for the most part a fascination and even admiration for the little terrestrial creatures. Even the botanist Joseph Hooker, Director for many years of Kew Royal Botanic Gardens in London, was impressed by Darwin's uncovering the industriousness of earthworms. Hooker wrote to Darwin:

> I had always looked on worms as amongst the most
> helpless and unintelligent members of the creation; and
> am amazed to find that they have a domestic life and
> public duties! [23]

Darwin's earlier books had provided raw material for the humorous cartoonists of *Punch* magazine. So also did Darwin's little book on earthworms. But now the tone had changed. Whereas two decades earlier *Punch* had turned Darwin into a laughable half-monkey, this time the cartoonist placed the elderly Darwin on a throne at the center of all of life. (See Figure 14.) Even though the cartoon was titled with the uncomplimentary remark "Man is but a worm," it depicted a clear evolution to the human race. Emerging out of chaos, first a worm appears, out of which reptile-like creatures evolve, then monkeys, then a caveman, then a British gentleman with top hat, and finally Darwin himself enthroned at the center.

More subtle than this nod of recognition to Darwin's achievements was the presence of that element that had made such evolution possible: At the base of the circle of evolution can be read the word's "Time's Meter," and in the background is a clock's face labeled "thousands of centuries." Time. Vast stretches of time.

An Unreturning Past

As he approached the end of his life, Charles Darwin had

Figure 14: Punch cartoon

established a legacy of over twenty books, a large family, many friendships, and the most important theory modern biology has ever seen. Throughout his adult life, despite his chronic illness, Charles Darwin always had a major scientific project to work on. Now, however, with the earthworms book behind him, given his age and decline in strength, he knew there were no further major projects ahead. During his lifetime, scientists had clearly stretched the Earth's timeline back at least a hundred-thousand years. But the time ahead for Darwin was now very short. In the autobiographical reflections penned toward the end of his life,

Charles Darwin, recalling the days when his children were very young, wrote, "I think with a sigh that such days can never return."[24]

In the same way that the past years of Darwin's life were a world he could no longer return to, so also did the past eons of fossilized species constitute an age that could never be returned to. Before Darwin, natural scientists of the previous century had imagined that Nature would always return to a set harmony of fixed species. After Darwin, scientists had to recognize that Nature was always changing, evolving, the past never returning.

In the end, after seventy-three years of life, Charles Darwin died at Down House, with members of his family nearby. At the very last, he was held by his beloved wife Emma, who had been his support through work and chronic illness for forty-two years.

Although many years before his death, Charles Darwin had abandoned attending church (leaving that regular practice to his wife), he nonetheless desired to be buried in the cemetery beside the modest country church at Downe. It was in that village church, after all, that were buried two of his and Emma's children as well as his brother Erasmus, who had died a year before Charles.

Charles Darwin's wish for a final resting place was, however, not to be. Larger forces were at play in British society. Even a decade before Darwin's death, many church leaders and all major scientists had come to accept some form of evolutionary explanation for life, even if they were not sure how large a part natural selection played.[25] The explanatory power of the new ideas in biology, following close upon the heels of the new geology, had begun transforming the halls of academia. Science had begun to have dominance over teaching Latin, Greek, and the classics. And what better way to celebrate that academic victory than to give the scientist Charles Darwin a funeral fit for a national hero!

Some of Darwin's former colleagues, working with some church leaders, quickly made alternative funeral arrangements, rather than Darwin's being buried in Downe. They got permission from Darwin's closest family for his body to be given a state funeral in London in Westminster Abbey. And so, despite his wishes, his body was lowered not into the soft soil of the Downe churchyard, but instead into an opening in the cold marble floor of a 14th-century cathedral. Sealed off from the soil with polished stone.

And while the scientists and friends and statesmen sat in Westminster Abbey, back in the village of Downe, in the churchyard of its old flint church, the earthworms made temporarily famous by Darwin continued their work beneath the soil. Just as they and their earthworm ancestors had done for over 100 million years.

And thousands of miles away, on the Galapagos Islands, iguanas, and giant tortoises, and tiny finches continued their own lives and endeavors, just as their ancestors had done for hundreds of millions of years.

And across the oceans encircling the Earth, barnacles, barely visible to the naked eye, continued their hidden lives, the way their barnacle ancestors had for half a billion years before them.

And all of them—humans and non-humans—were, and still are, "all netted together."

Chapter 16
When All the World's Not a Stage

In the early 1950's, the British Royal Air Force, as part of a rescue mission, began parachuting cats into the Pacific island of Borneo. Their bizarre action was the outcome of a chain of events that stands as an example of the environmental horror stories that became increasingly frequent in the second half of the 20th century.

The problem began when the World Health Organization had tried to eradicate mosquitoes by spraying DDT. But that insecticide also killed parasitic wasps that had been keeping a population of thatch-eating caterpillars in check. With the wasp population reduced, the caterpillar population exploded, and the thatch roofs on the houses of the native people began to disintegrate. As if that were not bad enough, DDT-poisoned insects were eaten by gecko lizards, which were in turn eaten by cats. With the cats thus poisoned to death, the rats multiplied, resulting in typhus and plague outbreaks.

Thus it was that the British Royal Air Force was called upon to parachute cats into Borneo in an urgent attempt to stop the unraveling of not only thatch houses but also the safety-net of life itself.[1]

The "Stage" Metaphor
Our environmental problems have caused many people to ask questions about what assumptions and sensibilities have been underlying Western culture over the past few centuries. One of the most pervasive attitudes uncovered has been the "stage" metaphor for Nature. (Throughout this book I am for clarity's sake capitalizing the word "Nature" when I refer to the non-human realm of other animals, plants, and the inanimate.) Modern Western thinking has usually viewed human history as taking place on a stage, with Nature being either the stage or backdrop for the human drama—thus making a strong distinction between human history and Nature.

As one leading professor of history, Herbert Butterfield, wrote in a book in 1950, the historian does not treat humanity "as essentially a part of nature" but instead "envisages [i.e., envisions] a world of human relations standing, so to speak, over against nature.... We may say that history is a human drama ... taking place as it were on the stage of nature."[2] Donald Worster, also a historian, examined the problems this approach had created, and explained in 1993 that it had become "the way we organize our academic life. Nature and history have become separate areas of specialization."[3] Worster graphically wrote:

> The *standard* account of American history has become
> a lot like the deodorized, fluorescent-lit, saran-
> wrapped supermarkets of the nation, where one can
> push a cart up and down the aisles every week and
> never be stimulated to wonder where the milk or bread
> comes from on which our politics, our heroes and
> villains, our social order, ... [and] our economic life,
> have fed.[4]

It is not just historians who had fallen prey to treating Nature as if it were only a detached backdrop for the human drama. It had become (and often remains) part of our modern, Western way of thinking.[5]

However, environmental problems, such as those requiring the Borneo cat-drop, have revealed the faultiness of that "stage" way of thinking. The science of ecology teaches us that our human lives are *inseparable* from Nature and deeply interpenetrated by it. The very oxygen each of us is breathing right now has been created by trees and other plants. The fact that each of us is able to move is made possible by our bodies' metabolizing the plants and animals we had for breakfast and dinner last night into the very elements of our own bodies. Nature is not merely a stage for our lives.

Beginning in the last quarter of the 20th century, a growing ecological awareness led to scientists, religious writers, and philosophers all examining humans' relationships with Nature. Much more than environmental problems have been explored. Those still-ongoing discussions center around several constellations of issues. This chapter will bring into focus some of those constellations one by one, beginning with those related more to the environment, and then moving on to those that involve human nature and spirituality.

Tracing the Un-ecological Strands

The wide-ranging discussions have led many writers to the conclusion that our environmental problems are not simply due to inefficient technology, but are instead rooted in our culture's attitudes toward Nature. We inhabit this Earth not only with our bodies and actions, but also with our minds, feelings, and sensibilities. A small vocabulary of terms has emerged, tracing the strands of thought that have contributed to our current situation. Here are those words, with a clarification of each, and a relevant sample quotation by some current writer.

Utilitarianism: The Scientific Revolution of the 17th century, as well as subsequent scientific knowledge, have gone hand-in-hand with technology. That coupling has helped cultivate an attitude that the value of things in Nature comes from their usefulness to us. That is, their **utilitarian value** (in contrast with their having any **intrinsic value** by themselves). *"Humans must inevitably be consumers of nature, but they can and ought sometimes be more admirers of nature.... Humans [can] enjoy natural things in as much diversity as possible—and enjoy them, at times, because such creatures flourish in themselves."*[6] (Holmes Rolston, III.)

Mechanical Worldview: With the expansion of our modern form of science in the 17th and 18th centuries, the non-human world was more and more viewed as operating mechanically, like a machine. *"[René] Descartes and other writers of the period abandoned any notion of nature as an organic entity and compared it to a mechanism, such as a clock (an image popularized by Robert Boyle).... Descartes stated...: 'There exists nothing in the whole of nature which cannot be explained in terms of purely physical causes, totally devoid of mind and thought.' "*[7] (Alister McGrath.) Descartes, one of the leading developers during that time of modern ways of thinking, preserved a place for human freedom—but only by drawing a strong contrast between humans, who have minds, and animals, which in his thinking did not.[8] (Such a mind-body divide has come to be referred to as **dualism**.)

History-Nature Split: During the 18th-century period we call the Enlightenment, human history came to be thought of as being that of progress forward brought about by human reason and science—in contrast to the recurring cycles of Nature, which more and more were thought of as being just in the background. That split came to infect other academic fields, including economics. So much so that by the 20th century, *"Nobel Prize winners could claim, without risk to reputations, that 'the world can, in effect, get along without natural resources.' "*[9] (J. R. McNeill.)

Urbanization: Over the past century-and-a half in the United States, the number of people living in cities and towns (rather than on farmlands) has grown from 20% to 80%.[10] Such urbanization has placed Nature and the land upon which people's lives depend further in the background of most people's thoughts. *"We no longer have a deep concept of place as a repository of meaning, history,... and sacred memory.... We are increasingly indoor people whose sense of place is indoor space and whose minds are increasingly shaped by electronic stimuli."*[11] (David W. Orr.)

Economism: As European society changed with the growth of science and technology, the 18th-century economist Adam Smith raised the question of how modern society should be arranged. In a nutshell, Smith's formula was that a society would become its best if individuals, acting in their own self-interest, seek greater wealth. Therefore, a society's success could be measured by the degree to which natural resources are moved into production and consumption as goods. In the 20th century, *"economists evolved Gross National Product (GNP)*[12] *as a measure of the amount of production, consumption and investment.... [But] GNP, measuring the size of an economy, includes many items that are not benefits to society as a whole. For example, the shorter the life of cars, and the more often they break down, the greater will be the amount of activity in an economy ... which is reflected in GNP figures."*[13] (Clive Ponting.)

Growthism: Despite E. F. Schumacher having reminded everybody with his 1989 book's title that *Small is Beautiful,*[14] "bigger" and "growth" remain favorable words in modern Western thought (and increasingly in non-Western countries as they become technologized). But the Earth is finite. And the number of species on this planet has been decreasing from human impact. Thus, human history and Nature in this regard have been put on different trajectories, even though we cannot live without air, water, and food from Nature.

Consumerism: Coupled with natural resources being turned into commodities, and economic growth seeming to be the formula for making society better, our roles in modern Western society have become increasingly that of being consumers. *"It's not surprising, I guess, that we muddle symbols and reality. We are told every day that owning a big car makes one an important person, that wearing fashionable clothes makes one more attractive, that having lots of things bought with credit cards makes one well off."*[15] (Donella Meadows.)

The re-examination of attitudes and sensibilities has also revealed ways that religion has been involved in Nature's being turned into a backdrop. Christianity has undergone the most intensive re-examination, it being the dominant faith-tradition in the modern West. The central finding is that over the past five-hundred years, Christianity has fallen prey to an **anthropocentrism**. That is, a human-centeredness, particularly in its focus having become narrowed down to human psychology or human society. As the theologian Elizabeth Johnson laments, "The theme of the natural world, called 'creation' when it is viewed in relation to God, got lost in Christian tradition."[16]

Why did this occur? Besides the broader cultural strands that have been outlined above, some inter-tangled strands within Christian history were influenced by changes in society and in science. From the earliest centuries of Christianity, one of the sources of revelation was considered to be Nature itself—what was sometimes called the "Book of Nature." That tradition helped keep Nature from falling into the background. However, after the 15th-century invention of Gutenberg's printing press, the book of Nature declined in importance as the Bible grew in importance and became the dominant source of revelation. Unfortunately, the Protestant Reformation (which overlapped the beginnings of the 17th-century Scientific Revolution) accelerated this decline of the "Book of Nature." The leading reformers held up the Bible as an alternative authority to that of the Roman Catholic hierarchy. The historian Peter Harrison explains that leading Protestant reformers such as "Luther and Calvin ... wished to argue that the Scripture was a *sufficient* source for our knowledge of God and his will."[17] Nature would more and more be turned over to science, and less and less be a source for encountering meanings about God and our relation to God.

The 20th-century theologian Jürgen Moltmann explains how this direction of Protestantism at first seemed helpful, but turned out to have been disastrous from our contemporary ecological standpoint:

> This Reformation tendency to interpret the biblical
> traditions in light of human and indeed personal
> questions of salvation was subsequently felt to be
> liberating, and is occasionally still seen as such
> today.... [But] theology's domain became the soul's
> assurance of salvation in the inner citadel of the
> heart.... This meant that the calamitous dichotomy
> between the subjectivity of human beings and the
> objective world of 'mere things' was deepened.[18]

This trend actually ran counter to the attitudes within the Bible about Nature. (Matters related to the Bible's contents in this regard are examined in the following Chapter 17, "A Lost Dimension of the Bible.")

Getting Beyond the "Guillotine"

As contemporary thinkers have realized that we cannot treat Nature as just a backdrop to the human drama, another constellation of issues under discussion has been what is called the is-ought problem or the is-ought fallacy. It is so named because it points out the error of thinking that because something *is*, therefore that is how I *ought* to behave. (Sometimes you might hear this fallacy called "the naturalistic fallacy," but in the field of philosophy that label is sometimes reserved for a more specific fallacy, and so I will stick with the more descriptive name of "the is-ought fallacy."[19])

That this leap from "is" to "ought" often involves an error in logic can be best illustrated by giving a statement in which the "is" involves something in human society. Many of us have heard someone say, "Everybody fudges on their taxes, so you shouldn't feel obliged to tell IRS about all your income." Notice how that statement leaps from a situation that supposedly *exists* to an assertion about how I *ought* to behave. But that the one logically (i.e., automatically) follows from the other is simply not the case. Even if everybody else in the U.S. did cheat, it would not *logically* follow that I should do likewise.

In the Western philosophical tradition, the is-ought fallacy was classically laid out by the 18th-century Scottish philosopher David Hume in his *Treatise on Human Nature*. Hume wrote how in reading works about morality, he often found that "the author proceeds for some time in ... [making] observations concerning human affairs; when of a sudden I am surpriz'd to find that" the author is making only statements that are "connected with an *ought*, or an *ought not*." Hume complains "that a reason should be given" for such a jump into moral statements, but usually no such reason is given.[20]

An example of the is-ought fallacy based on the social realm (such as the one about cheating on taxes) is more obvious in its flawed thinking. Things get trickier when we move to is-ought fallacies based on the biological realm. Here is where this logical fallacy involves matters of religion-science relationships. That is because today we turn to science to give us so much knowledge about the world that *is*, and religion has as one of its concerns that of how we *ought* to behave. Addressing the is-ought issue is thus one way of trying to find proper procedures for linking religion to science.

Here also is where Darwin's theory of evolution led to all sorts of erroneous applications that came to be called "social Darwinism." The various forms of social Darwinism looked at something that exists in the realm of Nature (such as competition for existence between different species), and then concluded that we humans should behave likewise (i.e., competitively), or else we would be resisting the progress of natural evolution. Or so it was claimed. But such a conclusion is simply not proven logically. Just because something exists in Nature does not mean that we human beings should aim to *imitate* it. The contemporary scholar Rod Preece expresses compactly in a visual way the core of the is-ought matter as it involves the non-human sphere:

> Nature provides no convenient passage for allowing
> itself to be used as a moral standard.[21]

(The way social Darwinism helped prompt anti-evolutionist's campaigns against Darwin's theory is laid out in Chapter 4, "An Awkward History.")

So solid did Hume's warning seem—and so extreme and offensive had been many of the offenses of social Darwinism become when viewed in hindsight—that the is-ought fallacy came to be nicknamed "Hume's guillotine." Facts on one side of the blade; ought's on the other.

Although knowing about the is-ought fallacy can keep us on guard against too easy leaps into false conclusions about how we should behave, the prevalence of cautions about the is-ought matter led to its *overuse*. So much so that philosophical thinking became even further cut off from the natural world. Nature became an even more distant backdrop. Why seek facts about Nature, or even about humans' biological nature, if moral decisions ("ought's") are in some self-enclosed sphere apart from the world that is? The professors Jan and Birgitta Tullberg are among recent thinkers who have criticized a simplified overuse of the is-ought thesis. They write that the fallacy

> is a popular ... thesis that can be used to support
> nonrational ideas.... If values and facts are "entirely
> different [from each other]," then the person bringing
> facts into a value discussion commits a fallacy.[22]

The Tullbergs thus point out how the overused "guillotine" had sometimes cut our "head" of values off from the "body" of facts about the world. But facts are obviously needed for good decision-making. As Roger Masters perceptively points out, "When the doctor prescribes a treatment, we don't normally object that this practice [improperly] bridges the logical distinction between the facts of diagnosis and the value of health."[23]

Faith-traditions have customarily seen morality as being in some way rooted in the nature of the world.[24] For centuries, Christian theological thought usually held that morality was not something of humankind's own making, but was grounded in the way God created us and the world. That line of thought reached its apex in the work of the 13th-century Thomas Aquinas. As a contemporary professor of philosophy summarizes it, Aquinas's view was that humans can discover what is moral "by rational reflection on the desires and behaviors that make human existence possible."[25] This was called a "natural law" morality. Although Aquinas emphasized human nature in this regard, in his view both it and Nature were created out of the same eternal law of God.[26]

(It was from this prior use of the phrase "natural law" for a natural ground for morality that 17th-century scientists developed the habit of referring to the recurring patterns they discovered in the physical universe as being the "laws of nature."[27] Nature was seen as being obedient to God's laws; more obedient than humans were.)

This general line of thinking about morality within human society continued into the 18th-century Enlightenment, which thought that human reason could uncover a universal set of "natural rights." By the 20th century, however, there was much skepticism about whether a universal ethic could be developed. Moreover, "existential philosophers, such as Sartre and Nietzsche, have [even] held that there is no such thing as human nature."[28] The isolation of human moral decision-making from the natural world had reached an extreme. Our "ought's" had been separated from an "is-ness" about the world. Hume's guillotine had descended.[29]

Fortunately, our modern environmental crisis came to our rescue, forcing many people into the realization that we cannot separate our human sphere from Nature. With the benefit of hindsight, we can now see more clearly another weakness in the natural-law tradition's effort to ground morality in some sort of knowledge about the world. As James Nash writes:

> One of the significant defects in the natural law tradition, both classical and contemporary versions, is that it generally forgot that humans are *ecological* animals.... Nearly all of the diverse expressions of this tradition,... have been strongly anthropocentric [i.e., human-centered].[30]

Thus has the ecologist Nash spotted how the is-ought matter is not just an abstract philosophical conundrum (nor just a caution about paying taxes). Instead, it is part of our modern predicament in imagining that our human lives could be lived apart from Nature.

So, the central question is: How do we re-discover a way of grounding our moral-making in facts about the natural world? How do we get beyond the seeming "guillotine"?

If we re-examine David Hume's classic quotation, we can see that his primary complaint was that people made the jump from "is" to "ought" statements without paying heed to the difference between the two types of statements. He does not say that there could be absolutely no *relationship* between the two. Notice also that Rod Preece's contemporary formulation says that there is "no convenient passage" from Nature to moral standards.[31] But there might be a complex passage we might find. There might be a roundabout passage to ethics and morals from the nature of ourselves and the rest of the natural world.

Among those thinkers who have re-examined philosophical matters in light of ecology, the most thorough and thoughtful has probably been the environmental ethicist Holmes Rolston, III. In one of his books, he provides some very helpful language for describing the type of passage from "is" to "ought" that we need. He suggests re-phrasing the question as, "Should we *follow* Nature?"[32] And he then parses different meanings of the word "follow," delving into which ones do and which ones do not seem sound. He is able to do so because "to follow" can have various meanings. For example, "to follow" something could mean to imitate it (in the way that social Darwinism incorrectly assumed that we should imitate certain behaviors of other species). But "to follow" something can also mean to be guided by it. The core of Rolston's conclusion is:

> It is difficult to propose that humans ought to follow
> nature in an *imitative* ethical sense.... [Nevertheless,]
> we take ourselves to nature and listen for its forms of
> expression.... In this ... sense we ought to follow
> nature, to make its value one among our goals; in so
> doing, our conduct is *guided* by nature.[33]

Rolston thus lays a logical foundation for our following Nature in the sense of being tutored by it.

An illuminative example of learning from Nature is provided by the eco-theologian Thomas Berry. The following example shows the relevance of this extended is-ought discussion, which might otherwise seem merely academic:

> As one woman told a group assembled in Florida after
> Hurricane Andrew, she did not consider herself a
> victim but a participant in this wild event in all its
> creative as well as its destructive aspects. The
> hurricane, she insisted, was telling us something. It
> was telling us how to build our houses if we wished to

dwell in this region. It was telling us to consider well
the winds and the sea, to mark well the fact that if we
live here we must obey the deeper laws of the place,
laws that cannot be overridden by any type of human
zoning.[34]

That Nature can be a guide in the sense of its tutoring us does
not mean that we are freed from the hard task of working out our
values in our relationships to it (drawing also upon aspects of our
human nature). For example, in the case of Florida hurricanes, we
have to work through the risks and costs, not just monetarily but
also in terms of both the expenditures of natural resources and the
social cost. And also, perhaps most importantly, in terms of what
values and sensibilities we are cultivating. Nevertheless, Nature
remains there as an "other"—something that is not us—that stands
ready to teach us. The professor of religious studies Jeffrey C.
Pugh expresses how Thomas Aquinas knew that:

The creation has a voice that is prior to our own, and
we do not hear it.... Thomas was able to see in ways
we cannot that things speak for themselves. Creation
has an eloquence that speaks for itself if we will
listen.[35]

Stories and Proverbs involving Nature

The is-ought fallacy still stands as a caution against making leaps
that have no logical foundation. We cannot simply imitate any
particular thing we see in the vastly variegated sphere we call
"Nature." So what then are we to make of our great inheritance of
forms of literature in which, with moral overtones, some parallel is
drawn between humans and animals? Such as children's stories,
fables, animal-tales, and proverbs—in which animals are put
forward as representing some qualities as moral guidance to
humans? Don't these sorts of literary forms often imply that
animal behavior can show us which human behavior is good, even
moral?

Those literary forms are not identical in their handling of
animals. But a quick look at fables such as Aesop's "The Tortoise
and the Hare" or "The Fox and the Grapes" will show that in them
the animal is merely a stand-in for some caricatured human
behavior. A particular human behavior is being projected onto the

animal, rather than Nature itself providing the moral standard.

In other literary forms, even when the depiction of an animal is less a caricature and more true to its real nature, something peculiar is again going on: The wisdom about which human qualities are favorable and unfavorable has *preceded* the selection of the animal to represent those qualities. Take for example, the Biblical proverb stating that ants "are smallest on earth yet wise beyond the wisest," with the example being given that ants "prepare their store of food in the summer." (Proverbs 30:24-25.)[36] The writer of that proverb would have already known that it was good for humans to store food during the growing time of the year, without having studied ants.

Such literary forms play a role closer to the way other analogies and metaphors operate. That is, the metaphor suggests that there are one or more similarities involved in the comparison being made, but we are required to intuit what they are. Metaphors thus pull us into the possibility of future growth in understanding and insights as we continue to engage with them.

Moreover, analogies to Nature such as these to animals, whatever literary form they come in, do not work just cognitively. They also work upon us emotionally, providing us delight and inspiration. As we make stories and proverbs about Nature more a part of our lives, we become more are a part of the immensely diverse living world. We feel more at home in it.[37]

Our Life and Spirit in Nature

There are thus many constellations of issues that have arisen out of our modern environmental awareness. The psychological and spiritual dimensions of some of these concerns crisscross a significant environmental matter. Namely, that surveys have revealed that the most environmentally concerned adults are not those who as children were taught the most about environmental damage. Instead, the most environmentally concerned adults are those who as children explored wild Nature, and thus came to love it.[38] Also, especially at elementary-level, education focused primarily on environmental damage can backfire because it induces in the child negative associations about Nature—what is called **ecophobia**. As Jennifer Sahn explains in her introduction to David Sobel's book *Beyond Ecophobia*:

> The key is in allowing for a close relationship to
> develop between children and the nature near home
> before laying the weight of the world's plight on their
> shoulders.[39]

So, it turns out that even when it comes to the environment, love is a greater motivation than is fear.

Nature is already part of our lives, whether we are conscious of it or not. The constellations of issues outlined in this chapter all demonstrate the inadequacy of thinking of the non-human world around us as just a stage or backdrop to the human drama. Nature is much more than "the environment" that we affect for better or for worse. The Christian ethicist Margaret Farley brings out the theological element of our relationship with Nature in this way:

> What we may need to do ... is, perhaps, for a time to
> turn away from ourselves and look around us. Only
> when we understand better what God is doing in the
> world of nature may we turn back to ourselves with
> greater wisdom about who we are.... We are
> profoundly interdependent with all other beings in
> nature, yet we are more dependent on the other beings
> than they are on us.[40]

Whether or not we think of the non-human sphere in that way, it has already been penetrating our lives. We might perceive this merely by reflecting upon the role that some element in Nature has played, and still plays, in human lives. Take flowers, for instance.

Flowers can be an earnest business for commercial flower-growers and florists. But it is a flower's enjoyable color, fragrance, and shape that capture an average person's attention. The humorist Mark Twain made the earnest observation that "Whatever a man's age, he can reduce it several years by putting a bright-colored flower in his buttonhole."[41] A wreath of flowers can soften the hard edge of a coffin, thus soothing the hearts of the bereaved. Despite the flower's fragility, symbolizing the transitoriness of life, its reproductive powers bring a hint of life into the acceptance of death. Again, Holmes Rolston:

> For longer than we can ever remember flowers have
> been flung up to argue against the forces of violence
> and death, because that is what they do in and of
> themselves, and thus they serve as so ready a sign for

any who encounter them in a pensive mood.[42]
With their colorful intensity and their message of new life, specific flowers have even gained a prominent role in many of the world's faith-traditions: The light-giving Golden Flower in Taoism. The lily of Easter resurrection in Christianity. And the lotus of life-giving tranquility in Buddhism.

Even beyond their being essential for the reproduction of many plants, flowers are more than a decorative backdrop for our human lives.

Chapter 17
A Lost Dimension of the Bible

In 1994, the noted Old Testament scholar Walter Brueggemann (an always thoughtful and frequently eloquent writer) published a confession. In a paper in *Harvard Theological Review*, Brueggemann yielded to the critique of a less-known Biblical scholar, J. Richard Middleton by writing:

> I am grateful to Richard Middleton for having
> commented upon my work with such care.... On the
> whole, I must *accept* the critique he makes.[1]

Although Walter Brueggemann's terse confession to his academic colleagues received no attention in the general news media, it was in its own way highly significant. And not just for Biblical scholarship. His confession was also significant as part of modern Western Christian theology's response to the effects of science, both bad and good.

The background to the problem was that 20th-century Bible scholarship had fallen under the spell of a way historians—all historians, not just Biblical ones—had come to view the world. Under the influence of modern science's way of thinking, modern Western thought had come to view human history as taking place on a stage with Nature as the stage or backdrop.

As one prominent general historian explained in 1950, "We may say that history is a human drama ... taking place as it were on the stage of nature."[2] That "stage" way of thinking had become widespread not only among historians and Biblical scholars but also among virtually all modern Christian theologians. For example, in 1946, exhibiting that way of thinking, the Christian theologian Emil Brunner wrote:

> The cosmic element in the Bible is never anything
> more than the *scenery* in which the history of mankind
> takes place.[3]

However, (as was explained in the preceding chapter) the "stage" way of thinking about history and Nature has been losing its credibility, and not just in the arena of Biblical scholarship. The faultiness of the "stage" metaphor is being recognized primarily because of our knowledge from the scientific field of ecology. That field reveals how much our human lives are deeply interrelated and interpenetrated by the inanimate and by non-human species of life. Nature is not just a surrounding sphere, backdrop, or stage.

(Throughout this book, for convenience sake, I am using the word "Nature" in the way we commonly use it to refer to plants, animals, and the inanimate—all of the non-human world.)

This chapter will demonstrate how the "stage" way of thinking so strongly influenced 20th-century Biblical scholarship and curricula that the dimension of Nature fell out of sight and became virtually lost. The "stage" way of thinking even came to distort the Biblical message. But in this chapter we will also see how modern science, which had contributed to the narrowing down of Biblical interpretation to a "stage" way of thinking, came to provide knowledge from the field of ecology that encouraged a restoration of the Bible's wider perspective about what we call "history" and "Nature."

Widespread Influence Upon Teaching Materials

Even if you have never heard of the Biblical scholar Brueggemann's confession (most people have not), nor heard the name Walter Brueggemann, you may have encountered in church-school classes the "stage" way of thinking in interpreting the Bible. That is because that way of thinking, having first dominated Biblical scholarship, spread into many widely used Biblical commentaries, handbooks, guides, and church curricula. Sometimes when we study the Bible (just as when we study events in general history classes), we use timelines marking off a series of events of human history in chronological order. And in history classes, we do not usually talk about what Nature is doing. Nature is virtually always just in the background, unnoticed.

Twentieth-century Biblical scholarship actually fell under the spell of an even more severe form of the "stage" way of viewing the world. In that more extreme form, Nature was not merely background but was even thought of *negatively*. Human history came to be seen as being on a linear track of progress, while Nature was imagined as being directionless, repetitive, seasonal cycles in the background. Day, night, day night. Summer, winter, summer, winter.

The consequences for Christian theology can hardly be under-stated. That is because, according to this narrowed way of thinking, God's caring in the Bible came to be thought of as being promises for progress in human history and society—and not promises involving Nature. Here is how that narrowed perspective is explained by the theologian Elizabeth Johnson:

> The modern construal [i.e., interpretation] of history ...
> was pressed into service in Protestant biblical
> interpretation to yield the religious assessment of
> history as the locus of God's mighty saving acts. By
> contrast, nature was seen as the realm of cyclic time
> where pagan deities reigned. Nature thus became not
> only a stage on which the drama of salvation history is
> played out; it even became a symbol of what human
> beings are rescued *from*.[4]

The Biblical scholar Walter Brueggemann even came to view the psalms in the Bible that celebrate all of God's creation as supposedly being oppressive, not liberating. It was at that point that the less-known Biblical scholar J. Richard Middleton called Brueggemann's hand, and Brueggemann's hand came up short.[5]

Not just psalms, but many more sections of the Bible were affected by "stage" thinking. The Bible is an immense collection of writings. And so, for the purposes of this chapter, we will concentrate on just two major themes that arch across the entire Bible. A number of the Biblical passages to be examined come from the Old Testament, which is the Hebrew Bible (*Tanakh*), and so they have implications for Judaism, not just Christianity.

Descriptions of God's Covenant

The first theme we will look at is that of covenant. (A covenant is like a contractual agreement.) It has been a major theme in inter-preting the Bible. Let us look at the entry on the word "Covenant" in *The Dictionary of Bible and Religion* (1986), which has been widely used by pastors and teachers. Its entry on "Covenant" reads in part:

> The term "covenant" translates a Hebrew word in the
> OT [i.e., Old Testament] whose primary meaning is "a
> binding pact" or "a compact".... Most often it refers to

the agreement between God and *humans*, for example,
Noah (Gen. 9:9-17).[6]

Similarly, an illustrated and annotated 1990 edition of the
Bible designed for a wide lay audience explains in the margin next
to the very same Biblical passage in Genesis.:

> The rainbow which appeared after the flood was
> symbolic of the covenant which God had made with
> Noah.... Whereas later, at Mount Sinai, God makes a
> second, more detailed, covenant,... here he extends
> grace to all mankind in a promise that he will never
> again disrupt the earth's natural cycle.[7]

But is God's covenant in Genesis 9:9-17 with "humans," with
"Noah," with "all mankind," as these two books have stated? Let
us examine the Biblical passage referred to, beginning one verse
earlier with verse 8 to get the context better. Notice *who* God is
making the covenant with. And notice the repeated phrases, something that is surely not accidental. (I have underlined phrases to
make spotting the repetitions easier.)

> Then God said to Noah and to his sons with him, "As
> for me, I am establishing my covenant with you and
> your descendants after you, and <u>with every living
> creature</u> that is with you, the birds, the domestic
> animals, and every animal of the earth with you, as
> many as came out of the ark. I establish my covenant
> with you, that never again shall <u>all flesh</u> be cut off by
> the waters of a flood, and never again shall there be a
> flood to destroy the earth." God said, "This is the sign
> of the covenant that I make between me and you and
> <u>every living creature</u> that is with you, for all future
> generations: I have set my bow in the clouds, and it
> shall be a sign of the covenant between me and the
> earth. When I bring clouds over the earth and the bow
> is seen in the clouds, I will remember my covenant that
> is between me and you and <u>every living creature</u> of <u>all
> flesh</u>; and the waters shall never again become a flood
> to destroy <u>all flesh</u>. When the bow is in the clouds, I
> will see it and remember the everlasting covenant
> between God and <u>every living creature</u> of <u>all flesh</u> that
> is on the earth." God said to Noah, "This is the sign of

the covenant that I have established between me and
<u>all flesh</u> that is on the earth."[8]

Who is this covenant with? Specifically listed at the passage's beginning are "you, the birds, the domestic animals, and every animal of the earth." As if that is not clear enough, four times God says the covenant is with "every living creature." The phrase "all flesh," which is repeated five times, is a Biblical phrase meaning all mortal beings, all mortal creatures, thus also emphasizing that the covenant is not just with humans.

Given these numerous, obviously intentional repetitions, how could the scholars who wrote the entries in the dictionary of the Bible and the annotated Bible not have been aware they were misrepresenting this covenant when they respectively wrote that it was God's agreement with "humans" and "mankind"? The explanation is the shrinking-down of modern Western Christian theology so that it has focused almost entirely on the human realm, with Nature becoming merely the stage or background for human history.

Not only has Nature become overlooked, the theological meaning of this foundational covenant has become distorted as a result.

Problems with "Stage" Interpretation of Bible

There are two major problems with the approach of interpreting the Bible as if Nature were merely the stage or background for human history. Already mentioned is how our modern knowledge about ecology shows humans' inescapable link with the non-human realm. But there is a second problem related to the Bible's own perspective. A very big problem.

It can be best explained by quoting from four books that have gotten beyond the modern "stage" way of thinking about Nature so as to better understand the Bible's perspective. Each of the following quotations will say essentially the same thing, but this point is so critical to the topic at hand that it deserves emphasizing.

First from the religious writer Ian Bradley, who at this point in his book is writing about the Old Testament, which was written in Hebrew:

There is no word in ancient Hebrew corresponding to
our word "nature" and that is simply because the

ancient Israelites had no concept of a separate world of nature existing over and against the world of human beings.[9]

And, from a book on Old Testament theology by the distinguished Biblical scholar John L. McKenzie:

There is no idea of nature and no word for nature in the Old Testament. [10]

And from a third scholar, who is writing about the entire Bible, Old Testament and New Testament:

The term "nature" does not appear in the Bible.[11]

And finally from Theodore Hiebert, professor at Harvard Divinity School:

Nature and society are so interdependent in the Bible that to distinguish them sharply or subordinate one to the other misrepresents biblical thought. Biblical languages, for example, possess no terms equivalent to the Western conceptions of nature and history, suggesting that this familiar modern distinction was not a part of a biblical thought.[12]

Our modern Western worldview—especially if influenced by the "stage" way of thinking—tends to make a two-part distinction:

- humans
- Nature

The Bible's perspective also makes a two-part distinction, but it is a quite different one (as Biblical scholars are now increasingly realizing). The Bible's distinction is:

- God
- the created world

That created world, the second part of the Bible's perspective, includes humans, non-human life, and the inanimate.

Consequences of the Bible's Unified Perspective

The implications of the Bible's quite different two-part distinction are profound. It means that an essential part of the Bible's very message about God is about God's reach far beyond the bounds of human history and human society. The message of the Bible is *intrinsically* related to all of the world, human and non-human. Nature is not an add-on.

Before leaving our Genesis text about the covenant, one more matter can be demonstrated using that passage. As explained earlier in this chapter, an extreme form of the "stage" way of thinking that came to dominate 20th-century Biblical scholarship was to see human history as being on a linear track of "progress," while Nature was imagined as being just purposeless repetitive, seasonal cycles in the background. According to that way of interpreting the Bible, God's caring came to be viewed as being promises for progress in human history, not promises involving Nature.

However, a closer examination of the Bible over the past few decades has shown that in the Bible, promises of the fulfillment of God's purpose *include* those cycles of Nature. One place that can be seen is in the verses that immediately follow the passage of Genesis quoted above. God's covenant-promise in verse 22 of that chapter of Genesis reads:

> As long as the earth endures, seedtime and harvest,
> cold and heat, summer and winter, day and night, shall
> not cease.[13]

So important are those repetitive cycles of "Nature" (as our modern view calls it) that the sustaining of "seedtime and harvest ... summer and winter" is part of the very promise God makes for a renewed creation. God knows the critical value of those cycles of Nature, affirms them, and even promises to sustain them. They are not merely a stage for a human drama. They are part of God's saving drama.

New Testament Theme of Salvation

Jesus and his earliest followers were Jews, and so they inherited many understandings about God from the books of the Old Testament that were the Hebrew scriptures. In the New Testament, animals and plants are not mentioned as frequently as in the Old Testament, but that is because the New Testament comes from a more urban world. What we should look for is not the number of times the non-human realm is mentioned but instead what is said about it. Let us look at one of the most important themes of the New Testament—salvation. Returning to our widely-used dictionary of the Bible, which was influenced by the "stage" way of thinking, we find that its entry on "Salvation" ends with this climactic statement:

> Salvation will not be achieved until God's purpose is

complete—for Jew as well as Gentile ... for all people
as well as believers (1 Cor. 15:25-28).[14]

How well does that explanation describe the New Testament's understanding of God's act of salvation, God's reconciliation through Christ? Let us first look at the very passage in 1 Corinthians mentioned in the dictionary's entry on "Salvation." Watch how many times the word "all" or the phrase "all things" are repeated (repetitions of the latter being underlined):

For he [Christ] must reign until he has put all his
enemies under his feet. The last enemy to be destroyed
is death. For "God has put <u>all things</u> in subjection
under his feet." But when it says, "<u>All things</u> are put in
subjection," it is plain that this does not include the
one who put <u>all things</u> in subjection under him. When
<u>all things</u> are subjected to him, then the Son himself
will also be subjected to the one who put <u>all things</u> in
subjection under him, <u>so that God may be all in all</u>.[15]

Five times this very passage cited by our dictionary says "all things." Not to mention the emphatic final phrase "so that God may be all in all." Given this repetition of "all things" over and over again, how is it possible that the seminary professor who wrote that dictionary entry on "Salvation" ended with the statement that "salvation will not be achieved until God's purpose is complete ... for all people."[16] The Bible's dramatic "all things" has become reduced to "all people" in the Bible dictionary.

This is another example of treating Nature as just the stage for the human drama—to the point that Nature, the non-human sphere, fell out of sight. It is identical to how, in regard to the covenant, the repeated phrase "with every living creature" fell outside a field of vision so narrowed down that it could see only the human drama.

Of course, the seminary professors and other Biblical scholars involved would have known the first part of the ancient Christian Apostles' Creed, which says that God is "Maker of heaven and earth." But what has happened is that after having God make heaven and earth, most modern Western Christian theology has narrowed God's *ongoing* relationship with creation to the human sphere. And a major cause has been its being influenced by the "stage" view of history. (Other causes for the narrowing down were explained near the first part of Chapter 16, "When All the World's Not a Stage.")

Of course, the Corinthians passage cited by the dictionary's "Salvation" entry might not be typical. So let us also look at a New Testament passage that is used fairly often in the Church. It is the opening of Paul's letter to Colossians, a hymn-like passage that talks about what God is reconciling to himself through Christ. Again, watch the repeated phrases:

> He [Christ] is the image of the invisible God, the
> firstborn of all creation; for in him <u>all things</u> <u>in heaven</u>
> <u>and on earth</u> were created, things visible and invisible,
> whether thrones or dominions or rulers or powers—<u>all</u>
> <u>things</u> have been created through him and for him. He
> himself is before <u>all things</u>, and in him <u>all things</u> hold
> together. He is the head of the body, the church; he is
> the beginning, the firstborn from the dead, so that he
> might come to have first place in everything. For in
> him all the fullness of God was pleased to dwell, and
> through him God was pleased to reconcile to himself
> <u>all things</u>, whether <u>on earth or in heaven</u>, by making
> peace through the blood of his cross.[17]

The repetition of the phrase "all things" five times is not sloppiness by the translators. There is a specific Greek word used in both the Corinthians and the Colossians passages. It is the Greek word *panta*.[18] (The meaning of "all" for *pan* shows up in our English word "panorama," a view taking in everything.)

In the Colossians passage, the twice-employed reference to both "earth" and "heaven" emphasizes that it is not just human society but everything that is being gathered up into God's great act of salvation.

The phrase "all things" is also employed in New Testament books by writers other than Paul when they too describe what God is gathering up into salvation through Christ. We find the same Greek word in the opening passage of the books of Hebrews, which is definitely written by someone other than Paul:

> Long ago God spoke to our ancestors in many and
> various ways by the prophets, but in these last days he
> has spoken to us by a Son, whom he appointed heir of
> <u>all things</u>, through whom he also created the worlds.

He is the reflection of God's glory and the exact
imprint of God's very being, and he sustains <u>all things</u>
by his powerful word.[19]

We also find the Greek word in the opening of the book of Ephesians, which most contemporary Biblical scholars think was a writer following in Paul's footsteps:

He [God] has made known to us the mystery of his
will, according to his good pleasure that he set forth in
Christ, as a plan for the fullness of time, to gather up
<u>all things</u> in him, <u>things in heaven and things on
earth</u>.[20]

Notice again not just the phrase "all things" but the cosmic character emphasized by "things in heaven and things on earth," which virtually matches a phrase in our Colossians passage.

This matter of God's salvation including animals can easily puzzle some people today. Admittedly, if my only mental image of salvation is, let us say, that of a person coming forward in a church sanctuary and professing faith in Jesus Christ, I could understandably be puzzled as to how such things as animals and plants are also being brought into God's great act of salvation. But there is an Old Testament background that helps explain the matter. Even in the Old Testament, God's saving is understood to cover all sorts of activities. Such as delivering people out of slavery (Exodus 14-15), or showing people a new well of water when they were in conflict over a single well (Gen. 26:21-22). In the Bible, salvation includes almost any kind of deliverance from danger or death— thus allowing for the movement of life into a richer, more fulfilled state of being. That is why, for example, Psalm 36 (part of the Hebrew Bible/*Tanakh*), in speaking to God, is able to explicitly say:

Your righteousness is like the mighty mountains, your
judgments are like the great deep; you save humans
and animals alike, O LORD.[21]

Persistence of the "Stage" Biblical Scholarship

The author of the Bible-dictionary entry quoted above is not the only one who had his field of vision so narrowed to the human sphere that it resulted in misleading statements about God's salvation. If we return to our illustrated and annotated Bible (the main editor of which taught at Princeton Seminary), and look at its comments on the story of the flood, we find this statement:

> The importance of this story lies not in the exact
> structure of the ark, but in the fact that God saved
> *Noah*.[22]

As still another example, here is a sentence from a 1966 book written by a seminary graduate who was a college professor:

> There exists in the New Testament the same basic
> assertions which appear in the Old, that salvation is a
> deliverance from whatever constitutes the primary
> threat to man's well being.[23]

Even if we did not catch the narrowed-down vision of the word "man's," we might have been alerted to the shortcoming of the latter book's theological perspective several pages earlier with this sentence;

> The narrative sections of the Old Testament include
> many examples of deliverance. Noah's family is saved
> from the flood.[24]

My assumption would be that it made a lot of difference to the animals who got onto the ark if God had merely saved "Noah's family" or "Noah," as these two books put it. (Not to mention what members of Noah's family would have had say if God had decided only to save "Noah," as the first book put it.)

Before we leave the matter of narrowed-down examples, it should be mentioned that the search for the historical Jesus that has occurred over more recent decades among some Biblical scholars is still within this narrowed-down form of modern Western Christianity. The search for the historical Jesus usually focuses on the political and social circumstances surrounding the life of Jesus of Nazareth. That is, it focuses on human society, the human realm. There is little in the historical-Jesus movement that addresses directly the involvement of God and Christ in the non-human part of the cosmos.

As an example, take the Biblical scholar Marcus Borg, whose highly readable books have proven so helpful to many contemporary Christians. Borg's *The Heart of Christianity* has no entry in its index for the words "Nature" or "ecology."[25] It does have an entry for "economy," but the three pages referred to concentrate only on human economy and society, with no mention at all of the natural resources on which human economies are ultimately based.

Borg's newer book, *Jesus: Uncovering the Life, Teachings, and Relevance of a Religious Revolutionary,* does not have an index of subjects.[26] But its scripture index, which has over 400 entries, has no listing for John 1:1-3a—the "Logos" passage— which is the key text in that Gospel for seeing God's work in Christ as being the work of God the Creator in all of the created world. Nor does its scripture index include the central New Testament passages that speak of God's work in Christ as redeeming "all things" in heaven and earth.

An examination of books by the other prominent writer of the historical-Jesus movement, John Dominic Crossan, yields very similar results. His *Jesus: A Revolutionary Biography,* for example, has no index entries for "Nature," "ecology," "creation," "Creator," "God," or "Logos."[27]

Restoring a Wider Vision

It is fortunate, however, that the problem of the modern narrowed-down vision was discovered. What comes through to us when we work to bring the wider dimension of the Bible back into sight is a more expansive picture of God. It is a picture of an even more generous God more intimately involved with the world in more ways. Therefore, if in reading the Bible we let animals, plants and the rest of the non-human cosmos become merely the scenery or props for a human drama, we miss out on the Bible's insights into what it sees God as being up to. (See inset list for just a few samples of Bible passages that could be read to help restore Nature to the Biblical drama.)

Let me demonstrate how the wider dimension can be lost by looking at a specific narrative in the Bible—the narrative that composes the Old Testament's Book of Ruth. In a famous and touching scene near the beginning of the Book of Ruth, Naomi is despondent because her husband and two grown sons, who have been the source of her security, have died. And so Naomi is returning to her homeland. But Ruth, a foreigner, pledges not to abandon her mother-in-law, saying, "Where you go, I will go; where you lodge, I will lodge."[28]

**Sample of Bible Passages
for Restoring Nature to the Biblical Drama**

A Fruitful Earth:
Genesis 1: 11-31
Humans from the Earth:
Genesis 2:7-8 & 2:15
The Ground Spoiled:
Genesis 4:8-12
The Earth Restored:
Genesis 7:1-9
Genesis 9:8-17
Further Restrictions:
Deuteronomy 22:6-7
Deuteronomy 20:19-20
Caring for Animals:
Exodus 23:4-5
Deuteronomy 25:4

A Shared Existence:
Hosea 4:1-3
Isaiah 24:4-5
Psalm 104
Psalm 96:9-13
Humans Not Everything:
Job 38:25-27
Job 38:41-39:6
Isaiah 1:3
Nurturing Cycles:
Genesis 8:20-22
Revelation 22:1-3
God's Caring for All:
Psalms 145:8-9, 14-16
*Vision of a Restored
Earth:*
Revelation 22:1-3

From this point, the story becomes a touching human drama in which Ruth works to restore her and her mother-in-law's security, in part by gaining a faithful husband Boaz. The common way of summarizing this story narrows its focus to the faithfulness of the human beings, particularly Ruth. As we follow the human story in that way, we can easily let the plants become just background scenery or props. But in fact, if we follow the plants (specifically grain) in the story, and watch closely who gives grain to whom, we will discover that it is in part *through* the plants that God is working.

The narrator of the Book of Ruth virtually never states explicitly how God does anything. But one exception is the statement toward the end of the story that after Boaz took Ruth for his wife,

"When they came together, the LORD made her conceive, and she bore a son."[29] In the book of Ruth's narrative, two pairs of carefully placed Hebrew words underscore how God saves Ruth and Naomi from their desperate situation by providing two things—not just a baby by Boaz, but also grain.[30] Thus is expressed the theological message that God, unseen, saves and restores people to new life by being the Giver of Life. And not just human life. Also plant life.

Are the plants just background "scenery"? No! Instead, in this narrative, the plants are a vehicle for God's caring presence, and are thus a very window into God.

Dealing with the "Dominion" Problem

Because our modern scientific technology has had so many environmentally damaging side-effects, discussions about the Bible and our relationships with the non-human realm almost inevitably elicit a question about human "dominion." Many Christians and Jews are embarrassed by the use of that English word in Genesis 1. They are bothered by it because they think it is giving the humans license to do as they please.

In fact, that passage is more easily dealt with than one might suppose. True, in Genesis 1:26-28, God does say to, "let them [humankind] have dominion" over animals. But even within the context of that narrative, "dominion" cannot mean license to do anything. That is because in that narrative of Genesis 1, the humans are *not* given permission to eat animals, but only eat plants.[31]

More important for recovering the Bible's true sense of the meaning of human dominion is the way that concept is developed throughout the rest of the Bible. The word usually translated "dominion" (Hebrew: *radah*) could be translated "kingship."[32] But in the Hebraic culture of the Old Testament, a person's being given kingship did not mean that person was being given license to do as they please. Moreover, as is apparent frequently in the Old Testament, there is a recognition that there is both good and bad kingship. (Today, even many children in church-school learn the story about how King David misused his power as king for selfish ends, and consequently had to repent of his wrongdoing.)

In the Biblical view, any person being given kingship was

being assigned a *responsibility*—a responsibility that involved being morally accountable to a higher authority: God. Over time, the Old Testament comes to depict the kind of kingship God prefers as being stewardship, or even servanthood. As just one example, Psalm 72 describes an ideal king (having "dominion") as being one who "has pity on the weak and the needy, and saves the lives of the needy."[33]

Kings were held accountable not only for ensuring that the poor and the powerless were not trampled upon, but also for upholding principles (codified in laws) that were meant to safeguard animals, plants, the land, the Earth. Old Testament directives about showing care even for animals include one form of the Sabbath commandment, which states, "Six days you shall do your work, but on the seventh day you shall rest, so that your ox and your donkey may have relief."[34]

The New Testament becomes even stronger on the theme of servanthood, even when speaking of kingship. For example, in Matthew 20:25-27, Jesus says to his Jewish disciples, "You know that the rulers of the Gentiles [i.e., non-Jews] lord it over them, and their great ones are tyrants over them. It will not be so among you; but whoever wishes to be great among you must be your servant, and whoever wishes to be first among you must be your slave."

A Holistic Cosmic Community

We should not, however, let our addressing the "dominion" passages, nor our concerns about the environment, lead us to thinking about Nature only in terms of our actions upon it, for bad or for good. The Bible can help remind us that the non-human sphere plays much larger roles in our lives. And in religion.

Nature can be a vehicle by which people come to know the glory of God. This shows up especially in psalms of praise. In Psalm 148, for example, wild animals, flying birds, cattle and creeping things, princes and rulers, men and women, mountains and hills, water and sky, sun, moon, and shining stars all praise God and express God's glory.

When we add such psalms to the other Bible passages examined and listed in this chapter, what emerges is a picture of the whole world, both human and non-human, as one cosmic community. As Ian Bradley puts it, there is:

> No concept of a separate world of nature existing over
> and against the world of human beings.... This leads to
> a profoundly holistic world picture [i.e., emphasizing
> the importance of the whole] in which humans take
> their place with every other creature in a state of utter
> dependence on God. There is a strong sense too of the
> interdependence of all creatures and an image of the
> world as a single cosmic community.[35]

Such a religious vision is coherent with what science today has
been telling us more and more.

Chapter 18
Reading the "Book" of Nature
in a Digital Age

About twenty years ago, a workshop for seminarians on the contemporary implications of their faith was being held in a retreat center in Texas. Like many church retreats, the conference was being held away from cities, in this case in a conference center that looked out upon a limestone bluff over the Frio River.

After more than a day of meetings, a most revealing incident occurred during one of the workshop sessions. The speaker, a prominent professor of religion, had been analyzing Biblical passages such as Genesis 1, in which the goodness of the world is repeatedly emphasized. But then a young women seminarian interrupted the speaker's chain of thought by standing up and saying something quite unexpected. She did not ask any of the typical questions, such as about the Hebrew words behind the English translation, or about the historical context in which the Biblical passages were written. Instead her words were:

Turn around. Look out the window.[1]

One reason that woman's request was so striking is that over the past five-hundred years, most of modern Western Christianity, including 20th-century Biblical scholarship, has narrowed its focus down to mostly the *human* sphere. Not, of course, that Christian theology had forgotten its ancient affirmation that God is "Maker of heaven and earth."[2] But what had happened is that most modern Western Christian theology narrowed its focus and its depiction of God's ongoing relationship with the natural world to the human sphere. In contrast, as the contemporary theologian Elizabeth Johnson explains:

Such amnesia about the cosmic world has not always been the case. In fact, for three-quarters of this history, creation [i.e., the universe] was actively present as an intrinsic part of theological reflection.[3]

In many periods and occasions in the first fifteen-hundred years of Christianity, a request such as that of the woman seminarian to "Turn around [and] look out the window" would not have been so surprising. That is because before Christianity became narrowed down to the human sphere, it possessed as a part of its tradition a concept that was frequently called the "Book of Nature." The metaphor of a "book" developed in Christianity in part as a way of expressing how the natural world can reveal truth about God, as a complement to the way that another book—the Bible—is able to do the same. Although that idea about the natural world can be found in a fundamental way in the Hebrew tradition even before Jesus, the Christian use of that idea begins in the New Testament, and extends from the first centuries of Christianity all the way to a few remnants of it in modern times.

(For the remainder of this chapter, the word "Nature" will be employed in it's everyday meaning of plants and animals and all the rest of the *non*-human world. I recognize, of course, that we humans are actually a part of the natural world. But by employing the world "Nature" in that everyday sense, I will be able to emphasize how opening the "Book of Nature," so to speak, involves turning our attention to things in the created world *other* than the human realm.)

This chapter will explore the Book-of-Nature tradition in the West: its past, the reasons for its decline, and the benefits of restoring it as part of religious and spiritual life.

Seeing beyond Nature's Ambiguity

I know it is possible that some readers might be thinking, "How can you claim that Nature can reveal God to us, when Nature can be so violent?" Sometimes when as a teacher I am asked that question, I do have to bite my tongue a bit and not reply sardonically, "You think Nature is especially violent? Have you watched the evening news on TV to see what *humans* are doing to each other?"

Nevertheless, the point of such a quite legitimate question needs to be dealt with. One way to do so would be to recognize that despite the injuries humans sometimes inflict, it is widely said by religious people today that the will of God can be at work through the actions of human beings. Similarly, it might be that we can learn how to discern God working through the non-human sphere.

And here, to begin with, is one way the metaphor of Nature as a "book" can be helpful. For, after all, as we grow up, we have to learn *how* to read books. We first learn the letters of the alphabet. We then learn to recognize words. We learn how grammar works. And we learn how, as we read, to listen for the thoughts and feelings and truths that *lie behind* the letters on the page. We hear in our head the mind of the writer even when our eyes see only bits of ink on paper (or on a Kindle screen). Similarly, the Book-of-Nature tradition in Christianity guided people in how to turn to Nature in such a way as to discern things about the world so as to attune themselves to God—which is not the world itself.

The Long Life of the Metaphor

One way to recover the wider dimension of Christianity would be to *redevelop* the Book-of-Nature tradition in a fashion appropriate for our contemporary world. A first step in doing that would be to know more about that tradition so as to appreciate it.

Of course, in Biblical times, because there were no books in the form of bound, rectangular sheets, we do not find the explicit metaphor of a "book" for the natural world. But we do find the idea behind that metaphor. Namely, that the natural world can in various ways be revelatory.

In the Old Testament (the Hebrew Bible/*Tanakh*), examples of this way of thinking are numerous, especially in the psalms. Such as Psalm 19, which opens by proclaiming:

> The heavens are telling the glory of God; and the
> firmament proclaims his handiwork. Day to day pours
> forth speech, and night to night declares knowledge.[4]

And the Old Testament prophet Isaiah declares:

> Holy, holy, holy is the LORD of hosts; the whole earth
> is full of his glory.[5]

Similarly, in the first chapter of the New Testament's book of Romans, the writer Paul assumes without question that:

> what can be known about God is plain ... because God
> has shown it.... Ever since the creation of the world
> [God's] eternal power and divine nature, invisible
> though they are, have been understood and seen
> through the things he has made.[6]

Also, down through centuries of Christianity, as books began to become available to some who could read, "book" became one of the metaphors to express that theological idea. Especially as books became a part of Christian devotional life, so also did "book" become a useful metaphor for how Nature can be a vehicle for maintaining our connection with God. For example, in the 3rd century, one of the early desert fathers, St. Anthony of the Desert wrote:

> My book is the nature of created things, and any time I
> wish to read the words of God, the book is before me.[7]

Other early Christian thinkers who were more influential than St. Anthony also engaged in very similar thinking. For example, St. Augustine wrote:

> Some people, in order to discover God, read books.
> But there is a great book: the very appearance of
> created things. Look above you! Look below you!
> Read it.[8]

In the latter part of the medieval period, Hugh of St. Victor wrote that:

> This whole visible world is a book written by the
> finger of God, that is, created by divine power; ... not
> derived by human will but instituted by divine
> authority to show forth the wisdom of the invisible
> things of God.[9]

And in the 13th century, Thomas Aquinas, one of the most influential of Christian theologians prior to the Scientific Revolution, used the "book" metaphor, writing succinctly:

> Sacred writings are bound in two volumes—that of
> creation and that of the Holy Scriptures.[10]

The Book-of-Nature tradition also continued into Protestantism. For example, the 16th-century reformer John Calvin wrote:

> In every part of the world, in heaven and on earth, he
> [God] has written and as it were engraved the glory of
> his power, goodness, wisdom and eternity.... For all
> creatures, from the firmament even to the center of the
> earth, could be witnesses and messengers of his glory
> to all men, drawing them on to seek him, and having
> found him, to do him service and honor.[11]

At roughly the same time, even some scientists (many of whom were devout Christians) employed the "book" metaphor to express their beliefs about God. For example, the early 17th-century revolutionary astronomer Johannes Kepler referred to:

the Book of Nature which is so highly praised in the
Holy Scriptures.[12]

And Kepler, drawing upon other imagery of Psalm 19 mentioned above, wrote of:

that Book of Nature in which God the Creator has
revealed and depicted His essence and what He wills
with man, in a wordless script.[13]

As another example of a science-religion conjunction in one person, we might note the example of Blaise Pascal in the 17th century, who was both a mathematician and a Christian writer. Although he did not use the word "book" explicitly, that metaphor was implied when Pascal wrote:

Those honor Nature well, who teach that she can speak
on everything, even on theology.[14]

Causes of Decline of the Metaphor

What happened then to such a vital and long-standing spiritual and theological tradition as the one demonstrated by these samples? The answer lies in that matter already mentioned: Namely, that over the past several centuries, Christianity has narrowed its focus to primarily the human sphere. That narrowing down has been a contrast to the Bible's perspective encompassing all of creation, and a contrast to the first 1500 years of Christianity.

Over the past few decades, our modern environmental crisis led to an extensive examination of Christian thought all the way back to the Bible and including it. That examination has revealed multiple causes behind the narrowing down of Christian thought. But three causes stand out:

• One main cause has been a retreat of Christian theology
from the realm of Nature under pressures from the
advancement of science. As science came to explain more
of the world in terms of natural laws, and as some of the
boundary lines between scientific and religious thought
shifted, most of Christianity found it easier to get out of
the "Nature" business, so to speak. Most modern Christian
theology abandoned the realm of Nature to science, and
retreated to the human sphere—focusing on the human

soul and psychology, or on human society. There it sought to stake out its own arena safe from these **scientific challenges**.

- A second cause behind the narrowing down (also beginning near the time of the Scientific Revolution), involved the invention of the printing press by Gutenberg in the 15th century. The first book to come off that printing press was the Bible, and it would lead to **an increased emphasis on the printed word** as the locus for the encounter with God. The Book of Nature declined in importance as the Bible grew in importance, with the Bible becoming the dominant or sole source of revelation. Unfortunately, the Protestant Reformation accelerated this decline of the Book of Nature in its reaction against Roman Catholicism. The leading Protestant reformers held up the Bible as an alternative authority to that of the Catholic hierarchy, and in doing so, accelerated that growing emphasis on the Bible as the source of revelation.

    Moreover, with the Bible becoming for most Western Christian theology the point of contact with God, Nature became isolated from God in Christian thought. Because, after all, animals cannot read the Bible. Animals thus increasingly seemed not to have any *ongoing* relationship with God.

- A third major cause has been that 20th-century Bible scholarship fell under the spell of a way historians (all historians, not just Biblical ones) had come to view history as being a human drama with **Nature as just the stage or backdrop** for the drama. That "stage" way of thinking that became part of modern thought dates back to the 18th-century period called the Enlightenment.

(It was, incidentally, that narrowed-down type of Biblical scholarship—an over-concentration on human history as interpreted through texts penned by humans—that frustrated that woman seminarian so much that she implored the speaker to "Turn around. Look out the window.")

One clarification should perhaps be made about the statement that modern Western Christianity became narrowed down to the human sphere. What is being referred to is not whether Christians are concerned about the treatment of the environment (even though the two matters can be related). What is being referred to is whether the non-human sphere is treated as an area of God's presence and ongoing activity—so that theology inevitably *includes* the non-human sphere in an integral way. That is what has gotten lost.

With such a narrowing-down of Christian thought to the human sphere (from multiple causes), it was inevitable that the Book-of-Nature tradition also became lost in the process. The loss of that "Book" theme was part of the very narrowing down.

Different Ways of Knowing

Having come to appreciate the long-standing Book-of-Nature tradition, we might turn to the prospects for such a component in our theology and spirituality today as one way of restoring the realm of Nature to Western religion. A difficulty, however, soon presents itself. Today, if you google "book of nature," you will find a number of articles that use that phrase. However, in most cases those articles represent an *inversion* of the manner in which the metaphor had been traditionally employed in Christianity. Most of those googled articles (and a few books) will be using the phrase "book of nature" to speak about contemporary scientific knowledge about the natural world, with an emphasis on the way science can complement religion's orientation toward the world.

In contrast, one of the strengths of the Book-of-Nature metaphor as previously employed by Christianity was to emphasize how even the uneducated could know and experience God's glory through everyday experiences as they allowed their minds and hearts to open to the message that God's creation could speak to them. As St. John Chrysostom wrote in the 4th century:

> If God had given instruction [only] by means of books,
> and of letters ... the illiterate man would have gone
> away without receiving any benefit.... This however
> cannot be said with respect to the heavens, but ... every
> man that walks upon the earth, shall hear this voice....
> Upon this volume the unlearned, as well as the wise
> man, shall be able to look, and whenever any one may
> chance to come, there looking upwards towards the
> heavens, he will receive a sufficient lesson from the

view of them.[15]

With science being such a powerful tool today, it can be easy to forget that science is not our only way of knowing the natural world. Therefore, one of the meanings of opening the Book of Nature today would be to attend ourselves to a firsthand, immediate experience of the sky, the light, the air, the grass, the trees, and the other life-forms around us.

For example, those retreatants at the conference beside the Frio River, in their breaks between sessions, had gained informally some knowledge about the immense geological timeline represented by the limestone cliffs. Such well-established scientific knowledge should always be accepted. But in opening the Book of Nature, such knowledge would need to be complemented with firsthand immediate experience of the cliffs' immense size, their color, their feel to the touch, as well as the feelings of awe experienced in viewing them, leading to contemplation and spiritual reflection.

Re-developing the Metaphor

Today, the time is ripe for re-exploring the value of the Book-of-Nature metaphor as a way of staying in touch with God. One reason is because we have so many kinds of books today, ranging from our traditional printed books to audio books to Kindle. Although sales of old-fashioned bound paper books remain strong, people today do not merely read words on a printed page of paper. We also put on earphones to listen to audio books. We search out links on web pages to locate books stored "on the cloud." And we tune into wi-fi to download digital ebooks.

Even before computers, the botanist George Washington Carver, inspired by radio technology, updated the idea of the Book of Nature when he wrote:

> I love to think of nature as an unlimited broadcasting
> station, through which God speaks to us every hour if
> we will only tune in.[16]

Taking a cue from Carver, we might remember the even greater number of radio, TV, and wi-fi signals all around us today, and think of Nature as continually sending out innumerable signals. With our wide variety of types of books today, our minds might be open to more flexibility in thinking through the variety of ways we might relate to Nature spiritually and theologically as if it were similar to some kind of "book."

Even though we live in what has been called the information age, we still do not read books just to get information. And so, as a way of beginning to redevelop the "book" metaphor, let us briefly look at just five different orientations during reading. Each of these can also be a way we can orient ourselves toward Nature theologically and spiritually. Each of these can be a way in which, by turning our attention to Nature as a "book," we can move ourselves into deeper relationship with God, the Divine. Each of these ways is quite different from science's orientation toward Nature.

- First, we sometimes read books in order **to relax and restore ourselves**. So also can turning our attention to Nature be restorative. As Jesus instructed his anxious disciples long ago, re-directing their attentions toward Nature, "Consider the lilies of the field."[17]
- We also read books **to commune with other hearts and minds**. Similarly, communing with Nature can be a way of communing with other kinds of beings, many of which make human existence possible. After all, the great irony our modern ecological knowledge points to is that while most species on this planet could do quite well without us, we could not exist if it were not for many of them.
- We sometimes read books **to be inspired**. Similarly, inspirational uplift is one of the most common and accessible benefits people experience from turning their attention to Nature. It might be from the beauty of a dramatic sunset, or the less obvious wonder at a bird in the backyard, a bird which can give delight.
- Sometimes when we read books we **become contemplative**—a shift of mood. So also as we turn our attention toward Nature with a particular orientation can we become contemplative. The 16th-century Protestant reformer John Calvin gave instruction on this very matter when he wrote:

  > While we contemplate in all creatures, as in
  > a mirror, those immense riches of his
  > [God's] wisdom, justice, goodness and

power, we should not merely run them over
cursorily and, so to speak, with a fleeting
glance, but we should ponder them at
length, turn them over in our mind
seriously and faithfully, and recollect them
repeatedly.[18]

• One other thing that sometimes occurs during reading is
that our minds and hearts **open into an expansive
awareness** of the world and our place in it. Such a
possibility of coming into an expansive awareness is true
with books made by human hands and with the Book of
Nature.

This list of orientations demonstrates how there are various depths
in which we can engage Nature spiritually. They range from a
simple but valuable refreshment to the deepest stilling of
awareness and quieting of our inner being, which can approach the
unsolicited mystic states that occasionally come to individuals.

Benefits of Recovering the Book of Nature

Turning our attention more often to Nature as a "book" by which
to relate to the Divine can be beneficial to contemporary religion
and spirituality in many ways, even beyond increasing our environmental concern. The following are just some of the benefits
that can come from turning our attention and thoughts more
frequently to Nature.

One benefit of revitalizing the Book-of-Nature tradition would
be to help reverse the narrowing-down of most Christianity to the
human sphere that occurred over the past few centuries. Any religion or theology that lets Nature just fall into the background will
become less and less credible as our ecological knowledge
reminds us of how our lives are continuously sustained by the
oxygen and water that has been produced by other species around
us. In fact, modern ecology tells us that as far as the life on this
planet goes, we humans are quite expendable! Expanding religion
to more actively include the non-human sphere can, therefore,
increase its credibility as it integrates that truth.

For Christianity, an additional benefit would be that of
restoring the exciting message repeatedly expressed in the New
Testament that God is gathering up into salvation not just humans

but "all things ... in heaven and ... on earth."[19] Because of that dimension in the New Testament, the contemporary theologian Sallie McFague reminds us:

> The scope of God's power and love is cosmological....
> Otherwise, God would not be God.[20]

Still another benefit would be to counter the Jesus-ism of too much of contemporary Christianity. Such Jesus-ism forgets Christianity's fundamental claim: Namely, that the love that Christian's have experienced through knowing Jesus Christ is the same love that is the sustaining Source for all of the natural world—all of God's creation.

Complementary to that benefit, expanding our theology to more actively incorporate the non-human realm would also provide an additional avenue for the ecumenical spirit. As the spiritual writer Matthew Fox puts it:

> No forest, no moon, no ocean, no field, can be labeled
> "Buddhist" or "Jewish" or "Muslim" or "Christian."[21]

Christians and Jews might also discover that Islam has as part of its tradition a quite vital component pointing to the natural world as being revelatory about God.[22]

Using the "Book of Nature" as one vehicle of revelation can also have the benefit of better engaging with people who are not grounded in any faith-tradition, but who have a more secular spirituality. Such people nonetheless in many cases have felt a sense of the sacred in Nature. Many centuries ago, even before our modern, secular culture, St. John Chrysostom recognized the universalism of the Book of Nature, writing:

> Before the giving of the scriptures, God ordered his
> dispensation toward us ... stretching out the heavens;
> and there openly unfolding a vast volume, useful alike
> to the simple and the wise, to the poor and the rich, to
> Scythians and to barbarians, and to all in general who
> dwell upon the earth.[23]

Still another benefit of recovering the Book of Nature can be that, as we turn our attention more frequently to Nature, we might become more receptive to its messages. We will feel increasingly the value of what it has to tell us. For, after all, one rule of thumb of spiritual development is that what we pay more attention to tends to become more valuable to us.

As we live more and more in a world of our own construction, we can become more and more awed by what we humans have created, and simultaneously experience less awe from encountering God's creation. All our modern gadgets, even as useful as they can sometimes be, catch our eyes and ears and demand our attention. And so, another benefit from cultivating a habit of being attentive toward Nature is that we can restore a proper perspective about ourselves. Such a restored perspective can include an awareness of who we are in relation to God. As Bill McKibben, a leading Christian writer on the environment put it:

> We live, all of a sudden, in an Astroturf world, and
> though an Astroturf world may have a God, he can't
> speak through the grass, or even be silent through it
> and let us hear.[24]

Having myself been a guest teacher in a number of different churches, I have noticed something. Enter almost any church-school classroom, and probably every furnishing in the room is something made by human beings. You will see a larger variety of objects made by God if you enter a public-school life-science classroom than if you enter a church-school classroom. We might ask ourselves: How does it affect our sense of God to have every item we see or touch in our church-schools be something we humans have made—and nothing (other than ourselves) that God has created?

Cultivating the practice of opening the Book of Nature can also have the benefit of strengthening Christian psychology and spirituality by addressing what has come to be called the "**nature-deficit disorder**" that infects our contemporary lifestyles. That phrase, coined by Richard Louv, points to the fact that people in the U.S. today have much less contact with the natural world than people traditionally had, even in the 19th century. That loss has had deleterious effects, especially upon children, in a number of ways (detailed in Louv's excellent book *Last Child in the Woods*).[25]

One final benefit that opening the Book of Nature and reading from it might bring is to counter the consumerism of our modern U.S. society. No matter which faith-tradition we relate to, or even if we have only a secular perspective regarding spirituality, our society tries to cast our identities in the mold of being consumers.

Something is very much lost there. Something about our deeper identity. The inverse psychological connection between consumption and an appreciation of Nature was detected two centuries ago by the poet William Wordsworth when he wrote:

Getting and spending, we lay waste our powers;
Little we see in Nature that is ours.[26]

A Vision: Becoming Whole through "Reading"

In summary, restoring and revitalizing the Book-of-Nature tradition would mean that we would cultivate the practice of looking up from our laptops and looking out the window more often. We would cultivate the practice of turning off the TV and the computer to watch instead the trees and birds and squirrels, letting ourselves become quiet and open as we did so.

We would use natural retreat settings (such as beside those majestic cliffs on the Frio River) not merely as a relaxing backdrop, but also as an opportunity to engage in *contemplation* of Nature. And also as a means of nesting and integrating our human stories, both secular and religious, into the larger story of the evolution of life on this planet.

We might bring objects from Nature into our religion's classrooms, and have children do the same, so as to reflect upon them, and thus keep our awareness expanded to encompass the non-human sphere.

Revitalizing the Book-of-Nature metaphor would mean that we would also return to our faith-tradition's scriptures to notice, study, and listen to the references to Nature that may have fallen into the background while we were focused on the human drama. (This matter is explored in Chapter 17, "A Lost Dimension of the Bible.")

Christians might even emulate Jesus in the way that his awareness of the vitality and creative power of animals and plants around him helped keep him in touch with the divine Power that sustains human lives and spirits as well.[27]

Having today many detailed studies of the historical Jesus in his social and political setting, we would return to the Bible not just to attend to the references to the non-human world, but also to ask what theological message is being conveyed by them. We would ask ourselves, for example: How do Jesus and the New

Testament writers see God's kingdom to be something being worked out in part through a universal divine creative Power—and not just through the power of human hands? With that added Biblical understanding and insight, we would be able to develop deeper and more insightful theological reflections.

One theological topic we might explore is the interplay between the insights we gain by attuning ourselves to the realm of Nature and the insights we gain by attuning ourselves to scriptural thought. That is, exploring how reading each of those two "books" informs our reading of the other.

And, by opening and reading the "Book of Nature" more often in more ways (restorative, inspirational, contemplative), we would also open ourselves more deeply to that divine creative Power that has moved throughout this universe long before human hands wrote any human-made book.

PART FIVE
Cosmic Dimensions

Life can only be understood backwards,
but it must be lived forwards.
— *Soren Kierkegaard*
(19th-century religious philosopher)

Whether in the intellectual pursuits of science
or in the mystical pursuits of the spirit,
the light beckons ahead and the purpose surging
in our natures responds.
—*Sir Arthur Eddington*
(20th-century astronomer)

Let knowledge grow from more to more,
But more of reverence in us dwell;
That mind and soul, according well,
May make one music as before.
— *Alfred, Lord Tennyson*
(19th-century poet)

Chapter 19
Belonging to
Earth and Cosmos

Jeffrey Sobosan, a professor of theology and an amateur night-sky watcher, confesses:

> There is something about the clear night sky that
> always works on me like the charmed talismans of an
> ancient sorcery. I can spend hours at a time looking up
> at it.[1]

Sobosan, however, also shares a troubling incident:

> I remember one of these disagreements with a mentor
> of mine, an old priest who had .... contributed
> brilliantly to his own specialty in theology, and now at
> the close of life had given himself over to what he
> once described as his first love, the study of the stars. I
> met him in a garden one evening, where he sat by his
> beloved telescope ... with a look of ineffable sadness in
> his eyes.... He spoke of the beauty of the universe ...
> but in striving after this beauty,... his mind had taken a
> savage turn ... toward the damning conclusion: the
> universe is void of meaning.[2]

These contrasting responses—delight as opposed to gloom—raise an important question: Can our sense that life is meaningful encompass our knowledge about the non-human realm of planet Earth and even of a mostly lifeless cosmos? That will be the question lying behind this chapter. It is a critical question because it involves many intersections between religion and science. It is also a vital question because, as the scholar of religion Karen Armstrong reminds us, "We are meaning-seeking creatures.... Humans fall very easily into despair if we don't find some significance in our lives."[3]

Meaning and Belonging

During the latter part of the 20th century, such a recognition of the importance of meaning to humans allowed for some pastors, rabbis, and other religious leaders to find common ground with social scientists, particularly in the field of psychology. The most helpful book has probably been Viktor Frankl's *Man's Search for Meaning*.[4] Frankl also created the psychotherapeutic method of logotherapy, which focuses on people's need for meaning. Ask a logotherapist how people find meaningfulness, and you might get a list of such things as:[5]

- in relationships with other people
- through using one's own creativity
- by cultivating a particular positive attitude

We can all probably recognize these avenues of meaning in our own lives or in the lives of people we know. But notice that none of these three avenues require us to think about the world beyond our human sphere. These avenues do not necessarily raise the question of whether there is any meaning to the larger world of Earth and cosmos that surrounds our human societies.

One way to expand our consciousness is to shift from the matter of meaning to explore questions about *belonging*. By definition, belonging entails a relationship to something larger. An individual person can belong to a group of people; in turn, that group can belong to something even larger. We human beings long to belong (as suggested by the common root of the words in the Middle English *longen*).

The matter of a sense of belonging is something our faith-traditions are accustomed to dealing with because, as Michael Barnes, a professor of religious studies, explains:

> As an answer to a feeling of being adrift without a true home or acceptance, religions can offer a God to belong to, a natural order to conform to, or, most especially, a community of companion believers in whatever form such a community takes.[6]

But the example of religions can remind us of a drawback that can occur with belonging to any social group: That group, even as it provides a sense of belonging for its own members, can become turned in upon itself. In the worst cases of religion, it becomes a cult. How can we prevent our faith-traditions from becoming parochial? Will the sense of belonging they provide become only provincial if it is not expanded to a sense of belonging to something larger?

One way to widen the circle of consciousness could be to widen it to include the non-human realm—especially because, in this ecological age, it has become a cliché that "everything is connected." But connections do not by themselves create a sense of belonging. A prisoner has connections to a prison-guard, but that does not mean the prisoner feels at home in the jail. Increasing the number of guards would increase the number of connections, but that would not necessarily mean the prisoner feels at home.

It is not easy to lay one's finger on what a sense of belonging consists of. Over my years of teaching, I have asked people about experiences in which they very quickly felt "at home," even though it might have been in an environment totally new to them. Sometimes, the people have mentioned there being a similarity to another place they once enjoyed—but not always. More often, people have expressed that their feeling of belonging included a sense of feeling safe, feeling at ease.

Seeking Help from Science

Most of modern Western religion has its focus narrowed primarily to the human sphere. We therefore frequently turn to science when talking about Nature,[7] the planet Earth, and the rest of the universe. But if we turn to many of those scientists who have had high media profiles over the past several decades, and ask them if they think the history of biological evolution, planet Earth, and the cosmos displays meaning and purpose, we get some disturbing replies. For example, the science promoter William B. Provine has made the claim that, "Modern science directly implies that there... is no ultimate meaning for humans."[8] And in the conclusion of his book *The First Three Minutes*, the Nobel-prize-winning physicist Steven Weinberg famously stated:

> It is almost irresistible for humans to believe ... that human life is not just a more-or-less farcical outcome of a chain of accidents reaching back to the first three minutes [after the Big Bang].... It is very hard to realize that all this is just a tiny part of an overwhelmingly hostile universe.... The more the universe seems comprehensible, the more it also seems pointless.[9]

Contrast that statement with the perspective of the creators of a quite different book, *The Hand of God*. It contains colorful photographs from the Hubble space-telescope, accompanied by Sharon Begley's introductory essay, in which she says that contemporary "discoveries of science ... [are providing] what in eras past only religion has offered: A sense of wonder, and of awe; a sense that the world is rational."[10]

Such opposite reactions—pointlessness or the possibility of glimpsing God—raise a question: Is such a contrast (similar to those of the stargazing Sobosan and his mentor priest) due simply to different temperaments? Or is there something else lying behind the contrasting reactions, something that tells us more about the relationships between religion and science?

What is not explained by such statements as Weinberg's that the universe seems "pointless" is that modern science has *removed* from its toolbox questions about overall purpose. (This self-limitation of science, as well as others, were explained in Chapter 6, "Ancient Wisdom Raises Her Head.") The consequence is that if you more and more view the world solely through the lens of science's knowledge, the world can easily come to look purposeless—because you have been using a toolbox from which purpose-seeking tools have been removed!

Because modern science has provided us more and more knowledge, it can give us the feeling that with that knowledge we are "getting to the bottom of things." But each scientific field (atomic physics, molecular biology, astronomy, etc.) is actually slicing through total reality at a particular level, and extracting that layer of knowledge about the world. Books about how to properly relate religion and science sometimes employ an analogy presented in the early 20th century by the astronomer Sir Arthur Eddington: Imagine that a scientific researcher is examining the deep ocean by using a net with 2-inch openings in it to draw up fish. The researcher will not catch 1-inch fish. And so, if that researcher forgets that their net has 2-inch openings, they might come to the incorrect conclusion that there are no 1-inch fish in the ocean.[11]

Scientific knowledge from each field of science is a mere slice out of our total intellectual knowledge of the world. Each slice is even smaller compared to our overall lived experience of the world. A poem by Walt Whitman, "When I Heard the Learn'd Astronomer," was quoted from in Chapter 6. In that poem, Whitman expressed how his listening to an astronomer describing the planets and stars objectively could not approach Whitman's own lived experience of being in "the mystical moist night-air, and from time to time," looking up "in perfect silence at the stars."[12] The contemporary philosopher Max Oelschlaeger explains the reason for what Whitman was experiencing and conveying. Even though science's methods do give us a specific type of knowledge, its methods are a fishing and straining of certain information out of the great sea of the world. Some "fish" are left behind. Oelschlaeger, using the pioneering scientific discoveries of Galileo as an example, writes:

> By using the telescope, Galileo's eyes gathered
> additional light, and the telescopic image itself was
> magnified, thus extending his mental vision.... What he
> lost was the sweeping field of view of the naked eye
> astronomy, the relation of the Milky Way to the starry
> sky.... And perhaps, in his intense concentration, he
> lost also the sounds and smells of the night and the
> awareness of himself as a conscious man beholding a
> grand and mysterious stellar spectacle.[13]

The professor of genetics Steve Jones reminds us of something even other scientists have admitted:

> Science cannot answer the question that philosophers
> —or children—ask; why are we here, what is the point
> of being alive, how ought we to behave.... Scientists
> are no more qualified to comment on them than is
> anyone else.[14]

Culture and a Loss of Depth

This paradox of modern science's "inability to answer childlike elementary questions," as the biologist Peter Medawar put it,[15] might lead us to reflections about how, beginning as children, we grow in cultural settings, and thereby hopefully gain a sense of belonging to something larger than our immediate family. Traditionally, faith-traditions initiated growing children not only into human society but also into all of the universe. In his book *The Hidden Heart of the Cosmos*, the cosmologist Brian Swimme makes some penetrating observations about modern Western culture:

> Where [today] are we initiated into the universe? To answer we need to reflect on what our children experience over and over again, at night, in a setting similar to those children in the past who gathered in the caves and listened to the chant of the elders.... The cave has been replaced with the television room and the chant with the advertisement.... Before a child enters first grade science class, and before entering in any real way into our religious ceremonies, a child will have soaked in thirty thousand advertisements.[16]

Science has brought numerous technological improvements, many of them great blessings. But if we look honestly at the present, we see that science has also helped turn modern cultures into consumer societies filled with consumer products. Because science's methods by themselves are not able to provide values or ethics, the marketplace has become a main determinant of what technology is created. Our relationships and identities within society have thus more and more become that of being consumers. Something is very much lost in such an approach toward life. And there is something lost in our sensibility toward the larger world that surrounds humankind. As the author N. Scott Momaday vividly put it, "We may be perfectly sure of where we are in relation to the supermarket and the next coffee break, but I doubt that any of us knows where he is in relation to the stars and to the solstices."[17]

Re-inhabiting the Earth

No matter which faith-tradition we identify with, or even if we identify with none, our modern societies can tempt us with the idea that we can increase our happiness, psychological stability, and sense of belonging by purchasing products. This is an additional reason for widening our consciousness to encompass our relationship to the Earth and cosmos that surround us. Doing so can build our spiritual relationship to things that are not manufactured in factories, nor even made by human hands—our relationship to something that existed long before there were human societies. There is a long Judeo-Christian precedent for such widening of spirituality beyond the human realm. (This was covered in the two preceding chapters, 17 and 18.) What Jozef Zycinskif writes about the first four books of the Christian New Testament could also be said about many other parts of the Bible:

> The Gospel view shows ... forcefully the connection
> with nature as a domain of the experience of God....
> Herds of sheep and nets filled with fish, the vine, the
> tares [i.e., weeds in the grain fields], and the shriveled
> fig tree speak of God. All of nature has a theological
> dimension, directing the attention of man in the
> direction of the unseen reality of the spirit.[18]

Again, we might ask if scientific knowledge can become part of a project of re-inhabiting the Earth with a deeper spiritual sense of belonging. The late biologist Stephen Jay Gould repeatedly reminded both scientists and non-scientists that, "Human purposes, meanings, and values [are] subjects that the factual domain of science ... can never resolve." But Gould did also write that the "domain of science might *illuminate*" such questions.[19] What illumination might science provide?

Here again, in quite a number of writers influenced by modern science, we find the claim that science has revealed the non-human world to be "hostile" territory (to use Weinberg's word). Instead of just admitting that science's methodology cannot address questions of purpose, the claim is made that the world *is* purposeless, and therefore alien to humankind. Such as this from the philosopher Jacques Monod:

> Science attacks values.... If he [humankind] accepts
> this message in its full significance, man must at last
> wake out of his millenary [i.e., thousand-year] dream
> and discover his total solitude, his fundamental
> isolation. He must realize that, like a gypsy, he lives on
> the boundary of an alien world.[20]

Is this planet Earth really "alien" to humankind? Are we really like interplanetary travelers who have landed on a strange, alien planet? There is an irony about such statements. That is because the modern sciences have revealed countless hidden continuities of humankind with other species of life, with the inanimate elements of our planet, and even with the rest of the universe. More continuities than people in the past could have ever known about! For example, we share **88%** of our genes with mice, **44%** of it with honeybees, and **25%** of it with rice plants.[21] The chemical elements that compose our bodies came out of the explosions of stars long, long ago. The person who puts to paper the notion that we live in a "hostile" or "alien" world is at that very moment having their life sustained through the air, water, and food from this Earth. Because we know about such continuities, the philosopher Mary Midgley criticized talk about our "alien" status, such as that of Jacques Monod. Midgley writes:

> It is hard to see any reasonable justification for simply denying the continuity of nature in [such a] way. The objection to doing so does not depend on a religious belief in God as Creator, though it is quite compatible with that belief. It rests simply on our kinship with the rest of the natural world around us ... so that our natural tendency to love and revere it is wholly appropriate part of our emotional constitution. We are not alien invaders in this world. We are at home in it.[22]

There is thus a disconnect, even a discord, between what science has revealed and those distancing views of the world that have been overtaken by modern science's objectifying methodology. Science employs that method (which can be traced back to René Descartes, an early promoter of science) to ensure that its findings will be testable and consistent regardless of which scientist is making the observations. But that demand for objectification can distort our perceptions if we forget it is only a scientific tool, and turn objectification into a way of trying to inhabit this Earth psychologically and spiritually. Such an approach does not just splits us off from the world, splitting mind from the natural world. It also splits our human selves—splitting mind from our other human faculties.

Midgley provides an explanation and an example:

> This demand to treat nature as pure object meant that even natural beings that were alive should in effect be treated as dead.... In France, where Descartes's message has been deeply absorbed, this idea still has great imaginative force. It lies at [the author] Sartre's peculiar vision of the natural world as absurdly loathsome, expressed, for instance, at the climax of his

novel *Nausea.*

In the passage Midgley refers to, Jean Sartre describes how, while "in the municipal park," he observed how the "root of the chestnut tree plunged into the ground underneath my bench," and he "no longer remembered that it was a root." He explains how he thus discovered his alienation—how "death itself would have been superfluous" because the essence of everything "is contingency," chance, and uncertainty. But Midgley observes:

> It is surely remarkable that this horrified sense of
> disconnectedness starts from a reaction to a *root*—
> something which, one would suppose, even a
> distracted metaphysician could see to be *connected*.
> But Sartre's despair is indeed what follows from
> accepting Descartes's sharp antithesis [i.e., opposition]
> between a world of mind [and] the realm of nature.[23]

One way the world's faith-traditions have cultivated our sense of rootedness in the Earth has been through prayers, liturgies, and rituals that nurture gratitude in response to our experiencing the Earth's benevolence in sustaining our human lives. The historian of cultures Thomas Berry, drawing upon both his Christian background and his reflecting upon the ecology of this planet, writes:

> As humans we are born of the Earth, nourished by the
> Earth, healed by the Earth. The natural world tells us: I
> will feed you, I will clothe you, I will shelter you, I
> will heal you.... For I offer you a communion with the
> divine, I offer you gifts that you can exchange with
> each other, I offer you flowers whereby you may
> express your reverence for the divine and your love for
> each other.[24]

Pain and Healing

Thomas Berry's statement that we are "healed by the Earth" could be read as simply referring to medicines created out of the minerals and living species of the Earth. But his reference to "communion with the divine" suggests something more. Even being physically well does not protect us from sorrow, nor ensure our sense of belonging. Can the Earth also heal our sorrows and allay our feelings of dislocation?

That question might seem strange to some people, but there is

Biblical precedent for it. One place in particular is the climactic scene of the Bible's book of Job. The man Job has endured more causes of sorrow than any human being should ever have to endure: His farm destroyed. His children killed. His health gone.[25] As if to make matters worse, even though he is in no way the cause of his sufferings, his insensitive friends assume he is, and tell him incessantly that bad things do not happen to good people. Job protests his innocence in a continuous lament until God appears. God, however, does not provide any explanation for Job's sufferings. Instead, of all things, God has Job contemplate different animals in the world about him. And even more puzzling, these animals are hardly warm and fuzzy, nor are they living easy, pretty lives.[26] And yet, a quietness comes upon Job.[27] A kind of inner peace that we have never seen in him before.

Once when I was teaching a class that drew upon that part of the Job story, I raised the question of why Job should now be calmed. I will never forget the answer one woman gave amid the silence of the rest of the class. She said, "Sometimes it is comforting not to be at the center of things." And indeed, up to that point, Job had been so concentrated upon himself, understandably so, given the immensity of his sufferings. But an inner shift occurs as is able to let that burden go—at the same moment in which he feels himself more a part of this all-surrounding Earth.

It is here on this earthly ground, as we expand our awareness beyond our human sphere, that we see animals that, like ourselves, are finding their own paths for their lives. It is here that we find that we are not alone in struggle and sorrow. And also find that we can share and celebrate our discoveries and our joys. It is here on this Earth, as we experience the cycles of seasons, and as we discover the life-cycles of other species, that we develop a sense of belonging for our own lives as they grow and fade.

Why the Cosmos?

If we affirm with the poet Robert Frost that, "Earth's the right place for love: / I don't know where it's likely to go better,"[28] then why should we even attempt to extend our sense of spiritual belonging any further than this Earth, the sun that warms it, and the moon that moves its tides? Why not just keep our mental focus on this planet, and forget about the vast number of lifeless planets and the incomprehensible stretches of uninhabited space between them? That might seem like a safer approach, but it detaches the Earth from its own home in the universe out of which it was born, as we now know from modern science.

Also, from the standpoint of all of the Western theistic faith-traditions (Judaism, Christianity, and Islam), it has been critical to affirm that God is the Creator and Sustainer of *all* that exists. The modern theologian Sallie McFague expresses that core idea when she writes that, "The scope of God's power and love is cosmological.... Otherwise, God would not be God."[29]

A cosmic scope can thus be a way of imaginatively widening our mental picture so that we remind ourselves that God's love is all-encompassing.

Moreover, 20th-century science's knowledge of the history of our universe provides all people a universal story—a story that people of all faith-traditions can share. It is an awesome narrative of how our universe began with a Big Bang, leading to the formation of galaxies, to our Sun, our planet Earth, and finally to life and the evolution of species upon it.

Because that often-repeated narrative has come out of the discoveries of modern science, it gives the appearance of being just facts, not prejudiced by human desires. But often overlooked is one critical way that narrative is unconsciously shaped by a human preference. Why is it told as a chain of events leading to the development of planet Earth? A narrative could be constructed just as scientifically that would lead to planet X in galaxy Y, or to planet Z. The choice of a meaningful narrative thread to follow is something that lies beyond the tools of modern science, as the theologian John Haught has pointed out.[30] But that is just as well. After all, what meaning could it bring to us if we did not follow the thread of the story that leads to life on Earth and even to us?

Scientists, when they tell the narrative of the universe following that thread, have thus allowed themselves to be not just scientists but also storytellers. It is an ancient art.

A New Home for Our Sacred Stories

Any exploration of the topic of belonging requires us to look at the roles stories play. As the professor of psychology John Teske succinctly states, "Myths, narratives, and stories engage human beings, produce their sense of identify and self-understanding, and shape their intellectual, emotional, and embodied lives."[31] All the elements of psychology Teske lists impinge upon when and where we feel (or do not feel) a sense of belonging.

Even though, with the help of modern science, we now possess a universal narrative that begins with the Big Bang and ends with ourselves as evolved creatures, how can we connect that grand narrative with the religious stories that have been passed down to us through our particular faith-traditions? (For most practicing Jews and Christians, that would be primarily narratives from the Bible.) In Chapter 17, "A Lost Dimension of the Bible," with the story of Ruth as a demonstration, we saw how to expand our awareness to see the significance of elements in Nature that are already in such stories, but which have often fallen into the back-ground.

There is another technique that can be employed even when there are not any Nature-elements explicitly mentioned in a religious narrative. It is the technique of *nesting*. We already commonly use that technique when we nest our individual faith-journeys within the larger narratives of our families and our religious communities. And nest those group-narratives within the story of humankind. In a similar fashion, we can imaginatively nest a religious story about human beings within the larger narrative of our living planet, and even within the story of the cosmos.

Let us look at how the theme of belonging in one Biblical narrative might be expanded through nesting to encompass the larger, cosmic narrative, even though that sphere is not explicitly mentioned in the text in the Old Testament (the Hebrew Bible/*Tanakh*). It is the narrative in Genesis 28:10-22, which takes place after the young Jacob has had to flee his home because he has deceived his father and taken advantage of his slower-witted brother in order to usurp his brother's rightful inheritance.

Although the immediate context is Jacob's fleeing from his enraged brother, there is a larger background to the young Jacob's situation (Gen. 25:22-27 & 27:1-45). There may be something else that Jacob is wanting to escape from. If we bring the terse Biblical narration into sharper mental focus, we could reasonably suspect that Jacob grew up in a dysfunctional family: An overbearing, secretly manipulating mother and a mostly passive father. One parent being partial to one son; the other parent partial to the other son. Even though Jacob deceived his father, he did so at his mother's instigation. Throughout Jacob's entire growing up, he has been imprisoned in a web of family dysfunctionality.

So where does he find himself now? By the time Jacob has gotten a safe distance from the home he has left behind and from his brother, night has fallen. Jacob must rest and sleep, even though he has no sleeping mat and no over-arching tent to shelter himself from the cool night air. Having been a mother's boy, and not having been an outdoorsman (Gen. 25:27), he might have never slept in the open before. As for a pillow, he finds nothing to use other than a hard rock (Gen. 28:11). We imagine him now, lying on his back, still a bit frightened, and very uncertain about the future that lies ahead. If there is a future at all. But he longs for something better, something more fulfilling than what his life has been.

And what does he see as he lies there on his back at night in the desert? It is quite likely that what he sees is a velvet-black sky shot through with more stars than he could have ever imagined. In that beautiful night sky, he experiences something much more expansive than anything he ever saw going to sleep in his family's tent. Jacob is over-arched by something not of his own making. Something grander than anything he ever tried to contrive or grasp for himself.

Jacob has no idea whether he will ever be able to return to his previous home. But now, as he begins to fall asleep, a feeling of peace and prospect for his life comes upon him. A sense of belonging to something larger. And once he is asleep, he will dream a wonderful dream that gives him a sense of promise, a sense of the possibility that a grand future for his life might lie ahead. And he feels that God is with him, and will remain with him (Gen. 28:12-15).

It is suitable that the dis-located Jacob should fall asleep in that way. Because, as the 20th-century philosopher Ernst Bloch once wrote:

> The wish at the heart of religion is still
> that the human being should feel at home
> in the mystery of existence.[32]

Chapter 20

Scientists and Mystics
in Dialogue

N ear the year 1900, the historian Henry Adams, a lover of
medieval arts, was exploring the great cathedral at Chartres,
France in order to write an appreciation of it. Once inside, like
countless people who had entered before him, he let his eyes
explore the 13th-century cathedral's immense stained-glass
windows in ruby reds glowing in the midst of watery blues. But
Adams was puzzled by one irregularity. Why was a small section
of windows toward the front of the interior composed not of those
glorious rich colors and expressive pictures, but instead of a
simple pattern in only grays? Even as an admirer of the culture of
the Middle Ages, he could only conclude that the reason for that
monochromatic art lay beyond our modern understanding. What
Henry Adams did not know was that the colorless section of
windows had originally been in the same brilliant colors as elsewhere in the cathedral, but had been replaced with the drab gray in
the 1700's. The drab section of windows had not been installed
during the medieval period, which we sometimes call "the Dark
Ages," but during the period we now call "the En*light*enment."[1]
For those who study the history of religion-science relationships, this otherwise minor incident of European history bears
special interest. It is the reverse of our contemporary caricature of
the Middle Ages as a period of religious gloom and ignorance in
contrast to the world we now live in, which we view as being
brightened through the coming of scientific knowledge. For
example, in his 1980 book *Cosmos*, based on his popular TV
series, the astronomer Carl Sagan left a timeline entirely blank
from the 500's to the 1500's, adding a comment that it was "a
thousand years of darkness."[2]
Nor should we imagine that Chartres cathedral's colorful
Middle-Age artwork was portraying just the glory of an other-
worldly afterlife. Among the scenes depicted are many of earthly
life, such as the stained-glass picture of shoemakers, who were

among those who contributed funds for building Chartres. (See black-and-white rendering in Figure 15.)

During the 20th century, the myth of continuous religion-science "warfare"—now discredited by historians—held sway. And that myth played into the way the past and the present were caricatured, as the historian Christine Garwood recently explained:

> The image of warfare between religion and science was as powerful as it was simplistic.... From the "Dark Ages" of superstition to the Enlightenment era and modern science, the scheme could have been named "progress from the past",... and the equation of science with truth and advance, and religion with error and backwardness, served [writers'] purposes only too well.[3]

Early in the 20th century, however, the historian Herbert Butterfield had spotted the misguided tendency in interpreting history in such a fashion. Borrowing the word "Whig" from the Whig progressive party in Britain of his day, Butterfield criticized what has come to be known as "the Whig interpretation of history."[4] It is a distorted view of history as progressing, usually inevitably, toward our own (of course more enlightened) way of seeing things today. Instead, we need to understand the past—in both religion and science—on its own terms the best we can. If we do not, we are likely to underrate the accomplishments of the past and overrate ourselves.

In this book's Introduction, we drew upon the Biblical story of Jacob and Esau to develop the metaphor of wrestling brothers for the variety of relationships between religion and science. We might return to that widely applicable story at this point to draw upon another feature of it. Namely, the alternations in dominance between the two siblings: Jacob seems for some time to have completely supplanted his brother. A shift in dominance has also occurred between religion and science. Before the academic turf wars of the latter 1800's in Britain and the U.S., religion had a dominant position in those countries and their universities. Today in most Western universities, the situation is inverted. Science now holds the dominant position. And especially during the first half of the 20th century, much popular writing about science took a *triumphalist* tone, declaring that science was giving humans

Figure 15: Shoemakers in window of Chartres cathedral
(This portrayal is positioned beneath a depiction of Jesus telling the
story of the Good Samaritan)

knowledge and power that would enable them to do without religion.[5]

Understanding through Dialogue

Fortunately, the past several decades have seen a variety of struc-tured, public forms of religion-science cooperation. (Jacob and his brother do re-connect after years apart.[6]) The Clergy Letter Project encourages churches, synagogues, and mosques to join in the annual Evolution Weekend to emphasize the compatibility of reli-gion and the theory of evolution.[7] And the John Templeton Foun-dation has sponsored numerous projects, as well as encouraging the voices of Scientists in Congregations.[8]

For the past few decades, discussions of religion-science relationships have often drawn upon Ian Barbour's very helpful categorization of four ways those fields can interrelate: Conflict, Independence, Dialogue, and Integration.[9] His categories remind us of the variety of relationships, as well as providing labels that are immediately recognizable.

The preceding chapters of the book you are reading have grappled with instances of conflict (easily caricatured), and have wrestled with instances of influence and even integration. This chapter will explore the value (and challenges) that might still come from further dialogue between religion and science, with an emphasis on the roles those two enterprises play within society. Therefore we might step back a bit and ask the question: What is dialogue? In one sense, we employ the word "dialogue" for any verbal exchange. However, among the many words we employ for forms of speech, "dialogue" stands on a spectrum between conversation and debate. Conversation can be a first step for people getting to know each other. Toward the other end of the spectrum (a step short of arguing and fighting) stands debating. Dialogue lies in between. In one specific use of the word, when true dialogue occurs, people move into a *mutual understanding* about significant matters, a shared level of comprehension they did not possess before the dialogue began.

So, let us imagine for awhile a dialogue between a mainstream, educated religious leader and a scientist well-versed in one field of the natural sciences.

Like any discussion between people whose enterprises have at times struggled with how to live together, time might be needed at first for the dialoguers to air some lingering grievances—some points of continued misinformation or misunderstanding. First, from our religious leader might come complaints about some of those small myths about religion-science history that help perpetuate the larger "warfare" myth:

- No, the ancient Library of Alexandria (mentioned in Chapter 1) did not come to an end because early Christianity opposed scientific learning.[10] In a nutshell, as one historian puts it, the Library "decayed as the result of neglect" by political rulers, leaving "no one left to tend and preserve it."[11]
- No, Giordano Bruno's execution by the 16th-century Roman Catholic Church was not for his advocating Copernicus's scientific proposal of how the Earth could revolve around the sun.[12] Bruno's use of a sun-centered model was not for scientific reasons but because he was a follower of the cult of Hermetism, which was based on the

ideas of ancient Egyptians who worshiped the sun. Bruno's worst offense was that, although a Roman Catholic priest, he had been traveling about Europe advocating occult magic, and teaching that Moses and Jesus were occult magicians.[13] Moreover, as one leading historian of science points out, "No scientist, to our knowledge, ever lost his life because of his scientific views."[14]

- No, the 16th-century Protestant reformer John Calvin did not denounce Copernicus by saying, "Who will venture to place the authority of Copernicus above that of the Holy Spirit?" (even though that bogus quotation is still repeated today).[15] The supposed quotation is pure fabrication, and is not to be found in Calvin's *Commentary on Genesis*, where it is supposed to have come from, nor anywhere else in Calvin's writings. It seems to have first appeared in a work by F. W. Farrar in 1886, as a part of late 19th-century turf wars in academia.[16]

Our imagined scientist would probably also have some grudges to air as the dialogue begins. Such as:

- No, scientists' calling evolution "the theory of evolution" does not mean that they think evolution is just a hypothesis with little to back it up.[17] For scientists, a theory is not just an idea or speculation, but is a unifying concept that connects various pieces of evidence. And an enormous amount of evidence from various fields of science grounds scientists' acceptance of evolution.[18]
- No, scientists (for the great part) are not trying to do away with religion. And most scientists think a religious urge to trust or have faith in God need not be put in opposition to a desire to understand more about the world scientifically.[19]

The Magnet of Truth

Hopefully, our two dialoguers might recognize that this effort to clear away myths demonstrates how they have a common desire. They both have a desire for truth.

On a practical level, if our dialoguers have children or a concern for children's development, they might discover a shared interest in how accurately textbooks and other books for the young represent the histories of both religion and science. (Such as how the common way of telling the Galileo story distorts the histories of *both* enterprises.)[20] On a broader level, our dialoguers can share a concern about the importance of truth in an age that easily leans toward a cynicism that thinks that truth is "just relative." Or thinks it is just political. The scientist Denis Alexander explains:

> Historically the scientific enterprise has strong
> Christian roots and Christians have a firm commitment
> to truth-telling about God's world. Most importantly,
> both science and Christianity are skeptical about
> relativistic theories of knowledge....[21]

Our current religion-science debates in the public arena can give the impression that Christianity is concerned only about particular religious truths, but Alexander's broader emphasis about truth has a long Christian legacy lying behind it. From even before the 4th century, when the bishop Ambrose of Milan wrote:

> All truth, no matter by whom it is uttered, comes from
> the Holy Spirit [i.e., God's Spirit].[22]

That legacy endured even beyond the Protestant reformer John Calvin in the 16th century, who wrote:

> If we recognize the Spirit of God as the unique
> fountain of truth, we shall never despise the truth
> wherever it may appear.[23]

Science and religion aim for different levels of understanding (as was explained in Chapter 5, "Two Windows onto the World"). Ian Barbour, having been a professor of both physics and religion, was well aware that "religion cannot claim to be scientific or to be able to conform to the standards of science." Nevertheless, religion might have a "spirit of inquiry," as he put it. There might be "a continual demand that our concepts and beliefs be closely related to what we have experienced."[24]

Such an approach, besides finding common ground between religion and science, can also make religion more appealing in our global age, in which our faith-traditions can too easily feel parochial. The contrasting universalism of scientific knowledge can compound this problem, as the cosmologist Hermann Bondi expresses:

> Perhaps the most striking feature of science is its
> universality.... It is in this respect that the contrast with
> religion is so total.... Science unites the world and

makes it possible for people of widely differing
backgrounds to work together and to cooperate.[25]
There thus lie ahead possibilities for intersections of interfaith
dialogue with religion-science dialogue.

Despite such mutuality that might emerge between our imagined religious leader and scientist during their dialogue, it could
prove quite helpful to have a third person—perhaps a philosopher
of science—facilitating the discussion.[26] That is because it is easy
for scientist-writers today, often without realizing it, to slip into
making assertions that seem as if they are part of scientific findings, but which really lie beyond the bounds of science. Over half-
a-century ago, the geneticist Sewall Wright reminded his fellow
scientists that, "Science deliberately accepts a rigorous limitation
of its activities to the description of the external aspect of events,"
and that "the scientist should not ... deceive himself or others into
thinking that he is giving an account of all of reality."[27] Nonetheless, numerous philosophers today who have examined the popular
books of scientists such as Richard Dawkins, Stephen Hawking,
Carl Sagan, Steven Weinberg, and Edward O. Wilson have pointed
out how all of them make personal assertions with the implication
(or sometimes outright claim) that such conclusions are derived
from science itself.[28]

Despite such stumbling blocks, there are considerable opportunities in our imagined religious leader and our scientist discussing
their common interest in truth. Our religious leader might even be
able to contribute a metaphysical observation that lies outside of
the realm of scientific observation. Namely, that even while we
and all the entities in the world pass away over the course of time,
truth grows. That seems counterintuitive. How can that be? The
theologian John Haught has explored this line of thinking previously developed by the philosopher and theologian Charles
Hartshorne. In Hartshorne's phrasing, it goes this way: At one
time, "there was once no such individual as myself," and so there
was no such truth that I existed. "But centuries after my death,
there will have been that very individual which I am"[29]—and thus
the new truth that I existed. The store of truth will thus have
expanded with the new truth that I lived—just as it expands with
each new being coming into existence.

Truth itself can thus be viewed as being greater than the

material world.

Making Mysticism Less Mysterious

Despite the more frequent and more varied dialogue between promoters of religion and promoters of science over the past few decades, communication is still cluttered with the derogatory use of a number of words. (The discordant use of several words is explained in this book's Glossary of Conflicting Usages.)

One word that has been employed in a pejorative sense in both religion and science, but which has begun to be restored to a more respectable status, is "mysticism." When I was growing up in the mid-20th century in a mainline Protestant denomination, the word "mysticism" was pulled up disparagingly to depict what a Christian should not be. Mystics were (supposedly) escapists who wanted to live in their own world of private, ecstatic experiences, rather than being concerned about and engaged in society.

Fortunately, mainline Protestantism has over the past half-century begun to better understand and appreciate the strands and vitalities within religion that can be called "mysticism" in a good sense. References to and brief quotations from such great mystics as Theresa of Ávila, Julian of Norwich, and Meister Eckhart are now sprinkled through many Protestant books about the spiritual and religious life. "Currently mysticism is attracting a degree of interest unrivaled since the late-medieval period," according to one teacher of Christian theology.[30]

Why bring up mysticism? One reason is because the mystic spirit (in a healthy sense) can be one element for correcting the direction of a Christianity that got thrown off course to some degree by the rise of modern science. As science expanded its ability to describe the operation of more and more of the world in terms of self-operating "natural laws," God frequently got shoved back into the past. (Some aspects of this challenge were explained in Chapter 6, "Ancient Wisdom Raises Her Head.") Restoring people's experience of God in the present is thus critical for modern Western Christianity. And the mystic strands in any faith-tradition emphasize people's experiencing the *immediacy* of their relationship with the Ultimate (whatever name it might be given).[31]

Nevertheless, even as recently as 2006, the word "mysticism" has had as one of its secondary dictionary definitions, "Vague, groundless speculation."[32] And so that word can be a handy slur for Whiggish promoters of the cliché of scientific knowledge ever-advancing by leaving religion behind in the historical dust. Given this awkward history of the word, perhaps the test of whether our two dialoguers have truly reached a point of communicating productively would be when they come to a clearer, shared understanding of mysticism in the way that term is now being used positively in Christianity. Clarity about mysticism might be one pinnacle to strive for.

Paradoxically, even though the meaning of "mysticism" in the healthy sense can be one of the most difficult matters upon which to reach understanding, the mystic strands in religion have turned out to be something upon which people of different faith-traditions have come to a greater recognition of their religious similarities. The voices of mystic poets travel across cultural and religious boundaries like sounds in the refreshingly cool night air.

If reaching clarity on the word "mysticism" is too challenging a pinnacle in religion-science dialogue, a closeness of understanding might be found in experiences of wonder at the intricacies of the natural world around us. During his adult life, the astronomer Carl Sagan, although never seeming to understand the character of theological language, did move toward an appreciation of how leaders in both religion and science could become allies in guarding against the destructive dangers of some scientific technologies.[33] Sagan headed a panel that led to the Union of Concerned Scientists' releasing a 1990 statement that took a noticeably religious tone in expressing many scientists' experiences of wonder—and perhaps of something more:

> As scientists, many of us have had profound
> experiences of awe and reverence before the
> universe.[34]

In passing, we might also notice how the context of this statement—a shared concern about the environment—demonstrates another avenue for mutuality between religion and science. Such instances of cooperation are why the theologian Elizabeth Johnson suggests that, "there is a fifth model of interaction that I would add to [Ian] Barbour's chart, namely *practical cooperation* for the preservation of the natural world."[35]

As wonderful as wonder is, and as wonderful as it is to have scientists express it, wonder is not always enough. As the theologian Celia Deane-Drummond points out, "If we simply accept wonder as the outcome of the evolutionary process [as explained by science], we are left without a clear sense of what to do with that wonderment."[36]

Keeping Awake

Gothic cathedrals such as Chartres were unified expressions of religion, art, and the latest scientific building technology. Although less famous than the Chartres cathedral, there is another piece of artwork from Christian European history that similarly demonstrates a linkage of religion and science. It is the elaborate clock installed in a cathedral in Strasbourg in 1843 to replace earlier versions made in the 14th and 16th centuries. (See Figure 16.) Although too baroque for most modern tastes, the clock epitomizes an earlier fascination with scientific technology that could construct mechanical clocks with increasing sophistication. Its being designed for a cathedral represented a confidence that the Maker of the universe was a Designer who infused the cosmos with clock-like natural laws that reason and scientific investigation could uncover.[37]

One small detail of the clock's design can easily go unnoticed. On top of the peak on the left side as you face it is a life-size rooster that comes to life at midday. That crowing bird announces the time, but it is also a reminder of every human being's vulnerability to moral failure. That is because in its heavily Christian culture, it was a reference to the Biblical story of Peter, the most enthusiastic of Jesus's followers, who repeatedly denies he ever knew Jesus after Jesus is arrested.[38] Peter recognizes his moral weakness when he is reminded by a crowing cock of Jesus's earlier prediction that Peter would fall away from the goodness Jesus embodies when times got tough (John 13:38 & 18:27).

Today, that little mechanical bird might remind us of two things. First, that in most nations of the modern West, we live in societies that are both secularized and pluralistic. People are less likely to recognize the Biblical symbolism of the Strasbourg clock's crowing cock, especially if they are of faith-traditions other than Christianity. Our discussions of religion-science relationships need to be sensitive to those multicultural challenges.

Figure 16: Clock in cathedral in Strasbourg

Secondly, that mechanical moral reminder on an elaborate mechanical device in a cathedral can remind us of the ever-present danger of science being employed not for good but for bad. We need to keep awake.

Today, the history of modern science is still frequently framed as a story of science every-advancing triumphantly, and so false turns and misuses of science are usually expunged from the record. A prime example is that today most books about evolution —even books about the development of scientific thought about it —have no index-entry for "eugenics." That movement, which aimed at improving the human race by controlling who had children and who did not, is now regarded as being pseudo-science.

But in the early 20th century, eugenics was not just an idea of some renegade scientist at work in his own garage. Setting aside the eugenic movement's success in Britain and Europe, and focusing on the U.S. alone, we can see that eugenics had the support of many scientists: Professors such as the sociologists Edward A. Ross at the University of Wisconsin and Charles Ellwood at the University of Missouri. Some psychologists, even one of the best known at the time, William McDougall from Harvard, endorsed it. Other nationally recognized psychologists who were supporters were Robert Yerkes and Lewis Terman. The biologist most behind it, the zoologist Charles Davenport, had taught at the University of Chicago. And as one contemporary historian explains:

> The eugenics movement achieved wide acceptance in
> the United States in the first thirty years of the
> twentieth century.... If the aim was human betterment,
> then science had provided the answer: eugenics.[39]

So popular was that movement that it led to laws in thirty states of the U.S. giving their governments the authority to sterilize certain criminals and mentally deficient people who were in public institutions.[40] In the U.S. alone, thousands of people were forcibly sterilized.

Expunging information about the eugenics movement from today's textbooks prevents us from learning how alert we need to be to ways that seemingly scientific knowledge can be used to endorse actions that will look misguided in hindsight.

Even when we are aware of such dangers, modern science's

method of relying on observations of the external world, coupled with its technological power to alter the world around us, inclines our minds toward thinking about ethics in terms of the effects our actions have upon the world around us. Recovering more of the traditional role religion has played, we would give more attention to the *internal* world—the attitudes, sensibilities, and other qualities that we are cultivating within ourselves. The theologian Celia Deane-Drummond encourages restoring a "virtue ethics" that would cultivate cardinal virtues of character:

> This does not mean that virtue ethics is not interested in particular actions, or for that matter the consequences of those actions. Rather, the fundamental ethical question of what I should do is expanded into related questions about who I am, who I should become, and how I should get there.[41]

A virtue ethics would not just consider the effect of social programs (such as eugenics), but would also encourage each of us to look within ourselves to examine what motivations we are cultivating. We have discovered how to shape the world around us in ways once never dreamed of. We are in comparison novices in learning how to shape ourselves from within.

Deane-Drummond is also among a fair number of Christian theologians who have called for breathing new life into the Biblical concept of wisdom. In the Bible, the spirit of Wisdom (sometimes personified as a woman) refers to both our best way of living and God's wisdom in how we and the world are made.[42] Besides being a concept that non-religious scientists might be able to recognize, the concept of wisdom has an advantage in its universality. Wisdom is a concept that people of all faith-traditions might recognize aspects of.

The Humanities and Our Humanness

Hopefully, one other thing that might emerge during our imagined dialogue is the realization that the religion-science divide is part of a broader divide between science and the humanities. That fact is virtually never mentioned in the general media's discussions about religion and science. Because modern Western religion has mostly turned the non-human sphere over to science, and because of science's dominance, it can be easy to get to thinking that science is our only way of getting real facts about the world. But we also learn about both ourselves and the world through the study of history, through biographies, and through other academic avenues. Even at times through literature. And, of course, through everyday experience. The contemporary biologist Francisco J. Ayala, who is also educated in theology, writes:

> In *The Myth of Sisyphus*, the great French writer Albert
> Camus asserted that we learn more about ourselves
> and the world from a relaxed evening's contemplation
> of the starry heavens and the scents of grass than from
> science's reductionistic ways. One needs not endorse
> such a contrasting claim in order to uphold the validity
> of the knowledge acquired by *non*-scientific modes of
> inquiry.[43]

One of the most intensely debated issues today between some scientists and disagreeing theologians still flies under the radar of the general media. Its is the issue of whether science, with its particular way of providing explanations, can with time absorb more and more of other academic fields, even the humanities and theology. The most ambitious attempt to put forward such a vision was Edward O. Wilson's 1998 book *Consilience*.[44] In a similar vein, in another one of his books Wilson asserted about science's methodology that, "the final decisive edge... will come from its capacity to explain traditional religion, its chief competitor, as a wholly material phenomenon."[45]

But numerous writers—both non-scientists and scientists— have criticized the very grounds for such an endeavor. The most extended critique has probably been made in a posthumous book by the scientist Stephen Jay Gould, in which he pointed out that:

> The sciences and humanities, by the basic logics of
> their disparate enterprises, do different things, each
> equally essential to human wholeness. We need this
> wholeness above all, but cannot achieve the goal by
> shearing off the legitimate differences ... that make our
> lives so varied, so irreducibly, and so fascinatingly,
> complex.... Wilson's model of consilience ...
> misconstrues the inherent nature of similarities and
> differences in these two intellectual ways ... by
> glossing [i.e., varnishing over] the differences in

pursuing the chimera of false unification.[46]

Today, all our academic areas of study, as well as all fields of the sciences, have become highly specialized. That specialization is why the number of writers who have degrees in both religion and science (such as Arthur Peacocke, John Polkinghorne, and Celia Deane-Drummond) are few in number. The specialization and splintering of our modern fields of academic knowledge can make it difficult for some scientists to really grasp what a particular field in the humanities is all about. For example, in his book *Consilience*, Wilson depicted the work of philosophy (a highly technical field dealing with the nature of knowledge and reasoning) as being "the contemplation of the unknown." But Gould, who was well-read in the humanities, pointed out that such a description "will ... either annoy or at least amuse some professional philosophers."[47]

The historian Ian F. McNeely explains that before the expansion of modern science, "scientists in Europe and Islam once saw the mastery and manipulation of nature as complementary, not antagonistic, to religious and humanistic understanding."[48] Using the same word "complementary," the American Association for the Advancement of Science has recognized that, "Many religious leaders and scientists alike view scientific investigation and religious faith as complementary components of a well-rounded life."[49]

But we might well ask: Is the purpose of a complementarity of science with religion, as well as with the other humanities, just so that we will have "well-rounded" lives? Didn't education in the humanities once have the purpose of helping people become more mature in character? Didn't it have the goal of developing qualities such as empathy, discernment, and good judgment? And developing wisdom? And maybe even reverence?

Art, Beauty, and Goodness

Looking back at the long course of 2,500 years of Western thought, we might be struck by the endurance of one particular concept. Namely, the idea, inspired in part by the ancient philosopher Plato, that there are three openings through which humans can know the Divine: Truth, Goodness, and Beauty.[50] Focusing on the last of these three—Beauty—brings us to the additional sphere of the arts, and what they might play in society.

In the great Gothic cathedrals (such as the one at Chartres) we see an integration of Christianity and the arts with the latest innovations in scientific engineering. A confluence, not a conflict, of three arenas of human endeavor: science, religion, and art. Notice the rough three-fold parallel to Truth, Goodness, and Beauty.

However, with the 17th-century rise of modern science, and with subsequent changes in thought and societies, the spheres split apart. The writer Ken Wilber explains, using the label "morals" for the sphere that overlaps much of religion:

> Where previously the spheres tended to be fused,
> modernity differentiated them and let each proceed at
> its own pace, with its own dignity.... The "bad news"
> of modernity was that these value spheres did not just
> peacefully separate, they often flew apart completely....
> This allowed a powerful and aggressive science to
> begin to invade and dominate the other spheres,
> crowding art and morals out of any serious
> consideration in approaching "reality."[51]

This splitting of the three spheres is evidenced by the way in contemporary Western culture that we tend to understand and interpret most art as being self-expression, rather than being an avenue to knowing truths about the world.

Among the three principle openings, Beauty has had its up's and down's in the West theologically, as the religion professor Frank Burch Brown explains:

> Although Christian theologians have reflected on
> beauty as well as on goodness, truth, and holiness, it is
> in fact beauty that they have most often slighted....
> Theologians [today, however,] increasingly recognize
> that aesthetic experience is a pervasive factor in our
> sense of the sacred, in our delight in creation (both
> human and divine), and in our moral imagination of
> good and evil.[52]

In religious thought, it has been considered critical to remember the link of Beauty to Goodness, not elevating Beauty alone. The modern classic about Beauty disjoined from Goodness is Oscar Wilde's *The Picture of Dorian Gray*, in which the main character makes a deal with the devil to preserve his youthful good looks, but meanwhile becomes corrupt and cruel from within.[53] The 20th-century writer Aldous Huxley, explaining the theological basis for that line of thought, writes that if a person "persists in worshiping the beauty in art and nature without going on to make himself capable, through selflessness, of apprehending Beauty as it is in the divine Ground, then he is only an idolater."[54] This is partly why classic Christian theology, even as it included Beauty as one opening into God, held to all *three* of the openings. Remembering the linkage to God helped pull the three principles together, not letting Beauty fly off on its own. The great medieval Christian theologian Thomas Aquinas saw God as the Ultimate Source of truth, goodness, and beauty, with the three being joined in God's own self.[55] And one of the sayings of Islam is, "God is beautiful and loves beauty."[56]

There is a grace in beauty itself. Encountering something beautiful can allay our anxious spirits, and give us a boost in facing our next step in life. We can encounter beauty in a painting or a piece of music. Our sense of grace can be even greater if the beauty is something in Nature itself, such as a sunset or a field of wildflowers. Such natural beauty can be more powerful because we know, at least subconsciously, that it was not constructed by human hands. We experience such natural beauty as a gift, something that need not have been. (Chapter 18 dealt with our need to read more often that "Book of Nature.")

Our modern three-way split of science, morals, and art places upon us the demand for self-integration in order to bring the divided aspects of the world together. Dialogue between spheres is not sufficient. The 20th-century theologian Charles Raven writes:

> All beauty, all truth, all goodness are the signs of
> [God's] presence and, potentially at least, the
> instruments of His purpose.... Hence [there is] the need
> in the full-grown man of the widest possible range of
> interests, so that he may dismiss nothing as common.[57]

Again, a concern for the character development of the individual person arises.

Finding Our Compass

This world can be a puzzling place. There are so many different entities in it, and so many of them have so much freedom, that the world can look chaotic. Similarly, our lives at times feel chaotic. Our modern, splintered spheres of learning do not make understanding this world any easier. How shall we orient our individual and communal life-journeys within the larger journeys of the world around us? What shall guide us as we wrestle with how to interrelate our varieties of knowledge from so many fields, as well as from our experiences of living? What shall guide us as we find our way through this world, sifting through everything?

All the world's great faith-traditions include teachings about the importance of cultivating the virtue of compassion as a way of learning to live better within this world.[58] Our world's faith-traditions still have much to share with one another.

For centuries, through all of the Middle Ages, the primary instrument for navigating on land was the hand-held astrolabe, a set of intricate, overlapping marked disks. In the 10th century, Gerbert of Aurillac—the future Pope Sylvester II—taught his students how to use that instrument, which had been greatly improved by Muslim scientists. Two-and-a-half centuries later, the Sufi mystic poet Rumi drew upon commonplace knowledge about that navigational tool to write that, "The astrolabe to the mysteries of God is love."[59] (Today, we would probably say, "The GPS to the mysteries of God is love.")

An enduring Christian hope (growing out of its Judaic roots) has been that each person will over time come to discern that there is a dimension that lies more deeply beneath the complexity of the world, and beneath the mundane challenges of life. A dimension lying partly hidden beneath the surface, but nevertheless sustaining all existence and all of life. And that Christian hope has also been that with time we will be able to rejoice in the same understanding that came to Julian of Norwich about the meaning of her visions that had at first been so puzzling to her. The understanding she expressed in the 14th century has become often quoted today:

> Do you wish to know your Lord's meaning in this
> thing? Know it well, love was his meaning. Who
> reveals it to you? Love. What did he reveal to you?
> Love. Why does he reveal it to you? For love. Remain
> in this, and you will know more of the same.[60]

Glossary of Conflicting Usages

Many current misunderstandings between religion and science are perpetuated because people in both enterprises use some of the same vocabulary but in quite different senses. Below are clarifications about words that are used in quite different ways, thus leading to conflict if the different uses of the word are not recognized.

belief:
In everyday English, we often use the word "believe" as a substitute for "think," particularly when saying that a person strongly thinks something to be the case. But a difficulty arises with that usage when a person thinks something that goes against scientific evidence to be the case. (Example: "The man believed a flying saucer had landed in his backyard yesterday afternoon.") With that usage, science is almost inevitably placed in conflict with belief (in this case, by looking for physical evidence that a heavy object had set down on the soft grass in the backyard, thus contradicting the man's belief).

However, a sound religious belief can *encompass* scientific knowledge, as well as knowledge derived through other means, such as everyday experience. Sound faith is not the opposite of knowing. When I step out my front door in the morning, I have to have a type of faith that the ground will support me. Yet that faith can encompass my knowledge about the ground's previous stability and about the unlikeliness of earthquakes where I live.

A sound religious belief is not holding to ideas in contradiction to facts. Instead, sound belief is embracing truths and values that we hold dear or love. That is shown by the word's origin: "Believed" has the same root as "be<u>loved</u>."

creation:
The general public frequently equates the religious concept that God "created" the world with the anti-evolutionist views of

creationists. But referring to the universe as "the creation" is, for many religious people, compatible with scientific knowledge. It is a complement to our knowledge about the beginnings of the universe, the appearance of life itself, and the evolution of species.

Nevertheless, the doctrine of creation (shared by Christianity, Judaism, and Islam) should not be confused with a mere statement of facts about events in the past. "Creation" is a theological interpretation pointing to existential truths, such as: That nothing in the universe has brought itself into being. That we humans share with all other beings dependency on God the Creator. And that our existence can be thought of as a gift, to which we can respond with gratitude.

Darwinism:
A most inconvenient term. To start with, we do not convert any other scientist's name into an "-ism." (I accept Newton's mathematical formula for gravity, but I do not say I believe in "Newtonianism," as if it were an ideology.)

Today, some scientists who are unsympathetic to religion promote their own packaged interpretations of evolution as "Darwinism." On the other hand, some people who object to ways the theory of evolution comes packaged in ideologies argue against "Darwinism." But that can make some scientists feel that the theory of evolution itself is under attack. (This is explained more in Chapter 9, "Opening Darwin's Gift.")

If anyone speaks or writes about "Darwinism," it would be best to inquire as to what they *specifically* mean.

mystery:
Countless TV programs tell us that contemporary science is "solving mysteries." That wording can put religion and science at odds because religions often nurture an awareness of our living in the midst of "mystery." However, the two enterprises' uses of the word will be different—provided religion is cultivating a sound approach toward knowledge.

Rather than saying that science is "solving mysteries," it would be clarifying to say that it is solving puzzles. That is, it is answering scientific questions. The danger for religion is that it will try to give the answer "God did it" to one of those as yet unanswered scientific questions. But that approach reduces God to a god of the gaps. That is, a god whose role continually shrinks as scientific knowledge expands, filling in previous gaps.

A sound religious sense of the word "mystery" aligns it more closely with the words "wonder" and "awe." In that sense, "mystery" points to the fact that our lives of faith are lived with an awareness of a depth that lies beyond any form of direct knowing. Even beyond science's kind of knowing. That greater sense of mystery is expressed by a question such as, "Why is there anything at all?"

naturalism:
Although this word is not a part of our everyday vocabulary, it lies on the dividing line of many current disagreements between advocates for religion and advocates for science. The issue in debates over "naturalism" is whether science is atheistic or whether it allows for God's presence in the natural world.

Those writers who try to resolve the conflict, such as mainline theologians, point out that we need to distinguish between two types of naturalism. Modern science does employ **methodological naturalism**, which is to say that its methods are those of looking for natural causes and effects that can be observed employing human senses. However, that form of naturalism is not the same as **philosophical naturalism**, which is the viewpoint that the natural things science identifies are the totality of all that is.

By emphasizing that science's naturalism need be only in its methodology (rather than being a philosophical stance), we allow room for religion and theology to depict God as being present in a dimension of depth that science cannot directly touch. (See this Glossary's entry on "mystery" about matters lying beyond science.)

theory:
Virtually always in ordinary English and in the media, the word "theory" is used to mean some idea that has not been proven. Scientists, however, use instead the word "hypothesis" to refer to an idea that needs testing, and which is of the type that science can test.

For scientists, a "theory" is not a hypothesis, but is a unifying concept that connects various pieces of evidence. Thus, scientists will speak of "the theory of gravity" not because there is no established evidence for gravity, but because that theory links the fall of an apple on Earth with the movements of planets in the solar system. It is in the same sense that science speaks of the "theory of evolution," because it links numerous pieces of evidence, from fields as varied as paleontology, anatomy, and genetics. (See the inset in Chapter 4, "An Awkward History," for samples of official religious statements accepting evolution.)

Reading Suggestions

The Notes section of this book demonstrates the extensive ongoing discussion at an academic level about religion-science relationships. Frequently, however, I have been approached by students who want something more introductory about a specific area. Below are the books I would recommend.

On Religion and Science in General:
Dixon, Thomas. *Science and Religion: A Very Short Introduction.* New York: Oxford University Press, 2008.

On Myths about the History of Science and Religion:
Numbers, Ronald L., editor. *Galileo Goes to Jail: And Other Myths about Science and Religion.* Cambridge, Mass.: Harvard University Press, 2009.

On the Symbolic Nature of Religious Language:
Tillich, Paul. *Dynamics of Faith.* New York: Harper Torchbooks, 1957.

On Interpreting the Bible:
Borg, Marcus. *Reading the Bible Again for the First Time: Taking the Bible Seriously but Not Literally.* San Francisco: HarperCollins, 2001.

On the Cultural Context of the Bible's Creation Narratives:
Hyers, Conrad. *The Meaning of Creation: Genesis and Modern Science.* Atlanta: John Knox Press, 1984.

On Hearing the Inner Meaning of the Bible's Miracle Stories:
John, Jeffrey. *The Meaning in the Miracles.* Grand Rapids, MI: William B. Eerdmans Publishing Co., 2001.

On Charles Darwin:
Aydon, Cyril. *Charles Darwin: The Naturalist Who Started a Scientific Revolution.* New York: Carroll & Graf Publishers, 2002.

On Evolution and Myths about It:
Smith, Cameron M. and Charles Sullivan. *The Top 10 Myths about Evolution.* Amherst, N.Y.: Prometheus Books, 2007.

On the History of the Evolution Controversies:
Giberson, Karl W. *Saving Darwin: How to Be a Christian and Believe in Evolution.* New York: HarperOne, 2008.

On the Misuse of Science, and Social Darwinism:
Gould, Stephen Jay. *The Mismeasure of Man.* New York: W.W. Norton & Co., 1981.

On Relating Evolution to Religion:
Haught, John F. *Responses to 101 Questions on God and Evolution.* New York: Paulist Press, 2001.

On the Difficulties with the Idea of "Intelligent Design":
Ayala, Francisco J. *Darwin and Intelligent Design.* Minneapolis: Fortress Press, 2006.

On Nature in the Bible:
The Green Bible: New Revised Standard Version. New York: HarperCollins, 2008. [Particularly the set of introductory essays, although the "Green Subject Index" can also be a useful tool.]

On Nature in the Bible and in Christian Theology:
Bradley, Ian. *God is Green: Ecology for Christians.* New York: Doubleday, 1990.

On Suffering, Perishability, and their Religious Implications:
Tillich, Paul. *The Shaking of the Foundations.* New York: Charles Scribner's Sons, 1948. [Particularly the chapters "On the Transitoriness of Life" and "Nature, Also, Mourns for a Lost Good."]

On the Cosmos's History and its Implications for Humans:
Swimme, Brian. *The Hidden Heart of the Cosmos: Humanity and the New Story.* New York: Orbis Books, Maryknoll, 1996.

Acknowledgments

The Notes section demonstrates the extensive, ongoing discussions about religion-science relationships, without which this book would not have been possible. The names of writers listed there should be considered an extension of this Acknowledgments page, even though I cannot thank them all personally.

I want to express my appreciation of John F. Haught and his visits to Houston over the past years to speak on and discuss theology at more than one venue.

I express my gratitude to all my students who, over the course of many years, have so attentively listened to my presentations and engaged in thoughtful discussion. Especially those of Central Presbyterian Church, Covenant Church, the Church and Society Class of St. Philip Presbyterian Church, and the Foundation for Contemporary Theology.

I am very appreciative of my copy editor for her help with my manuscript. Any mistakes I introduced into or did not spot in the galley proofs are my own.

And I am especially thankful for friends and family who encouraged me in this project.

Picture Credit

Notes

*Most of these Notes consist of listings of sources either for quotations or for other facts presented in this book. Where these Notes include additional material, it has been placed in **bold** for the convenience of readers who would like a few more tidbits of information.*

Introduction

1 Jon Balchin. *Science: 100 Scientists Who Changed the World.* New York: Enchanted Lion Books, 2003. p. 109.

2 Lawrence Principe. Quoted in Joshua M. Moritz. *Considering God's Works,* "Lecture 4: The War that Never Was—Exploding the Myth of the Historical Conflict Between Christianity and Science." Available through Scientists in Congregations. https://vimeo.com/77023999 (emphasis added)

3 David C. Lindberg and Ronald L. Numbers. "Beyond War and Peace: A Reappraisal of the Encounter Between Christianity and Science." *Perspectives on Science and Christian Faith* 39.3 (9/1987): pp. 140-149.

4 Amy McCaig, News release March 13, 2015. "Nearly 70 percent of evangelicals do not view religion and science as being in conflict." http://news.rice.edu/2015/03/13/nearly70percentofevangelicalsdonotview religionandscienceasbeinginconflict/#sthash.4yHXuHbJ.dpuf

5 David Ruth, News release February 16, 2014. "Misconceptions of science and religion found in new study."

6 Cary Funk and Becka A. Alper. **"Highly religious Americans are less likely than others to see conflict between faith and science."** http://www.pewinternet.org/2015/10/22/science-and-religion/? utm_source=Pew+Research+Center&utm_campaign=70a524fbc3- Weekly_Oct_22_201510_22_2015&utm_medium=email&utm_term=0_ 3e953b9b70-70a524fbc3-399622637.

7 Genesis 25:22 (NRSV).

8 Based on Gauguin's letter to Vincent Van Gogh, on or about July 22, 1888.

9 There are many lists of the multiple aspects of religions, but this list of seven is condensed from Michael J. Reiss. "The Relationship between Evolutionary Biology and Religion." *Evolution*, Vol. 63, No. 7 (July 2009). p. 1936. Available at http://www.jstor.org/stable/40306267.

10 **I write "practicing Jews" because, strictly speaking, the term "Jews" refers to an ethnic group, the members of which may or may not follow practices of Judaism. As one historian explains, "Some contemporary Jews would describe themselves as atheists ... rejecting any belief in God and eschewing [i.e., avoiding] religious practices."** (Geoffrey Cantor. "Modern Judaism." In *Science and Religion around the World*, edited by John Hedley Brooke & Ronald L.

Numbers. New York: Oxford University Press, 2011. p. 45.)

11 Allan D. Austin. *African Muslims in Antebellum America*. New York: Routledge, 1997. pp. 3-5.

12 John Michael Ziman. "Natural sciences." *The Norton Dictionary of Modern Thought*, edited by Alan Bullock, et al. New York: W.W. Norton & Co., 1999. pp. 564-565.

13 **Before modern times, early scientists were called "natural philosophers." But today the word "philosopher" is used with a quite different meaning, and so it could be confusing. Therefore, I employ today's closest equivalent—"scientist."**

Part One

Epigraph 1: Heidi A. Campbell and Heather Looy. *A Science and Religion Primer*. Grand Rapids, MI: Baker Academic, 2009. p. 11.

Epigraph 2: Colin A. Russell. "The Conflict of Science and Religion." In *The History of Science and Religion in the Western Tradition*, edited by Gary B. Ferngren, pp. 12-17. New York: Garland Publishing, Inc., 2000. pp. 12, 15.

Epigraph 3: Soren Kierkegaard. *Life*. Quoted in *Familiar Quotations*, edited by John Bartlett. 14th edition Boston: Little, Brown and Co., 1968. p. 676a.

Chapter 1

1 Robert J. Schadewald. "Flat-Earthism." In *The History of Science and Religion in the Western Tradition: An Encyclopedia*, edited by Gary B. Ferngren. New York: Garland Publishing, Inc., 2000. p. 412.

2 Aristotle. *On the Heavens* (Book II, 350 B.C.E.) Quoted in Christine Garwood. *Flat Earth: The History of an Infamous Idea*. New York: St. Martin's Press, 2007. p. 15. Source re. Aquinas: Lesley B. Cormack "Myth 3: That Medieval Christians taught that the Earth was Flat." In *Galileo Goes to Jail: And Other Myths about Science and Religion*, edited by Ronald L. Numbers. Cambridge, Mass.: Harvard University Press, 2009. p. 31.

3 **Although during these centuries scientists were called "natural philosophers," today the word "philosopher" is used with a quite different meaning. Therefore, I employ today's closest equivalent —"scientist."**

4 Lesley B. Cormack. "Myth 3." In *Galileo Goes to Jail*. p. 32.

5 Jeffrey Burton Russell. *Inventing the Flat Earth: Columbus and Modern Historians*. New York: Praeger, 1991. pp. 9-11.

6 Robert J. Schadewald. "Flat-Earthism." In *The History of Science and Religion in the Western Tradition: An Encyclopedia*. p. 412.

7 Washington Irving. *History of the Life and Voyages of Christopher Columbus*, 1828. Quoted in Denis Alexander. *Rebuilding the Matrix: Science and Faith in the 21st Century*. Grand Rapids, MI: Zondervan, 2001. p. 25.

8 Joseph Chiari. *Christopher Columbus*. New York: Gordian Press, 1979.

9 **Frequently, it is said that the pivotal date regarding church-state relationships was 312 C.E., when Emperor Constantine converted to Christianity. However, he did not make Christianity the official religion, and even granted freedom of worship to all in 313 with the Edict of Milan. And so, really more significant are the year 391 and Theodosius's action against non-Christian temples, as well as the year 438, which was the date of the harsh Theodosian Code.** (Source: *The Oxford Dictionary of the Christian Church*, edited by F. L. Cross. New York: Oxford Univ. Press, 1974. pp.1361 & 915.)

10 Karen Armstrong. *The Bible: A Biography*. New York: Atlantic Monthly Press, 2007. pp. 108-117.

11 Alister E. McGrath. *Christian Theology: An Introduction*, 4th edition. Malden, MA: Blackwell Publishing, 2007. p. 196.

12 David C. Lindberg. "Science and the Early Christian Church." *Isis*, Vol. 74 (Dec., 1983), pp. 509-530. Available at http://www.jstor.org/stable/232210.

13 Justin Martyr. *Second Apology*, Chapter 13. Available at http://www.catholicchurchdoctrine.com/wpcontent/uploads/2013/11/SaintJustinMartyrTheSecondApology.pdf.

14 Augustine. *The Literal Meaning of Genesis*, I, 42-43. Trans. by John Hammond Taylor. Quoted in *The History of Science and Religion in the Western Tradition: An Encyclopedia*. p. 280.

15 **"Plato uses the phrase *sophos kagathos* ('the wise and good'), perhaps basing this on the earlier stock phrase *kalos kagathos* ('the beautiful and good')."** — Alister E. McGrath. The *Open Secret: A New Vision for Natural Theology*. Malden, MA: Blackwell Publishing, 2008. p. 228n22.

16 Thomas Cahill. *Sailing the Wine-Dark Sea: Why the Greeks Matter.* New York: Nan A. Talese, Doubleday, 2003. p. 187.

17 **Because of our current concerns about patriarchal dominance over women, I should add that we probably should not read the "handmaiden" metaphor as being one of female submission to the male. Most likely, the female word "handmaiden" was chosen to describe a helping role for science because the Latin word *philosophia* for science is grammatically feminine. As was also the Latin word *theologia* for theology. So, if there is any gender implied by the metaphor, it would be one of feminine Theology being helped by feminine Science.** (Source: David C. Lindberg. "Medieval Science and Its Religious Context." *Osiris*, 2nd Series, Vol. 10. 1995. p. 72n25.)

18 Edward Grant. "Science and Theology in the Middle Ages." In *God and Nature: Historical Essays on the Encounter between Christianity and Science*, edited by David C. Lindberg and Ronald L. Numbers. Berkeley: University of California Press, 1986. p. 50.

19 William Shakespeare. *Julius Caesar*, I, ii, 134.

20 Augustine. *The City of God*, trans. Marcus Dods. New York: The Modern Library, 1950. V, p. 144.

21 Peter M. Hess. "Natural History." In *The History of Science and Religion in the Western Tradition: An Encyclopedia*. p. 501.

22 **St. Anthony of the Desert, also called St. Anthony of Egypt and St. Anthony the Great.** In a story told by Evagrius Ponticus in *Praktikos*, 92. Quoted in Thomas Merton. *The Wisdom of the Desert* (New York: New Directions, 1960), Saying CIII.

23 Joy Hakim. *The Story of Science: Aristotle Leads the Way*. Washington: Smithsonian Books, 2004. pp. 200-201.

24 Sources: M. Postan. "Why Was Science Backward in the Middle Ages?" In *A Short History of Science*. Garden City, N.Y. 1951. p. 12. And: James Hannam. *God's Philosophers: How the Medieval World Laid the Foundations of Modern Science*. London: Iron Books, 2009.

25 Daniel J. Boorstin. *The Seekers: The Story of Man's Continuing Quest to Understand His World*. New York: Random House, 1998. p. 81.

26 Michael H. Shank. "Myth 2: That the Medieval Christian Church Suppressed the Growth of Science." In *Galileo Goes to Jail: And Other Myths about Science and Religion*. pp. 22, 21, & 22.

27 "Fides quaerens intellectulm," which began his book *Proslogion*. (Source: Jeffrey C. Pugh. *The Matrix of Faith: Reclaiming a Christian Vision*. New York: Crossroad Publishing Co., 2001. pp. 54 & 62.)

28 Dard Hunter. *Papermaking: The History and Technique of an Ancient Craft*. New York: Dover Publications, Inc., 1947. pp. 60 & 470.

29 Alister E McGrath. *The Foundations of Dialogue in Science and Religion*. Malden, Mass.: Blackwell Publishers, 1998. p. 123.

30 John Calvin. *Commentary on the Psalms*, edited by James Anderson. Grand Rapids, Mich.: Baker, 1981. p. 86. Quoted in *Is God a Creationist? The Religious Case Against Creation-Science*, edited by Roland Mushat Frye. (New York: Charles Scribner's Sons, 1983), p. 202.

31 R. Hooykaas. "The Rise of Modern Science: When and Why?" *The British Journal for the History of Science*, Vol. 20, No. 4 (Oct. 1987), p. 455. (emphasis added)

32 Francis Bacon. *Advancement of Learning*, 1605. Available at: https://en.wikisource.org/wiki/The_Advancement_of_Learning.

33 Galileo Galilei. *The Assayer*, 1623. Quoted in Denis Alexander. *Rebuilding the Matrix: Science and Faith in the 21st Century* (Grand Rapids, MI: Zondervan, 2001), p. 80.

34 St. Anthony of the Desert. In a story told by Evagrius Ponticus in *Praktikos*, 92.

35 Edward B. Davis. "Myth 13: That Isaac Newton's Mechanistic Cosmology Eliminated the Need for God." In *Galileo Goes to Jail: And Other Myths about Science and Religion*. pp. 115ff.

36 John Hedley Brooke. *Science and Religion: Some Historical Perspectives*. Cambridge: Cambridge University Press, 1991. pp. 135-

139. (**Most of Newton's religious writings were not published during his lifetime.** [Source: Patrick McDonald. "Newton, Isaac." In *A Science and Religion Primer,* edited by Heidi A. Campbell & Heather Looy. Grand Rapids, MI: Baker Academic, 2009. p. 159.])

37 Karen Armstrong. *The Case for God.* New York: Alfred A. Knopf, 2009. p. 227.

38 From Genesis 28:15a (NRSV). (emphasis added)

39 **Examples of this advance guard of atheists in the latter 18th century are Claude d'Holbach and Denis Diderot, who is known more for his creation of the first modern encyclopedia.** (John Hedley Brooke and Ronald L. Numbers, editors. *Science and Religion around the World.* New York: Oxford University Press, 2011. pp. 254-261.)

40 Thomas Paine. *Age of Reason,* 1794. Quoted in Joshua M. Moritz. *Considering God's Works, Lecture 4: The Myth that Never Was.* Available online through Scientists in Congregations. http://www.scientistsincongregations.org/resources/videolibrary/.

41 David C. Lindberg. *The Beginnings of Western Science: The European Scientific Tradition in Philosophical, Religious, and Institutional Context, 600 B.C. to A.D. 1450.* Chicago: Univ. of Chicago Press, 1992. pp. 53-54.

42 **Philosophy textbooks usually translate these four names as being respectively the material, efficient, formal, and final causes. But I have found in my teaching that those labels are confusing because of changes in our ordinary use of those words.**

43 Richard Tarnas. *The Passion of the Western Mind: Understanding the Ideas That Have Shaped Our World View.* New York: Ballantine Books, 1991. p. 484n11.

44 **In the case of the house being constructed, it would of course be recognized that the people involved had individual purposes for their actions. However, modern science, taking an external or objective approach, would describe those people in terms of matter and external interactions. It is in this sense that the question of overall purpose ("Why should there be anything at all?") was eliminated.**

45 Ronald L. Numbers. "Introduction." In *Galileo Goes to Jail: And Other Myths about Science and Religion.* p. 6.

46 Timothy Larsen. "War Is Over, If You Want It: Beyond the Conflict between Faith and Science." *Perspectives on Science and Christian Faith,* Vol. 60, No. 3 (Sept. 2008). pp. 147-155.

47 Thomas Henry Huxley. *Collected Essays,* Vol. II, p. 52. Quoted in Frank M. Turner. "The Victorian Conflict between Science and Religion: A Professional Dimension." *Isis,* Vol. 69. No. 3 (Sept. 1978), p. 358. Available at http://www.jstor.org/stable/231040.

48 Jeffrey Burton Russell. *Inventing the Flat Earth: Columbus and Modern Historians.* pp. 38-49.

49 **Two examples are the 5th-grade textbook *America: Past and Present,***

and the 8th-grade textbook *We the People: A History of the United States of America.* They both perpetuate the myth (in Draper's book) that before Columbus, people believed the Earth was flat. (Source: Joshua M. Moritz *Considering God's Works, Lecture 4: The Myth that Never Was.*) And a college textbook, *A History of Civilization Prehistory to 1715*, incorrectly states that ancient Greeks' knowledge about the Earth's sphericity was lost in the Middle Ages.

50 Source: https://en.wikipedia.org/wiki/World_War_I_casualties.

51 J. Marston. "A National Survey of Students' Opinions on Science and Faith," Sept. 1997. Quoted in Denis Alexander. *Rebuilding the Matrix: Science and Faith in the 21st Century.* p. 30.

Chapter 2

1 One example of the use of a Copernicus-deathbed scene for the opening of a book is: Barbara A. Somervill. *Nicolaus Copernicus: Father of Modern Astronomy.* Minneapolis: Compass Point Books, 2005.

2 The extremely misleading statement is in: Mark Henderson, and Joanne Baker & Tony Crilly. *100 Most Important Science Ideas: Key Concepts in Genetics, Physics and Mathematics.* Buffalo, NY: Firefly Books, 2009. p. 161.

3 **Although during these centuries early scientists were called "natural philosophers," today the word "philosopher" is used with a quite different meaning. Therefore, I employ today's closest equivalent —"scientist."**

4 Jack Repcheck. *Copernicus' Secret: How the Scientific Revolution Began.* New York: Simon & Schuster, 2007. p. 57. **(Copernicus declined the invitation to revise the calendar because he thought more research needed to be done.)**

5 That misleading book is: Robin S. Doak. *Galileo: Astronomer and Physicist.* Minneapolis: Compass Point Books, 2005. p. 95.

6 Yuksel A. Aslandogan: "Religion vs. Science: Galileo vs. Aristotle?" (Interview with Lynn Mitchell, Ph.D.) *The Fountain.* Issue 70 (July-Aug. 2009). pp. 46ff.

7 Isaac Asimov. *Breakthroughs in Science.* Boston: Houghton Mifflin Co., 1959. pp. 36-37.

8 **The two known professors were Cesare Cremonini and Giulio Libri.** Source: J. L. Heilbron. *Galileo.* N.Y.: Oxford Univ. Press, 2010. pp. 195-196. Sources: re others: Steven Shapin: *The Scientific Revolution.* Chicago: University of Chicago Press, 1996. p. 73.

9 Heather Couper and Nigel Henbest. *The History of Astronomy.* Buffalo, NY: Firefly Books, 2007. p. 146.

10 Patricia Fara. *Science: A Four Thousand Year History.* New York: Oxford Univ. Press, 2009. pp. 115-116.

11 Owen Gingerich. "The Galileo Affair." *Scientific American*, May 1982. Available at: http://ftp.beitberl.ac.il/~bbsite/misc/ezer_anglit/klali/01_20.doc. p. 1.

12 Michael Hoskin. "From Geometry to Physics: Astronomy Transformed."
   Hoskin, Michael, ed. *The Cambridge Illustrated History of Astronomy*.
   Cambridge: Cambridge Univ. Press, 1997. p. 92-93.
13 Caption to illustration in Roland H. Bainton. *Christianity*. Boston:
   Houghton Mifflin Co., 1992. p. 327.
14 Dennis R. Danielson. "Myth 6: That Copernicanism Demoted Humans
   from the Center of the Cosmos." In Numbers, Ronald L., ed. *Galileo
   Goes to Jail: And Other Myths about Science and Religion*. Cambridge,
   Mass.: Harvard University Press, 2009. pp. 50-58.
15 Owen Gingerich. "The Galileo Affair." p. 2.
16 Owen Gingerich. "Truth in Science: Proof, Persuasion, and the Galileo
   Affair." *Perspectives on Science and Christian Faith*, Vol. 55 No. 2
   (June 2003). p. 85.
17 **A convincing observation of stellar parallax did not occur until 1838.**
   Source: Ibid., p. 86.
18 **Brahe's model, published in 1588, was based on his own sightings
   and on tabulations by Copernicus, but Brahe rejected Copernicus's
   solution of having the Earth move in part because no stellar parallax
   could be observed.**
19 Michael Hoskin. "From Geometry to Physics: Astronomy Transformed."
   p. 129.
20 Christopher M. Graney. "A True Demonstration: Bellarmine and the
   Stars as Evidence Against Earth's Motion in the Early Seventeenth
   Century." *Logos*, 14:3 (Summer 2011). pp. 72-75.
21 Will and Ariel Durant. *The Story of Civilization, Part VII: The Age of
   Reason Begins*. New York: Simon and Schuster, 1961. p. 605.
22 Richard G. Olson. *Science and Religion, 1450-1900: From Copernicus
   to Darwin*. Baltimore: Johns Hopkins Univ. Press, 2004. p. 17.
23 **The particular passages that seemed to some people to need
   interpretation in this regard were Joshua 10:13, Psalm 93:1, and
   Psalm 104:5.**
24 John Hedley Brooke. *Science and Religion: Some Historical
   Perspectives*. New York: Cambridge University Press, 1991. pp. 78-79.
25 Council of Trent, April 8, 1546. Quoted in Richard G. Olson. *Science
   and Religion, 1450-1900: From Copernicus to Darwin*. pp. 12-13.
26 **It was Father Luigi Maraffi, the Dominican Preacher General, who
   sent the letter of apology to Galileo.** It is quoted in: David Whitehouse,.
   Renaissance Genius: Galileo Galilei & His Legacy to Modern Science.
   New York: Sterling Publishing, 2009. pp. 108-111.
27 **There was no indication in *Revolutions'* original publication that the
   "Introduction to the Reader" had been written by the editor,
   Andreas Osiander.** Source: Owen Gingerich. "Truth in Science: Proof,
   Persuasion, and the Galileo Affair." p. 81.
28 Cardinal Bellarmine. Letter of April 12, 1615 to Carmelite priest Paolo
   Antonio Foscarini. Quoted in Olaf Pedersen. *The Book of Nature*. p. 49.

(emphasis added)

29 Michael Sharratt. *Galileo: Decisive Innovator.* Cambridge: Cambridge Univ. Press, 1994. p. 116.
30 Ron Naylor. "Galileo's Tidal Theory." *Isis,* Vol. 98, No. 1 (March 2007), pp. 1-22. Available at http://www.jstor.org/stable/10.1086/512829.
31 Hal Hellman. *Great Feuds in Science: Ten of the Liveliest Disputes Ever.* New York: John Wiley & Sons, Inc., 1998. p. 12.
32 The heart of the Decree of 1616 is quoted in Will and Ariel Durant. *The Story of Civilization, Part VII: The Age of Reason Begins.* p. 608.
33 Stillman Drake. *Galileo: Pioneer Scientist.* Toronto: Univ. of Toronto Pres, 1990. p. 176.
34 David Whitehouse. *Renaissance Genius: Galileo Galilei & His Legacy to Modern Science.* New York: Sterling Publishing, 2009. p. 145.
35 Michael Hoskin. "From Geometry to Physics: Astronomy Transformed." p. 130.
36 **Galileo's book was also behind the times scientifically in not including the astronomer Kepler's groundbreaking discovery that planets' orbits are elliptical (i.e., oval) rather than circular.**
37 Francis Collins. *The Language of God: A Scientist Presents Evidence for Belief.* New York: Free Press, 2006. p. 155.
38 Hal Hellman. *Great Feuds in Science: Ten of the Liveliest Disputes Ever.* p. 13.
39 Dava Sobel. *Galileo's Daughter.* New York: Walker and Co., 1999. p. 225.
40 Stillman Drake. *Galileo: Pioneer Scientist.* p. 203.
41 Maurice A. Finocchiaro. "Myth 8: That Galileo was Imprisoned and Tortured for Advocating Copernicanism." In Numbers, Ronald L., ed. *Galileo Goes to Jail: And Other Myths about Science and Religion.* Cambridge, Mass.: Harvard University Press, 2009. pp. 68-78.
42 The misleading statement is in: Robert Youngson. *Scientific Blunders: A Brief History of How Wrong Scientists Can Sometimes Be.* New York: Carroll & Graf, 1998. p. 291.
43 A clear, compact summary regarding the 1616 documents is: Denis Alexander. *Rebuilding the Matrix: Science and Faith in the 21st Century.* Grand Rapids, MI: Zondervan, 2001. p. 119.
44 Galileo Galilei, from trial documents. *The Trial of Galileo: Essential Documents,* trans. & ed. by Maurice A. Finocchiaro. Indianapolis: Hackett Publishing Co., 2014. p. 127.
45 Ibid. Also: Richard J. Blackwell. *Behind the Scenes at Galileo's Trial.* Notre Dame, Indiana: University of Notre Dame Press, 2006. p. 12.
46 Thomas Dixon. *Science and Religion: A Very Short Introduction.* New York: Oxford University Press, 2008. p. 30.
47 Rivka Feldhay. *Galileo and the Church: Political Inquisition or Critical Dialogue?* Cambridge: Cambridge Univ. Press, 1995.
48 Stillman Drake. *Galileo: Pioneer Scientist.* p. 176.

49 Timothy Moy. "The Galileo Affair." In *Science and Religion: Are They Compatible?, edited by Paul* Kurtz. Amherst, N.Y.: Prometheus Books, 2003. p. 141.

50 A similar conclusion is made by Edith W. Hetherington. & Norriss S. *Astronomy and Culture.* Santa Barbara, Cal.: Greenwood Press, 2009. p. 167.

51 Galileo Galilei, letter to Nicolas-Claude Fabri de Peiresc, March 16, 1635. Quoted in Dava Sobel. *Galileo's Daughter.* p. 349. (emphasis added)

52 Voltaire. "Descartes and Newton" (1728). Quoted in Maurice A. Finocchiaro. "Myth 8: That Galileo was Imprisoned and Tortured for Advocating Copernicanism." p. 68.

53 Maurice A. Finocchiaro. "Myth 8: That Galileo was Imprisoned and Tortured for Advocating Copernicanism." pp. 73-74.

54 Ibid., p. 74. Also: James Brodrick,. *Galileo: The Man, his Work, his Misfortune.* New York: Harper and Row, 1964. pp. 141-144.

55 Dava Sobel. *Galileo's Daughter.* pp. 353-354.

56 Alister McGrath. *Dawkins' God.* Malden, MA: Blackwell Publishing, 2005. pp. 140-141.

Chapter 3

1 Alfred, Lord Tennyson. "In Memoriam," 56, st. 4. (Published 1850.) **The surrounding verses read:**
   Trusted God was love indeed
   And love Creation's final law –
   Though Nature, red in tooth and claw
   With ravine, shrieked against his creed –

2 Ibid., LV, stanza 2.

3 **Tennyson's friend was the brilliant and handsome Arthur Hallam (1811-1833), who Tennyson met at Trinity College, Cambridge, and who died at the age of 22. Tennyson worked on the poem, which became quite popular among Victorians, over the course of 17 years.**

4 Karl W. Giberson. *Saving Darwin: How to Be a Christian and Believe in Evolution.* New York: HarperOne, 2008. pp. 48-52.

5 J. R. Lucas, "Wilberforce and Huxley: A Legendary Encounter." *The Historical Journal,* 22, 2 (1979), pp. 313-330. Available at http://www.jstor.org/stable/2638867.

6 *The Athenaeum.* Quoted in G. S. Carter, *A Hundred Years of Evolution.* London, 1957. p. 70. Taken from J. R. Lucas, "Wilberforce and Huxley: A Legendary Encounter."

7 **Although Wilberforce's review came out a few days after the debate, it was written five months previously, given that it was 17,000 words long, and given the time required for typesetting and publication.**

8 Charles Darwin, in a letter to Joseph Hooker, July, 1860. *The Life and Letters of Darwin,* 2:324. Quoted in J. R. Lucas. "Wilberforce and Huxley." pp. 317-320.

9   Frederick Temple, sermon at the University Church to BAAS delegates, 1860. "The Present Relations of Science to Religion." Oxford: Parker, 1960. 8,17. Quoted in William E. Phipps, *Darwin's Religious Odyssey* (Harrisburg, Pennsylvania: Trinity Press International, 2002), p. 91.

10 Charles Kingsley, quoted in *Origin of Species,* second edition, 1860. Chap. XV.

11 **The most quoted statement by someone who accepts the theory of evolution but who depicts atheism as its inevitable consequence is by the biologist Richard Dawkins, who wrote, "Darwin made it possible to be an intellectually fulfilled atheist."** (Richard Dawkins. *The Blind Watchmaker.* New York and London: W. W. Norton, 1987. p. 6.)

12 From Darwin's commenting upon Herschel's remark in Darwin's letter to Charles Lyell, Dec. 12, 1859. *Life and Letters of Darwin*, vol. II. p. 241.

13 Francisco J. Ayala. *Darwin's Gift to Science and Religion*. Washington, D.C.: John Henry Press, 2007. pp. 4 & 157. (emphasis added)

14 William Paley. *Natural Theology*, 1802.

15 Aubrey Moore. "The Christian Doctrine of God." In *Lux Mundi*, 12th ed., edited by C. Gore. London: John Murray, 1890, 1891. p. 73. Quoted in Christopher Southgate. *The Groaning of Creation: God, Evolution, and the Problem of Evil* (Louisville: Westminster John Knox Press, 2008), pp. 10-11.

16 Charles Darwin. *The Origin of Species*, 1859. Chapter III.

17 Holmes Rolston, III. *Science and Religion: A Critical Survey.* Philadelphia: Temple University Press, 1987. p. 134.

18 J. R. Illingworth, "The Problem of Pain: Its Bearing on Faith in God," in *Lux Mundi: A Series of Studies in the Religion of the Incarnation*, 3rd ed., edited by Charles Gore. London: John Murray,, repr. 1890. pp. 113-126. Quoted in Christopher Southgate, *The Groaning of Creation.* p. 1.

19 Aubrey Moore. "The Christian Doctrine of God." p. 73. Quoted in Christopher Southgate, *The Groaning of Creation.* pp. 10-11.

Chapter 4

1   **The Tennessee Supreme Court's statement was that "nothing is to be gained by prolonging the life of this bizarre case."** Scopes v. State, 154 Tenn. 105 (1927) Jan, 1927. Available at http://darrow.law.umn.edu/documents/Scopes%201926.pdf.

2   **I use the word "leading" here in the sense of those two individuals being preeminent in the public eye because of their fame even before the trial, and, therefore, their overshadowing the other members of the defense and prosecution teams.**

3   Ted Peters and Martinez Hewlett. *Can You Believe in God and Evolution? A Guide for the Perplexed.* Nashville: Abingdon Press, 2006. p. 46.

4   **The fine print on this early fundamentalist concept of inerrancy, at least among its more sophisticated thinkers such as Warfield, was that the Bible was to be considered as being "inerrant" if it was**

understood as it were *meant* to be understood. That qualification allowed for recognizing parts of the Bible as being figurative, thus allowing for non-literal readings of Genesis.

5   Benjamin Warfield, lecture, Dec. 1888. Quoted in Mark A. Noll. *A History of Christianity in the United States and Canada* (Grand Rapids, MI: William B. Eerdmans Publishing Co., 1992), p. 371.

6   Genesis 7-8.

7   **The Tennessee law was the Butler Act, passed in 1925.**

8   Scopes trial transcript. Quoted in Ronald L. Numbers. *Darwinism Comes to America*. Cambridge, Mass.: Harvard University Press, 1998. p. 80.

9   Karl W Giberson. *Saving Darwin: How to Be a Christian and Believe in Evolution.* New York: HarperOne, 2008. pp. 49-51.

10 William Jennings Bryan. "Prince of Peace," 1904. pp. 266-268. Quoted in Edward J. Larson. *Summer for the Gods: The Scopes Trial and America's Continuing Debate Over Science and Religion* (New York: Basic Books, 2006), p. 39.

11 John D. Rockefeller. *National Life and Character*, p. 85. Quoted in R. Hofstadter. *Social Darwinism in American Thought* (Boston: Beacon, 1983), p. 45. Taken from Cameron M. Smith & Charles Sullivan. *The Top 10 Myths about Evolution.* (New York: Prometheus Books, 2007), p. 154.

12 Andrew Carnegie. *The Gospel of Wealth and Other Timely Essays*, 1900. New York. Chap. 2. Excerpted in *Darwin: A Norton Critical Edition*, edited by PhilipAppleman. New York: W.W. Norton & Co., third ed., 1970. p. 396.

13 Ibid., p. 387.

14 Ibid., p. 398.

15 William Jennings Bryan. INN-1896-08-29_01 Quoted in Michael Kazin. "The Forgotten Forerunner." *The Wilson Quarterly* Vol. 23, No. 4 (Autumn, 1999). p. 28. Available at http://www.jstor.org/stable/40259961.

16 Richard Milner. *The Encyclopedia of Evolution: Humanity's Search for Its Origins*. New York: Facts On File, 1990. p. 424.

17 Herbert Spencer. *Social Statics*, 1851. pp. 79-80. Quoted in Richard Hofstadter, *Social Darwinism in American Thought*. Chap. 2. Excerpted in *Darwin: A Norton Critical Edition*, edited by PhilipAppleman. p. 392.

18 Indiana statute, 1907. Quoted in Carl N. Degler. *In Search of Human Nature: The Decline and Revival of Darwinism in American Social Thought* (New York: Oxford Univ. Press), 1991. p. 45.

19 One of the few good sources about the eugenics movement in the U.S. is: Bill Bryson. *One Summer: America, 1927*. New York: Doubleday, 2013. pp. 362-370.

20 William Jennings Bryan. "Prince of Peace," 1904. p. 266-268. Quoted in Edward J. Larson. *Summer for the Gods.* p. 39.

21 George. W. Hunter. *A Civic Biology.* New York: American, 1914. Quoted

in Edward J. Larson. *Summer for the Gods*. p. 27.

22 Frederick Lewis Allen. *Only Yesterday: An Informal History of the 1920's*. New York: John Wiley & Sons, Inc., 1931, 1959.

23 Ronald L. Numbers. "The Creationists." In *God and Nature: Historical Essays on the Encounter between Christianity and Science*, edited by David C. Lindberg and Ronald L. Numbers. Berkeley: University of California Press, 1986. pp. 394 & 403.

24 More examples such as these can be found in *The Prism and the Rainbow: A Christian Explains Why Evolution I Not a Threat*, by Joel W Martin. Baltimore: Johns Hopkins Univ. Press., 2010. pp. 111-121.

25 **The Edwards vs. Aguillard decision upheld a pivotal 1982 District Court decision called McLean vs. Arkansas Board of Education.**

26 **The official name of the case was "Kitzmiller vs. Dover School Board."**

27 Charles Darwin. *The Descent of Man*, 1871.

28 **Sometimes the is-ought fallacy is called "the naturalistic fallacy." But in the field of philosophy, that label is reserved for a more specific fallacy, and so I use the more descriptive name of the is-ought fallacy.**

29 Charles A Gallagher & Cameron D Lippard, editors. *Race and Racism in the United States, Vol. 4: An Encyclopedia of the American Mosaic*. 2014. p. 40.

30 Buck v. Bell decision, May 2, 1927. Page 274 U.S. 207. Available at http://supreme.justia.com/cases/federal/us/274/200/case.html.

31 Karl W. Giberson. *Saving Darwin*. pp. 74-75.

Part Two

Epigraph 1: W.T. Stace. *Religion and the Modern Mind*. New York: J. B. Lippincott Company, 1952. p. 97.

Epigraph 2: Abraham Joshua Heschel. *God in Search of Man*. New York: Harper and Row, 1955. p. 3.

Chapter 5

1 **The numeral for zero, having originated in India, also made its way into Europe through the Muslim world, but was slower in working its way into European culture.**

2 Nancy Marie Brown. *The Abacus and the Cross: The Story of the Pope Who Brought the Light of Science to the Dark Ages*. New York: Basic Books, 2010.

3 Huston Smith in an interview by Bill Moyers. "A Personal Philosophy," April 26, 1996. http://billmoyers.com/content/a-personal-philosophy-the-wisdom-of-faith-with-huston-smith/.

4 One place John Haught did so was as an expert witness in the 2005 trial Kitzmiller v. Dover Area School District. http://www.talkorigins.org/faqs/dover/day5pm.html#day5pm7.

5 National Academy of Sciences. *Teaching About Evolution and the*

Nature of Science. Washington, D.C.: National Academy Press, 1998. Quoted in Kenneth R Miller. *Finding Darwin's God: A Scientist's Search for Common Ground Between God and Evolution* (New York: HarperCollins, 1999), p. 169.

6   John F. Haught. *Responses to 101 Questions on God and Evolution*. New York: Paulist Press, 2001. p. 57.

7   Ian G. Barbour. *Religion and Science: Historical and Contemporary Issues*. San Francisco: HarperSanFrancisco, 1997. pp. 106-112, 130-136.

8   National Academy of Sciences. *Teaching About Evolution and the Nature of Science*.

9   Ian G. Barbour. *Religion and Science: Historical and Contemporary Issues*. p. 29.

10 Huston Smith. *Forgotten Truth: The Primordial Tradition*. New York: Harper & Row, 1976. pp. 14-16.

11 René Descartes. *Discourse on Method*, Meditation III, 1637. Available at http://oregonstate.edu/instruct/phl302/texts/descartes/meditations/Meditat ion3.html.

12 **In contemporary Christian theology, this classic differentiation between what are called "signs" and what are called "symbols" is in: Paul Tillich. *Dynamics of Faith*. New York: Harper Torchbooks, 1957.** pp. 41-45.

13 James R. Moore. *The Post-Darwinian Controversies: A Study of the Protestant Struggle to Come to Terms with Darwin in Great Britain and America, 1870-1900*. London: Cambridge University Press, 1979, 1981. p. 77. (emphasis added)

14 The many layers of experience from "within" are explored in: Ken Wilber. *The Marriage of Sense and Soul: Integrating Science and Religion*. New York: Random House, 1998. pp. 64, 69-72.

15 Keith Ward. *God: A Guide for the Perplexed*. Oxford: Oneworld Publications, 2002. pp. 1-2.

16 e. g. Paul Tillich. *Systematic Theology*, Vol. 1. Chicago: Univ. of Chicago Press, 1951. p. 235.

17 Alister E. McGrath. *Christian Theology: An Introduction*, 4th edition. Malden, MA: Blackwell Publishing, 2007. pp. 193-197.

18 e. g. Paul Tillich. *The New Being*. New York: Charles Scribner's Sons, 1955. pp. 152-160.

19 Troy Wilson Organ. *Western Approaches to Eastern Philosophy*. Athens, Ohio: Ohio University Press, 1975. p. 144.

20 Paul Tillich. *Dynamics of Faith*. p. 10.

21 e. g. Paul Tillich. *A History of Christian Thought*. New York: Simon & Schuster; 1968. p. 202.

22 AAAS Program of Dialogue between Science and Religion brochure, 1995. (emphasis added) Quoted in Dorothy Nelkin. "God Talk: Confusion between Science and Religion: Posthumous Essay." *Science, Technology & Human Values*, Vol. 29. No. 2 (Spring, 2004), p. 144.

23 Paul Tillich. "Science and Theology: A Discussion with Einstein." In *Theology of Culture*, edited by Robert C. Kimball. New York: Oxford University Press, 1964. p. 131.

24 Paul Tillich. "Science and Theology: A Discussion with Einstein." p. 132. (emphasis added)

25 Peter Harrison. "Miracles, Early Modern Science, and Rational Religion." *Church History*. Vol. 75, No. 3 (Sept. 2006), pp. 506. Available at http://www.jstor.org/stable/27644815.

26 *The Oxford English Dictionary*. Oxford: Clarendon Press, 1933, 1961. Vol. X, p. 187.

27 An examination of Hume's writing on miracles in its social context is: Denis Alexander. *Rebuilding the Matrix: Science and Faith in the 21st Century*. Grand Rapids, MI: Zondervan, 2001. pp. 429-432.

28 Peter Harrison. "Miracles, Early Modern Science, and Rational Religion." pp. 493 & 494.

29 Ibid., pp. 493 & 494.

30 Ibid., pp. 495-496.

31 Ibid., p. 493. **(Most modern translations of the Bible—even the New King James Version—have mostly or entirely eliminated use of the English word "miracle.")**

32 Augustine. *City of God*, X.12. Quoted in Ibid., pp. 496n9.

33 Paul Tillich. "Science and Theology: A Discussion with Einstein." p. 128. (emphasis added)

34 Irenaeus. *Sermons*. Quoted in *Eternal Quest: Vol. 1, The Search for God*. David Manning White, ed. New York: Paragon House, 1991. p. 31. (edited for inclusive language)

35 **"NOMA" stood for "nonoverlapping magisteria."** Stephen Jay Gould. *Rocks of Ages: Science and Religion in the Fullness of Life*. New York: The Ballantine Publishing Group, 1964.

36 **On a webpage discussion after his book was published, Gould clarified that in his scheme, "The two magisteria bump right up against each other.... Many of our deepest questions call upon aspects of both for different parts of a full answer."** http://www.pointofinquiry.org/tom_flynn_the_science_vs_religion_warfa re_thesis/.

Chapter 6

1 Condensed from: Diane Karay Tripp. *Trusted Voices: Spiritual Wisdom from Lost Generations of Women*. Louisville, KY: Witherspoon Press, 2009. p. ix.

2 Proverbs 8:12 (NRSV). (emphasis added)

3 Lawrence O. Richards. *New International Encyclopedia of Bible Words*. Grand Rapids, MI: Zondervan, 1991. p. 629.

4 e.g. Langdon Gilkey. *Creationism on Trial: Evolution and God at Little Rock*. Minneapolis: Winston Press, 1985. p. 173.

5 Karen Armstrong. *The Case for God*. New York: Alfred A. Knopf, 2009.

pp. 212 & 216.

6 Charlene Spretnak. *The Resurgence of the Real: Body, Nature, and Place in a Hypermodern World*. New York: Routledge, 1997. pp. 135ff.

7 Walt Whitman. "When I Heard the Learn'd Astronomer." *Complete Poetry and Selected Prose*, edited by James E. Miller, Jr. Boston: Houghton Mifflin Co., 1959. p. 196.

8 John F. Haught. *Deeper Than Darwin: The Prospect for Religion in the Age of Evolution*. Cambridge, MA.: Westview Press, 2003. p. 44.

9 Huston Smith. *Forgotten Truth: The Primordial Tradition*. New York: Harper & Row, 1976. pp. 14-16.

10 Richard Dawkins. *A Devil's Chaplain*. London: Weidenfield & Nicholson, 2003. p. 34. Quoted in Alister McGrath. "Has Science Eliminated God?—Richard Dawkins and the Meaning of Life." *Science & Christian Belief* Vol. 17, No. 2 (2005). p. 117.

11 From the 1995 AAAS Program of Dialogue between Science and Religion brochure. Quoted in Dorothy Nelkin. "God Talk: Confusion between Science and Religion.: Posthumous Essay." *Science, Technology & Human Values* Vol. 29. No. 2 (Spring, 2004), p. 144.

12 **Scientists who study animal behavior are currently divided as to whether or not in describing certain animal behaviors they should give a localized purpose within the animal as a causal explanation. But even when that type of description is employed, those scientists still do not give a purpose in the larger sense, such as giving an explanation of what is the purpose of evolution, or the purpose of life.**

13 e.g. Niles Eldredge. *The Triumph of Evolution and the Failure of Creationism*. New York: W. H. Freeman and Company, 2001. p. 127.

14 Stephen Jay Gould. "Impeaching a Self-Appointed Judge." *Scientific American* (1992) 267 (1), pp. 118-121. Quoted in Alister McGrath. "Has Science Eliminated God?" p. 121.

15 *Time* magazine cover, Nov. 13, 2006.

16 Gary E. Schwartz with William L. Simon. *The G.O.D. Experiments: How Science Is Discovering God in Everything, Including Us*. New York: Atria Books, 2006.

17 Victor J. Stenger. *God, The Failed Hypothesis: How Science Shows That God Does Not Exist*. Amherst, N.Y.: Prometheus Books, 2007.

18 Linwood Urban. *A Short History of Christianity*, Revised and Expanded Edition. New York: Oxford University Press, 1995. p. 180.

19 John F. Haught. *Is Nature Enough? Meaning and Truth in the Age of Science*. New York: Cambridge University Press, 2006. esp. pp. 42-51.

20 Elizabeth A. Johnson. "Losing and Finding Creation in the Christian Tradition." In *Christianity and Ecology*, edited by Dieter T. Hessel & Rosemary Radford Ruether. Cambridge, Mass.: Harvard University Press, 2000. p. 4. (emphasis added)

21 Jawaharlal Nehru, 1947. Quoted in Mary Midgley. "Visions, Secular and

Sacred." *The Hastings Center Report* Vol. 25, No. 5 (Sept.-Oct., 1995), pp. 20-27. Available at http://www.jstor.org/stable/3562790.

22 Mary Midgley. "Visions, Secular and Sacred." p. 22.

23 Such simplifications from evolutionary psychology are critiqued in: *Alas, Poor Darwin: Arguments Against Evolutionary Psychology*, edited by Hilary & Steven Rose. New York: Harmony Books, 2000.

24 Stephen Jay Gould. "Caring Groups and Selfish Genes." *The Panda's Thumb: More Reflections in Natural History*. New York: W.W. Norton & Co. 1980. p. 91.

25 Richard Dawkins. *The Selfish Gene*. New York: Oxford University Press, 1989. p. 127. Quoted in Terence L. Nichols. *The Sacred Cosmos: Christian Faith and the Challenge of Naturalism*. Grand Rapids, MI: Brazos Pres, 2003. p. 97.

26 John Stuart Mill. "Principles of Political Economy, with Some of Their Applications to Social Philosophy." Quoted in Diane B. Paul & Benjamin Day. "John Stuart Mill: Innate Differences,and the Regulation of Reproduction." *Stud. Hist. Phil. Biol. & Biomed. Sci.* 39 (2008). p. 223. Available at http://www.dianebpaul.com/uploads/2/3/2/9/23295024/js_mill.pdf.

27 John Macquarrie. *Thinking about God*. New York: Harper & Row, 1975. p. 133.

28 Charlene Spretnak. *The Resurgence of the Real*. p. 137.

29 Johann Gottfried von Herder. Quoted in Ken Wilber. *The Marriage of Sense and Soul: Integrating Science and Religion*, New York: Random House, 1998. p. 94.

30 Mary Midgley. "Visions, Secular and Sacred." pp. 23 & 22.

31 Natalie Angier. "A One-Way Trip to Mars? Many Would Sign Up." *New York Times*, Dec. 8, 2014.

32 John Hedley Brooke. *Science and Religion: Some Historical Perspectives*. New York: Cambridge University Press, 1991. p. 337.

33 Ian G Barbour. *Religion in an Age of Science*. San Francisco: HarperSanFrancisco, 1990. p. xiii.

34 Charlene Spretnak. *States of Grace: The Recovery of Meaning in the Postmodern Age*. San Francisco: HarperSanFrancisco, 1991. pp. 156-157.

35 **Judaism, Christianity, and Islam are called "Abrahamic" faith-traditions because they all trace their lineage to the ancient patriarch Abraham.**

36 **Just some scriptural examples expressing the need for people to embody concern for those who are less fortunate are Leviticus 19:34 in the Hebrew Bible/*Tanakh*, Matthew 25:37-40 in the Christian New Testament, and verse 4:36 in Islam's Qur'an.**

37 Charlene Spretnak. *States of Grace*, p. 159.

Chapter 7

1 **Although commonly referred to as "The Jefferson Bible," Jefferson's**

assemblage was titled *The Life and Morals of Jesus of Nazareth*.

2 Thomas Jefferson. Letter to William Short, August 4, 1820. *American History: From Revolution to Reconstruction and Beyond*. http://www.let.rug.nl/usa/presidents/thomasjefferson/lettersofthomasjeffe rson/jefl261.php.

3 Karen Armstrong. *The Bible: A Biography*. New York: Grove Press, 2007. p. 183.

4 Mark A. Noll. *A History of Christianity in the United States and Canada*. Grand Rapids, MI: William B. Eerdmans Publishing Co., 1992. pp. 154 & 156.

5 John Calvin. *Commentary on the Psalms* (at re. Psalm 136:7), edited by James Anderson. Grand Rapids, MI.: Baker, 1981. p. 86. Quoted in Roland Mushat Frye, editor. *Is God a Creationist? The Religious Case Against Creation Science* (New York: Charles Scribner's Sons, 1983), p. 202.

6 Presbyterian Church U.S. "Evolution and the Bible." Office of Theology and Worship, GA Minutes 1969: 5962. Available at http://www.presbyterianmission.org/ministries/theologyandworship/evol ution.

7 Hugh Ross. *The Genesis Question: Scientific Advances and the Accuracy of Genesis*. Colorado Springs, Colorado: NavPress, 1998. p. 59.

8 Augustine. *The Literal Meaning of Genesis*. 5.3.6. (Source: Louis Lavallee. "Augustine on the Creation Days." *JETS* 32/4 [Dec. 1989]. pp. 459-460.) **(Unfortunately, rather than having the Vulgate translation of the Bible, Augustine had a poor Latin translation of Genesis 2:4, which put at a disadvantage his finding a way to reconcile the two creation narratives.)**

9 Origen. *De Principiis* 4.1.16. One translation is in *The Writings of Origen*, trans. by Frederick Crombie. Edinburgh: T.&T. Clark, 1869. pp. 316-317.

10 Further explication of the theological meanings in each of these narratives can be found in any good annotated Bible, such as *The New Oxford Annotated Bible* or *The HarperCollins Study Bible*.

11 W. Sibley Towner. *Genesis*. Louisville: Westminster John Knox Press, 2001. p. 14.

12 Ian G. Barbour. *When Science Meets Religion*. San Francisco: HarperSanFrancisco, 2000. p. 50.

13 John Polkinghorne. *Science and Theology: An Introduction*. Minneapolis: Fortress Press, 1998. pp. 79-80.

14 Psalm 104:14 & 30 (NRSV).

15 **Modern Biblical scholars have deciphered how the Noah narrative in the Bible was constructed out of two different traditions, but the two original narratives have been snugly intertwined (rather than being placed one after the other, as was the case with Genesis's two creation narratives).**

16 Charles Darwin. *Origin of Species*, 1859. Chapter XI.

17 Karl W Giberson. *Saving Darwin: How to Be a Christian and Believe in Evolution.* New York: HarperOne, 2008. pp. 49-51.

18 **The primary New Testament passages upon which the ascension of Jesus is based are Luke 24:50-51 and Acts 1:69, both by the same writer. There is also a brief mention of it in the final ending for Mark at Mark 16:19.**

19 **The complete Ephesians 4:9-10 (NRSV) passage reads:**
   (When it says, "He ascended," what does it mean but that he had also descended into the lower parts of the earth? He who descended is the same one who ascended far above all the heavens, so that he might fill all things.)

20 Marcus J. Borg. *Speaking Christian: Why Christian Words Have Lost Their Meaning and Power—And How They Can Be Restored.* New York: HarperCollins, 2011. p. 179-180. (emphasis added)

21 Ibid.

22 Mary Augusta (Mrs. Humphrey) Ward. *Robert Elsmore.* Lincoln, Neb., 1969. p. 414. Quoted in Karen Armstrong. *The Bible: A Biography.* p. 197.

23 Lawrence Boadt. "The Pentateuch," In *The Catholic Study Bible.* New York: Oxford University Press, 1990. p. RG 41.

24 Frank Burch Brown. "Aesthetics." In *New & Enlarged Handbook of Christian Theology,* edited by Donald W. Musser & Joseph L. Price. Nashville: Abingdon Press, 2003. p. 22.

25 United Presbyterian Church in the United States of America. Presbyterian Confession of 1967, section titled "The Bible." Louisville: Office of the General Assembly, 2002. p. 257. (emphasis added)

26 Shirley C. Guthrie. *Christian Doctrine*, Revised Edition. Louisville, KY: Westminster/John Knox Press, 1994. pp. 13-14.

Chapter 8

1 **Darwin was taken on board to be the gentleman dining-companion for the upper-class captain Robert Fitzroy. Not too far into the voyage, the ship's official naturalist quit, and Darwin took over the task of collecting plant and animal samples for scientific study.**

2 **Part of that statement by Charles Kingsley is quoted in the current book in Chapter 3, "Tempest in a British Teapot."**

3 Charles Darwin. Letter to Asa Gray, 1860. In *The Correspondence of Charles Darwin* 8, 1860. Cambridge: Cambridge University Press, 1993. p. 224.

4 Ibid.

5 Charles Darwin. *The Autobiography of Charles Darwin, 18091882. With original omissions restored, Edited with Appendix and Notes by his granddaughter, Nora Barlow.* New York: W. W. Norton & Co., 1958. pp. 92-94.

6 Charles Darwin. Letter to Joseph Hooker, July 12, 1870. In *More Life*

and Letters of Charles Darwin. London: John Murray, 1888. 1:321.

7   Charles Darwin. From Darwin's private memorial written a week after Annie's death. Quoted in Cyril Aydon. *Charles Darwin: The Naturalist Who Started a Scientific Revolution* (New York: Carroll & Graf Publishers, 2002), p. 178.

8   Randal Keynes. *Darwin, His Daughter and Human Evolution.* New York: Riverhead Books, 2001. pp. 17 & 254.

9   Francis Darwin. Quoted in Randal Keynes. *Darwin, His Daughter and Human Evolution.* p. 102.

10 **Some biographers have concluded, based on a few indications, that Charles Darwin's doubts about some of the Church's depictions of God's power began with the death of Charles's father two-and-a-half years before the death of Annie.**

11 Proverbs 12:21. *King James Version* of the Bible.

12 Tombstone at Malvern. Quoted in Cyril Aydon. *Charles Darwin: The Naturalist Who Started a Scientific Revolution.* p. 179.

13 Emma Darwin. Letter to Charles Darwin, June 1861. In Darwin Correspondence Project, http.//www.darwinproject.ac.uk, Letter 3169.

14 Charles Darwin. *Autobiography.* p. 90.

15 Ibid.

16 Charles Darwin. Letter to Joseph Hooker, Nov. 27, 1963. Quoted in Randal Keynes. *Darwin, His Daughter and Human Evolution.* p. 302.

17 *Articles of Religion.* **Although interpretation of the text of the Articles did not require so strict a reading, it did seem to be implied by the title of Article XVIII: "Of obtaining eternal Salvation only by the Name of Christ."**

18 Emma Darwin. Quoted in Randal Keynes,. *Darwin, His Daughter and Human Evolution.* p. 64. (emphasis added)

19 Charles Darwin. Quoted in Randal Keynes, *Darwin, His Daughter and Human Evolution.* p. 65.)

20 Charles Darwin. *Autobiography.* p. 87.

21 Charles Darwin. Letter to Joseph Hooker, Nov. 27, 1963. Quoted in Randal Keynes, *Darwin, His Daughter and Human Evolution.* p. 302.

22 Charles Darwin. *Autobiography*, pp. 88, 89.

23 Charles Darwin. *Origin of Species,* 1859. Chap. III.

24 Charles Darwin. Quoted in David Quammen, *The Reluctant Mr. Darwin: An Intimate Portrait of Charles Darwin and the Making of His Theory of Evolution* (New York: W. W. Norton Co., 2006), pp. 252-253.

Chapter 9

1   Thomas Henry Huxley. *Life and Letters of Thomas Henry* Huxley, edited by Leonard Huxley. London, 1900. p. 461. Quoted in Susan Jacoby. *Freethinkers: A History of American Secularism.* (New York: Henry Holt and Company, 2004), pp. 134-135.

2   **The most famous example being Thomas Henry Huxley's distortive claim that, "Extinguished theologians lie about the cradle of every**

science." (*Collected Essays*, Vol. II, p. 52. Quoted in Frank M. Turner. "The Victorian Conflict between Science and Religion: A Professional Dimension." *Isis*, Vol. 69. No. 3 [Sept. 1978], p. 358. Available at http://www.jstor.org/stable/231040.)

3 Susan Jacoby. *Freethinkers*. p. 135.

4 Arthur Peacocke. *Evolution: The Disguised Friend of Faith?* Philadelphia: Templeton Foundation Press, 2004.

5 John F. Haught. "Darwin's Gift to Theology." In *Evolutionary and Molecular Biology: Scientific Perspectives on Divine Action*, edited by Robert John Russell, et al. Vatican City: Vatican Observatory Publications, 1998. pp. 393-418.

6 Langdon Gilkey. *Creationism on Trial: Evolution and God at Little Rock.* Minneapolis: Winston Press, 1985.

7 John F. Haught. *God After Darwin: A Theology of Evolution*. Boulder: Westview Press, 2000, 2008. (The last chapter of the updated edition is about the Dover trial.)

8 Ted Peters and Martinez Hewlett. *Can You Believe in God and Evolution? A Guide for the Perplexed*. Nashville: Abingdon Press, 2006. p. x. (emphasis added)

9 Richard Dawkins. *The Selfish Gene*. New York: Oxford University Press, 1989. p. 127. Quoted in Terence L. Nichols. *The Sacred Cosmos: Christian Faith and the Challenge of Naturalism* (Grand Rapids, MI: Brazos Press, 2003), p. 97.

10 Marilynne Robinson. "Consequences of Darwinism." *Salmagundi*, No. 114/115 (spring/summer 1997), p. 27. Available at http://www.jstor.org.houstontx.idm.oclc.org/stable/pdf/40548960.pdf.

11 Edward O. Wilson. *On Human Nature*. Quoted in John Polkinghorne and Nicholas Beale. *Questions of Truth: Fifty-one Responses to Questions about God, Science, and Belief* (Louisville: Westminster John Knox Press, 2009), p. 78.

12 John Polkinghorne and Nicholas Beale. *Questions of Truth*. pp. 78-79.

13 Richard Dawkins. *The Blind Watchmaker*. New York & London: W.W. Norton, 1987. p. 6. Quoted in Ted Peters and Martinez Hewlett. *Can You Believe in God and Evolution?* p. 29.

14 William B. Provine. *Origins Research* 16, No. 1 (1994). Quoted in *The Religion and Science Debate: Why Does It Continue*, edited by Harold W. Attridge. New Haven: Yale University Press, 2009. p. 46.

15 Richard Dawkins. Introduction to *The Origin of Species and The Voyage of the 'Beagle'* by Charles Darwin. New York: Alfred A. Knopf, 2003. p. ix.

16 Phillip E Johnson. *Darwin on Trial*. Washington, D.C.: Regnery Gateway, 1991.

17 Phillip Johnson. On American Family Radio, Jan 10, 2003. Quoted in Mark Isaak. *The Counter-Creationism Handbook* (Berkeley: University of California Press, 2007), p. 280.

18 The official name of the trial was "Kitzmiller v. Dover Area School District."

19 American Association for the Advancement of Science. Statement approved by Board of Directors, Oct., 2002. Available through archived news release of Nov. 6, 2002. http://www.aaas.org/news/.

20 Andrew Robinson, Michael Robert Negus and Christopher Southgate. "Theology and Evolutionary Biology." In *God, Humanity and the Cosmos*, edited by Christopher Southgate. T & T Clark International, 2011. pp. 184-185.

21 The phrase "god of the gaps" caught on after appearing in 1955 in the mathematician and religious author Charles Coulson's *Science and Christian Belief*. But the problems it pointed to were summarized, even using the word "gaps," in 1894 by the evangelist Henry Drummond (*The Ascent of Man*). And the pastor Dietrich Bonhoeffer condemned it in a May 29, 1944 letter to Eberhard Bethge (in Bonhoeffer's *Letters and Papers from Prison*).

22 Michael J. Behe. *Darwin's Black Box: The Biochemical Challenge to Evolution*. New York: Free Press, 1996.

23 Paul Tillich. *A History of Christian Thought*, New York: Simon & Schuster, 1968. pp. 456-457.

24 Francisco J. Ayala. *Darwin's Gift to Science and Religion*. Washington, D.C.: John Henry Press, 2007. p. 157. (emphasis added)

25 James A. Wiseman. *Theology and Modern Science: Quest for Coherence*. New York: Continuum, 2002. pp. 64-65.

26 "Panentheism." *Oxford Concise Dictionary of the Christian Church*, 2nd edition. E. A. Livingstone, editor. New York: Oxford Univ. Press, 2000. p. 378.

27 Ephesians 4:6 (NRSV).

28 Thomas Aquinas. *Summa Theologiae* I, Question 8, article 1, Reply to Objection 2, 1:34. Quoted in Terence L. Nichols. *The Sacred Cosmos: Christian Faith and the Challenge of Naturalism*. Grand Rapids, MI: Brazos Press, 2003. p. 232n20.

29 Martin Luther. *Luthers Werke Kritische Gesamtausgabe (Schriften)*. Weimar. 23.134.34. Quoted in H. Paul Santmire. *The Travail of Nature: The Ambiguous Ecological Promise of Christian Theology* (Minneapolis: Fortress Press, 1985), p. 129.

30 William C Placher. *The Domestication of Transcendence: How Modern Thinking about God Went Wrong*. Louisville, KY: Westminster John Knox Press, 1996. p. 128.

31 Christopher Southgate. *God, Humanity and the Cosmos*, edited by Christopher Southgate. New York: T & T Clark International, 2011. p. 248.

32 William E. Phipps. *Supernaturalism in Christianity: Its Growth and Cure*. Mercer University Press, 2008. p. xii.

33 Christopher Southgate. *God, Humanity and the Cosmos*, edited by

Christopher Southgate. p. 248.

34 Hans Kung. *The Beginning of All Things: Science and Religion*. Grand Rapids, MI: William B. Eerdmans Publishing Co., 2005. p. 106. (Kung is referring to a statement in Augustine's *Confessions*, Chap. 7.)

35 William Wordsworth. "Lines Composed a Few Miles Above Tintern Abbey," 1798. line 96.

36 Alister E. McGrath. *Christian Theology: An Introduction*, 4th edition. Malden, MA: Blackwell Publishing, 2007. pp. 193-198.

37 International Theological Commission."Communion and Stewardship: Human Persons Created in the Image of God." Available at http://www.vatican.va/roman_curia/congregations/cfaith/cti_documents/r c_con_cfaith_doc_20040723_communionstewardship_en.html. (The joint letter by the three scientists was addressed to Pope Benedict, and was dated July 12, 2005.)

38 Greek Interlinear Bible. Scripture4all Foundation, 2010. www.scripture4all.org.

39 Jürgen Moltmann. *Science and Wisdom*. Minneapolis: Fortress Press, 2003. p. 61.

40 Ted Peters. "Evolution, Evil, and the Theology of the Cross." *Svensk Theologisk Kvartalskrift*. Arg. 83 (2007). p. 113.

41 Anne. M. Clifford. "Darwin's Revolution in *The Origin of Species*: A Hermeneutical Study of the Movement from Natural Theology to Natural Selection." In *Evolutionary and Molecular Biology: Scientific Perspectives on Divine Action*, edited by Robert John Russell, et al. Vatican City: Vatican Observatory Publications, 1998. pp. 301-302.

42 Lonnie D. Kliever. *The Shattered Spectrum: A Survey of Contemporary Theology*. Atlanta: John Knox Press, 1981. pp. 98-99.

43 Ibid., pp. 105 & 107.

44 John F. Haught. *The Promise of Nature: Ecology and Cosmic Purpose.* New York: Paulist Press, 1993.

Part Three

Epigraph 1: Caption to cartoon "A Logical Refutation of Mr. Darwin's Theory." *Punch*, April, 1871.

Epigraph 2: Paul Tillich. *Systematic Theology*, Vol. II. London: SCM Press, 1978. p. 95.

Chapter 10

1 Remark by unnamed wife of a canon of Worcester Cathedral. In *Bloomsbury Treasury of Quotations*, edited by John Daintith. London: Bloomsbury Publishing, 1994. p. 241.

2 Psalm 8:3-4a (NRSV).

3 John Macquarrie. "Original Sin." In *The Dictionary of Bible and Religion*, edited by William H. Gentz. Nashville: Abingdon Press, 1986. pp. 761-763.

4 Holmes Rolston, III. "Does Nature Need to Be Redeemed?" *Zygon*, vol

29, no. 2 (June 1994). p. 205.

5 **Another example is Jay McDaniel writing, "We cannot follow this route [of a 'Fall'], for we have to acknowledge that ... predator-prey relations existed long before the early hominids [human-like species] appeared."** (Jay B. McDaniel. "Can Animal Suffering be Reconciled with Belief in an All-Loving God?" Quoted in *Animals on the Agenda: Questions about Animals for Theology and Ethics*, edited by Andrew Linzey & Dorothy Yamamoto. [London: SCM Press Ltd., 1998.] p. 117.)

6 John F. Haught. "Evolution and The Suffering of Sentient Life." In *The Evolution of Evil*, edited by Gaymon Bennett, et al. Göttingen: Vandenhoeck & Ruprecht, 2008. p. 203.

7 Psalm 145:9 (NRSV).

8 John Henry. "Atheism." In *The History of Science and Religion in the Western Tradition: An Encyclopedia*, edited by Gary B. Ferngren. New York: Garland Publishing, Inc., 2000. pp. 208-214.

9 **Although countless books call Mendel a monk, he was a friar in the Abbey of St. Thomas, where he "found a supportive scientific community," as one contemporary historian states.** (Simon Mawer. *Gregor Mendel: Planting the Seeds of Genetics*. New York: Abrams, 2006. p. 30.)

10 James Turner. *Without God, Without Creed: The Origins of Unbelief in America*. Baltimore: Johns Hopkins University Press, 1985. p. 205.

11 Ibid., p. 205.

12 **An 1888 observation by J. R. Illingworth in this regard was quoted in Chapter 3, "Tempest in a British Teapot."**

13 Fyodor Dostoevsky [Dostoyevsky]. *The Brothers Karamazov, A New Translation by Ignat Arsey.* Oxford: Oxford University Press, 1880, Eng. ed. 1998. pp. 306-308. Quoted in Christopher Southgate. *The Groaning of Creation: God, Evolution, and the Problem of Evil* (Louisville: Westminster John Knox Press, 2008), p. 13.

14 Christopher Southgate. *The Groaning of Creation: God, Evolution, and the Problem of Evil*. p. 13.

15 John F. Haught. "Nature and Purpose." Religion Online. http://www.religion-online.org/showchapter.asp?title=2063&C=1834.

16 Lonnie D. Kliever. "Dax and Job: The Refusal of Redemptive Suffering." *Dax's Case: Essays in Medical Ethics and Human Meaning*, edited by Lonnie D. Kliever. Dallas: Southern Methodist University Press, 1989. p. 187ff.

17 Albert Schweitzer. *Memoirs of Childhood and Youth*, 1926. p. 40. In *Albert Schweitzer: An Anthology*, edited by Charles R. Joy. Boston: The Beacon Press, 1947. p. 274.

Chapter 11

1 Benjamin Disraeli, 1864 speech at Sheldonian Theatre at Oxford. In *Familiar Quotations*, edited by John Bartlett. Boston: Little, Brown and Co., 1968. p. 612b.

2   Arthur Peacocke. *Evolution: The Disguised Friend of Faith?*
    Philadelphia: Templeton Foundation Press, 2004. p. 179.
3   Genesis 2:4b through Genesis 3:24.
4   Mark Twain. "The Mysterious Stranger." In *The Wit and Wisdom of
    Mark Twain: A Book of Quotations.* Mineola, N.Y.: Dover Publications,
    1999. p. 1.
5   William Schwenck Gilbert. *Iolanthe*, II.
6   Gloria L. Schaab. *The Creative Suffering of the Triune God: An Evolutionary
    Theology.* New York: Oxford University Press, 2007. p. 11.
7   Francisco J. Ayala. *Darwin's Gift to Science and Religion.* Washington,
    D.C.: John Henry Press, 2007. pp. 155-158.
8   Timothy Anders. *The Evolution of Evil: An Inquiry into the Ultimate
    Origins of Human Suffering.* Chicago: Open Court, 1994. p. 21.
9   William Shakespeare. Line by Prospero in *The Tempest.* IV, i, 188-189.
10 Heather Looy. "Evolutionary Psychology." In *A Science and Religion
    Primer,* edited by Heidi A. Campbell & Heather Looy. Grand Rapids, MI:
    Baker Academic, 2009. p. 105. **(The discussions about sociobiology
    and evolutionary psychology have not been made any easier because
    of memories about how, in the first half of the 20th century, racist
    ideas distorted the work of some scientists. The historical
    background to this sad history is looked at from a particular angle in
    Chapter 12, "Darwin, Race, Slavery, Science, and the Tree of Life.")**
11 Stephen Jay Gould. *Ever Since Darwin: Reflections in Natural Science.*
    New York: W. W. Norton & Co., 1977. p. 251.
12 Ibid., p. 256.
13 Timothy Anders. *The Evolution of Evil.* p. 120.
14 Charles Hartshorne. *Omnipotence and other Theological Mistakes.*
    Albany: State University of New York, 1984. p. 91.
15 Donald B. Caine. *Within Reason: Rationality and Human Behavior.* New
    York: Vintage Books, 1999. back cover.
16 David Eagleman. *The Brain: The Story of You.* New York: Pantheon
    Books, 2015. pp. 151-152.
17 Charles Hartshorne. *Omnipotence and other Theological Mistakes.* p.
    128.
18 Ibid., p. 128.
19 Athanasius. *Orations against the Arians*, 2.78, trans. by Khaled
    Anatolios. London & New York: Routledge, 2004. pp. 171-174. Quoted
    in Denis Edwards. "The Redemption of Animals in an Incarnational
    Theology." In *Creaturely Theology: On God, Humans and Other
    Animals,* edited by Celia Deane-Drummond & David Clough. London:
    SCM Press, 2009. p. 83.
20 Thomas Aquinas. *Commentary on St. Paul's Epistle to the Ephesians, In
    Eph. 3, lectio 5,* trans. by Matthew Lamb. Quoted in Matthew Fox. *The
    Coming of the Cosmic Christ* (San Francisco: Harper & Row, 1980), p.
    75.

21 Two instances of the phrase "image of God" are just repetitions in the same passage (Genesis 1:26-27), underscoring its not being a widely used concept in the Bible. The other instances are Genesis 9:6, 1 Corinthians 11:7, and James 3:9. As a further example of the flexibility of that metaphor, in the New Testament, the emphasis shifts away from applying the phrase to human beings, applying it instead to Christ. (Source: "image of God." In *Harper's Bible Dictionary*, edited by Paul J. Achtemelier. San Francisco: Harper & Row, 1985. pp. 418-419.)

22 W. Sibley Towner. *Genesis*. Louisville: Westminster John Knox Press, 2001. p. 26.

23 Bernhard W. Anderson. "The Earth is the Lord's: An Essay on the Biblical Doctrine of Creation." In *Is God a Creationist? The Religious Case Against Creation-Science*, edited by Roland Mushat Frye. New York: Charles Scribner's Sons, 1983. p. 191.

24 George Matheson. *Searchings in the Silence*. London: Cassell, 1895. pp. 215-216. Quoted in Ian Bradley. *God is Green: Ecology for Christians*. (New York: Doubleday, 1990), p. 96.

25 Ibid., p. 96.

26 May Kendall. "Lay of the Trilobite," 1887. Quoted in Mark Pallen. *The Rough Guide to Evolution* (New York: Rough Guides Ltd., 2009), p. 252.

Chapter 12

1 Darwin was taken on board to be the gentleman dining-companion for the upper-class captain Robert Fitzroy. After the ship's official naturalist quit part way into the voyage, Darwin took over the task of collecting samples for scientific study.

2 Tim McCaskell. "A History of Race/ism." Equity Dept., Toronto District School Board, 1996. p. 2. Available at http://ocasi.org/sites/default/files/A%20History%20of%20Race.doc.

3 Ibid., p. 6.

4 Ibid., p. 8.

5 Charles Darwin. *Voyage of the Beagle*, 1838-1843. Chap. XXI.

6 Ibid. Chap. XXI.

7 Charles Darwin. Letter to Asa Gray, June 5, 1861. Available at http://www.darwinproject.ac.uk. Letter 3176.

8 The word "brothers" is used in the New Testament as an expression of community (and therefore sometimes translated "sisters and brothers" in the inclusively worded NRSV translation). It is used at least 90 times in that part of the Bible.

9 Randal Keynes. *Annie's Box: Charles Darwin, his Daughter and Human Evolution*. London: Fourth Estate: 2001. Plate 1.

10 Pope Paul III's declaration was the 1537 papal bull *Sublimis Deus*.

11 Pope Paul III. *Sublimis Deus*, 1537. Papal Encyclicals Online. http://www.papalencyclicals.net/Paul03/p3subli.htm.

12 Tim McCaskell. "A History of Race/ism." pp. 8-9.

13 The racist, compartmentalized diagram was in *Types of Mankind*, 1855, by Josiah Nott and George Gliddon.

14 Edward Lurie. "Louis Agassiz and the Races of Man." *Isis* Vol. 45, No. 3 (Sept., 1954), pp. 232ff. Available at http://www.jstor.org/stable/226710 .

15 Charles Darwin. *Origin of Species*, first edition, 1859. Chapter 4.

16 Ibid., Chapter 14.

17 The cartoon, with a poem titled "Monkeyana," appeared in *Punch* magazine in May 1861.

18 James Hunt. "On the Application of the Principle of Natural Selection to Anthropology," 1866. pp. 339-340. Quoted in Adrian Desmond & James Moore. *Darwin's Sacred Cause: How a Hatred of Slavery Shaped Darwin's Views on Human Evolution* (Boston: Houghton Mifflin, 2009). pp. 352-353.

19 Charles Darwin. *Descent of Man*, 1871; 2nd edition 1874. Chap. XXI.

20 Charles Darwin. *Descent of Man*, 2nd edition 1874. Chapter XX.

21 Ibid., Chapter VII. (Darwin's use of the lower-case "n" in "negro" in this quotation is consistent with common usage in his day, and should not be misinterpreted as being condescending.)

22 That evolutionary diagram of human lineage that was distorted by racially prejudiced views was in the geologist Alexander Winchell's 1878 book *Adamites and Preadamites*.

23 At one point, Descartes wrote, "Doubtless when the swallows come in spring, they operate like clocks. The actions of honey bees are of the same nature, and the discipline of cranes in flight, and of apes in fighting." (René Descartes. Letter to the Marquess of Newcastle, 1646. *Philosophical Letters*, trans. Anthony Kenny. Oxford: Clarendon Press,1970. p. 207. [Quoted in James A. Wiseman. *Theology and Modern Science: Quest for Coherence*. New York: Continuum, 2002. p.82.])

24 The phrase "all flesh" appears 35 times in the NRSV translation of the Bible.

25 James Turner. *Reckoning With The Beast: Animals, Pain and Humanity in the Victorian Mind*. Baltimore: The Johns Hopkins University Press, 1980, p. 4.

26 Ibid., pp. 5-13.

27 Jeremy Bentham. *An Introduction to the Principles of Morals and Legislation*, 1780. Quoted in James Turner, *Reckoning With The Beast*. p. 13.

28 Charles Darwin. *Descent of Man*, first edition, 1871. Chapter III.

29 Charles Darwin. *Descent of Man*, Concluding Remarks. (emphasis added)

30 Charles Darwin. *Notebooks* p. 228 (B231). Quoted in Adrian Desmond & James Moore. *Darwin's Sacred Cause*. p. 115.

31 Stephen Jay Gould. *The Mismeasure of Man*. New York: W. W. Norton & Co., 1981.

Chapter 13

1 John Dunlop. *The Dunlop Papers*, i. *Autobiography of John Dunlop*, edited by J.G. Dunlop, 1932. p. 186. Quoted in Keith Thomas. *Man and the Natural World: A History of the Modern Sensibility* (New York: Pantheon Books, 1983), p. 141.

2 James A. Wiseman. *Theology and Modern Science: Quest for Coherence.* New York: Continuum, 2002. pp. 79-84.

3 Ibid., pp. 89-90.

4 **It is because the early church insisted on Jesus's being human that the 2nd-century Apostles' Creed (still used today) emphasized aspects of Jesus's life that reveal his physical humanness—that he "was conceived... born... crucified, [was] dead, and buried."**

5 John Macquarrie. *Jesus Christ in Modern Thought.* Philadelphia: Trinity Press Intl., 1991. esp. pp. 159-160. **(Early Christianity maintained that Jesus was fully human by rejecting the alternative positions of Docetism [the view that Jesus only appeared to have a human body] and Apollinarianism [the view that Jesus had a human body but not a human mind and emotions].)**

6 Mary Midgley. "One World, But a Big One." *Journal of Consciousness Studies* 3 (1996). Quoted in Charles L. Birch. "Processing Towards Life." http://religion-online.org/showarticle.asp?title=2861.

7 James F. Kasting and David Catling. "Evolution of a Habitable Planet." *Annual Review of Astronomy and Astrophysics* Vol. 41 (2003). pp. 429-460. Available at http://cips.berkeley.edu/events/planets-life-seminar/kasting.pdf.

8 Psalm 104:10-11a (NRSV).

9 Psalm 42:1 (NRSV).

10 John F. Haught. "Evolution and The Suffering of Sentient Life." In *The Evolution of Evil*, edited by Gaymon Bennett, et al. Göttingen: Vandenhoeck & Ruprecht, 2008. p.193.

11 Ian G. Barbour. *Religion and Science: Historical and Contemporary Issues.* San Francisco: HarperSanFrancisco, 1997. pp. 223 & 225. **(These secondary forces within evolution include the "Baldwin effect," but are not confined to it.)**

12 Hildegard of Bingen. In *Meditations with Hildegard of Bingen*, edited by Gabriele Uhlein. Santa Fe: Bear & Co., 1983. p. 31.

13 Johann Wolfgang von Goethe. "Gedichte," in *Sämtliche Werke.* Zurich, 1950. p. I:409.

14 Alfred North Whitehead. *Science and the Modern World.* New York: The Free Press, 1925. pp. 191-192.

15 Psalm 118:5 (NRSV). **Other examples of "broad place" (or "make room for us") are Psalm 18:19, Psalm 31:8, Psalm 66:12, and Genesis 26:21-22.**

16 Psalm 36:6 (NRSV). (emphasis added)

17 Psalm 104:24, 27-28 (NRSV).

18 Greek Interlinear Bible.
    http://www.scripture4all.org/OnlineInterlinear/Greek_Index.htm.
19 Romans 8:22-23 (NRSV).
20 Roger Hazelton. "Salvation." In *A Handbook of Christian Theology*,
    edited by Marvin Halverson. New York: Meridian Books, Inc., 1958. p.
    337. (emphasis added)
21 M. K. Gandhi. *Young India*, 11-10-28. Quoted in *Gleanings from the
    writings of Mahatma Gandhi bearing on God, God-Realization and the
    Godly way*, edited by R. K. Prabhu. Available at
    http://www.north24parganasurbancongress.in/pdf/truth_is_god.pdf.
22 R. E. Davies and R. H. Koch. "All the Observed Universe has
    Contributed to Life." *Philosophical Transactions: Biological Sciences*
    Vol. 334, No. 1271 (Dec. 30, 1991), pp. 391-403. Available at
    http://www.jstor.org/stable/55573.
23 **One scientist who particularly develops the concept of emergence for
    an educated lay reader is Stuart A. Kauffman, in his a bit
    challenging book *Reinventing the Sacred: A New View of Science,
    Reason, and Religion*. New York: Basic Books, 2008.**
24 Aaron Slloman. "Emergent property." In *The Norton Dictionary of
    Modern Thought*, edited by Alan Bullock, et al. New York: W.W. Norton
    & Co., 1999. p. 266.
25 Steve McIntosh. *Evolution's Purpose: An Integral Interpretation of the
    Scientific Story of Our Origins*. New York: SelectBooks, Inc., 2012. p. 8.
26 Francis Crick. *The Astonishing Hypothesis: The Scientific Search for the
    Soul*. New York: Charles Scribner's Sons, 1994. p. 3. Quoted in Mikael
    Stenmark. "What Is Scientism?" *Religious Studies* Vol. 33, No. 1 (Mar.,
    1997). p. 23. (emphasis added) Available at
    http://www.jstor.org/stable/20008069.
27 Stephen Jay Gould. *The Hedgehog, the Fox, and the Magister's Pox:
    Mending the Gap between Science and the Humanities*. New York:
    Harmony Books, 2003. p. 221.
28 John F. Haught. *Responses to 101 Questions on God and Evolution*. New
    York: Paulist Press, 2001. pp. 49-50.
29 Ibid., p. 109.
30 Marcus Borg. *Speaking Christian: Why Christian Words Have Lost Their
    Meaning and Power—And How They Can Be Restored*. New York:
    HarperCollins Publishers, 2011. p. 39.
31 Paul Tillich. *The Eternal Now*. New York: Charles Scribner's Sons. pp.
    122-132.
32 Meister Eckhart. Quoted in Sallie McFague. *The Body of God: An
    Ecological Theology*. (Minneapolis: Fortress Press, 1993), p. 98.
33 John Muir. In *John Muir In His Own Words*, edited by Peter Browning.
    Lafayette, Cal.: Great West Books, 1988. # 308.

Part Four

Epigraph 1: John Ray. *The Wisdom of God Manifested in the Works of*

Creation, 1691.

Epigraph 2: Thomas Aquinas. *Summa theologiae (1266-1273) I.* q. 47. a. 1. Quoted in Matthew Fox, *Sheer Joy: Conversations with Thomas Aquinas on Creation Spirituality* (New York: Jeremy P. Tarcher/Putnam, 1992), p. 123.

Chapter 14

1 Rachel Carson. *Silent Spring*. Boston: Houghton Mifflin Co., 1962. p. 7.

2 **The slogan was that of the DuPont Corporation.**

3 John Muir, July 27, 1869. In *John Muir in His Own Words*, edited by Peter Browning. Lafayette, Calif.: Great West Books, 1988. #63.

4 **One 1945 photograph advertising insecticide for home use showed a mother spraying it right over her baby's crib.** Reproduced in: George Shea. *Rachel Carson: Founder of the Environmental Movement*. Detroit: Thomson Gale, 2006. p. 8.

5 Lynn White, Jr. "The Historical Roots of Our Ecologic Crisis." *Science*, Vol. 155, 3767, (March 10, 1967). pp. 1203-1207. **(White used the word "ecologic" in the way we would today say "ecological.")**

6 **Before 1967, very few 20th-century Christian theologians addressed such environmental connections. One exception was Joseph Sittler, but he dealt mainly with how Christianity should *respond* to environmental concerns, rather than focusing on how Christianity might have influenced technology's approach toward Nature, as was the case after Lynn White's wake-up call.**

7 John Calvin. *Commentary on Genesis*. Grand Rapids: Baker Books, 2003. At Gen. 1:26.

8 Rachel Carson. *Silent Spring*. p. 297.

9 Peter Harrison. "Subduing the Earth: Genesis 1, Early Modern Science, and the Exploitation of Nature." *The Journal of Religion*, Vol. 79. No. 1 (Jan. 1999). esp. pp. 90 & 96. Available at http://www.jstor.org/stable/1207043.

10 Lynn White, Jr. "The Historical Roots of Our Ecologic Crisis."

11 **An early (1984) use of "eco-justice" by the theologian Philip Joranson was directed toward the idea that the Earth should be given justice. But over time, the term "eco-justice" or "ecojustice" came to be used more to emphasize the interpenetration of environmental and social matters.**

12 Lynn White, Jr. "The Historical Roots of Our Ecologic Crisis."

13 Saint Francis of Assisi. "Canticle of Brother Sun [or Canticle of the Sun]." The original Umbrian text and a translation are available at en.wikipedia.org.

14 The interviewer was Jane Howard. "The Gentle Storm Center: A Calm Appraisal of Silent Spring." *Life*, October 12, 1962, pp. 109-110. Quoted in Mark Lytle. *The Gentle Subversive: Rachel Carson, Silent Spring, and the Rise of the Environmental Movement* (New York: Oxford University Press, 2007), pp. 177-178.

15 Ezra Taft Benson. In a communication to Dwight Eisenhower. Quoted in
Linda J. Lear, "Rachel Carson's *Silent Spring.*" *Environmental History
Review* 17 (Summer 1993): 2348. Available at
http://www.history.vt.edu/Barrow/Hist3706/readings/lear.html.

16 Hildegard of Bingen. In *Meditations with Hildegard of Bingen*, edited by
Gabriele Uhlein. Santa Fe: Bear & Co., 1983. p. 79.

17 Rachel Carson. *Silent Spring.* p. 297.

18 Hildegard of Bingen. In *Meditations with Hildegard of Bingen.* p. 71.
(emphasis added)

19 Francis Bacon. *Novum Organon, or True Directions Concerning The
Interpretation Of Nature*, 1620. CXXIX. Available at
http://www.constitution.org/bacon/nov_org.htm.

20 Rachel Carson. *Silent Spring.* p. 296.

21 Francis Bacon. *Novum Organon.* CXXIX.

22 Rachel Carson. In television interview "The Silent Spring of Rachel
Carson," April 3, 1963. Quoted in *The New York Times* Obituary of April
15, 1964.

23 Francis Bacon. "De Augmentis Scientiarum," 1623, and "The Masculine
Birth of Time," 1603. Quoted in Carolyn Merchant. *The Death of
Nature: Women, Ecology and the Scientific Revolution* (San Francisco:
HarperSanFrancisco, 1989), p. 169 & 170. **(Today, there is a widely
circulated claim that Bacon said that Nature should be "placed on
the rack." But that supposed quotation is spurious, Bacon not having
used that phrase. However, given the context of his time, the imagery
Bacon employed to describe the extracting of Nature's secrets would,
in all probability, have had overtones of the coercive methods of
some prosecutors.** [Source: Carolyn Merchant. "The Scientific
Revolution and *The Death of Nature.*" *Isis*, 97 (1996). p. 518.])

24 Stephen Bede Scharper. *Redeeming the Time: A Political Theology of the
Environment.* New York: Continuum, 1997. pp. 133-134.

25 **As an example, although *Silent Spring* was filled with more scientific
data than most lay readers were accustomed to, the *Time* magazine
review of her book (Sept. 18, 1962) called it "hysterical ... [an]
emotional and inaccurate outburst."** Quoted in J.E. deSteiguer. *The
Origins of Modern Environmental Thought* (Tuscon: University of
Arizona Press, 2006), p. 35.

26 Hildegard of Bingen. Quoted in Charles Singer, "The Visions of
Hildegard of Bingen." *Yale Journal of Biology and Medicine* 78 (2005):
p. 70. Available at
http://www.ncbi.nlm.nih.gov/pmc/articles/PMC2259136/pdf/16197730.p
df.

27 Hildegard of Bingen. In *Meditations with Hildegard of Bingen.* p. 65.

Chapter 15

1 Emma Darwin. Letter to Henrietta Darwin, June 1877. *Emma Darwin: A
Century of Family Letters, 1792-1896*, II, edited by Henrietta Litchfield.

N.Y.: D. Appledon and Co., 1915. p. 226. Quoted in Deborah Heiligman. *Charles and Emma: The Darwins' Leap of Faith* (New York: Henry Holt and Co.), 2009. p. 219.

2   Augustine of Hippo. *Confessions*. XI, 14.

3   Paul Tillich. "On the Transitoriness of Life." In *The Shaking of the Foundations*. New York: Charles Scribner's Sons, 1948. p. 35.

4   Stuart McCready, editor. *The Discovery of Time*. Naperville, Ill.: Sourcebooks, Inc., 2001. esp. p. 189.

5   **The variety of ways of interpreting the Bible, as well as the principle of accommodation that was used to allow for non-literal readings of the Bible—even its creation narratives—were explained in Chapter 1 ("Exposing the 'Warfare' Myth").**

6   Karl W Giberson. *Saving Darwin: How to Be a Christian and Believe in Evolution.* New York: HarperOne, 2008. pp. 49-51.

7   **The term "deep time" came into parlance after the American writer John McPhee used it in 1981 in his study of geological thought titled *Basin and Range*.**

8   James Hutton. *Theory of the Earth*, 1788. Quoted in Langdon Gilkey. *Nature, Reality, and the Sacred: The Nexus of Science and Religion* (Minneapolis: Fortress Press, 1993), p. 19.

9   Percy Bysshe Shelley. "Peter Bell the Third," 1819. Quoted in *A Dictionary of Environmental Quotations*, edited by Barbara K. Rodes, et al. (Baltimore: Johns Hopkins Univ. Press, 1992), 6:6.

10 Cecil Frances Alexander. "All Things Bright and Beautiful," 1848. Quoted in Keith Thomson. *Before Darwin: Reconciling God and Nature* (New Haven: Yale Univ. Press, 2005), p. 244.

11 Rebecca Stott. *Darwin and the Barnacle*. New York: W. W. Norton & Co., 2003.

12 Charles Darwin. *Origin of Species*. London: John Murray, 1859. Chapter 4.

13 Isaac Watts. "Our God, Our Help in Ages Past," 1719.

14 Alfred Tennyson. "In Memoriam," 1850. 55, stanza 2 & 56, stanza 1. **In that poem, Tennyson referred to a species as a "type," and wrote:**
    Are God and Nature then at strife,
       That Nature lends such evil dreams?
       So careful of the type she seems,
    So careless of the single life ...
    So careful of the type? but no.
       From scaped cliff and quarried stone
       She cries, "A thousand types are gone:
    I care for nothing, all shall go."

15 Charles Darwin. *Notebooks* p. 228 (B231).

16 René Descartes. (AT 5:277; K 244) Quoted in Daisie and Michael Radner. *Animal Consciousness* (Amherst, New York: Prometheus Books, 1996), p. 80.

17 **One of the most specific statements Darwin ever made about his beliefs, written late in his life, was, "I for one must be content to remain an Agnostic."** (Charles Darwin. *The Autobiography of Charles Darwin, 1809-1882. With original omissions restored, Edited with Appendix and Notes by his granddaughter, Nora Barlow.* New York: W. W. Norton & Co., 1958. p. 94.) (Darwin's religious struggles are detailed in Chapter 8, "Unfinished Odysseys, Darwin's and Ours.")

18 **In 1879, in response to a letter he received from John Fordyce, Darwin replied that it was "absurd to doubt that a man may be an ardent Theist & an evolutionist." And Darwin gave Charles Kingsley and Asa Gray as examples.** (Letter of May, 7 1879. Available at http://www.darwinproject.ac.uk/entry-12041.)

19 Charles Darwin. Quoted in Adrian Desmond & James Moore. *Darwin* (London: Michael Joseph, Penguin Group, 199), p. 657.

20 Charles Darwin. *The Formation of Vegetable Mould, through the Action of Worms.* London: John Murray, 1881. Chapter I.

21 Ibid., Chapter VII.

22 **The biologist Ernst Haeckel coined the term "oekology" (now spelled "ecology" in English) in 1866, deriving the name from the Greek word *oikos* or "house" to indicate the study of the "homes" or niches animals occupy.** (Richard Milner. *The Encyclopedia of Evolution: Humanity's Search for Its Origins.* New York: Facts On File, 1990. p. 151.)

23 Joseph Hooker. Letter to Brian Hodgson, April 10, 1881. In *Life and Letters of Sir Joseph Dalton Hooker.* Available at https://archive.org/stream/lifelettersofsir02hookrich/lifelettersofsir02hoo krich_djvu.txt.

24 Charles Darwin. *The Autobiography of Charles Darwin, 1809-1882.* p. 97.

25 Peter J. Bowler. *Evolution: The History of an Idea.* Berkeley: Univ. of California Press, 2009. pp. 24-25.

Chapter 16

1 Amory B. Lovins. "Making Security Profitable." In *Crisis and the Renewal of Creation: World and Church in the Age of Ecology,* edited by Jeffrey Golliher & William Bryant Logan. New York: Continuum, 1996. p. 101.

2 Herbert Butterfield. *Christianity and History.* New York: Charles Scribner's Sons, 1950. Quoted in Bernard W. Anderson. *The Unfolding Drama of the Bible* (Philadelphia: Fortress Press, 1957, 1988), pp. 23-24.

3 Donald Worster. *The Wealth of Nature: Environmental History and the Ecological Imagination.* New York: Oxford University Press, 1993. p. 19.

4 Ibid., p. 19. (emphasis added)

5 **This history-Nature split also shows up in modern psychiatry's and psychotherapy's heavy concentration on our relationships with other**

humans (parents, family, friends, colleagues)—often ignoring our relationships with Nature, upon which the life of all those humans depends.

6   Holmes Rolston, III. *A New Environmental Ethics: The Next Millennium for Life on Earth.* New York: Routledge, 2012. p. 115.

7   Alister McGrath. *The Reenchantment of Nature: The Denial of Religion and the Ecological Crisis.* New York: Doubleday, 2002. pp. 109 & 122.

8   James A Wiseman. *Theology and Modern Science: Quest for Coherence.* New York: Continuum, 2002. p. 82.

9   J. R. McNeill. *Something New Under the Sun: An Environmental History of the Twentieth-Century World.* New York: W.W. Norton & Company, 2000. (He is quoting the 1974 Nobel laureate Robert Solow.)

10 Holmes Rolston, III. *A New Environmental Ethics.* p. 48.

11 David W. Orr. *Earth in Mind.* Washington, DC: Island Press, 1994. p. 163.

12 A similar measurement of Gross Domestic Product (GDP) is used today, but Ponting's observation about the limitations of these economic measurements is just as apt.

13 Clive Ponting. *A Green History of the World: The Environment and the Collapse of Great Civilizations.* New York: Penguin Books, 1991. p. 156.

14 E. F. Schumacher. *Small Is Beautiful: Economics as if People Mattered.* New York: HarperCollins, 1989.

15 Donella H. Meadows. *The Global Citizen.* Washington, DC: Island Press, 1991.

16 Elizabeth A. Johnson. "Losing and Finding Creation in the Christian Tradition." In *Christianity and Ecology,* edited by Dieter T. Hessel & Rosemary Radford Ruether. Cambridge, Mass.: Harvard University Press, 2000. p. 4.

17 Peter Harrison. "The Bible and the Emergence of Modern Science." *Science & Christian Belief* Vol. 18 No. 2 (2006). p. 124. Available at http://epublications.bond.edu.au/cgi/viewcontent.cgi?article=1068&context=hss_pubs.

18 Jürgen Moltmann. *God in Creation.* Minneapolis: Fortress Press, 1985. p. 35.

19 Most philosophers reserve the phrase "naturalistic fallacy" for a more specific type of problem laid out and so named by the philosopher G. E. Moore in his *Principia Ethica* in 1903. He critiqued thinking that reduced "good" to something of another category, such as "pleasant" or "useful." The is-ought formulation is more useful for exploring questions about the relationship of humans to Nature than is Moore's concern.

20 David Hume. *A Treatise on Human Nature,* 1740. Oxford: Clarendon Press, 1978. p. 469. Quoted in Denis Alexander. *Rebuilding the Matrix: Science and Faith in the 21st Century* (Grand Rapids, MI: Zondervan, 2001), p. 391.

21 Rod Preece. *Animals and Nature: Cultural Myths, Cultural Realities.* Vancouver: UBC Press, 1999. p. 48.

22 Jan and Birgitta S. Tullberg. "A Critique of the Naturalistic Fallacy Thesis." *Politics and the Life Sciences*, Vol. 20, No. 2 (Sept., 2001), pp. 165, 166. Available at http://www.jstor.org.houstontx.idm.oclc.org/stable/pdf/4236638.pdf.

23 Roger Masters. *The Nature of Politics.* New Haven, CT: Yale University Press, 1989. p. xv. Quoted in ibid., p. 170.

24 **In philosophical Taoism, the grounding of morality in Nature is expressed through a double meaning of the word *tao*, usually translated as "way." The *tao* is the best *way* for us to behave based on the *way* the natural world is.**

25 Craig A. Boyd. "Natural Law Morality." In *A Science and Religion Primer*, edited by Heidi A. Campbell and Heather Looy. Grand Rapids, MI: Baker Academic, 2009. p. 151. (Thomas Aquinas used the phrase "natural law" in his *Summa Theologica*, Part II, Sect. 1, q. 91, art. 2.)

26 Samuel Enoch Stumpf. "Natural Law." In *A Handbook of Christian Theology.* New York: Living Age Books, 1958. p. 246.

27 John Hedley Brooke. *Science and Religion: Some Historical Perspectives.* New York: Cambridge University Press, 1991. pp. 117-151.

28 Craig a. Boyd. "Natural Law Morality." In *A Science and Religion Primer.* p. 152.

29 **A major exception being Roman Catholic Thomistic theology, which carried on natural-law thinking similar to Thomas Aquinas's.**

30 James A. Nash. "Seeking Moral Norms in Nature: Natural Law and Ecological Responsibility." In *Christianity and Ecology.* pp. 232 & 228. (emphasis added)

31 Rod Preece. *Animals and Nature.* p. 48.

32 **Rolston does not capitalize "Nature," as I have been doing to indicate the non-human sphere, but the environmental and ecological context of his question and his analysis of it indicate that is the sense in which he is for the most part using the word.**

33 Holmes Rolston, III. *Environmental Ethics: Duties to and Values in the Natural World.* Philadelphia: Temple University Press, 1988. pp. 38 & 41. (emphasis added)

34 Thomas Berry. *The Great Work: Our Way into the Future.* New York: Bell Tower, 1999. p. 51.

35 Jeffrey C. Pugh. *The Matrix of Faith: Reclaiming a Christian Vision.* New York: Crossroad Publishing Co., 2001. p. 91.

36 Translation is that of *The Revised English Bible.* Oxford University Press, 1989.

37 **Most writing about animals that has come out of our modern environmental crisis has been concerned about animal rights or the possibilities of species becoming extinct. An exception has been the work of Paul Shepard, who has perceptively examined the**

interpenetrations of animals with human thought and culture. Such as in his book *Thinking Animals: Animals and the Development of Human Intelligence.* Athens, GA: University of Georgia Press, 1978, 1998.

38 Nancy M. Wells. "Nature and the Life Course: Pathways from Childhood Nature Experiences to Adult Environmentalism." *Children, Youth and Environments* 16;1. (2006). Available at http://promiseofplace.org/research_attachments/Wells2006Natureandthe LifeCourse.pdf.

39 Jennifer Sahn. Introduction in *Beyond Ecophobia: Re-claiming the Heart in Nature Education* by David Sobel. Great Barrinton, MA: The Orion Society, 1996.

40 Margaret A. Farley. "Religious Meanings for Nature and Humanity." In *The Good in Nature and Humanity: Connecting Science, Religion, and Spirituality with the Natural World.*, edited by Stephen R. Kellert and Timothy J. Farnham. Washington: Island Press, 2002. p. 110.

41 Mark Twain. "The American Claimant." In *The Wit and Wisdom of Mark Twain: A Book of Quotations*. New York: Dover Publications, 1999. p. 29. (spelling modernized)

42 Holmes Rolston III. "The Pasqueflower." *Natural History* 88, no. 4 (April 1979): pp. 616. Available at https://dspace.library.colostate.edu/bitstream/handle/10217/37703/Pasque flower.pdf?sequence=1.

Chapter 17

1 Walter Brueggemann. "Israel's Creation Faith." *The Book That Breathes New Life: Scriptural Authority and Biblical Theology*. Minneapolis: Fortress Press, 2005. p. 156. (emphasis added)

2 Herbert Butterfield. *Christianity and History*. New York: Charles Scribner's Sons, 1950. Quoted in Bernard W. Anderson. *The Unfolding Drama of the Bible* (Philadelphia: Fortress Press, 1957, 1988), pp. 23-24.

3 Emil Brunner. *Revelation and Reason*. Philadelphia: Westminster, 1946. p. 33n. Quoted in Terence E. Fretheim. *God and World in the Old Testament: A Relational Theology of Creation* (Nashville: Abingdon Press, 2005), p. 250. (emphasis added)

4 Elizabeth A. Johnson. "Losing and Finding Creation in the Christian Tradition." In *Christianity and Ecology*, edited by Dieter T. Hessel & Rosemary Radford Ruether. Cambridge, Mass.: Harvard University Press, 2000. p. 10.

5 Addl. source: William P. Brown. *The Ethos of the Cosmos: The Genesis of Moral Imagination in the Bible*. Grand Rapids, MI: William P. Eerdmans Publishing Co., 1999. p. 23- 24.

6 John R. McRay. "Covenant." In *The Dictionary of Bible and Religion*, edited by William H. Gentz. Nashville: Abingdon Press, 1986. p. 229. (emphasis added)

7 *The Reader's Digest Bible*, Bruce M. Metzger, gen. editor. New York:

Reader's Digest Association, 1990. p. 32.

8 Genesis 9:8-17 (NRSV).

9 Ian Bradley. *God is Green: Ecology for Christians*. New York: Image Books, 1990. p. 19.

10 John L. McKenzie. *A Theology of the Old Testament*. Garden City, N.Y.: Doubleday & Co., Inc., 1974. pp. 195-196.

11 Peter Coates. *Nature: Western Attitudes Since Ancient Times*. Berkeley: University of California Press, 1998. p. 203n36.

12 Theodore Hiebert. "Nature and Ecology." In *The Oxford Companion to the Bible*, edited by Bruce M. Metzger, et al. New York: Oxford University Press, 1993. p. 550.

13 Genesis 8:22 (NRSV).

14 Ralph P. Martin. "Salvation." In *The Dictionary of Bible and Religion*. p. 922.

15 1 Corinthians 15:25-28 (NRSV).

16 Ralph P. Martin. "Salvation." In *The Dictionary of Bible and Religion*. p. 922.

17 Colossians 1:15-20 (NRSV).

18 Interlinear Greek Bible. Available at http://www.scripture4all.org/OnlineInterlinear/Greek_Index.htm.

19 Hebrews 1:1-3a (NRSV).

20 Ephesians 1:9-10 (NRSV).

21 Psalm 36:6 (NRSV).

22 *The Reader's Digest Bible*. p. 31. (emphasis added)

23 E. Ashby Johnson. *Saved—from What?* Richmond, Virginia: John Knox Press, 1966. p. 36.

24 Ibid., p. 30.

25 Marcus J. Borg. *The Heart of Christianity: Rediscovering a Life of Faith*. San Francisco: HarperSanFrancisco, 2003.

26 Marcus J. Borg. J*esus: Uncovering the Life, Teachings, and Relevance of a Religious Revolutionary*. San Francisco: HarperSanFrancisco, 2006.

27 John Dominic Crossan. *Jesus: A Revolutionary Biography*. San Francisco: HarperSanFrancisco, 1994.

28 From Ruth 1:16 (NRSV).

29 Ruth 4:13b (NRSV).

30 **The two revealing pairs both express the narrative's movement from desolation to fullness. But the Hebrew word-pairs are obscured in most English translations by the use of different English words rather than matching words. The first pair is a Hebrew word that could be translated as "lads," expressing that Naomi first lost her two "lads" (sons) in Ruth 1:5, but was provided a new "lad" (grandchild) in Ruth 4:13-17. The other pair expresses how in the beginning of the story, after the famine, Naomi returns to her homeland "empty" in Ruth 1:20-21. But later, in Ruth 3:15-17, she is given through Ruth grain from Boaz, who told Ruth to not go back**

to Naomi "empty"(i.e., empty-handed). (Source: Edward E. Campbell, Jr. *The Anchor Bible: Ruth.* New York: Doubleday, 1975. p. 13.)

31 **Later in Genesis, God gives the humans permission to eat animals— but with a restriction (Gen. 9:3-4) so that people will not forgot that all life is a gift from God, not something that humans own. The following verses (Gen 9:5-6) show that there is a concern that without such an awareness, humans will spill human blood.**

32 Lawrence O. Richards. *Encyclopedia of Bible Words.* Grand Rapids: Zondervan, 1991. p. 538.

33 Psalm 72:13 (NRSV).

34 Exodus 23:12a (NRSV).

35 Ian Bradley. *God is Green.* p 19.

Chapter 18

1 Source of incident, and prominent religious speaker: Jay McDaniel. "The Sacred Whole: An Ecumenical Protestant Approach." In *The Greening of Faith: God, the Environment, and the Good Life,* edited by John E. Carroll, et al. Hanover: University Press of New England, 1997. p. 110.

2 **The Apostles' Creed (dating back to the second century C.E).**

3 Elizabeth A. Johnson. "Losing and Finding Creation in the Christian Tradition." In *Christianity and Ecology,* edited by Dieter T. Hessel & Rosemary Radford Ruether. Cambridge, Mass.: Harvard University Press, 2000. p. 4.

4 Psalm 19:14a (NRSV).

5 Isaiah 6:3 (NRSV).

6 Romans 1:19-20a (NRSV).

7 **St. Anthony of the Desert, also called St. Anthony of Egypt and St. Anthony the Great (250?-350?).** In a story told by Evagrius Ponticus in *Praktikos,* 92. [The quotation can also be found in Thomas Merton, *The Wisdom of the Desert* (New York: New Directions, 1960) Saying CIII.]

8 St. Augustine, *De Civitate Dei,* Book 16. Quoted in *The Green Bible: New Revised Standard Version* (New York: HarperCollins, 2006), p. I-100.

9 Hugh of St. Victor. *De sacramentis,* Book I, Pars VI, chap. 5 [PL 176, 266–7]. Quoted in G. Tanzella-Nitti. "The Two Books Prior to the Scientific Revolution." *Perspectives on Science and Christian Faith* Vol. 57, No. 3 (Sept. 2005). p. 239.

10 Thomas Aquinas. *Sermons on the Two Precepts of Charity and the Ten Precepts of the Law,* 1273. 6.5, p. 129.

11 John Calvin. *Opera Selecta* 9:793, 795. Quoted in H. Paul Santmire. *The Travail of Nature: The Ambiguous Ecological Promise of Christian Theology* (Minneapolis: Fortress Press, 1985), p. 128.

12 Johannes Kepler. *Mysterium Cosmographicum,* Praefatico; *Ges. Werke* I (1938) 5. Quoted in Olaf Pedersen. *The Book of Nature* (Vatican Observatory Foundation, 1992), p. 44.

13 Johannes Kepler. *Epitome Astronomiae Copernicanae,* 1618. *Ges. Werke*

VII (1952) 25. Quoted in Olaf Pedersen. *The Book of Nature.* p. 44.
(Kepler's use of "wordless" is a reference to Psalm 19's recognition that Nature's message is *metaphorically* speech by saying, "Day to day pours forth speech [yet] there is no speech, nor are there words." [Ps. 19:2-3a (NRSV).]

14 Blaise Pascal. *Pensees,* 1670. Quoted in Barbara K. Rodes, et al., eds. *A Dictionary of Environmental Quotations* (Baltimore: Johns Hopkins Univ. Press, 1992), 117.2.

15 St. John Chrysostom. Homily IX, 5, 162-3. *The Homilies of S. John Chrysostom, on The Statutes, to the People of Antioch,* A Library of the Fathers of the Holy Catholic Church. Oxford: Parker, 1842. Quoted in Ted Peters & Gaymon Bennett. *Bridging Science and Religion* (London: SCM Press, 2002), pp. 127-128.

16 George Washington Carver. Quoted in Shirley A. Jones, editor. *The Mind of God & Other Musings: The Wisdom of Science* (San Rafael, Cal.: Classic Wisdom Collection, 1994), p. 56.

17 **From Matthew 6:28b (NRSV). With the surrounding verses, the words of Jesus read: "And why do you worry about clothing? Consider the lilies of the field, how they grow; they neither toil nor spin, yet I tell you, even [King] Solomon in all his glory was not clothed like one of these. But if God so clothes the grass of the field, which is alive today and tomorrow is thrown into the oven, will he not much more clothe you—you of little faith?"**

18 John Calvin. *Institutes.* 1.14.21. Quoted in H. Paul Santmire. *The Travail of Nature.* pp. 128-129.

19 **This example of the key phrase "all things" [Greek *ta panta*] is from Ephesians 1:10 (NRSV). Other examples can be found in Colossians 1:15-20, Hebrews 1:13, and 1 Corinthians 15:25-28.**

20 Sallie McFague. "An Ecological Christology: Does Christianity Have It?" In *Christianity and Ecology.* p. 37.

21 Matthew Fox. *One River, Many Wells: Wisdom Springing from Global Faiths.* New York: Jeremy P. Tarcher/Putnam, 2000. p. 28.

22 **As just one example, this line from the *Qur'an* (Koran): "In the water that Allah sends down from the clouds and quickens therewith the earth after its death and scatters therein all kind of beasts, and in the course of the winds, and the clouds pressed into service between the heaven and the earth, are indeed Signs for a people who understand."** (*The Qur'an*, trans. Muhammad Zafrulla Khan. 26. Quoted in Matthew Fox. *One River, Many Wells.* p. 38.)

23 St. John Chrysostom. Homily X. 3,175. *The Homilies of S. John Chrysostom, on The Statutes, to the People of Antioch.* Quoted in Ted Peters & Gaymon Bennett. *Bridging Science and Religion.* 228 n.9.

24 Bill McKibben. *The End of Nature.* New York: Random House, 1989. p. 80.

25 Richard Louv. *Last Child in the Woods: Saving Our Children from*

Nature-Deficit Disorder. Chapel Hill, NC: Algonquin Books of Chapel Hill, 2005.

26 William Wordsworth. "The World is Too Much With Us," 1806. Quoted in Robert J. Begiebing & Owen Grumbling, editors. *The Literature of Nature: The British and American Traditions* (Medford, NJ: Plexus Publishing, Inc., 1990), p. 69.

27 **Jesus even sees the vital connection between every single sparrow and the life-giving God—a divine matrix of life in which every creature's life is supported: "Are not two sparrows sold for a penny? Yet not one of them will fall to the ground apart from your Father." (Matthew 10:29, NRSV).**

Part Five

Epigraph 1: Soren Kierkegaard. *Life.* Quoted in *Familiar Quotations*, edited by John Bartlett. 14th edition Boston: Little, Brown and Co., 1968. p. 676a.

Epigraph 2: Sir Arthur Eddington. Quoted in *The Mind of God & Other Musings*, edited by Shirley Jones. San Rafael, CA., 1994. p. 50.

Epigraph 3: Alfred, Lord Tennyson. "In Memoriam," 1850. Prologue, stanza 7.

Chapter 19

1 Jeffrey G. Sobosan. *Romancing the Universe: Theology, Science, and Cosmology.* Grand Rapids, MI: William B. Eerdmans Publishing Co., 1999. p. 1.

2 Ibid., p. 97.

3 Karen Armstrong. "Think Again: God." *Foreign Policy*, Nov./Dec. 2009. Available at http://foreignpolicy.com/2009/10/15/thinkagaingod/.

4 Viktor Frankl. *Man's Search for Meaning.* Boston: Beacon Press, 1959.

5 This list of three avenues was provided by Michael Winters in response to a question following his lecture "Viktor Frankl: At the Intersection of Psychology and Spirituality" at an event of the Foundation for Contemporary Theology on Feb. 11, 2015.

6 Michael H. Barnes. *In the Presence of Mystery: An Introduction to the Story of Human Religiousness.* Mystic, CN: TwentyThird Publications, 1990. p. 132.

7 As elsewhere in this book I am using the capitalized word "Nature" to refer to the non-human realm of animals, plants, and the inanimate.

8 William B. Provine. "Evolution and the Foundation of Ethics," *MBL Science* 3. 1988. p. 28. Quoted in Mikael Stenmark. "Evolution, Purpose and God" (*Ars Disputandi*, Vol. 1, 2001), p. 1.

9 Steven Weinberg. *The First Three Minutes*, updated. ed. New York: Basic Books, 1977, 1993. p. 154.

10 Sharon Begley, introduction in *The Hand of God: Thoughts and Images Reflecting the Spirit of the Universe*, edited by Michael Reagan. Kansas City, Missouri: Andrews McNeel Publishing, 1999. p. 28.

11 Arthur Eddington. *The Philosophy of Physical Science*. Cambridge: Cambridge Univ. Press, 1939. p. 16.

12 Walt Whitman. "When I Heard the Learn'd Astronomer." *Complete Poetry and Selected Prose*, edited by James E. Miller, Jr. Boston: Houghton Mifflin Co., 1959. p. 196.

13 Max Oelschlaeger. *The Idea of Wilderness*. New Haven: Yale University Press, 1991. pp. 111-113.

14 Steve Jones. Quoted in Denis R. Alexander. "Science: Friend or Foe?" *Cambridge Paper* series, Vol. 4, No 3 (Sept. 1995). Available at http://www.cis.org.uk/upload/Resources/General/Alexander_Science_Fri end_or_Foe.pdf.

15 P. B. Medawar. *The Limits of Science*. New York: Harper & Row, 1984. p. 59.

16 Brian Swimme. *The Hidden Heart of the Cosmos: Humanity and the New Story*. New York: Orbis Books, Maryknoll, 1996. p. 13.

17 N. Scott Momaday. *The Man Made of Words: Essays, Stories, Passages*. New York: St. Martin's Press, 1997. pp. 47-48.

18 Jozef Zycinskif. *God and Evolution: Fundamental Questions of Christian Evolutionism*. Washington, D.C.: Catholic University of America Press, 2006. p. 148.

19 Stephen Jay Gould. *Rocks of Ages: Science and Religion in the Fullness of Life*. New York: The Ballantine Publishing Group, 1999. p. 4. (emphasis added)

20 Jacques Monod. *Chance and Necessity*, trans. by A. Wainhouse. London: Fontana, 1974. p. 160. Quoted in Mary Midgley. "Criticizing the Cosmos." In *Is Nature Ever Evil? Religion, Science and Value*, edited by Willem B. Drees. (London: Routledge, 2003), p. 12.

21 Carl Zimmer. "Genes Are Us. And Them." *National Geographic*. http://ngm.nationalgeographic.com/2013/07/125explore/sharedgenes.

22 Mary Midgley. "Criticizing the Cosmos." op. cit., p. 21.

23 Mary Midgley. *Science as Salvation: A Modern Myth and its Meaning*. London: Routledge, 1992. pp. 48-49. (emphasis added)

24 Thomas Berry. *Evening Thoughts: Reflections on Earth as Sacred Community*, edited by Mary Evelyn Tucker. San Francisco: Sierra Club Books, 2006. p. 139.

25 Job 1:13-19 & 2:7.

26 Job 38:39 through 39:30.

27 Job 40:3-5.

28 Robert Frost. "Birches." In *Complete Poems of Robert Frost*. New York: Holt, Rinehart and Winston, 1967. p. 153.

29 Sallie McFague. "An Ecological Christianity: Does Christianity Have It?" In *Christianity and Ecology*, edited by Dieter T. Hessel & Rosemary Radford Ruether, pp. 29-46. Cambridge, Mass.: Harvard University Press, 2000. p. 37.

30 John F. Haught. *Is Nature Enough? Meaning and Truth in the Age of*

Science. New York: Cambridge University Press, 2006. pp. 46-47.
31 John A. Teske. "Neuromythology: Brains and Stories." Paper prepared for Science and Religion: Global Perspectives, June 48, 2005. p. 1. Available at http://metanexus.net/archive/conference2005/pdf/teske.pdf.
32 Ernst Bloch. *The Principle of Hope*, 1954, 1959. Quoted in Jurgen Moltmann. *God in Creation: A New Theology of Creation and the Spirit of God* (Minneapolis: Fortress Press, 1993), p. 321.

Chapter 20

1 Curtis Cate. "René Descartes." *Makers of Modern Thought*, edited by Bruce Mazlish. American Heritage Publishing Co., Inc., 1972. p. 123. **(Historians are divided over the reason or reasons for the change of windows. My interest here lies in the way our modern culture thinks about itself and other time periods, even using buildings as emblems, as in the incident involving Thomas Henry Huxley that opened Chapter 9, "Opening Darwin's Gift.")**
2 Carl Sagan. *Cosmos*. New York: Random House, 1980. p. 335.
3 Christine Garwood. *Flat Earth: The History of an Infamous Idea*. New York: St. Martin's Press, 2007. pp. 11-12.
4 Herbert Butterfield. "The Whig Interpretation of History," 1931. Available at http://cdn.preterhuman.net/texts/literature/general/Butterfield %20(Herbert)%20The%20Whig%20Interpretation%20of %20History.pdf.
5 Mary Midgley. *The Myths We Live By*. New York: Routledge, 2003. pp. 13-17.
6 Genesis 33:1-15.
7 http://www.theclergyletterproject.org/.
8 https://www.templeton.org/. And http://www.scientistsincongregations.org/.
9 Ian G. Barbour. *Religion in an Age of Science*. San Francisco: HarperSanFrancisco, 1990. pp. 3-30.
10 **The biggest disseminator of this myth about the Library of Alexandria was Carl Sagan's 1980 TV series *Cosmos* and the companion book. (Carl Sagan. *Cosmos*. pp. 20 & 333-336.) Sagan entangled the story of the Library with a myth about Hypatia, who actually died because she got caught in the middle of a political fight, not because Christianity was against education.**
11 Ian F. McNeely, with Lisa Wolverton. *Reinventing Knowledge: From Alexandria to the Internet*. New York: W.W. Norton & Co., 2008. p. 35.
12 Just one example of this common mislead is: Paul Mason. *Galileo*. Chicago: Heinemann Library, 2001. pp. 23-24.
13 Jole Shackelford. "Myth 7: That Giordano Bruno Was the First Martyr of Modern Science." In *Galileo Goes to Jail: And Other Myths about Science and Religion*, edited by Ronald L. Numbers, pp. 59-67. Cambridge, Mass.: Harvard University Press, 2009.

14 Ronald L. Numbers. *Galileo Goes to Jail: And Other Myths about Science and Religion.* p. 6.
15 One book that repeats this fabricated statement is: Catherine M. Andronik. *Copernicus: Founder of Modern Astronomy.* Berkeley Heights, NJ: Enslow Publishers, 2002. p. 62.
16 Alister E. McGrath. *The Foundations of Dialogue in Science and Religion.* Malden, Mass.: Blackwell Publishers, 1998. p. 17.
17 **The 2004 Dover trial occurred after anti-evolutionists mandated that science teachers in public schools read a statement to their classes that included the assertion that, "Because Darwin's Theory is a theory,... [it] is not a fact."** (Source: Francisco J. Ayala. *Darwin and Intelligent Design.* Minneapolis: Fortress Press, 2006. p. 99.)
18 Cameron M. Smith and Charles Sullivan. *The Top 10 Myths about Evolution.* Amherst, N.Y.: Prometheus Books, 2007. pp. 25-42.
19 Elaine Howard Ecklund and Jerry Z. Park. "Conflict between Religion and Science among Academic Scientists?" *Journal for the Scientific Study of Religion,* Vol. 48, No. 2 (Jun., 2009): pp. 276-292. Available at http://www.jstor.org/stable/40405617.
20 The complexities of the actual Galileo affair were explained in Chapter 2, "The Galileo Story: Great Drama, Mostly False."
21 Denis R. Alexander. "Science: Friend or Foe?" *Cambridge Paper* series, Vol. 4, No 3 (Sept. 1995). Available at http://www.cis.org.uk/upload/Resources/General/Alexander_Science_Fri end_or_Foe.pdf.
22 Ambrose of Milan. Quoted in Ted Peters and Martinez Hewlett, *Evolution from Creation to New Creation* (Nashville: Abingdon Press, 2003), p. 121.
23 John Calvin. *Institutes of the Christian Religion.* 2.2.15 (1:273-274). Quoted in *The Doubleday Christian Quotation Collection,* compiled by Hannah Ward, and Jennifer Wild (New York: Doubleday, 1997), p. 90.
24 Ian G. Barbour. *Religion and Science: Historical and Contemporary Issues.* San Francisco: HarperSanFrancisco, 1997. p. 159.
25 Sir Hermann Bondi. "Uniting the World—Or Dividing It: Which Outlook Is Truly Universal, which Parochial in the Extreme?" In *Science and Religion: Are They Compatible?,* edited by Paul Kurtz. Amherst, N.Y.: Prometheus Books, 2003. pp. 145, 146, 148.
26 **One example of an excellent religion-science discussion that benefited from a facilitator (Thomas Matus) is transcribed in: Fritjof Capra & David Steindl-Rast.** *Belonging to the Universe: Explorations on the Frontiers of Science and Spirituality.* San Francisco: HarperSanFrancisco, 1991.
27 Sewall Wright. "Gene and Organism." In *American Naturalist,* 87 (1953), pp. 5-18. Quoted in Charles L. Birch, *Nature and God* (Philadelphia: The Westminster Press, 1965), p. 49.
28 The most balanced and thorough examination of these scientists' books

is: Karl Giberson & Mariano Artigas. *Oracles of Science: Celebrity Scientists versus God and Religion*. New York: Oxford University Press, 2007.

29 Charles Hartshorne. *The Logic of Perfection*. LaSalle, Ill.: Open Court Publishing Co., 1962. p. 250. Quoted in John F. Haught. *The Cosmic Adventure: Science, Religion and the Quest for Purpose* (New York: Paulist Press, 1984), p. 111.

30 James R. Price III. "Mysticism." In *New & Enlarged Handbook of Christian Theology*, edited by Donald W. Musser & Joseph L. Price. Nashville: Abingdon Press, 2003. p. 336.

31 Margaret Lewis Furse. *Mysticism: Window on a World View*. Nashville: Abingdon, 1977. pp. 13-18, 36.

32 *The American Heritage Dictionary of the English Language*, Fourth Edition. New York: Houghton Mifflin Co., 2006. p. 1164. **(The 2011 edition of this dictionary substituted a less harsh secondary definition, hopefully an indication that the word "mysticism" is less often being used as a slur.)**

33 Karl Giberson & Mariano Artigas. *Oracles of Science*. Chap. 4.

34 Union of Concerned Scientists. "Preserving and Cherishing the Earth: An Appeal for Joint Commitment in Science and Religion." Quoted in David Suzuki. *The Sacred Balance: Rediscovering Our Place in Nature* (Vancouver: Greystone Books, 1997), p. 27.

35 Elizabeth E. Johnson. *Ask the Beasts: Darwin and the God of Love*. London: Bloomsbury, 2014. p. 11.

36 Celia E. Deane-Drummond. *The Ethics of Nature*. Malden, MA: Blackwell Publishing, 2004. p. 218. Available at http://www.researchgate.net/profile/Celia_Deanedrummond/publication/30067726_The_ethics_of_nature/links/54e33e360cf2d90c1d9c4dec.pdf.

37 Günther Oestmann. "The Strasbourg Cathedral Clock." Jan., 1999. p. 13. Available at www.researchgate.net/publication/263060347.

38 Ibid., p. 7.

39 Nathan Hallanger. "Eugenics and the Question of Religion." In *The Evolution of Evil*, ed. by Gaymon Bennett, et al., pp. 301-317. Göttingen: Vandenhoeck & Ruprecht, 2008. pp. 315, 317.

40 Bill Bryson. *One Summer: America, 1927*. New York: Doubleday, 2013. pp. 362-370.

41 Celia Deane-Drummond. "Wisdom with Justice." *Ethics In Science And Environmental Politics* (Jan. 2002). p. 67. Available at http://www.researchgate.net/profile/Celia_Deanedrummond/publication/26386710_Wisdom_with_justice/links/54e33e380cf2d90c1d9c4df1.pdf.

42 **Examples of this joint meaning for wisdom are Proverbs 8:4-12 and Proverbs 8:22-34.**

43 Francisco J. Ayala. "Darwin's Devolution: Design Without Designer." In *Evolutionary and Molecular Biology: Scientific Perspectives on Divine Action*, ed. by Robert John Russell, et al. Vatican City: Vatican

Observatory Publications, 1998. p. 115. (emphasis added)

44 Edward O Wilson. *Consilience: The Unity Of Knowledge.* New York: Knopf, 1998.

45 The methodology Wilson was referring to is "scientific naturalism." Edward O. Wilson. *On Human Nature.* Cambridge, Mass.: Harvard Univ. Press, 1978. p. 192. Quoted in Karl W. Giberson and Donald A. Yerxa, *Species of Origins.* p. 131.

46 Stephen Jay Gould. *The Hedgehog, the Fox, and the Magister's Pox: Mending the Gap between Science and the Humanities.* New York: Harmony Books, 2003. pp. 5 & 262.

47 Ibid., p. 218.

48 Ian F. McNeely, with Lisa Wolverton. *Reinventing Knowledge.* p. xxi.

49 American Association for the Advancement of Science. "Questions and Answers on Evolution." (no date). Available at: http://www.wwf.gr/images/pdfs/pe/Darwin_QA_Evolution.pdf.

50 Steve McIntosh. *Evolution's Purpose: An Integral Interpretation of the Scientific Story of Our Origins.* New York: SelectBooks, Inc., 2012. pp. 82-84.

51 Ken Wilber. *The Marriage of Sense and Soul: Integrating Science and Religion.* New York: Random House, 1998. pp. 11-13, 56.

52 Frank Burch Brown. "Aesthetics." In *New & Enlarged Handbook of Christian Theology,* edited by Donald W. Musser & Joseph L. Price, pp. 19-23. Nashville: Abingdon Press, 2003. pp. 19 & 21.

53 Oscar Wilde. *The Picture of Dorian Gray,* 1891.

54 Aldous Huxley. *The Perennial Philosophy.* New York: Harper & Brothers, 1945. p. 138.

55 In various writings of Aquinas. Quoted in *Sheer Joy: Conversations with Thomas Aquinas on Creation Spirituality,* edited by Matthew Fox. New York: Jeremy P. Tarcher/Putnam, 1992. pp. 269 & 102-107.

56 Hadith of Muslim. In *World Scripture: A Comparative Anthology of Sacred Texts.* New York: Paragon House, 1991. p. 88.

57 Charles E. Raven. *Natural Religion and Christian Theology.* Cambridge: Cambridge Univ. Press, 1953. p. 178.

58 **One source of samples of the elevation of compassion in many faith-traditions is: Karen Armstrong.** *Twelve Steps To A Compassionate Life.* **New York: Alfred A. Knopf, 2010.**

59 Jalalluddin Rumi. *The Mathnawi,* trans. Reynold Alleyne Nicholson. (My rendering slightly altered from this translation.) p. 30 (Book 1, No. 110). Available at http://tbm100.org/Lib/Rum11.pdf.

60 Julian of Norwich. *Showings* (sometimes titled *Revelations of Divine Love*), trans. by Edumnd Colledge & James Walsh. New York: Paulist Press, 1978. Chapter 86. p. 342.

Index

Some key words are placed in **bold** type. So also is the page number on which the meaning of that word is explained. Page numbers that are <u>underlined</u> refer to the Timeline of Christianity and Science (Figure 3 in Chapter 1).

Ordering information:
http://bruceyaeger.blogspot.com

CPSIA information can be obtained
at www.ICGtesting.com
Printed in the USA
FSOW02n2222040516
20068FS

9 781367 809925